WRITE GREAT CODE
Volume 1: Understanding
the Machine

WRITE GREAT CODE

CODE

Volume 1:
Understanding the Machine

by Randall Hyde

**NO STARCH
PRESS**

San Francisco

Printed on recycled paper in the United States of America

2 3 4 5 6 7 8 9 10 – 07 06 05

No Starch Press and the No Starch Press logo are registered trademarks of No Starch Press, Inc. Other product and company names mentioned herein may be the trademarks of their respective owners. Rather than use a trademark symbol with every occurrence of a trademarked name, we are using the names only in an editorial fashion and to the benefit of the trademark owner, with no intention of infringement of the trademark.

Publisher: William Pollock
Managing Editor: Karol Jurado
Cover and Interior Design: Octopod Studios
Developmental Editor: Hillel Heinstein
Technical Reviewer: Mark de Wever
Copyeditor: Andy Carroll
Compositor: Riley Hoffman
Proofreader: Stephanie Provines

For information on book distributors or translations, please contact No Starch Press, Inc. directly:

No Starch Press, Inc.
555 De Haro Street, Suite 250, San Francisco, CA 94107
phone: 415-863-9900; fax: 415-863-9950; info@nostarch.com; http://www.nostarch.com

Library of Congress Cataloguing-in-Publication Data

Hyde, Randall.
  Write great code : understanding the machine / Randall Hyde.
      p. cm.
  ISBN 1-59327-003-8
1. Computer programming. 2. Computer architecture. I. Title.
  QA76.6.H94 2004
  005.1--dc22
                                        2003017502

BRIEF CONTENTS

CONTENTS IN DETAIL

1
WHAT YOU NEED TO KNOW TO WRITE GREAT CODE

2
NUMERIC REPRESENTATION

3
BINARY ARITHMETIC AND BIT OPERATIONS

4
FLOATING-POINT REPRESENTATION

5
CHARACTER REPRESENTATION

6
MEMORY ORGANIZATION AND ACCESS

7
COMPOSITE DATA TYPES AND MEMORY OBJECTS

8
BOOLEAN LOGIC AND DIGITAL DESIGN

9
CPU ARCHITECTURE

10
INSTRUCTION SET ARCHITECTURE

11
MEMORY ARCHITECTURE AND ORGANIZATION

12
INPUT AND OUTPUT (I/O)

THINKING LOW-LEVEL, WRITING HIGH-LEVEL
405

A
ASCII CHARACTER SET
407

INDEX
411

ACKNOWLEDGMENTS

A book such as the one you are now holding is rarely the work of one person, even if only one name appears on the cover. Producing this book has been a team effort, and I would like to take this opportunity to acknowledge the other individuals who have contributed greatly to its quality.

Mary Philips, a wonderful friend who helped proofread several of the earlier chapters.

Bill Pollock, who read and offered suggestions for Chapters 1 through 6.

Karol Jurado, my editor, who shepherded this project from conception to production.

Hillel Heinstein, the developmental editor, who kept this book on the right track and helped clean up the writing.

Andy Carroll, the copyeditor, who also helped improve my writing.

Mark de Wever, the technical reviewer, who caught a large number of little typos and technical problems to help ensure the accuracy of the material.

Riley Hoffman, who handled the page layout chores and helped ensure that the book (including the listings) was readable.

Stephanie Provines, whose proofreading caught several typographical and layout errors.

Leigh Sacks, who has done a great job of marketing this book and my earlier book, *The Art of Assembly Language.*

And of course, all the great people at No Starch Press who've been supportive of this project from the very beginning.

Last, but not least, I would like to thank my wife, Mandy, who allowed me to get away with not spending as much time working around the house as I should have, so that I could get this book out the door.

Thanks to all of you,
Randall Hyde

1

WHAT YOU NEED TO KNOW TO WRITE GREAT CODE

Write Great Code will teach you how to write code you can be proud of, code that will impress other programmers, code that will satisfy customers and prove popular with users, and code that people (customers, your boss, and so on) won't mind paying top dollar to obtain. In general, the volumes in the Write Great Code series will discuss how to write software that achieves legendary status, eliciting the awe of other programmers.

1.1 The Write Great Code Series

Write Great Code: Understanding the Machine is the first of four volumes in the Write Great Code series. Writing great code requires a combination of knowledge, experience, and skill that programmers usually obtain only after years of mistakes and discoveries. The purpose of this series is to share with both new and experienced programmers a few decade's worth of observations and experience. I hope that these books will help shorten the time and reduce the frustration that it takes to learn things "the hard way."

This first volume, *Understanding the Machine*, is intended to fill in the low-level details that are often skimmed over in a typical computer science or engineering curriculum. The information in this volume is the foundation upon which great software is built. You cannot write efficient code without this information, and the solutions to many problems require a thorough grounding in this subject. Though I'm attempting to keep each volume as independent as possible of the others, *Understanding the Machine* might be considered a prerequisite for all the following volumes.

The second volume, *Thinking Low-Level, Writing High-Level*, will immediately apply the knowledge gained in this first volume. *Thinking Low-Level, Writing High-Level* will teach you how to analyze code written in a high-level language to determine the quality of the machine code that a compiler would generate for that code. Armed with this knowledge, you will be able to write high-level language programs that are nearly as efficient as programs handwritten in assembly language. High-level language programmers often get the mistaken impression that optimizing compilers will always generate the best machine code possible, regardless of the source code the programmer gives them. This simply isn't true. The statements and data structures you choose in your source files can have a big impact on the efficiency of the machine code a compiler generates. By teaching you how to analyze the machine code your compiler generates, *Thinking Low-Level, Writing High-Level* will teach you how to write efficient code without resorting to assembly language.

There are many other attributes of great code besides efficiency, and the third volume in this series, *Engineering Software*, will cover some of those. *Engineering Software* will discuss how to create source code that is easily read and maintained by other individuals and how to improve your productivity without burdening you with the "busy work" that many software engineering books discuss. *Engineering Software* will teach you how to write code that other programmers will be happy to work with, rather than code that causes them to use some choice words about your capabilities behind your back.

Great code *works*. Therefore, I would be remiss not to include a volume on testing, debugging, and quality assurance. Whether you view software testing with fear or with disgust, or you feel it's something that only junior engineers should get stuck doing, an almost universal truth is that few programmers properly test their code. This generally isn't because programmers actually find testing boring or beneath them, but because they simply don't know *how* to test their programs, eradicate defects, and ensure the quality of their code. As a result, few applications receive high-quality testing, which has led the world at large to have a very low opinion of the software engineering profession. To help overcome this problem, the fourth volume in this series, *Testing, Debugging, and Quality Assurance,* will describe how to efficiently test your applications without all the drudgery engineers normally associate with this task.

1.2 What This Volume Covers

In order to write great code, you need to know how to write efficient code, and to write efficient code, you must understand how computer systems execute programs and how abstractions found in programming languages map to the low-level hardware capabilities of the machine. This first volume teaches you the details of the underlying machine so you'll know how to write software that best uses the available hardware resources. While efficiency is not the only attribute great code possesses, inefficient code is never great. So if you're not writing efficient code, you're not writing great code.

In the past, learning great coding techniques has required learning assembly language. While this is not a bad approach, it is overkill. Learning assembly language involves learning two related subjects: (1) machine organization and (2) programming in assembly language. While learning assembly language programming helps, the real benefits of learning assembly language come from learning machine organization at the same time. Few books have taught machine organization without also teaching assembly language programming. To rectify this problem, this book teaches machine organization independently of assembly language so you can learn to write great code without the excessive overhead of learning assembly language.

"So what is machine organization?" you're probably wondering. Well, machine organization is a subset of computer architecture, and this book concentrates on those parts of computer architecture and machine organization that are visible to the programmer or are helpful for understanding why system architects chose a particular system design. The goal of learning machine organization is not to enable you to design your own CPU or computer system, but to teach you how to make the most efficient use of existing computer designs.

"Okay, so what is machine organization?" you're probably *still* asking. Well, a quick glance at the table of contents will give you an idea of what this subject is all about. Let's do a quick run-through of the book.

Chapters 2, 4, and 5 deal with basic computer data representation — how computers represent signed and unsigned integer values, characters, strings, character sets, real values, fractional values, and other numeric and nonnumeric quantities. If you do not have a solid understanding of how computers represent these various data types internally, it's difficult to understand why some operations that use these data types are so inefficient. And if you don't realize they're inefficient, you'll likely use them in an inappropriate fashion and the resulting code will not be *great.*

Chapter 3 discusses binary arithmetic and bit operations used by most modern computer systems. Because these operations are generally available in programming languages, Chapter 3 also offers several insights into how you can write better code by using arithmetic and logical operations in ways not normally taught in beginning programming courses. Learning standard "tricks" such as these is part of how you become a *great programmer*.

Chapter 6 begins a discussion of one of the more important topics in this book: memory organization and access. Memory access is a common performance bottleneck in modern computer applications. Chapter 6 provides an introduction to memory, discussing how the computer accesses its memory, and describing the performance characteristics of memory. This chapter also describes various machine code *addressing modes* that CPUs use to access different types of data structures in memory. In modern applications, poor performance often occurs because the programmer does not understand the ramifications of memory access in their programs, and Chapter 6 addresses many of these ramifications.

Chapter 7 returns to the discussion of data types and representation by covering composite data types and memory objects. Unlike the earlier chapters, Chapter 7 discusses higher-level data types like pointers, arrays, records, structures, and unions. All too often programmers use large composite data structures without even considering the memory and performance issues of doing so. The low-level description of these high-level composite data types will make clear their inherent costs enabling you to use them in your programs sparingly and wisely.

Chapter 8 discusses Boolean logic and digital design. This chapter provides the mathematical and logical background you'll need to understand the design of CPUs and other computer system components. Although this particular chapter is more hardware oriented than the previous chapters, there are still some good ideas that you can incorporate into *really great code*. In particular, this chapter discusses how to optimize Boolean expressions, such as those found in common high-level programming language statements like if, while, and so on.

Continuing the hardware discussion begun in Chapter 8, Chapter 9 discusses CPU architecture. Although the goal of this book is not to teach you how to design your own CPU, a basic understanding of CPU design and operation is absolutely necessary if you want to write great code. By writing your code in a manner consistent with the way a CPU will execute that code, you'll get much better performance using fewer system resources. By writing your applications at odds with the way CPUs execute code, you'll wind up with slower, resource-hogging programs.

Chapter 10 discusses CPU instruction set architecture. Machine instructions are the primitive units of execution on any CPU, and the time spent during program execution is directly determined by the number and type of machine instructions the CPU executes. Understanding how computer architects design machine instructions can provide valuable insight into why certain operations take longer to execute than others. Once you understand the limitations of machine instructions and how the CPU interprets them, you can use this information to turn mediocre code sequences into great code sequences.

Chapter 11 returns to the subject of memory, covering memory architecture and organization. This chapter will probably be one of the most important to the individual wanting to write fast code. It describes the memory hierarchy and how to maximize the use of cache and other fast memory components. Great code avoids *thrashing*, a common source of performance problems in modern applications. By reading this chapter you will learn about thrashing and how to avoid low-performance memory access in your applications.

Chapter 12, "Input and Output," describes how computer systems communicate with the outside world. Many peripheral (input/output) devices operate at much lower speeds than the CPU and memory. You can write the fastest executing sequence of instructions possible, and still have your application run slowly because you don't understand the limitations of the I/O devices in your system. Chapter 12 presents a discussion of generic I/O ports, system buses, buffering, handshaking, polling, and interrupts. It also discusses how to effectively use many popular PC peripheral devices, including keyboards, parallel (printer) ports, serial ports, disk drives, tape drives, flash storage, SCSI, IDE/ATA, USB, and sound cards. Understanding the impact of these devices on your applications can help you write great, *efficient* code.

1.3 Assumptions This Volume Makes

For the purposes of this book, you should be reasonably competent in at least one imperative (procedural) programming language. This includes C and C++, Pascal, BASIC, and assembly, as well as languages like Ada, Modula-2, FORTRAN, and the like. You should be capable, on your own, of taking a small problem description and working through the design and implementation of a software solution for that problem. A typical semester or quarter course at a college or university (or several months' experience on your own) should be sufficient background for this book.

At the same time, this book is not language specific; its concepts transcend whatever programming language(s) you're using. To help make the examples more accessible to readers, the programming examples in this book will rotate among several languages (such as C/C++, Pascal, BASIC, and assembly). Furthermore, this book does not assume that you use or know any particular language. When presenting examples, this book explains exactly how the code operates so that even if you are unfamiliar with the specific programming language, you will be able to understand its operation by reading the accompanying description.

This book uses the following languages and compilers in various examples:

- C/C++: GCC, Microsoft's Visual C++, Borland C++
- Pascal: Borland's Delphi/Kylix
- Assembly language: Microsoft's MASM, HLA (the High Level Assembler), Gas (on the PowerPC)
- BASIC: Microsoft's Visual Basic

You certainly don't need to know all these languages or have all these compilers to read and understand the examples in this book. Often, the examples appear in multiple languages, so it's usually safe to ignore a specific example if you don't completely understand the syntax of the language the example uses.

1.4 Characteristics of Great Code

What do we mean by *great code*? Different programmers will have different definitions for great code, so it is impossible to provide an all-encompassing definition that will satisfy everyone. However, there are certain attributes of great code that nearly everyone will agree upon, and we'll use some of these common characteristics to form our definition. For our purposes, here are some attributes of great code:

- Uses the CPU efficiently (which means the code is fast)
- Uses memory efficiently (which means the code is small)
- Uses system resources efficiently
- Is easy to read and maintain
- Follows a consistent set of style guidelines
- Uses an explicit design that follows established software engineering conventions
- Is easy to enhance
- Is well-tested and robust (meaning that it works)
- Is well-documented

We could easily add dozens of items to this list. Some programmers, for example, may feel that great code must be portable, that it must follow a given set of programming style guidelines, or that it must be written in a certain language (or that it must *not* be written in a certain language). Some may feel that great code must be written as simply as possible, while others may feel that great code is written quickly. Still others may feel that great code is created on time and under budget. You can probably think of additional characteristics.

So what is great code? Here is a reasonable definition:

> Great code is software that is written using a consistent and
> prioritized set of good software characteristics. In particular,
> great code follows a set of rules that guide the decisions a
> programmer makes when implementing an algorithm as
> source code.

Two different programs do not have to follow the same set of rules (that is, they need not possess the same set of characteristics) in order for both to be great programs. As long as they each consistently obey their particular set of rules, they can both be examples of great code. In one environment, a great program may be one that is portable across different CPUs and operating systems. In a different environment, efficiency (speed) may be the primary goal, and portability may not be an issue. Both could be shining examples of great code, even though their goals might be mutually exclusive. Clearly, neither program would be an example of great code when examined according to the rules of the other program; but as long as the software consistently follows the guidelines established for that particular program, you can argue that it is an example of great code.

1.5 The Environment for This Volume

Although this book presents generic information, parts of the discussion will necessarily be specific to a particular system. Because the Intel Architecture PCs are, by far, the most common in use today, this book will use that platform when discussing specific system-dependent concepts. However, those concepts will still apply to other systems and CPUs (for example, the PowerPC CPU in the Power Macintosh or some other RISC CPU in a Unix box) though you may well need to research the solution for your specific platform when an example does not explicitly apply to your system.

Most examples appearing in this book run under both Windows and Linux. This book attempts to stick with standard library interfaces to the operating system (OS) wherever possible, and it makes OS-specific calls only when the alternative is to write "less than great" code.

Most of the specific examples in this book run on a late-model Intel Architecture (including AMD) CPU under Windows or Linux, with a reasonable amount of RAM and other system peripherals normally found on a late-model PC. The concepts, if not the software itself, will apply to Macs, Unix boxes, embedded systems, and even mainframes.

1.6 For More Information

No single book can completely cover everything about machine organization that you need to know in order to write great code. This book, therefore, concentrates on those aspects of machine organization that are most pertinent for writing great software, providing the 90 percent solution for those who are interested in writing the best possible code. To learn that last 10 percent of machine organization, you're going to need additional resources.

- Learn assembly language. Fluency in at least one assembly language will fill in many missing details that you just won't get by learning machine organization alone. Unless you plan on using assembly language in your software systems, you don't necessarily have to learn assembly language on the platform(s) to which you're targeting your software. Probably your best bet, then, is to learn 80x86 assembly language on a PC. The Intel Architecture isn't the best, but there are lots of great software tools for learning assembly language (for example, the High Level Assembler) that simply don't exist on other platforms. The point of learning assembly language here is not so you can write assembly code, but rather to learn the assembly paradigm. If you know 80x86 assembly language, you'll have a good idea of how other CPUs (such as the PowerPC or the IA-64 family) operate. Of course, if you need to write assembly code, you should learn the assembly language for the CPU you'll be using. An excellent choice for learning assembly language is another book of mine, *The Art of Assembly Language*, available from No Starch Press.

- Study advanced computer architecture. Machine organization is a subset of the study of computer architecture, but space limitations prevent covering machine organization and computer architecture in complete detail within this book. While you may not need to know how to design your own CPUs, studying computer architecture may teach you something you've missed in the presentation of machine organization in this book. *Computer Architecture: A Quantitative Approach* by Hennessy and Patterson is a well-respected textbook that covers this subject matter.

2

NUMERIC REPRESENTATION

High-level languages shield programmers from the pain of dealing with low-level numeric representation. Writing great code, however, requires a complete understanding of how computers represent numbers. Once you understand internal numeric representation, you'll discover efficient ways to implement many algorithms and see the pitfalls associated with many common programming practices. Therefore, this chapter looks at numeric representation to ensure you completely understand what your computer languages and systems are doing with your data.

2.1　What Is a Number?

Having taught assembly language programming for many years, I've discovered that most people don't understand the fundamental difference between a number and the representation of that number. Most of the time this confusion is harmless. However, many algorithms depend upon the internal and external representations we use for numbers to operate correctly and efficiently. If you do not understand the difference between the abstract concept of a number and the representation of that number, you'll have trouble understanding, using, or creating such algorithms. Fully understanding this difference could take you from creating some mediocre code to creating great code.

A *number* is an intangible, abstract, concept. It is an intellectual device that we use to denote quantity. Let's say I were to tell you that "some book has one hundred pages." You could touch the pages — they are tangible. You could even count those pages to verify that there are one hundred of them. However, "one hundred" is simply an abstraction that I would be applying to the book as a way of describing its size.

The important thing to realize is that the following is *not* one hundred:

100

This is nothing more than ink on paper forming certain lines and curves. You might recognize this sequence of symbols as a representation of one hundred, but this is not the actual value 100. It's just three symbols appearing on this page. It isn't even the only representation for one hundred — consider the following, which are all different representations of the value one hundred:

100	decimal representation
C	Roman numeral representation
$\mathbf{64_{16}}$	base 16/hexadecimal representation
$\mathbf{1100100_2}$	base two/binary representation
$\mathbf{144_8}$	base eight/octal representation
one hundred	English representation

The representation of a number is (generally) some sequence of symbols. For example, the common representation of the value one hundred, "100," is really a sequence of three numeric digits: the digit *1* followed by the digit *0* followed by a second *0* digit. Each of these digits has some specific meaning, but we could have just as easily used the sequence "64" to represent the value one hundred. Even the individual digits that comprise this representation of 100 are not numbers. They are numeric digits, tools we use to represent numbers, but they are not numbers themselves.

Now you may be wondering why we should even care whether a sequence of symbols like "100" is the actual value one hundred or just the representation of this value. The reason for this distinction is that you'll encounter several different sequences of symbols in a computer program that look like numbers (meaning that they look like "100"), and you don't want to confuse them with actual numeric values. Conversely, there are many different representations for the value one hundred that a computer could use, and it's important for you to realize that they are equivalent.

2.2 Numbering Systems

A *numbering system* is a mechanism we use to represent numeric values. In today's society, people most often use the *decimal numbering system* (base 10) and most computer systems use binary representation. Confusion between the two can lead to poor coding practices. So to write great code, you must eliminate this confusion.

To appreciate the difference between numbers and their representations, let's start with a concrete discussion of the decimal numbering system. The Arabs developed the decimal numbering system we commonly use today (indeed, the ten decimal digits are known as *Arabic numerals*). The Arabic system uses a *positional notation system* to represent values with a relatively small number of different symbols. That is, the Arabic representation takes into consideration not only the symbol itself, but the position of the symbol in a sequence of symbols, a scheme that is far superior to other, nonpositional, representations. To appreciate the difference between a positional system and a nonpositional system, consider the tally-slash representation of the number 25 in Figure 2-1.

Figure 2-1: Tally-slash representation of 25

The tally-slash representation uses a sequence of *n* marks to represent the value *n*. To make the values easier to read, most people arrange the tally marks in groups of five, as in Figure 2-1. The advantage of the tally-slash numbering system is that it is easy to use when counting objects. The disadvantages include the fact that the notation is bulky, and arithmetic operations are difficult. However, without question, the biggest problem with the tally-slash representation is the amount of physical space this representation consumes. To represent the value *n* requires some amount of space that is proportional to *n*. Therefore, for large values of *n*, the tally-slash notation becomes unusable.

2.2.1 The Decimal Positional Numbering System

The decimal positional notation (base 10) represents numbers using strings of Arabic numerals. The symbol immediately to the left of the decimal point in the sequence represents some value between zero and nine. If there are at least two digits, then the second symbol to the left of the decimal point represents some value between zero and nine times ten. In the decimal positional numbering system each digit appearing to the left of the decimal point represents a value between zero and nine times an increasing power of ten (see Figure 2-2).

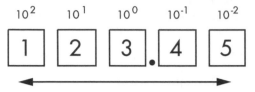

The magnitude associated with each digit is relative to its distance from the decimal point.

Figure 2-2: A positional numbering system

When you see a numeric sequence like "123.45," you don't think about the value 123.45; rather, you generate a mental image of this quantity. In reality, 123.45 represents:

$$1 \times 10^2 + 2 \times 10^1 + 3 \times 10^0 + 4 \times 10^{-1} + 5 \times 10^{-2}$$

or

$$100 + 20 + 3 + 0.4 + 0.05$$

To get a clear picture of how powerful this notation is, consider the following facts:

- The positional numbering system, using base 10, can represent the value ten in one-third the space of the tally-slash system.
- The base-10 positional numbering system can represent the value one hundred in about 3 percent of the space of the tally-slash system.
- The base-10 positional numbering system can represent the value one thousand in about 0.3 percent of the space of the tally-slash system.

As the numbers grow larger, the disparity becomes even greater. Because of the compact and easy-to-recognize notation, positional numbering systems are quite popular.

2.2.2 Radix (Base)

Human beings developed the decimal numbering system because it corresponds to the number of fingers ("digits") on their hands. However, the decimal numbering system isn't the only positional numbering system possible. In fact, for most computer-based applications, the decimal numbering system isn't even the best numbering system available. Again, our goal of writing great code requires that we learn to "think like the machine," and that means we need to understand different ways to represent numbers on our machines. So let's take a look at how we represent values in other bases.

The decimal positional numbering system uses powers of ten and ten unique symbols for each digit position. Because decimal numbers use powers of ten, we call such numbers "base-10" numbers. By substituting a different set of numeric digits and multiplying those digits by powers of some base other than 10, we can devise a different numbering system to represent our numbers. The base, or *radix*, is the value that we raise to successive powers for each digit to the left of the *radix point* (note that the term *decimal point* only applies to decimal numbers).

As an example, we can create a base-8 numbering system using eight symbols (0–7) and powers of eight (base 8, or *octal*, was actually a common representation on early binary computer systems). The base-8 system uses successive powers of eight to represent values. Consider the octal number 123_8 (the subscript denotes the base using standard mathematical notation), which is equivalent to 83_{10}:

$$1 \times 8^2 + 2 \times 8^1 + 3 \times 8^0$$

or

$$64 + 16 + 3$$

To create a base-n numbering system, you need n unique digits. The smallest possible radix is two (for this scheme). For bases two through ten, the convention is to use the Arabic digits zero through $n - 1$ (for a base-n system). For bases greater than ten, the convention is to use the alphabetic digits a..z[1] or A..Z (ignoring case) for digits greater than nine. This scheme supports numbering systems through base 36 (10 numeric digits and 26 alphabetic digits). No agreed-upon convention exists for symbols beyond the 10 Arabic numeric digits and the 26 alphabetic digits. Throughout this book, we'll deal with base-2, base-8, and base-16 values because base 2 (binary) is the native representation most computers use, and base 16 is more compact than base 2. Base 8 deserves a short discussion because it was a popular numeric representation on older computer systems. You'll find many programs that use these three different bases, so you'll want to be familiar with them.

2.2.3   The Binary Numbering System

If you're reading this book, chances are pretty good that you're already familiar with the base-2, or *binary*, numbering system; nevertheless, a quick review is in order. The binary numbering system works just like the decimal numbering system, with two exceptions: binary only uses the digits 0 and 1 (rather than 0–9), and binary uses powers of two rather than powers of ten.

Why even worry about binary? After all, almost every computer language available allows programmers to use decimal notation (automatically converting decimal representation to the internal binary representation).

[1] The ".." notation, taken from Pascal and other programming languages, denotes a range of values. For example, "a..z" denotes all the lowercase alphabetic characters between *a* and *z*.

Despite computer languages being able to convert decimal notation, most modern computer systems talk to I/O devices using binary, and their arithmetic circuitry operates on binary data. For this reason, many algorithms depend upon binary representation for correct operation. Therefore, a complete understanding of binary representation is necessary if you want to write great code.

2.2.3.1 Converting Between Decimal and Binary Representation

In order to allow human beings to work with decimal representation, the computer has to convert between the decimal notation that humans use and the binary format that computers use. To appreciate what the computer does for you, it's useful to learn how to do these conversions manually.

To convert a binary value to decimal, we add 2^i for each "1" in the binary string, where i is the zero-based position of the binary digit. For example, the binary value 11001010_2 represents:

$$1 \times 2^7 + 1 \times 2^6 + 0 \times 2^5 + 0 \times 2^4 + 1 \times 2^3 + 0 \times 2^2 + 1 \times 2^1 + 0 \times 2^0$$

or

$$128 + 64 + 8 + 2$$

or

$$202_{10}$$

To convert decimal to binary is almost as easy. Here's an algorithm that converts decimal representation to the corresponding binary representation:

1. If the number is even, emit a zero. If the number is odd, emit a one.
2. Divide the number by two and throw away any fractional component or remainder.
3. If the quotient is zero, the algorithm is complete.
4. If the quotient is not zero and the number is odd, insert a one before the current string. If the quotient is not zero and the number is even, prefix your binary string with zero.
5. Go back to step 2 and repeat.

2.2.3.2 Making Binary Numbers Easier to Read

As you can tell by the equivalent representations, 202_{10} and 11001010_2, binary representation is not as compact as decimal representation. Because binary representation is bulky, we need some way to make the digits, or bits, in binary numbers easier to read.

In the United States, most people separate every three digits with a comma to make larger numbers easier to read. For example, 1,023,435,208 is much easier to read and comprehend than 1023435208. We'll adopt a similar convention in this book for binary numbers. We will separate each group of four binary bits with an underscore. For example, we will write the binary value 10101111110110010_2 as $1010\_1111\_1011\_0010_2$.

2.2.3.3 Binary Representation in Programming Languages

This chapter has been using the subscript notation embraced by mathematicians to denote binary values (the lack of a subscript indicates the decimal base). While this works great in word processing systems, most program text editors do not provide the ability to specify a numeric base using a subscript. Even if a particular editor does support this feature, very few programming language compilers would recognize the subscript. Therefore, we need some way to represent various bases within a standard ASCII text file.

Generally, only assembly language compilers ("assemblers") allow the use of literal binary constants in a program. Because there is a wide variety of assemblers out there, it should come as no surprise that there are many different ways to represent binary literal constants in an assembly language program. Because this text presents examples using MASM and HLA, it makes sense to adopt the conventions these two assemblers use.

MASM treats any sequence of binary digits (zero and one) that ends with a "b" or "B" as a binary value. The "b" suffix differentiates binary values like "1001" and the decimal value of the same form (one thousand and one). Therefore, the binary representation for nine would be "1001b" in a MASM source file.

HLA prefixes binary values with the percent symbol (%). To make binary numbers more readable, HLA also allows you to insert underscores within binary strings:

%11_1011_0010_1101

2.2.4 The Hexadecimal Numbering System

Binary number representation is verbose. Because reading and writing binary values is awkward, programmers often avoid binary representation in program source files, preferring hexadecimal notation. Hexadecimal representation offers two great features: it's very compact, and it's easy to convert between binary and hexadecimal. Therefore, software engineers generally use hexadecimal representation rather than binary to make their programs more readable.

Because hexadecimal representation is base 16, each digit to the left of the hexadecimal point represents some value times a successive power of 16. For example, the number 1234_{16} is equal to:

$$1 \times 16^3 + 2 \times 16^2 + 3 \times 16^1 + 4 \times 16^0$$

or

$$4096 + 512 + 48 + 4$$

or

$$4660_{10}$$

Hexadecimal representation uses the letters *A* through *F* for the additional six digits it requires (above and beyond the ten standard decimal digits, 0–9). The following are all examples of valid hexadecimal numbers:

$$234_{16} \quad DEAD_{16} \quad BEEF_{16} \quad 0AFB_{16} \quad FEED_{16} \quad DEAF_{16}$$

2.2.4.1 Hexadecimal Representation in Programming Languages

One problem with hexadecimal representation is that it is difficult to differentiate hexadecimal values like "dead" from standard program identifiers. Therefore, most programming languages use a special prefix or suffix character to denote the hexadecimal radix for constants appearing in your source files. Here's how you specify literal hexadecimal constants in several popular languages:

- The C, C++, C#, Java, and other C-derivative programming languages use the prefix "0x" to denote a hexadecimal value. Therefore, you'd use the character sequence "0xdead" for the hexadecimal value $DEAD_{16}$.

- The MASM assembler uses an "h" or "H" suffix to denote a hexadecimal value. This doesn't completely resolve the ambiguity between certain identifiers and literal hexadecimal constants; "deadh" still looks like an identifier to MASM. Therefore, MASM also requires that a hexadecimal value begin with a numeric digit. So for hexadecimal values that don't already begin with a numeric digit, you would add "0" to the beginning of the value (adding a zero to the beginning of any numeric representation does not alter the value of that representation). For example, use "0deadh" to unambiguously represent the hexadecimal value $DEAD_{16}$.

- Visual Basic uses the "&H" or "&h" prefix to denote a hexadecimal value. Continuing with our current example ($DEAD_{16}$), you'd use "&Hdead" to represent this hexadecimal value in Visual Basic.

- Pascal (Delphi/Kylix) uses the symbol $ as a prefix for hexadecimal values. So you'd use "$dead" to represent our current example in Delphi/Kylix.

- HLA similarly uses the symbol $ as a prefix for hexadecimal values. So you'd also use "$dead" to represent $DEAD_{16}$ with HLA. HLA allows you to insert underscores into the middle of a hexadecimal number to make it easier to read, for example "$FDEC_A012."

In general, this text will use the HLA/Delphi/Kylix notation for hexadecimal numbers except in examples specific to some other programming language. Because there are several C/C++ examples in this book, you'll frequently see the C/C++ notation, as well.

2.2.4.2 Converting Between Hexadecimal and Binary Representations

On top of being a compact way to represent values in code, hexadecimal notation is also popular because it is easy to convert between the binary and hexadecimal representations. By memorizing a few simple rules, you can mentally convert between these two representations. Consider Table 2-1.

Table 2-1: Binary/Hexadecimal Conversion Chart

Binary	Hexadecimal
%0000	$0
%0001	$1
%0010	$2
%0011	$3
%0100	$4
%0101	$5
%0110	$6
%0111	$7
%1000	$8
%1001	$9
%1010	$A
%1011	$B
%1100	$C
%1101	$D
%1110	$E
%1111	$F

To convert the hexadecimal representation of a number into binary, substitute the corresponding four binary bits for each hexadecimal digit. For example, to convert $ABCD into the binary form %1010_1011_1100_1101, convert each hexadecimal digit according to the values in Table 2-1:

A	B	C	D	Hexadecimal
1010	1011	1100	1101	Binary

To convert the binary representation of a number into hexadecimal is almost as easy. The first step is to pad the binary number with zeros to make sure it is a multiple of four bits long. For example, given the binary number 1011001010, the first step would be to add two zero bits to the left of the number so that it contains 12 bits without changing its value. The result is

001011001010. The next step is to separate the binary value into groups of four bits: 0010_1100_1010. Finally, look up these binary values in Table 2-1 and substitute the appropriate hexadecimal digits, which are $2CA. Contrast this with the difficulty of converting between decimal and binary or decimal and hexadecimal!

2.2.5   The Octal (Base-8) Numbering System

Octal (base-8) representation was common in early computer systems. As a result, you may still see people use the octal representation now and then. Octal is great for 12-bit and 36-bit computer systems (or any other size that is a multiple of three). However, it's not particularly great for computer systems whose bit size is some power of two (8-bit, 16-bit, 32-bit, and 64-bit computer systems). As a result, octal has fallen out of favor over the past several decades. Nevertheless, some programming languages provide the ability to specify numeric values in octal notation, and you can still find some older Unix applications that use octal, so octal is worth discussing here.

2.2.5.1   Octal Representation in Programming Languages

The C programming language (and derivatives like C++ and Java), Visual Basic, and MASM support octal representation. You should be aware of the notation various programming languages use for octal numbers in case you come across it in programs written in these languages.

- In C, you specify the octal base by prefixing a numeric string with a zero. For example, "0123" is equivalent to the decimal value 83_{10} and is definitely not equivalent to the decimal value 123_{10}.

- MASM uses a "Q" or "q" suffix to denote an octal number (Microsoft/Intel probably chose "Q" because it looks like an "O" and they didn't want to use "O" or "o" because of the possible confusion with zero).

- Visual Basic uses the "&O" (that's the letter *O*, not a zero) prefix to denote an octal value. For example, you'd use "&O123" to represent the decimal value 83_{10}.

2.2.5.2   Converting Between Octal and Binary Representation

Converting between binary and octal is similar to converting between binary and hexadecimal, except that you work in groups of three bits rather than four. See Table 2-2 for the list of binary and octal equivalent representations.

To convert octal into binary, replace each octal digit in the number with the corresponding three bits from Table 2-2. For example, when converting 123q into a binary value the final result is %0_0101_0011:

```
1   2   3
001 010 011
```

Table 2-2: Binary/Octal Conversion Chart

Binary	Octal
%000	0
%001	1
%010	2
%011	3
%100	4
%101	5
%110	6
%111	7

To convert a binary number into octal, you break up the binary string into groups of three bits (padding with zeros, as necessary), and then you look up each triad in Table 2-2 and substitute the corresponding octal digit.

If you've got an octal value and you'd like to convert it to hexadecimal notation, convert the octal number to binary and then convert the binary value to hexadecimal.

2.3 Numeric/String Conversions

Because most programming languages (or their libraries) provide automatic numeric/string conversions, beginning programmers are often unaware that this conversion is even taking place. In this section we'll consider two conversions: from string to numeric form and from numeric form to string.

Consider how easy it is to convert a string to numeric form in various languages. In each of the following statements, the variable i can hold some integer number. The input from the user's console, however, is a string of characters. The programming language's run-time library is responsible for converting that string of characters to the internal binary form the CPU requires.

```
cin >> i;      // C++
readln( i );   // Pascal
input i        // BASIC
stdin.get(i);  // HLA
```

Because these statements are so easy to use, most programmers don't consider the cost of using such statements in their programs. Unfortunately, if you have no idea of the cost of these statements, you'll not realize how they can impact your program when performance is critical. The reason for exploring these conversion algorithms here is to make you aware of the work involved so you will not make frivolous use of these conversions.

To simplify things, we'll discuss unsigned integer values and ignore the possibility of illegal characters and numeric overflow. Therefore, the following algorithms actually understate the actual work involved (by a small amount).

Use this algorithm to convert a string of decimal digits to an integer value:

1. Initialize a variable with zero; this will hold the final value.
2. If there are no more digits in the string, then the algorithm is complete, and the variable holds the numeric value.
3. Fetch the next digit (going from left to right) from the string.
4. Multiply the variable by ten, and then add in the digit fetched in step 3.
5. Go to step 2 and repeat.

Converting an integer value to a string of characters takes even more effort. The algorithm for the conversion is the following:

1. Initialize a string to the empty string.
2. If the integer value is zero, then output a *0*, and the algorithm is complete.
3. Divide the current integer value by ten, computing the remainder and quotient.
4. Convert the remainder (always in the range 0..9) to a character, and concatenate the character to the end of the string.
5. If the quotient is not zero, make it the new value and repeat steps 3–5.
6. Output the characters in the reverse order they were placed into the string.

The particulars of these algorithms are not important. What is important to note is that these steps execute once for each output character and division is very slow. So a simple statement like one of the following can hide a fair amount of work from the programmer:

```
printf( "%d", i );    // C
cout << i;            // C++
print i               // BASIC
write( i );           // Pascal
stdout.put( i );      // HLA
```

To write great code you don't need to eschew the use of numeric/string conversions. They are an important part of computation, and great code will need to do these conversions. However, a great programmer will be careful about the use of numeric/string conversions and only use them as necessary.

Note that these algorithms are only valid for unsigned integers. Signed integers require a little more effort to process (though the extra work is almost negligible). Floating-point values, however, are far more difficult to convert between string and numeric form. That's something to keep in mind when writing code that uses floating-point arithmetic.

2.4 Internal Numeric Representation

Most modern computer systems are binary computer systems and, therefore, use an internal binary format to represent values and other objects. However, most systems cannot represent just any binary value. Instead, they are only capable of efficiently representing binary values of a given size. If you want to write great code, you need to make sure that your programs use data objects that the machine can represent efficiently. The following sections describe how computers physically represent values.

2.4.1 Bits

The smallest unit of data on a binary computer is a single *bit*. Because a bit can represent only two different values (typically zero or one) you may get the impression that there are a very small number of items you can represent with a single bit. Not true! There are an infinite number of two-item combinations you can represent with a single bit. Here are some examples (with arbitrary binary encodings I've created):

- Zero (0) or one (1)
- False (0) or true (1)
- Off (0) or on (1)
- Male(0) or female (1)
- Wrong (0) or right (1)

You are *not* limited to representing binary data types (that is, those objects that have only two distinct values). You could use a single bit to represent any two distinct items:

- The numbers 723 (0) and 1,245 (1)
- The colors red (0) and blue (1)

You could even represent two unrelated objects with a single bit. For example, you could use the bit value zero to represent the color red and the bit value one to represent the number 3,256. You can represent *any* two different values with a single bit. However, you can represent *only two* different values with a single bit. As such, individual bits aren't sufficient for most computational needs. To overcome the limitations of a single bit, we create *bit strings* from a sequence of multiple bits.

2.4.2 Bit Strings

As you've already seen in this chapter, by combining bits into a sequence, we can form binary representations that are equivalent to other representations of numbers (like hexadecimal and octal). Most computer systems, however, do not let you collect together an arbitrary number of bits. Instead, you have to work with strings of bits that have certain fixed lengths. In this section we'll discuss some of the more common bit string lengths and the names computer engineers have given them.

A *nibble* is a collection of four bits. Most computer systems do not provide efficient access to nibbles in memory. However, nibbles are interesting to us because it takes exactly one nibble to represent a single hexadecimal digit.

A *byte* is eight bits and it is the smallest addressable data item on many CPUs. That is, the CPU can efficiently retrieve data on an 8-bit boundary from memory. For this reason, the smallest data type that many languages support consumes one byte of memory (regardless of the actual number of bits the data type requires).

Because the byte is the smallest unit of storage on most machines, and many languages use bytes to represent objects that require fewer than eight bits, we need some way of denoting individual bits within a byte. To describe the bits within a byte, we'll use *bit numbers*. Normally, we'll number the bits in a byte, as Figure 2-3 shows. Bit 0 is the *low-order (LO) bit* or *least significant bit*, and bit 7 is the *high-order (HO) bit* or *most significant bit* of the byte. We'll refer to all other bits by their number.

Figure 2-3: Bit numbering in a byte

The term *word* has a different meaning depending on the CPU. On some CPUs a word is a 16-bit object. On others a word is a 32-bit or 64-bit object. In this text, we'll adopt the 80x86 terminology and define a word to be a 16-bit quantity. Like bytes, we'll number the bits in a word starting with bit number zero for the LO bit and work our way up to the HO bit (bit 15), as in Figure 2-4. When referencing the other bits in a word, use their bit position number.

Figure 2-4: Bit numbers in a word

Notice that a word contains exactly two bytes. Bits 0 through 7 form the LO byte, bits 8 through 15 form the HO byte (see Figure 2-5).

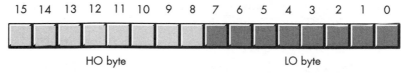

HO byte   LO byte

Figure 2-5: The two bytes in a word

A *double word* is exactly what its name implies, a pair of words (sometimes you will see "double word" abbreviated as "dword"). Therefore, a double-word quantity is 32 bits long, as shown in Figure 2-6.

Figure 2-6: Bit layout in a double word

A double word contains a pair of words and a set of four bytes, as Figure 2-7 shows.

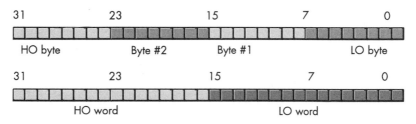

HO byte   Byte #2   Byte #1   LO byte

HO word   LO word

Figure 2-7: Bytes and words in a double word

Most CPUs efficiently handle objects up to a certain size (typically 32 or 64 bits on contemporary systems). That does not mean you can't work with larger objects — it simply becomes less efficient to do so. For that reason, you typically won't see programs handling numeric objects much larger than about 128 or 256 bits. Because 64-bit integers are available in some programming languages, and most languages support 64-bit floating-point values, it does make sense to describe a 64-bit data type; we'll call these *quad words*. Just for the fun of it, we'll use the term *long word* for 128-bit values. Few languages today support 128 bit values,[2] but this does give us some room to grow.

Of course, we can break quad words down into 2 double words, 4 words, 8 bytes, or 16 nibbles. Likewise, we can break long words down into 2 quad words, 4 double words, 8 words, or 16 bytes.

On Intel 80x86 platforms there is also an 80-bit type that Intel calls a *tbyte* (for 10-byte) object. The 80x86 CPU family uses tbyte variables to hold extended precision floating-point values and certain binary-coded decimal (BCD) values.

---

[2] HLA, for example, supports 128-bit values.

In general, with an n-bit string you can represent up to 2^n different values. Table 2-3 shows the number of possible objects you can represent with nibbles, bytes, words, double words, quad words, and long words.

Table 2-3: Number of Values Representable with Bit Strings

Size of Bit String (in Bits)	Number of Possible Combinations (2^n)
4	16
8	256
16	65,536
32	4,294,967,296
64	18,446,744,073,709,551,616
128	340,282,366,920,938,463,463,374,607,431,768,211,456

2.5   Signed and Unsigned Numbers

The binary number $0...00000^3$ represents zero, $0...00001$ represents one, $0...00010$ represents two, and so on towards infinity. But what about negative numbers? To represent signed values, most computer systems use the two's complement numbering system. The representation of signed numbers places some fundamental restrictions on those numbers, so it is important to understand the difference in representation between signed and unsigned numbers in a computer system to use them efficiently.

With n bits we can only represent 2^n different objects. As negative values are objects in their own right, we'll have to divide these 2^n combinations between negative and non-negative values. So, for example, a byte can represent the negative values −128..−1 and the non-negative values 0..127. With a 16-bit word we can represent signed values in the range −32,768..+32,767. With a 32-bit double word we can represent values in the range −2,147,483,648..+2,147,483,647. In general, with n bits we can represent the signed values in the range -2^{n-1} to $+2^{n-1}-1$.

The two's complement system uses the HO bit as a *sign bit*. If the HO bit is zero, the number is non-negative; if the HO bit is one, the number is negative. Here are some examples using 16-bit numbers:

```
$8000 (%1000_0000_0000_0000) is negative because the HO bit is one
$100 (%0000_0001_0000_0000) is non-negative because the HO bit is zero
$7FFF (%0111_1111_1111_1111) is non-negative
$FFFF (%1111_1111_1111_1111) is negative
$FFF (%0000_1111_1111_1111) is non-negative
```

---

[3] The ellipses ("...") have the standard mathematical meaning: repeat a string of zeros an indefinite number of times.

To negate a two's complement number, you can use the following algorithm:

1. Invert all the bits in the number, that is, change all the zeros to ones and all the ones to zeros.
2. Add one to the inverted result (ignoring any overflow).

For example, these are the steps to compute the 8-bit equivalent of the decimal value −5:

%0000_0101	Five (in binary)
%1111_1010	Invert all the bits
%1111_1011	Add one to obtain −5 (in two's complement form)

If we take −5 and negate it, the result is 5 (%0000_0101), just as we expect:

%1111_1011	Two's complement for −5
%0000_0100	Invert all the bits
%0000_0101	Add one to obtain 5 (in binary)

Here are some 16-bit examples and their negations:
First, negate 32,767 ($7fff):

$7FFF:	%0111_1111_1111_1111	+32,767, the largest 16-bit positive number.
	%1000_0000_0000_0000	Invert all the bits (8000h)
	%1000_0000_0000_0001	Add one (8001h or −32,767)

First, negate 16,384 ($4000):

$4000:	%0100_0000_0000_0000	16,384
	%1011_1111_1111_1111	Invert all the bits ($BFFF)
	%1100_0000_0000_0000	Add one ($C000 or −16,384)

And now negate −32,768 ($8000):

$8000:	%1000_0000_0000_0000	−32,768, the smallest 16-bit negative number.
	%0111_1111_1111_1111	Invert all the bits ($7FFF)
	%1000_0000_0000_0000	Add one ($8000 or −32768)

$8000 inverted becomes $7FFF, and after adding one we obtain $8000! Wait, what's going on here? −(−32,768) is −32,768? Of course not. However, the 16-bit two's complement numbering system cannot represent the value +32,768. In general, you cannot negate the smallest negative value in the two's complement numbering system.

2.6 Some Useful Properties of Binary Numbers

It's worth learning a few interesting facts about binary values that you might find useful in your programs. Here are some useful properties:

1. If bit position zero of a binary (integer) value contains one, the number is an odd number; if this bit contains zero, then the number is even.

2. If the LO n bits of a binary number all contain zero, then the number is evenly divisible by 2^n.

3. If a binary value contains a one in bit position n, and zeros everywhere else, then that number is equal to 2^n.

4. If a binary value contains all ones from bit position zero up to (but not including) bit position n, and all other bits are zero, then that value is equal to 2^n-1.

5. Shifting all the bits in a number to the left by one position multiplies the binary value by two.

6. Shifting all the bits of an unsigned binary number to the right by one position effectively divides that number by two (this does not apply to signed integer values). Odd numbers are rounded down.

7. Multiplying two n-bit binary values together may require as many as $2*n$ bits to hold the result.

8. Adding or subtracting two n-bit binary values never requires more than $n+1$ bits to hold the result.

9. Inverting all the bits in a binary number (that is, changing all the zeros to ones and all the ones to zeros) is the same thing as negating (changing the sign) of the value and then subtracting one from the result.

10. Incrementing (adding one to) the largest unsigned binary value for a given number of bits always produces a value of zero.

11. Decrementing (subtracting one from) zero always produces the largest unsigned binary value for a given number of bits.

12. An n-bit value provides 2^n unique combinations of those bits.

13. The value 2^n-1 contains n bits, each containing the value one.

You should probably memorize all the powers of two from 2^0 through 2^{16}, as these values come up in programs all the time. Table 2-4 lists their values.

Table 2-4: Powers of Two

n	2^n
0	1
1	2
2	4
3	8
4	16
5	32
6	64
7	128
8	256

Table 2-4: Powers of Two (continued)

n	2^n
9	512
10	1,024
11	2,048
12	4,096
13	8,192
14	16,384
15	32,768
16	65,536

2.7 Sign Extension, Zero Extension, and Contraction

Many modern high-level programming languages allow you to use expressions involving integer objects with differing sizes. So what happens when your two operands in an expression are of different sizes? Some languages will report an error, other languages will automatically convert the operands to a common format. This conversion, however, is not free, so if you don't want your compiler going behind your back and automatically inserting conversions into your otherwise great code, you should be aware of how compilers deal with such expressions.

With the two's complement system, a single negative value will have different representations depending on size of the representation. You cannot arbitrarily use an 8-bit signed value in an expression involving a 16-bit number; a conversion will be necessary. This conversion, and its converse (converting a 16-bit value to 8 bits) are the *sign extension* and *contraction* operations.

Consider the value −64. The 8-bit two's complement value for this number is $C0. The 16-bit equivalent of this number is $FFC0. Clearly, these are not the same bit pattern. Now consider the value +64. The 8- and 16-bit versions of this value are $40 and $0040, respectively. It should be obvious that extending the size of negative values is done differently than extending the size of non-negative values.

To *sign extend* a value from some number of bits to a greater number of bits is easy — just copy the sign bit into the additional HO bits in the new format. For example, to sign extend an 8-bit number to a 16-bit number, simply copy bit seven of the 8-bit number into bits 8..15 of the 16-bit number. To sign extend a 16-bit number to a double word, simply copy bit 15 into bits 16..31 of the double word.

You must use sign extension when manipulating signed values of varying lengths. For example, when adding a byte quantity to a word quantity, you will need to sign extend the byte to 16 bits before adding the two numbers. Other operations may require a sign extension to 32 bits.

Table 2-5: Sign Extension Examples

8 Bits	16 Bits	32 Bits	Binary (Two's Complement)
$80	$FF80	$FFFF_FF80	%1111_1111_1111_1111_1111_1111_1000_0000
$28	$0028	$0000_0028	%0000_0000_0000_0000_0000_0000_0010_1000
$9A	$FF9A	$FFFF_FF9A	%1111_1111_1111_1111_1111_1111_1001_1010
$7F	$007F	$0000_007F	%0000_0000_0000_0000_0000_0000_0111_1111
n/a	$1020	$0000_1020	%0000_0000_0000_0000_0001_0000_0010_0000
n/a	$8086	$FFFF_8086	%1111_1111_1111_1111_1000_0000_1000_0110

When processing unsigned binary numbers, *zero extension* lets you convert small unsigned values to larger unsigned values. Zero extension is very easy — just store a zero in the HO byte(s) of the larger operand. For example, to zero extend the 8-bit value $82 to 16 bits you just insert a zero for the HO byte yielding $0082.

Table 2-6: Zero Extension Examples

8 Bits	16 Bits	32 Bits	Binary
$80	$0080	$0000_0080	%0000_0000_0000_0000_0000_0000_1000_0000
$28	$0028	$0000_0028	%0000_0000_0000_0000_0000_0000_0010_1000
$9A	$009A	$0000_009A	%0000_0000_0000_0000_0000_0000_1001_1010
$7F	$007F	$0000_007F	%0000_0000_0000_0000_0000_0000_0111_1111
n/a	$1020	$0000_1020	%0000_0000_0000_0000_0001_0000_0010_0000
n/a	$8086	$0000_8086	%0000_0000_0000_0000_1000_0000_1000_0110

Many high-level language compilers automatically handle sign and zero extension. The following examples in C demonstrate how this works:

```
signed char sbyte;    // Chars in C are byte values.
short int sword;      // Short integers in C are *usually* 16-bit values.
long int sdword;      // Long integers in C are *usually* 32-bit values.
    . . .
sword = sbyte;   // Automatically sign extends the 8-bit value to 16 bits.
sdword = sbyte;  // Automatically sign extends the 8-bit value to 32 bits.
sdword = sword;  // Automatically sign extends the 16-bit value to 32 bits.
```

Some languages (such as Ada) may require an explicit cast from a smaller size to a larger size. You'll have to check the language reference manual for your particular language to see if this is necessary. The advantage of a language that requires you to provide an explicit conversion is that the compiler never does anything behind your back. If you fail to provide the conversion yourself, the compiler emits a diagnostic message so you'll be made aware that your program will need to do additional work.

The important thing to realize about sign and zero extension is that they aren't always free. Assigning a smaller integer to a larger integer may require more machine instructions (taking longer to execute) than moving data between two like-sized integer variables. Therefore, you should be careful about mixing variables of different sizes within the same arithmetic expression or assignment statement.

Sign contraction, converting a value with some number of bits to the same value with a fewer number of bits, is a little more troublesome. Sign extension never fails. Given an m-bit signed value you can always convert it to an n-bit number (where $n > m$) using sign extension. Unfortunately, given an n-bit number, you cannot always convert it to an m-bit number if $m < n$. For example, consider the value -448. As a 16-bit hexadecimal number, its representation is $FE40. Unfortunately, the magnitude of this number is too large to fit into eight bits, so you cannot sign contract it to eight bits.

To properly sign contract one value to another, you must look at the HO byte(s) that you want to discard. First, the HO bytes must all contain either zero or $FF. If you encounter any other values, you cannot sign contract the value. Second, the HO bit of your resulting value must match *every* bit you've removed from the number. Here are some examples of converting 16-bit values to 8-bit values:

```
$FF80 (%1111_1111_1000_0000) can be sign contracted to $80 (%1000_0000).
$0040 (%0000_0000_0100_0000) can be sign contracted to $40 (%0100_0000).
$FE40 (%1111_1110_0100_0000) cannot be sign contracted to 8 bits.
$0100 (%0000_0001_0000_0000) cannot be sign contracted to 8 bits.
```

Contraction is somewhat difficult in a high-level language. Some languages, like C, will simply store the LO portion of the expression into a smaller variable and throw away the HO component (at best, the C compiler may give you a warning during compilation about the loss of precision that may occur). You can often quiet the compiler, but it still doesn't check for invalid values. Typically, you'd use code like the following to sign contract a value in C:

```
signed char sbyte;    // Chars in C are byte values.
short int sword;      // Short integers in C are *usually* 16-bit values.
long int sdword;      // Long integers in C are *usually* 32-bit values.
  . . .
sbyte = (signed char) sword;
sbyte = (signed char) sdword;
sword = (short int) sdword;
```

The only safe solution in C is to compare the result of the expression to an upper and lower bounds value before attempting to store the value into a smaller variable. Unfortunately, such code tends to get unwieldy if you need to do this often. Here's what the preceding code might look like with these checks:

```
if( sword >= -128 && sword <= 127 )
{
    sbyte = (signed char) sword;
}
else
{
    // Report appropriate error.
}

// Another way, using assertions:

assert( sdword >= -128 && sdword <= 127 )
sbyte = (signed char) sword;

assert( sdword >= -32768 && sdword <= 32767 )
sword = (short int) sword;
```

As you can plainly see, this code gets pretty ugly. In C/C++, you'd probably want to turn this into a macro (#define) or a function so your code would be a bit more readable.

Some high-level languages (such as Pascal and Delphi/Kylix) will automatically sign contract values for you and check the value to ensure it properly fits in the destination operation.[4] Such languages will raise some sort of exception (or stop the program) if a range violation occurs. Of course, if you want to take corrective action, you'll either need to write some exception handling code or resort to using an if statement sequence similar to the one in the C example just given.

2.8 Saturation

Saturation is another way to reduce the size of an integer value. Saturation is useful when you want to convert a larger object to a smaller object and you're willing to live with possible loss of precision. If the value of the larger object is not outside the range of the smaller object, you can convert the value via saturation by copying the LO bits of the larger value into the smaller object. If the larger value is outside the smaller object's range, then you *clip* the larger value by setting it to the largest (or smallest) value within the range of the smaller data type.

When converting a 16-bit signed integer to an 8-bit signed integer, if the 16-bit value is in the range −128..+127 you simply copy the LO byte into the 8-bit object. If the 16-bit signed value is greater than +127, then you clip the value to +127 and store +127 into the 8-bit object. Likewise, if the value is less than −128, you clip the final 8-bit object to −128. Saturation works the same

---

[4] Borland's compilers require the use of a special compiler directive to activate this check. By default, the compiler does not do the bounds check.

way when clipping 32-bit values to smaller values. If the larger value is outside the range of the smaller value, then you simply clip the value to the closest value that you can represent with the smaller data type.

If the larger value is outside the range of the smaller value, there will be a loss of precision during the conversion. While clipping the value is never desirable, sometimes this is better than raising an exception or otherwise rejecting the calculation. For many applications, such as audio or video, the clipped result is still recognizable to the end user, so this is a reasonable conversion scheme in such situations.

As a result, many CPUs support saturation arithmetic in their special "multimedia extension" instruction sets. On the Intel 80x86 processor family, for example, the MMX instruction extensions provide saturation capabilities. Most CPUs' standard instruction sets, as well as most high-level languages, do not provide direct support for saturation, but saturation is not difficult. Consider the following Pascal/Delphi/Kylix code that uses saturation to convert a 32-bit integer to a 16-bit integer:

```
var
    li  :longint;
    si  :smallint;
        . . .
    if( li > 32767 ) then

        si := 32767;

    else if( li < -32768 ) then

        si := -32768;

    else
        si := li;
```

2.9 Binary-Coded Decimal (BCD) Representation

The *binary-coded decimal* (BCD) format, as its name suggests, encodes decimal values using a binary representation. The 80x86 CPU family provides several machine instructions that convert between BCD and pure binary formats. Common general-purpose high-level languages (like C/C++, Pascal, and Java) rarely support decimal values. However, business-oriented programming languages (like COBOL and many database languages) support this data type. So if you're writing code that interfaces with a database or some language that supports decimal arithmetic, you may need to deal with BCD representation.

BCD values consist of a sequence of nibbles, with each nibble representing a value in the range 0..9. Of course, you can represent values in the range 0..15 using a nibble; the BCD format, however, uses only 10 of the possible 16 values. Each nibble represents a single decimal digit in a BCD value, so with a single byte we can represent values containing two decimal digits (0..99), as shown in Figure 2-8. With a word, we can represent values having four decimal digits (0..9999). Likewise, a double word can represent up to eight decimal digits.

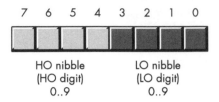

Figure 2-8: BCD data representation in a byte

As you can see, BCD storage isn't particularly efficient. An 8-bit BCD variable can represent values in the range 0..99 while that same eight bits, holding a binary value, could represent values in the range 0..255. Likewise, a 16-bit binary value can represent values in the range 0..65535 while a 16-bit BCD value can only represent about a sixth of those values (0..9999). Inefficient storage isn't the only problem with BCD, though. BCD calculations also tend to be slower than binary calculations.

At this point, you're probably wondering why anyone would ever use the BCD format. The BCD format does have two saving graces: it's very easy to convert BCD values between the internal numeric representation and their decimal string representations, and it's also very easy to encode multidigit decimal values in hardware when using BCD — for example, when using a set of dials with each dial representing a single digit. For these reasons, you're likely to see people using BCD in embedded systems (such as toaster ovens and alarm clocks) but rarely in general-purpose computer software.

A few decades ago people mistakenly thought that calculations involving BCD (or just decimal) arithmetic were more accurate than binary calculations. Therefore, they would often perform important calculations, like those involving dollars and cents (or other monetary units) using decimal-based arithmetic. While it is true that certain calculations can produce more accurate results in BCD, this statement is not true in general. Indeed, for most calculations the binary representation is more accurate. For this reason, most modern computer programs represent all values (including decimal values) in a binary form. For example, the Intel 80x86 floating-point unit (FPU) supports a pair of instructions for loading and storing BCD values. Internally, however, the FPU converts these BCD values to binary. It only uses BCD as an external data format (external to the FPU, that is). This generally produces more accurate results.

2.10 Fixed-Point Representation

One thing you may have noticed by now is that this discussion has dealt mainly with integer values. A reasonable question to ask is how one represents fractional values. There are two ways computer systems commonly represent numbers with fractional components: fixed-point representation and floating-point representation.

Back in the days when CPUs didn't support floating-point arithmetic in hardware, fixed-point arithmetic was very popular with programmers writing high-performance software that dealt with fractional values. The software overhead necessary to support fractional values in a fixed-point format is less than that needed to do the same calculation using a software-based floating-point computation. However, as the CPU manufacturers added floating-point units (FPUs) to their CPUs to support floating-point in hardware, the advantages of fixed-point arithmetic waned considerably. Today, it's fairly rare to see someone attempt fixed-point arithmetic on a general-purpose CPU that supports floating-point arithmetic. It's usually more cost effective to use the CPU's native floating-point format.

Although CPU manufacturers have worked hard at optimizing the floating-point arithmetic on their systems, reducing the advantages of fixed-point arithmetic, carefully written assembly language programs can make effective use of fixed-point calculations in certain circumstances and the code will run faster than the equivalent floating-point code. Certain 3D gaming applications, for example, may produce faster computations using a 16:16 (16-bit integer, 16-bit fractional) format rather than a 32-bit floating-point format. Because there are some very good uses for fixed-point arithmetic, this section discusses fixed-point representation and fractional values using the fixed-point format (Chapter 4 will discuss the floating-point format).

Fractional values fall between zero and one, and positional numbering systems represent fractional values by placing digits to the right of the radix point. In the binary numbering system, each bit to the right of the binary point represents the value zero or one multiplied by some successive negative power of two. Therefore, when representing values with a fractional component in binary, we represent that fractional component using sums of binary fractions. For example, to represent the value 5.25 in binary, we would use the following binary value:

101.01

The conversion to decimal yields:

$$1 \times 2^2 + 1 \times 2^0 + 1 \times 2^{-2} = 4 + 1 + 0.25 = 5.25$$

When using a fixed-point binary format you choose a particular bit in the binary representation and implicitly place the binary point before that bit. For a 32-bit fixed-point format you could place the binary point before (or after) any of the 32 bits. You choose the position of the binary point based on the number of significant bits you require in the fractional portion of the number. For example, if your values' integer components can range from 0 to 999, you'll need at least 10 bits to the left of the binary point to represent this range of values. If you require signed values, you'll need an extra bit for the sign. In a 32-bit fixed-point format, this leaves either 21 or 22 bits for the fractional part, depending on whether your value is signed.

Fixed-point numbers are a small subset of the real numbers. Because there are an infinite number of values between any two integer values, fixed-point values cannot exactly represent every value between two integers (doing so would require an infinite number of bits). With fixed-point representation, we have to approximate most of the real numbers. Consider the 8-bit fixed-point format that uses six bits for the integer portion and two bits for the fractional component. The integer component can represent values in the range 0..63 (or any other 64 values, including signed values in the range −32..+31). The fractional component can only represent four different values, typically 0.0, 0.25, 0.5, and 0.75. You cannot exactly represent 1.3 with this format; the best you can do is approximate 1.3 by choosing the value closest to 1.3 (which is 1.25). Obviously, this introduces error. You can reduce this error by adding additional bits to the right of the binary point in your fixed-point format (at the expense of reducing the range of the integer component or adding additional bits to your fixed-point format). For example, if you move to a 16-bit fixed-point format using an 8-bit integer and an 8-bit fractional component, then you can approximate 1.3 using the following binary value:

1.01001101

The decimal equivalent is as follows:

---

1 + 0.25 + 0.03125 + 0.15625 + 0.00390625 = 1.30078125

As you can see, adding more bits to the fractional component of your fixed-point number will give you a more accurate approximation of this value (the error is only 0.00078125 using this format compared to 0.05 in the previous format).

However, when using a fixed-point binary numbering system, there are certain values you can never accurately represent regardless of how many bits you add to the fractional part of your fixed-point representation (1.3 just happens to be such a value). This is probably the main reason why people (mistakenly) feel that decimal arithmetic is more accurate than binary arithmetic (particularly when working with decimal fractions like 0.1, 0.2, 0.3, and so on).

To contrast the comparative accuracy of the two systems, let's consider a fixed-point decimal system (using BCD representation). If we choose a 16-bit format with eight bits for the integer portion and eight bits for the fractional portion, we can represent decimal values in the range 0.0 to 99.99 with two decimal digits of precision to the right of the decimal point. We can exactly represent values like 1.3 in this BCD notation using a hex value like $0130 (the implicit decimal point appears between the second and third digits in this number). As long as you only use the fractional values 0.00..0.99 in your computations, this BCD representation is, indeed, more accurate than the binary fixed-point representation (using an 8-bit fractional component). In general, however, the binary format is more accurate.

The binary format lets you exactly represent 256 different fractional values, whereas the BCD format only lets you represent 100 different fractional values. If you pick an arbitrary fractional value, it's likely the binary fixed-point representation provides a better approximation than the decimal format (because there are over two and a half times as many binary versus decimal fractional values). The only time the decimal fixed-point format has an advantage is when you commonly work with the fractional values that it can exactly represent. In the United States, monetary computations commonly produce these fractional values, so programmers figured the decimal format is better for monetary computations. However, given the accuracy most financial computations require (generally four digits to the right of the decimal point is the minimum precision serious financial transactions require), it's usually better to use a binary format.

For example, with a 16-bit fractional component, the decimal/BCD fixed-point format gives you exactly four digits of precision; the binary format, on the other hand, offers over six times the resolution (65,536 different fractional values rather than 10,000 fractional values). Although the binary format cannot exactly represent some of the values that you can exactly represent in decimal form, the binary format does exactly represent better than six times as many values. Once you round the result down to cents (two digits to the right of the decimal point), you're definitely going to get better results using the binary format.

If you absolutely, positively, need to exactly represent the fractional values between 0.00 and 0.99 with at least two digits of precision, the binary fixed-point format is not a viable solution. Fortunately, you don't have to use a decimal format; there are other binary formats that will let you exactly represent these values. The next couple of sections describe such formats.

2.11 Scaled Numeric Formats

Because the decimal (BCD) formats can exactly represent some important values that you cannot exactly represent in binary, many programmers have chosen to use decimal arithmetic in their programs despite the better precision and performance of the binary format. However, there is a better numeric representation that offers the advantages of both schemes: the exact representation of certain decimal fractions combined with the precision of the binary format. This numeric format is also efficient to use and doesn't require any special hardware. What's this wonderful format? It's the *scaled numeric* format.

One advantage of the scaled numeric format is that you can choose any base, not just decimal, for your format. For example, if you're working with ternary (base-3) fractions, you can multiply your original input value by three (or some power of three) and exactly represent values like $1/_3$, $2/_3$, $4/_9$, $7/_{27}$, and so on. You cannot exactly represent any of these values in either the binary or decimal numbering systems.

The scaled numeric format uses fast, compact integer arithmetic. To represent fractional values, you simply multiply your original value by some value that converts the fractional component to a whole number. For example, if you want to maintain two decimal digits of precision to the right of the decimal point, simply multiply your values by 100 upon input. This translates values like 1.3 to 130, which we can exactly represent using an integer value. Assuming you do this calculation with all your fractional values (and they have the same two digits of precision to the right of the decimal point), you can manipulate your values using standard integer arithmetic operations. For example, if you have the values 1.5 and 1.3, their integer conversion produces 150 and 130. If you add these two values you get 280 (which corresponds to 2.8). When you need to output these values, you simply divide them by 100 and emit the quotient as the integer portion of the value and the remainder (zero extended to two digits, if necessary) as the fractional component. Other than the need to write specialized input and output routines that handle the multiplication and division by 100 (as well as dealing with the decimal point), this scaled numeric scheme is almost as easy as doing regular integer calculations.

Of course, do keep in mind that if you scale your values as described here, you've limited the maximum range of the integer portion of your numbers by a like amount. For example, if you need two decimal digits of precision to the right of your decimal point (meaning you multiply the original value by 100), then you may only represent (unsigned) values in the range 0..42,949,672 rather than the normal range of 0..4,294,967,296.

When doing addition or subtraction with a scaled format, you must ensure that both operands have the same scaling factor. That is, if you've multiplied the left operand of an addition operator by 100, you must have multiplied the right operand by 100 as well. Ditto for subtraction. For example, if you've scaled the variable i10 by ten and you've scaled the variable j100 by 100, you need to either multiply i10 by ten (to scale it by 100) or divide j100 by ten (to scale it down to ten) before attempting to add or subtract these two numbers. When using the addition and subtraction operators, you ensure that both operands have the radix point in the same position (and note that this applies to literal constants as well as variables).

When using the multiplication and division operators, the operands do not require the same scaling factor prior to the operation. However, once the operation is complete, you may need to adjust the result. Suppose you have two values you've scaled by 100 to produce two digits of precision after the decimal point and those values are i = 25 (0.25) and j = 1 (0.01). If you compute k = i * j using standard integer arithmetic, the result you'll get is 25 (25 × 1 = 25). Note that the actual value should be 0.0025, yet the result appearing in i seems to be 0.25. The computation is actually correct; the problem is understanding how the multiplication operator works. Consider what we're actually computing:

$$(0.25 \times (100)) \times (0.01 \times (100))$$
$$=$$
$$0.25 \times 0.01 \times (100 \times 100) \quad // \text{ commutative laws allow this}$$
$$=$$
$$0.0025 \times (10,000)$$
$$=$$
$$25$$

The problem is that the final result actually gets scaled by 10,000. This is because both i and j have been multiplied by 100 and when you multiply their values, you wind up with a value multiplied by 10,000 (100 × 100) rather than 100. To solve this problem, you should divide the result by the scaling factor once the computation is complete. For example, k = i * j/100. The division operation suffers from a similar (though not the exact same) problem. Suppose we have the values m = 500 (5.0) and n = 250 (2.5) and we want to compute k = m/n. We would normally expect to get the result 200 (2.0, which is 5.0/2.5). However, here's what we're actually computing:

$$(5 \times 100) / (2.5 \times 100)$$
$$=$$
$$500/250$$
$$=$$
$$2$$

At first blush this may look correct, but don't forget that the result is really 0.02 after you factor in the scaling operation. The result we really need is 200 (2.0). The problem here, of course, is that the division by the scaling factor eliminates the scaling factor in the final result. Therefore, to properly compute the result, we actually need to compute k = 100 * m/n so that the result is correct.

Multiplication and division place a limit on the precision you have available. If you have to premultiply the dividend by 100, then the dividend must be at least 100 times smaller than the largest possible integer value or an overflow will occur (producing an incorrect result). Likewise, when multiplying two scaled values, the final result must be 100 times less than the maximum integer value or an overflow will occur. Because of these issues, you may need to set aside additional bits or work with small numbers when using scaled numeric representation.

2.12 Rational Representation

One big problem with the fractional representations we've seen is that they are not exact; that is, they provide a close approximation of real values, but they cannot provide an exact representation for all rational values.[5] For example, in binary or decimal you cannot exactly represent the value $1/3$. You could switch to a ternary (base-3) numbering system and exactly represent $1/3$, but then you wouldn't be able to exactly represent fractional values like $1/2$ or $1/10$. What we need is a numbering system that can represent any reasonable fractional value. Rational representation is a possibility in such situations.

Rational representation uses pairs of integers to represent fractional values. One integer represents the numerator (n) of a fraction, and the other represents the denominator (d). The actual value is equal to n/d. As long as n and d are "relatively prime" with respect to one another (that is, they are not both evenly divisible by the same value) this scheme provides a good representation for fractional values within the bounds of the integer representation you're using for n and d. In theory, arithmetic is quite easy; you use the same algorithms to add, subtract, multiply, and divide fractional values that you learned in grade school when dealing with fractions. The only problem is that certain operations may produce really large numerators or denominators (to the point where you get integer overflow in these values). Other than this problem, however, you can represent a wide range of fractional values using this scheme.

2.13 For More Information

Donald Knuth's *The Art of Computer Programming, Volume Two: Seminumerical Algorithms* is probably the seminal text on number systems and arithmetic. For more information on binary, decimal, fixed-point, rational, and floating-point arithmetic, you'll want to take a look at that text.

---

[5] It is not possible to provide an exact computer representation of an irrational number, so we won't even try.

3

BINARY ARITHMETIC
AND BIT OPERATIONS

Understanding how computers represent data in binary is a prerequisite to writing software that works well on those computers. Of equal importance, of course, is understanding how computers operate on binary data. Exploring arithmetic, logical, and bit operations on binary data is the purpose of this chapter.

3.1 Arithmetic Operations on Binary and Hexadecimal Numbers

Because computers use binary representation, programmers who write great code often have to work with binary (and hexadecimal) values. Often, when writing code, you may need to manually operate on two binary values in order to use the result in your source code. Although calculators are available to compute such results, you should be able to perform simple arithmetic operations on binary operands by hand.

Hexadecimal arithmetic is sufficiently painful that a hexadecimal calculator belongs on every programmer's desk (or, at the very least, use a software-based calculator that supports hexadecimal operations, such as the Windows calculator). Arithmetic operations on binary values, however, are actually easier than decimal arithmetic. Knowing how to manually compute binary arithmetic results is essential because several important algorithms use these operations (or variants of them). Therefore, the next several subsections describe how to manually add, subtract, multiply, and divide binary values, and how to perform various logical operations on them.

3.1.1   Adding Binary Values

Adding two binary values is easy; there are only eight rules to learn. (If this sounds like a lot, just realize that you had to memorize approximately 200 rules for decimal addition!) Here are the rules for binary addition:

- 0 + 0 = 0
- 0 + 1 = 1
- 1 + 0 = 1
- 1 + 1 = 0 with carry
- Carry + 0 + 0 = 1
- Carry + 0 + 1 = 0 with carry
- Carry + 1 + 0 = 0 with carry
- Carry + 1 + 1 = 1 with carry

Once you know these eight rules you can add any two binary values together. Here are some complete examples of binary addition:

```
      0101
    + 0011
    ------
```

Step 1: Add the LO bits (1 + 1 = 0 + carry).

```
        c
      0101
    + 0011
    ------
         0
```

Step 2: Add the carry plus the bits in bit position one (carry + 0 + 1 = 0 + carry).

```
        c
      0101
    + 0011
    -------
        00
```

Step 3: Add the carry plus the bits in bit position two (carry + 1 + 0 = 0 + carry).

```
      c
    0101
  + 0011
  ------
     000
```

Step 4: Add the carry plus the bits in bit position three (carry + 0 + 0 = 1).

```
    0101
  + 0011
  ------
    1000
```

Here are some more examples:

```
  1100_1101       1001_1111       0111_0111
+ 0011_1011     + 0001_0001     + 0000_1001
-----------     -----------     -----------
1_0000_1000       1011_0000       1000_0000
```

3.1.2 Subtracting Binary Values

Binary subtraction is also easy; like addition, binary subtraction has eight rules:

- $0 - 0 = 0$
- $0 - 1 = 1$ with a borrow
- $1 - 0 = 1$
- $1 - 1 = 0$
- $0 - 0 -$ borrow $= 1$ with a borrow
- $0 - 1 -$ borrow $= 0$ with a borrow
- $1 - 0 -$ borrow $= 0$
- $1 - 1 -$ borrow $= 1$ with a borrow

Here are some complete examples of binary subtraction:

```
    0101
  - 0011
  ------
```

Step 1: Subtract the LO bits (1 − 1 = 0).

```
    0101
  - 0011
  ------
       0
```

Step 2: Subtract the bits in bit position one (0 − 1 = 1 + borrow).

```
    0101
 −  0011
     b
 ------
     10
```

Step 3: Subtract the borrow and the bits in bit position two (1 − 0 − b = 0).

```
    0101
 −  0011
 ------
    010
```

Step 4: Subtract the bits in bit position three (0 − 0 = 0).

```
    0101
 −  0011
 ------
    0010
```

Here are some more examples:

```
  1100_1101      1001_1111      0111_0111
− 0011_1011    − 0001_0001    − 0000_1001
-----------    -----------    -----------
  1001_0010      1000_1110      0110_1110
```

3.1.3 Multiplying Binary Values

Multiplication of binary numbers is also very easy. It's just like decimal multiplication involving only zeros and ones (which is trivial). Here are the rules you need to know for binary multiplication:

- $0 \times 0 = 0$
- $0 \times 1 = 0$
- $1 \times 0 = 0$
- $1 \times 1 = 1$

Using these four rules, multiplication is done the same way you'd do decimal multiplication (in fact, if you just follow the rules for decimal multiplication on your binary values you'll actually get the correct results, because the rules for decimal multiplication involving the zero and one digits are identical). Here are some examples of binary multiplication:

```
      1010
   ×  0101
   -------
```

Step 1: Multiply the LO bit of the multiplier times the multiplicand.

```
      1010
   ×  0101
   -------
      1010     (1 × 1010)
```

Step 2: Multiply bit one of the multiplier times the multiplicand.

```
      1010
   ×  0101
   -------
      1010     (1 × 1010)
      0000     (0 × 1010)
   -------
     01010     (partial sum)
```

Step 3: Multiply bit two of the multiplier times the multiplicand.

```
      1010
   ×  0101
   -------
    001010     (previous partial sum)
     1010      (1 × 1010)
   -------
    110010     (partial sum)
```

Step 4: Multiply bit three of the multiplier times the multiplicand.

```
      1010
   ×  0101
   -------
    110010     (previous partial sum)
    0000       (0 × 1010)
   -------
   0110010     (product)
```

3.1.4 Dividing Binary Values

Like multiplication of binary numbers, binary division is actually easier than decimal division. You use the same (longhand) division algorithm, but binary division is easier because you can trivially determine whether the divisor goes into the dividend during each step of the longhand division algorithm. Figure 3-1 on the next page shows the steps in a decimal division problem.

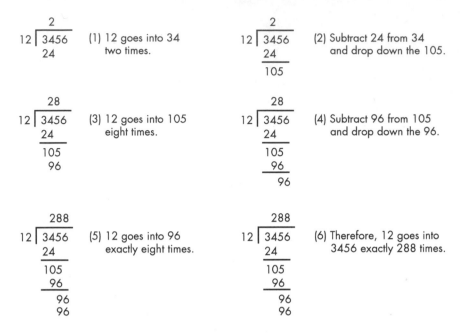

```
      2                                              2
12 | 3456      (1) 12 goes into 34        12 | 3456      (2) Subtract 24 from 34
     24            two times.                  24            and drop down the 105.
                                              ___
                                              105
```

```
     28                                            28
12 | 3456      (3) 12 goes into 105       12 | 3456      (4) Subtract 96 from 105
     24            eight times.                24            and drop down the 96.
    ___                                       ___
    105                                       105
     96                                        96
                                              ___
                                               96
```

```
    288                                           288
12 | 3456      (5) 12 goes into 96        12 | 3456      (6) Therefore, 12 goes into
     24            exactly eight times.        24            3456 exactly 288 times.
    ___                                       ___
    105                                       105
     96                                        96
    ___                                       ___
     96                                        96
     96                                        96
```

Figure 3-1: Decimal division (3456/12)

This algorithm is actually easier in binary because at each step you do not have to guess how many times 12 goes into the remainder nor do you have to multiply 12 by your guess to obtain the amount to subtract. At each step in the binary algorithm, the divisor goes into the remainder exactly zero or one times. As an example, consider the division of 27 (11011) by three (11) as shown in Figure 3-2.

```
       1
11 | 11011        11 goes into 11 one time.
     11
```

```
       1
11 | 11011        Subtract out the 11 and bring down the zero.
     11
     ___
     00
```

```
      10
11 | 11011        11 goes into 00 zero times.
     11
     ___
     00
     00
```

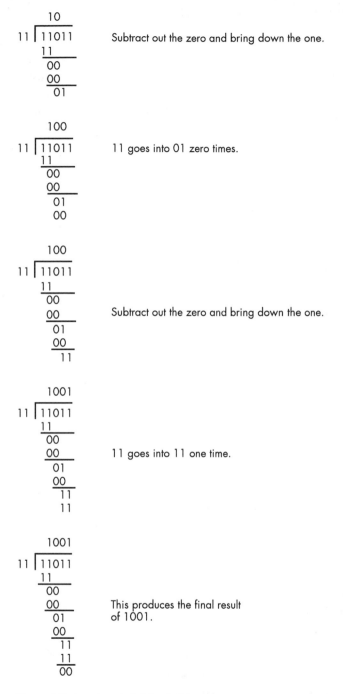

Figure 3-2: Longhand division in binary

3.2 Logical Operations on Bits

There are four main logical operations we'll need to perform on hexadecimal and binary numbers: AND, OR, XOR (exclusive-or), and NOT. Unlike the arithmetic operations, a hexadecimal calculator isn't necessary to perform these operations.

The logical AND, OR, and XOR operations accept two single-bit operands and compute the following results:

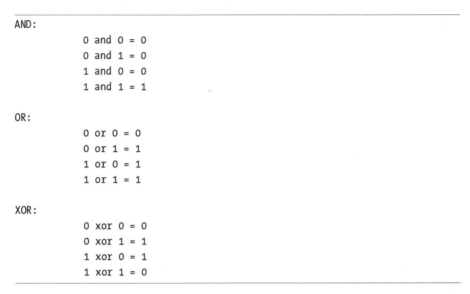

```
AND:
        0 and 0 = 0
        0 and 1 = 0
        1 and 0 = 0
        1 and 1 = 1

OR:
        0 or 0 = 0
        0 or 1 = 1
        1 or 0 = 1
        1 or 1 = 1

XOR:
        0 xor 0 = 0
        0 xor 1 = 1
        1 xor 0 = 1
        1 xor 1 = 0
```

Table 3-1, Table 3-2, and Table 3-3 show the *truth tables* for the AND, OR, and XOR operations. A truth table is just like the multiplication tables you encountered in elementary school. The values in the left column correspond to the left operand of the operation. The values in the top row correspond to the right operand of the operation. The value located at the intersection of the row and column (for a particular pair of input values) is the result.

Table 3-1: AND truth table

AND	0	1
0	0	0
1	0	1

Table 3-2: OR truth table

OR	0	1
0	0	1
1	1	1

Table 3-3: XOR truth table

XOR	0	1
0	0	1
1	1	0

In plain English, the logical AND operation translates as, "If the first operand is one and the second operand is one, the result is one; otherwise the result is zero." We could also state this as "If either or both operands are zero, the result is zero." The logical AND operation is useful for forcing a zero result. If one of the operands is zero, the result is always zero regardless of the value of the other operand. If one of the operands contains one, then the result is the value of the other operand.

Colloquially, the logical OR operation is, "If the first operand or the second operand (or both) is one, the result is one; otherwise the result is zero." This is also known as the *inclusive-OR* operation. If one of the operands to the logical-OR operation is one, the result is always one. If an operand is zero, the result is always the value of the other operand.

In English, the logical XOR operation is, "If the first or second operand, but not both, is one, the result is one; otherwise the result is zero." If one of the operands is a one, the result is always the *inverse* of the other operand.

The logical NOT operation is unary (meaning it accepts only one operand). The truth table for the NOT operation appears in Table 3-4. This operator simply inverts (reverses) the value of its operand.

Table 3-4: NOT truth table

NOT	0	1
	1	0

3.3 Logical Operations on Binary Numbers and Bit Strings

The logical functions work on single-bit operands. Because most programming languages manipulate groups of 8, 16, or 32 bits, we need to extend the definition of these logical operations beyond single-bit operands. We can easily extend logical functions to operate on a *bit-by-bit* (or *bitwise*) basis. Given two values, a bitwise logical function operates on bit zero of both operands producing bit zero of the result; it operates on bit one of both operands producing bit one of the result, and so on. For example, if you want to compute the bitwise logical AND of two 8-bit numbers, you would logically AND each pair of bits in the two numbers:

```
%1011_0101
%1110_1110
----------
%1010_0100
```

This bit-by-bit execution also applies to the other logical operations, as well. The ability to force bits to zero or one using the logical AND and OR operations, and the ability to invert bits using the logical XOR operation, is very important when working with strings of bits (such as binary numbers). These operations let you selectively manipulate certain bits within a value while leaving other bits unaffected. For example, if you have an 8-bit binary value X and you want to guarantee that bits four through seven contain zeros, you could logically AND the value X with the binary value %0000_1111. This bitwise logical AND operation would force the HO four bits of X to zero and leave the LO four bits of X unchanged. Likewise, you could force the LO bit of X to one and invert bit number two of X by logically ORing X with %0000_0001 and then logically exclusive ORing (XORing) X with %0000_0100. Using the logical AND, OR, and XOR operations to manipulate bit strings in this fashion is known as *masking* bit strings. We use the term *masking* because we can use certain values (one for AND, zero for OR and XOR) to "mask out" or "mask in" certain bits in an operand while forcing other bits to zero, one, or their inverse.

Several languages provide operators that let you compute the bitwise AND, OR, XOR, and NOT of their operands. The C/C++/Java language family uses the ampersand (&) operator for bitwise AND, the pipe (|) operator for bitwise OR, the caret (^) operator for bitwise XOR, and the tilde (~) operator for bitwise NOT. The Visual Basic and Delphi/Kylix languages let you use the and, or, xor, and not operators with integer operands. From 80x86 assembly language, you can use the AND, OR, NOT, and XOR instructions to do these bitwise operations.

```
// Here's a C/C++ example:

    i = j & k;    // Bitwise AND
    i = j | k;    // Bitwise OR
    i = j ^ k;    // Bitwise XOR
    i = ~j;       // Bitwise NOT
```

3.4   Useful Bit Operations

Although bit operations may seem a bit abstract, they are quite useful for many non-obvious purposes. The following subsections describe some of their useful properties of using the logical operations in various languages.

3.4.1   *Testing Bits in a Bit String Using AND*

You can use the bitwise AND operator to test individual bits in a bit string to see if they are zero or one. If you logically AND a value with a bit string that contains a one in a certain bit position, the result of the logical AND will be zero if the corresponding bit contains a zero, and the result will be nonzero if that bit position contains one. Consider the following C/C++ code that checks an integer value to see if it is odd or even by testing if bit zero of the integer:

```
IsOdd = (ValueToTest & 1) != 0;
```

In binary form, here's what this bitwise AND operation is doing:

```
xxxx_xxxx_xxxx_xxxx_xxxx_xxxx_xxxx_xxxx  // Assuming ValueToTest is 32 bits
0000_0000_0000_0000_0000_0000_0000_0001  // Bitwise AND with the value one
----------------------------------------
0000_0000_0000_0000_0000_0000_0000_000x  // Result of bitwise AND
```

The result is zero if the LO bit of ValueToTest contains a zero in bit position zero. The result is one if ValueToTest contains a one in bit position one. This calculation ignores all other bits in ValueToTest.

3.4.2   Testing a Set of Bits for Zero/Not Zero Using AND

You can also use the bitwise AND operator to check a set of bits to see if they are all zero. For example, one way to check to see if a number is evenly divisible by 16 is to see if the LO four bits of the value are all zeros. The following Delphi/Kylix statement uses the bitwise AND operator to accomplish this:

```
IsDivisibleBy16 := (ValueToTest and $f) = 0;
```

In binary form, here's what this bitwise AND operation is doing:

```
xxxx_xxxx_xxxx_xxxx_xxxx_xxxx_xxxx_xxxx  // Assuming ValueToTest is 32 bits
0000_0000_0000_0000_0000_0000_0000_1111  // Bitwise AND with $F
----------------------------------------
0000_0000_0000_0000_0000_0000_0000_xxxx  // Result of bitwise AND
```

The result is zero if and only if the LO four bits of ValueToTest are all zero, because ValueToTest is evenly divisible by 16 only if its LO four bits all contain zero.

3.4.3   Comparing a Set of Bits Within a Binary String

The AND and OR operations are particularly useful if you need to compare a subset of the bits in a binary value against some other value. For example, you might want to compare two 6-bit values found in bits 0, 1, 10, 16, 24, and 31 of a pair of 32-bit values. The trick is to set all the uninteresting bits to zero and then compare the two results.[1]

---

[1] It's also possible to set all the uninteresting bits to ones via the OR operation, but the AND operator is often more convenient.

Consider the following three binary values; the "x" bits denote bits whose values we don't care about:

```
%1xxxxxx0xxxxxxx1xxxxx0xxxxxxxx10
%1xxxxxx0xxxxxxx1xxxxx0xxxxxxxx10
%1xxxxxx1xxxxxxx1xxxxx1xxxxxxxx11
```

If we compare the first and second binary values (assuming we're only interested in bits 31, 16, 10, 1, and 0), we should find that the two values are equal. If we compare either of the first two values against the third value, we'll find that they are not equal. Furthermore, if we compare either of the first two values against the third, we should discover that the third value is greater than the first two. In C/C++ and assembly, this is how we could compare these values:

```
// C/C++ example

    if( (value1 & 0x81010403) == (value2 & 0x81010403))
    {
        // Do something if bits 31, 24, 16, 10, 1, and 0 of
        //  value1 and value2 are equal
    }

    if( (value1 & 0x81010403) != (value3 & 0x81010403))
    {
        // Do something if bits 31, 24, 16, 10, 1, and 0 of
        //  value1 and value3 are not equal
    }

// HLA/x86 assembly example:

    mov( value1, eax );        // EAX = value1
    and( $8101_0403, eax );    // Mask out unwanted bits in EAX
    mov( value2, edx );        // EDX = value2
    and( $8101_0403, edx );    // Mask out the same set of unwanted bits in EDX
    if( eax = edx ) then       // See if the remaining bits match

        // Do something if bits 31, 24, 16, 10, 1, and 0 of
        //  value1 and value2 are equal

    endif;

    mov( value1, eax );        // EAX = value1
    and( $8101_0403, eax );    // Mask out unwanted bits in EAX
    mov( value3, edx );        // EDX = value2
    and( $8101_0403, edx );    // Mask out the same set of unwanted bits in EDX
```

```
if( eax <> edx ) then     // See if the remaining bits do not match

    // Do something if bits 31, 24, 16, 10, 1, and 0 of
    //  value1 and value3 are not equal

endif;
```

3.4.4 Creating Modulo-n Counters Using AND

The AND operation lets you create efficient *modulo-n counters*. A modulo-n counter counts from zero[2] to some maximum value and then resets to zero. Modulo-n counters are great for creating repeating sequences of numbers such as $0, 1, 2, 3, 4, 5, \ldots n{-}1, 0, 1, 2, 3, 4, 5, \ldots n{-}1, 0, 1, \ldots$. You can use such sequences to create circular queues and other objects that reuse array elements upon encountering the end of the data structure. The normal way to create a modulo-n counter is to add one to the counter, divide the result by n, and then keep the remainder. The following code examples demonstrate the implementation of a modulo-n counter in C/ C++, Pascal, and Visual Basic:

```
cntr = (cntr + 1 ) % n;    // C/C++
cntr := (cntr + 1) mod n;  // Pascal/Delphi/Kylix
cntr = (cntr + 1) Mod n    `` Visual Basic
```

The problem with this particular implementation is that division is an expensive operation, requiring far more time to execute than operations such as addition. In general, you'll find it more efficient to implement modulo-n counters using a comparison rather than the remainder operator. Here's a Pascal example:

```
cntr := cntr + 1;      // Pascal example
if( cntr >= n ) then
    cntr := 0;
```

For certain special cases, however, you can increment a modulo-n counter more efficiently and conveniently using the AND operation. You can use the AND operator to create a modulo-n counter when n is a power of two. To create such a modulo-n counter, increment your counter and then logically AND it with the value $n = 2^m{-}1$ ($2^m{-}1$ contains ones in bit positions $0..m{-}1$ and zeros everywhere else). Because the AND operation is usually much faster than a division, AND-driven modulo-n counters are much more efficient than those using the remainder operator. Indeed, on most CPUs, using the AND operator is quite a bit faster than using an if statement. The following examples show how to implement a modulo-n counter for $n = 32$ using the AND operation:

---

[2] Actually, they could count down to zero as well, but usually they count up.

```
//Note: 0x3f = 31 = 2^5 − 1, so n = 32 and m = 5

    cntr = (cntr + 1) & 0x3f;      // C/C++ example
    cntr := (cntr + 1) and $3f;    // Pascal/Delphi/Kylix example
    cntr = (cntr + 1) And &h3f     ` Visual Basic example
```

The assembly language code is especially efficient:

```
inc( eax );                        // Compute (eax + 1) mod 32
and( $1f, eax );
```

3.5   Shifts and Rotates

Another set of logical operations on bit strings are the *shift* and *rotate* operations. These functions can be further broken down into *shift lefts, rotate lefts, shift rights,* and *rotate rights.* These operations turn out to be very useful in many programs.

The shift left operation moves each bit in a bit string one position to the left, as shown in Figure 3-3. Bit zero moves into bit position one, the previous value in bit position one moves into bit position two, and so on.

Figure 3-3: Shift left operation (on a byte)

There are two questions that arise: "What goes into bit zero?" and "Where does the HO bit wind up?" We'll shift a zero into bit zero, and the previous value of the HO bit will be the *carry* out of this operation.

Several high-level languages (such as C/C++/C#, Java, and Delphi/Kylix) provide a shift left operator. In the C language family, this operator is <<. In Delphi/Kylix, you use the shl operator. Here are some examples:

```
// C:

        cLang = d << 1;    // Assigns d shifted left one position to
                           //   variable "cLang"
```

```
// Delphi:

        Delphi := d shl 1; // Assigns d shifted left one position to
                           //   variable "Delphi"
```

Shifting the binary representation of a number one position to the left is equivalent to multiplying that value by two. Therefore, if you're using a programming language that doesn't provide an explicit shift left operator, you can usually simulate this by multiplying a binary integer value by two. Although the multiplication operation is usually slower than the shift left operation, most compilers are smart enough to translate a multiplication by a constant power of two into a shift left operation. Therefore, you could write code like the following in Visual Basic to do a shift left:

```
vb = d * 2
```

A shift right operation is similar to a shift left, except we're moving the data in the opposite direction. Bit seven moves into bit six; bit six moves into bit five; bit five moves into bit four; and so on. During a shift right, we'll move a zero into bit seven, and bit zero will be the carry out of the operation (see Figure 3-4). C, C++, C#, and Java use the >> operator for a shift right operation. Delphi/Kylix uses the shr operator. Most assembly languages also provide a shift right instruction (shr on the 80x86).

Figure 3-4: The shift right operation (on a byte)

Shifting an unsigned binary value right divides that value by two. For example, if you shift the unsigned representation of 254 ($FE) one place to the right, you get 127 ($7F), exactly as you would expect. However, if you shift the 8-bit two's complement binary representation of −2 ($FE) one position to the right, you get 127 ($7F), which is *not* correct. To divide a signed number by two using a shift, we must define a third shift operation: *arithmetic shift right*. An arithmetic shift right operation does not modify the value of the HO bit. Figure 3-5 shows the arithmetic shift right operation for an 8-bit operand.

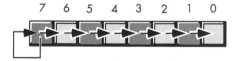

Figure 3-5: Arithmetic shift right operation (on a byte)

This generally produces the result you expect for two's complement signed operands. For example, if you perform the arithmetic shift right operation on −2 ($FE), you get −1 ($FF). Note, however, that this operation always rounds the numbers to the closest integer that is *less than or equal to the actual result*. If you arithmetically shift right −1 ($FF), the result is −1, not zero. Because −1 is less than zero, the arithmetic shift right operation rounds towards −1. This is not a "bug" in the arithmetic shift right operation; it just uses a different (though valid) definition of integer division. The bottom line, however, is that you probably won't be able to use a signed division operator as a substitute for arithmetic shift right in languages that don't support arithmetic shift right, because most integer division operators round towards zero.

One problem with the shift right operation in high-level languages is that it's rare for a high-level language to support both the logical shift right and the arithmetic shift right. Worse still, the specifications for certain languages leave it up to the compiler's implementer to decide whether to use an arithmetic shift right or a logical shift right operation. Therefore, it's only safe to use the shift right operator on values whose HO bit will cause both forms of the shift right operation to produce the same result. If you need to guarantee that a shift right is a logical shift right or an arithmetic shift right operation, then you'll either have to drop down into assembly language or you'll have to handle the HO bit manually. Obviously, the high-level code gets ugly really fast, so a quick in-line assembly statement might be a better solution if your program doesn't need to be portable across different CPUs. The following code demonstrates how to simulate a 32-bit logical shift right and arithmetic shift right in languages that don't guarantee the type of shift they use:

```
// Written in C/C++, assuming 32-bit integers, logical shift right:
    // Compute bit 30.
    Bit30 = ((ShiftThisValue & 0x80000000) != 0) ? 0x40000000 : 0;
    // Shifts bits 0..30.
    ShiftThisValue = (ShiftThisValue & 0x7fffffff) >> 1;
    // Merge in Bit #30.
    ShiftThisValue = ShiftThisValue | Bit30;

// Arithmetic shift right operation

    Bits3031 = ((ShiftThisValue & 0x800000000) != 0) ? 0xC0000000 : 0;
    // Shifts bits 0..30.
    ShiftThisValue = (ShiftThisValue & 0x7fffffff) >> 1;
    // Merge bits 30/31.
    ShiftThisValue = ShiftThisValue | Bits3031;
```

Many assembly languages also provide various rotate instructions that recirculate bits through an operand by taking the bits shifted out of one end of the operation and shifting them into the other end of the operand. Few high-level languages provide this operation; fortunately, you won't need it very often. If you do, you can synthesize this operation using the shift operators available in your high-level language:

```
// Pascal/Delphi/Kylix Rotate Left, 32-bit example:
    // Puts bit 31 into bit 0, clears other bits.
    CarryOut := (ValueToRotate shr 31);
    ValueToRotate := (ValueToRotate shl 1) or CarryOut;
```

Assembly language programmers typically have access to a wide variety of shift and rotate instructions. For more information on the type of shift and rotate operations that are possible, consult my assembly language programming book, *The Art of Assembly Language* (No Starch Press).

3.6 Bit Fields and Packed Data

CPUs generally operate most efficiently on byte, word, and double-word data types;[3] but occasionally you'll need to work with a data type whose size is something other than 8, 16, or 32 bits. In such cases, you may be able to save some memory by *packing* different strings of bits together as compactly as possible, without wasting any bits to align a particular data field on a byte or other boundary.

Consider a date of the form "04/02/01." It takes three numeric values to represent this date: month, day, and year values. Months, of course, use the values 1..12. It will require at least four bits (a maximum of 16 different values) to represent the month. Days use the range 1..31. Therefore, it will take five bits (a maximum of 32 different values) to represent the day entry. The year value, assuming that we're working with values in the range 0..99, requires seven bits (representing up to 128 different values). Four plus five plus seven is 16 bits, or two bytes. In other words, we can pack our date data into two bytes rather than the three that would be required if we used a separate byte for each of the month, day, and year values. This saves one byte of memory for each date stored, which could be a substantial saving if you need to store many dates. You might arrange the bits as shown in Figure 3-6.

Figure 3-6: Short packed date format (16 bits)

MMMM represents the four bits making up the month value, DDDDD represents the five bits making up the day, and YYYYYYY is the seven bits that hold the year. Each collection of bits representing a data item is a *bit field*. We could represent April 2, 2001, with $4101:

0100	00010	0000001	= %0100_0001_0000_0001 or $4101
04	02	01	

Although packed values are *space efficient* (that is, they use little memory), they are *computationally inefficient* (slow!). The reason? It takes extra instructions to unpack the data from the various bit fields. These extra instructions take time to execute (and additional bytes to hold the instructions); hence, you must carefully consider whether packed data

---

[3] Some RISC CPUs only operate efficiently on double-word values, so the concept of bit fields and packed data may apply to any object less than 32 bits in size on such CPUs.

fields will save you anything. The following sample HLA/x86 code demonstrates the effort that must go into packing and unpacking this 16-bit date format.

```
program dateDemo;

#include( "stdlib.hhf" )

static
    day:        uns8;
    month:      uns8;
    year:       uns8;

    packedDate: word;

begin dateDemo;

    stdout.put( "Enter the current month, day, and year: " );
    stdin.get( month, day, year );

    // Pack the data into the following bits:
    //
    // 15 14 13 12 11 10  9  8  7  6  5  4  3  2  1  0
    //  m  m  m  m  d  d  d  d  d  y  y  y  y  y  y  y

    mov( 0, ax );
    mov( ax, packedDate );   //Just in case there is an error.
    if( month > 12 ) then

        stdout.put( "Month value is too large", nl );

    elseif( month = 0 ) then

        stdout.put( "Month value must be in the range 1..12", nl );

    elseif( day > 31 ) then

        stdout.put( "Day value is too large", nl );

    elseif( day = 0 ) then

        stdout.put( "Day value must be in the range 1..31", nl );

    elseif( year > 99 ) then

        stdout.put( "Year value must be in the range 0..99", nl );
```

```
    else

        mov( month, al );
        shl( 5, ax );
        or( day, al );
        shl( 7, ax );
        or( year, al );
        mov( ax, packedDate );

    endif;

    // Okay, display the packed value:

    stdout.put( "Packed data = $", packedDate, nl );

    // Unpack the date:

    mov( packedDate, ax );
    and( $7f, al );          // Retrieve the year value.
    mov( al, year );

    mov( packedDate, ax );  // Retrieve the day value.
    shr( 7, ax );
    and( %1_1111, al );
    mov( al, day );

    mov( packedDate, ax );  // Retrieve the month value.
    rol( 4, ax );
    and( %1111, al );
    mov( al, month );

    stdout.put( "The date is ", month, "/", day, "/", year, nl );

end dateDemo;
```

Keeping in mind the Y2K[4] problem, adopting a date format that only supports a two-digit year is rather foolish. So consider a better date format, shown in Figure 3-7.

Figure 3-7: Long packed date format (32 bits)

---

[4] Year 2000, a software engineering disaster that occurred because programmers in the 1900s encoded dates using only two digits and then discovered they couldn't differentiate 1900 and 2000 when the year 2000 came along.

Because there are more bits in a 32-bit variable than are needed to hold the date, even accounting for years in the range 0–65,535, this format allots a full byte for the month and day fields. Because these two fields are bytes, an application can easily manipulate them as byte objects, reducing the overhead to pack and unpack these fields on those processors that support byte access. This leaves fewer bits for the year, but 65,536 years is probably sufficient (you can probably assume that your software will not be in use 63,000 years from now).

Of course, you could argue that this is no longer a packed date format. After all, we needed three numeric values, two of which fit just nicely into one byte each and one that should probably have at least two bytes. Because this "packed" date format consumes the same four bytes as the unpacked version, what is so special about this format? Well, in this example packed effectively means *packaged* or *encapsulated*. This particular packed format does not use as few bits as possible; by packing the data into a double-word variable the program can treat the date value as a single data value rather than as three separate variables. This generally means that it requires only a single machine instruction to operate on this data rather than three separate instructions.

Another difference you will note between this long packed date format and the short date format appearing in Figure 3-6 is the fact that this long date format rearranges the Year, Month, and Day fields. This is important because it allows you to easily compare two dates using an unsigned integer comparison. Consider the following HLA/assembly code:

```
mov( Date1, eax );         // Assume Date1 and Date2 are double-word variables
if( eax > Date2 ) then     //  using the Long Packed Date format.

    << do something if Date1 > Date2 >>

endif;
```

Had you kept the different date fields in separate variables, or organized the fields differently, you would not have been able to compare Date1 and Date2 in such a straightforward fashion. This example demonstrates another reason for packing data, even if you don't realize any space savings — it can make certain computations more convenient or even more efficient (contrary to what normally happens when you pack data).

Some high-level languages provide built-in support for packed data. For example, in C you can define structures like the following:

```
struct
{
    unsigned bits0_3   :4;
    unsigned bits4_11  :8;
    unsigned bits12_15 :4;
    unsigned bits16_23 :8;
    unsigned bits24_31 :8;
} packedData;
```

This structure specifies that each field is an unsigned object that holds four, eight, four, eight, and eight bits, respectively. The ":n" item appearing after each declaration specifies the minimum number of bits the compiler will allocate for the given field.

Unfortunately, it is not possible to provide a diagram that shows how a C/C++ compiler will allocate the values from a 32-bit double word among the fields. No (single) diagram is possible because C/C++ compiler implementers are free to implement these bit fields any way they see fit. The arrangement of the bits within the bit string is arbitrary (for example, the compiler could allocate the bits0_3 field in bits 28..31 of the ultimate object). The compiler can also inject extra bits between fields as it sees fit. The compiler can use a larger number of bits for each field if it so desires (this is actually the same thing as injecting extra padding bits between fields). Most C compilers attempt to minimize the injection of extraneous padding, but different C compilers (especially on different CPUs) do have their differences. Therefore, any use of C/C++ struct bit field declarations is almost guaranteed to be nonportable, and you can't really count on what the compiler is going to do with those fields.

The advantage of using the compiler's built-in data-packing capabilities is that the compiler automatically handles packing and unpacking the data for you. For example, you could write the following C/C++ code, and the compiler would automatically emit the necessary machine instructions to store and retrieve the individual bit fields for you:

```
struct
{
    unsigned year  :7;
    unsigned month :4;
    unsigned day   :5;
} ShortDate;
        . . .
    ShortDate.day = 28;
    ShortDate.month = 2;
    ShortDate.year = 3;   // 2003
```

3.7 Packing and Unpacking Data

The advantage of packed data types is efficient memory use. Consider the Social Security identification number in use in the United States. This is a nine-digit code that normally takes the following form (each "X" represents a single decimal digit):

```
XXX-XX-XXXX
```

If we encode a Social Security number using three separate (32-bit) integers, it will take 12 bytes to represent this value. That's actually more than the 11 bytes needed to represent the number using an array of characters. A better solution is to encode each field using short (16-bit) integers. Now it takes only 6 bytes to represent the Social Security number. Because the middle field in the Social Security number is always between 0 and 99, we can actually shave one more byte off the size of this structure by encoding the middle field with a single byte. Here's a sample Delphi/Kylix record structure that defines this data structure:

```
SSN :record

        FirstField:  smallint;  // smallints are 16 bits in Delphi/Kylix
        SecondField: byte;
        ThirdField:  smallint;

end;
```

If we drop the hyphens in the Social Security number, you'll notice that the result is a nine-digit number. Because we can exactly represent all values between 0 and 999,999,999 (nine digits) using 30 bits, it should be clear that we could actually encode any legal Social Security number using a 32-bit integer. The problem is that some software that manipulates Social Security numbers may need to operate on the individual fields. This means that you have to use expensive division, modulo, and multiplication operators in order to extract fields from a Social Security number you've encoded in a 32-bit integer format. Furthermore, it's a bit more painful to convert Social Security numbers to and from strings when using the 32-bit format. The advantage of using bit fields to hold a value is that it's relatively easy to insert and extract individual bit fields using fast machine instructions, and it's also less work to create a standard string representation (including the hyphens) of one of these fields. Figure 3-8 provides a straightforward implementation of the Social Security number packed data type using a separate string of bits for each field (note that this format uses 31 bits and ignores the HO bit).

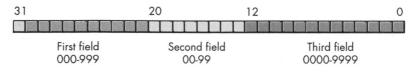

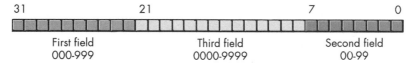

Figure 3-8: Social Security number packed fields encoding

As you'll soon see, fields that begin at bit position zero in a packed data object are the ones you can most efficiently access. So it's generally a good idea to arrange the fields in your packed data type so that the field you access most often begins at bit zero. Of course, you'll have to determine which field you access most often on an application-by-application basis. If you have no idea which field you'll access most often, you should try to assign the fields so they begin on a byte boundary. If there are unused bits in your packed type, you should attempt to spread them throughout the structure so that individual fields begin on a byte boundary and have those fields consume multiples of eight bits.

We've only got one unused bit in the Social Security example shown in Figure 3-8, but it turns out that we can use this extra bit to align two fields on a byte boundary and ensure that one of those fields occupies a bit string whose length is a multiple of eight bits. Consider Figure 3-9, which shows a rearranged version of our Social Security number data type.

Figure 3-9: A (possibly) improved encoding of the Social Security number

One problem with the data format shown in Figure 3-9 is that we can't sort Social Security numbers in an intuitive fashion by simply comparing 32-bit unsigned integers.[5] Therefore, if you intend to do a lot of sorting based on the entire Social Security number, the format in Figure 3-8 is probably a better format.

If this type of sorting isn't important to you, the format in Figure 3-9 has some advantages. This packed type actually uses eight bits (rather than seven) to represent SecondField (along with moving SecondField down to bit position zero); the extra bit will always contain zero. This means that SecondField consumes bits 0..7 (a whole byte) and ThirdField begins on a byte boundary (bit position eight). ThirdField doesn't consume a multiple of eight bits, and FirstField doesn't begin on a nice byte boundary, but we've done fairly well with this encoding, considering we only had one extra bit to play around with.

---

[5] "Intuitive" meaning that the first field is the most significant portion of the value, the second field is the next most significant, and the third field is the least significant component of the number.

The next question is, "How do we access the fields of this packed type?" There are two separate activities here. We need the ability to retrieve, or *extract*, the packed fields, and we need to be able to *insert* data into these fields. The AND, OR, and SHIFT operations provide the tools for this.

When actually operating on these fields, it's convenient to work with three separate variables rather than working directly with the packed data. For our Social Security number example, we can create the three variables FirstField, SecondField, and ThirdField. We can then extract the actual data from the packed value into these three variables, operate on these variables, and then insert the data from these three variables back into their fields when we're done.

Extracting the SecondField data from the packed format shown in Figure 3-9 is easy (remember, the field aligned to bit zero in our packed data is the easiest one to access). All you have to do is copy the data from the packed representation to the SecondField variable and then mask out all but the SecondField bits using the AND operation. Because SecondField is a 7-bit value, we can create the mask as an integer containing all one bits in positions zero through six and zeros everywhere else. The following C/C++ code demonstrates how to extract this field into the SecondField variable (assuming packedValue is a variable holding the 32-bit packed Social Security number):

```
SecondField = packedValue & 0x7f;    // 0x7f = %0111_1111
```

Extracting fields that are not aligned at bit zero takes a little more work. Consider the ThirdField entry in Figure 3-9. We can mask out all the bits associated with the first and second fields by logically ANDing the packed value with %_11_1111_1111_1111_0000_0000 ($3F_FF00). However, this leaves the ThirdField value sitting in bits 8 through 21, which is not convenient for various arithmetic operations. The solution is to shift the masked value down eight bits so that it's aligned at bit zero in our working variable. The following Pascal/Delphi/Kylix code shows how one might do this:

```
SecondField := (packedValue and $3fff00) shr 8;
```

As it turns out, you can also do the shift first and then do the logical AND operation (though this requires a different mask, $11_1111_1111_1111 or $3FFF). Here's the C/C++ code that extracts SecondField using that technique:

```
SecondField = (packedValue >> 8) & 0x3FFF;
```

Extracting a field that is aligned against the HO bit, as the first field is in our Social Security packed data type is almost as easy as accessing the data aligned at bit zero. All you have to do is shift the HO field down so that it's aligned at bit zero. The logical shift right operation automatically fills in the HO bits of the result with zeros, so no explicit masking is necessary. The following Pascal/Delphi code demonstrates this:

```
FirstField := packedValue shr 18; // Delphi's shift right is a logical
                                  //  shift right.
```

In HLA/x86 assembly language, it's actually quite easy to access the second and third fields of the packed data format in Figure 3-9. This is because we can easily access data at any arbitrary byte boundary in memory. That allows us to treat both the second and third fields as though they both are aligned at bit zero in the data structure. In addition, because the SecondField value is an 8-bit value (with the HO bit always containing zero), it only takes a single machine instruction to unpack the data, as shown here:

```
movzx( (type byte packedValue), eax );
```

This instruction fetches the first byte of packedValue (which is the LO 8 bits of packedValue on the 80x86), and it zero extends this value to 32 bits in EAX (movzx stands for "move with zero extension"). The EAX register, therefore, contains the SecondField value after this instruction executes.

Extracting the ThirdField value from our packed format isn't quite as easy, because this field isn't an even multiple of eight bits long. Therefore, we'll still need a masking operation to clear the unused bits from the 32-bit result we produce. However, because ThirdField is aligned on a byte (8-bit) boundary in our packed structure, we'll be able to avoid the shift operation that was necessary in the high-level code. Here's the HLA/x86 assembly code that extracts the third field from our packedValue object:

```
mov( (type word packedValue[1]), ax );  // Extracts bytes 1 & 2
                                         //  from packedValue.
and( $3FFF, eax );                       // Clears all the undesired bits.
```

Extracting FirstField from the packedValue object in HLA/x86 assembly code is identical to the high-level code; we'll simply shift the upper ten bits (which comprise FirstField) down to bit zero:

```
mov( packedValue, eax );
shr( 21, eax );
```

Inserting a field into a packed structure is only a little more complicated than extracting a field. Assuming the data you want to insert appears in some variable and contains zeros in the unused bits, inserting a field into a packed object requires three operations. First, if necessary, you shift the field's data to the left so its alignment matches the corresponding field in the packed object. The second step is to clear the corresponding bits in the packed structure. The final step is to logically OR the shifted field into the packed object. Figure 3-10 on the next page displays the details of this operation.

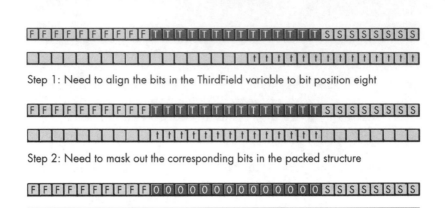

Step 1: Need to align the bits in the ThirdField variable to bit position eight

Step 2: Need to mask out the corresponding bits in the packed structure

Step 3: Need to logically OR the two values to produce the final result

Final Result

Figure 3-10: Inserting ThirdField into the Social Security packed type

Here's the C/C++ code that accomplishes the operation shown in Figure 3-10:

```
packedValue = (packedValue & 0xFFc000FF) | (ThirdField << 8 );
```

You'll note that $FFC000FF is the hexadecimal value that corresponds to all zeros in bit positions 8 through 21 and ones everywhere else.

3.8   For More Information

My book, *The Art of Assembly Language*, provides additional information on bit processing, including several algorithms for counting bits, reversing the bits in an object, merging two bit strings, coalescing sets of bits, and spreading bits out across some value. Please see that text for more details on these low-level bit operations. Donald Knuth's *The Art of Computer Programming, Volume Two: Seminumerical Algorithms* provides a discussion of various arithmetic operations (addition, subtraction, multiplication, and division) that you may find of interest.

4

FLOATING-POINT REPRESENTATION

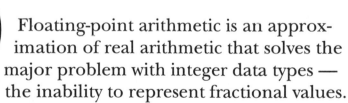

Floating-point arithmetic is an approximation of real arithmetic that solves the major problem with integer data types — the inability to represent fractional values. Although floating-point arithmetic is often slower than integer arithmetic, modern CPUs incorporate well-designed floating-point units, thus reducing the performance difference between integer and floating-point arithmetic.

For this reason, the stigma surrounding floating-point arithmetic has diminished since the days when floating-point results were computed using software (rather than hardware). One unfortunate aspect of floating-point's increasing popularity is that many programmers do not understand the inherent limitations of the floating-point format. Floating-point arithmetic is but an approximation of real arithmetic. The inaccuracies present in this approximation can lead to serious defects in application software if an engineer is not aware of the problems associated with these approximations. In order to write great software that produces correct results when using floating-point arithmetic, programmers must be aware of the machine's underlying numeric representation and of how floating-point arithmetic approximates real arithmetic.

4.1 Introduction to Floating-Point Arithmetic

Floating-point numbers provide only an approximation of real numbers. This is because there is an infinite number of possible real values, while floating-point representation uses a finite number of bits (and, therefore, can only represent a finite number of different values). When a given floating-point format cannot exactly represent some real value, the floating-point number must instead use the closest value that it can exactly represent. This section describes how the floating-point format works so you can better understand the problems with these approximations.

Consider a couple of problems with integer and fixed-point formats. Integers, of course, cannot represent any fractional values. Another problem with most integer representations is that they can only represent values in the range $0..2^n-1$ or $-2^{n-1}..2^{n-1}-1$. Fixed-point formats provide the ability to represent fractional values, but at the expense of the range of integer values you can represent. This problem, which the floating-point format solves, is the issue of *dynamic range*.

Consider a simple 16-bit unsigned fixed-point format that uses 8 bits for fractional component and 8 bits for the integer component of the number. The integer component can represent values in the range 0..255, and the fractional component can represent the values zero and fractions between 2^{-8} and 1 (with a resolution of about 2^{-8}). Suppose, now, that for a string of calculations you only need two bits to represent the fractional values 0.0, 0.25, 0.5, and 0.75. Unfortunately, the extra six bits in the fractional part of the number go to waste. Wouldn't it be nice if we could utilize those bits in the integer portion of the number to extend its range from 0..255 to 0..16,383? Well, that's the basic concept behind the floating-point representation. In a floating-point value, the radix point (binary point) can freely float between digits in the number as needed. So if in a 16-bit binary number you only need two bits of precision for the fractional component of the number, the binary point can float down between bits 1 and 2 in the number, allowing the format to utilize bits 2 through 15 for the integer portion. In order to support a floating-point format, the numeric representation needs one additional field — a field that specifies the position of the radix point within the number. This extra field is equivalent to the *exponent* present when using scientific notation.

To represent real numbers, most floating-point formats use some number of bits to represent a *mantissa* and a smaller number of bits to represent an *exponent*. The mantissa is a base value, that usually falls within a limited range (for example, between zero and one). The exponent is a multiplier that when applied to the mantissa produces values outside this range. The result of separating the number into these two parts is that floating-point numbers can only represent numbers with a specific number of *significant* digits. As you will soon see, if the difference between the smallest and largest exponent is greater than the number of significant digits in the mantissa (and it usually is), then the floating-point representation cannot exactly represent all the integers between the smallest and largest values the floating-point format can represent.

To easily see the impact of limited-precision arithmetic, we will adopt a simplified *decimal* floating-point format for our examples. Our floating-point format will provide a mantissa with three significant digits and a decimal exponent with two digits. The mantissa and exponents are both signed values, as shown in Figure 4-1.

Figure 4-1: Simple floating-point format

Note that this particular floating-point representation can approximate all the values between 0.00 and 9.99×10^{99}. However, this format certainly cannot exactly represent all values in this range (that would take 100 digits of precision!). To represent a value like 9,876,543,210, the floating-point format in Figure 4-1 would have to approximate this value with 9.88×10^{9} (or 9.88e + 9 in programming language notation, which this book will generally use from this point forward).

The big advantage of the mantissa/exponent configuration is that a floating-point format can represent values across a wide range. There is a subtle disadvantage to this scheme, however: you cannot *exactly* represent as many different values with a floating-point format as you can with an integer format. This is because the floating-point format can provide multiple representations (that is, different bit patterns) for the same value. In the simplified decimal floating-point format shown in Figure 4-1, for example, 1.00e + 1 and 0.10e + 2 are different representations of the same value. As there are a finite number of different representations possible (given a finite number of bits or digits), whenever a single value has two possible representations, that's one less different value the format can represent.

Furthermore, the floating-point format, a form of scientific notation, complicates arithmetic somewhat. When adding and subtracting two numbers in scientific notation, you must adjust the two values so that their exponents are the same. For example, when adding 1.23e1 and 4.56e0, you could convert 4.56e0 to 0.456e1 and then add them. This produces 1.686e1. Unfortunately, the result does not fit into the three significant digits of our current format, so we must either *round* or *truncate* the result to three significant digits. Rounding generally produces the most accurate result, so let's round the result to obtain 1.69e1. As you can see, the lack of *precision* (the number of digits or bits maintained in a computation) affects the *accuracy* (the correctness of the computation).

In the previous example, we were able to round the result because we maintained *four* significant digits *during* the calculation. If our floating-point calculation were limited to three significant digits *during* computation, we would have had to truncate the last digit of the smaller number, obtaining 1.68e1, which is even less correct. Therefore, to improve the accuracy of floating-point calculations, it is necessary to use extra digits during the calculation. These extra digits are known as *guard digits* (or *guard bits* in the case of a binary format). They greatly enhance accuracy during a long chain of computations.

The accuracy lost during a single computation usually isn't bad unless you are greatly concerned about the accuracy of your computations. However, if you compute a value that is the result of a sequence of floating-point operations, the error can *accumulate* and greatly affect the computation itself. For example, suppose we add 1.23e3 and 1.00e0. Adjusting the numbers so their exponents are the same before the addition produces 1.23e3 + 0.001e3. The sum of these two values, even after rounding, is 1.23e3. This might seem perfectly reasonable to you; after all, if we can only maintain three significant digits, adding in a small value shouldn't affect the result. However, suppose we were to add 1.00e0 to 1.23e3 *ten times*. The first time we add 1.00e0 to 1.23e3 we get 1.23e3. Likewise, we get this same result the second, third, fourth . . . and tenth time we add 1.00e0 to 1.23e3. On the other hand, had we added 1.00e0 to itself ten times, then added the result (1.00e1) to 1.23e3, we would obtain a different result, 1.24e3. This is an important thing to know about limited-precision arithmetic:

> *The order of evaluation can affect the accuracy of the result.*

Your results will be better when adding or subtracting numbers if their relative magnitudes (that is, the sizes of the exponents) are similar. If you are performing a chain calculation involving addition and subtraction, you should attempt to group the operations so that you can add or subtract values whose magnitudes are close to one another before adding or subtracting values whose magnitudes are not as close.

Another problem with addition and subtraction is that you can wind up with *false precision*. Consider the computation 1.23e0 − 1.22e0. This produces 0.01e0. Although this is mathematically equivalent to 1.00e − 2, this latter form suggests that the last two digits are both exactly zero. Unfortunately, we only have a single significant digit after this computation, which is in the hundredths place. Indeed, some FPUs or floating-point software packages might actually insert random digits (or bits) into the LO positions. This brings up a second important rule concerning limited-precision arithmetic:

> *Whenever subtracting two numbers with the same signs or adding two numbers with different signs, the accuracy of the result may be less than the precision available in the floating-point format.*

Multiplication and division do not suffer from these same problems because you do not have to adjust the exponents before the operation; all you need to do is add the exponents and multiply the mantissas (or subtract the exponents and divide the mantissas). By themselves, multiplication and division do not produce particularly poor results. However, they tend to exacerbate any accuracy error that already exists in a value. For example, if you multiply 1.23e0 by 2, when you should be multiplying 1.24e0 by 2, the result is even less accurate than it was. This brings up a third important rule when working with limited-precision arithmetic:

> *When performing a chain of calculations involving addition, subtraction, multiplication, and division, try to perform the multiplication and division operations first.*

Often, by applying normal algebraic transformations, you can arrange a calculation so the multiplication and division operations occur first. For example, suppose you want to compute the following:

```
x × (y + z)
```

Normally you would add y and z together and multiply their sum by x. However, you will get a little more accuracy if you first transform the previous equation to get the following:

```
x × y + x × z
```

This way you can compute the result by performing the multiplications first.[1]

Multiplication and division have other problems, as well. When multiplying two very large or very small numbers, it is quite possible for *overflow* or *underflow* to occur. The same situation occurs when dividing a small number by a large number, or when dividing a large number by a small number. This brings up a fourth rule you should attempt to follow when multiplying or dividing values:

> *When multiplying and dividing sets of numbers, try to multiply and divide numbers that have the same relative magnitudes.*

Comparing floating-point numbers is very dangerous. Given the inaccuracies present in any computation (including converting an input string to a floating-point value), you should *never* compare two floating-point values to see if they are equal. In a binary floating-point format, different computations that produce the same (mathematical) result may differ in their least significant bits. For example, adding 1.31e0 + 1.69e0 should produce 3.00e0. Likewise, adding 1.50e0 + 1.50e0 should produce 3.00e0. However, were you to compare (1.31e0 + 1.69e0) against (1.50e0 + 1.50e0) you might find that these sums are *not* equal to one another. The test for equality succeeds if and

---

[1] Of course, the drawback is that you must now perform two multiplications rather than one, so the result may be slower.

only if all bits (or digits) in the two operands are the same. Because it is not necessarily true that two seemingly equivalent floating-point computations will produce exactly equal results, a straight comparison for equality may fail when, algebraically, such a comparison should succeed.

The standard way to test for equality between floating-point numbers is to determine how much error (or tolerance) you will allow in a comparison, and then check to see if one value is within this error range of the other. The straightforward way to do this is to use a test like the following:

```
if( (Value1 >= (Value2 - error)) and (Value1 <= (Value2 + error)) then . . .
```

A more efficient way to handle this is to use a statement of the form:

```
if( abs(Value1 - Value2) <= error ) then . . .
```

You must exercise care when choosing the value for *error*. This should be a value slightly greater than the largest amount of error that will creep into your computations. The exact value will depend upon the particular floating-point format you use and the magnitudes of the values you are comparing. So the final rule is this:

> *When comparing two floating-point numbers for equality, always compare the values to see if the difference between two values is less than some small error value.*

Checking two floating-point numbers for equality is a very famous problem, and almost every introductory programming text discusses this issue. Perhaps less well known is the fact that comparing for less than or greater than creates the same problems. Suppose that a sequence of floating-point calculations produces a result that is only accurate to within plus or minus error, even though the floating-point representation provides better accuracy than error suggests. If you compare such a result against some other calculation computed with less accumulated error, and those two values are very close to one other, then comparing them for less than or greater than may produce incorrect results.

For example, suppose that some chain of calculations in our simplified decimal representation produces the result 1.25, which is only accurate to plus or minus 0.05 (that is, the real value could be somewhere between 1.20 and 1.30). Also assume that a second chain of calculations produces the result 1.27, which is accurate to the full precision of our floating-point result (that is, the actual value, before rounding, is somewhere between 1.265 and 1.275). Now, if we compare the result of the first calculation (1.25) against the value of the second calculation (1.27), we will find that the first calculation is less than the result of the second. Unfortunately, given the inaccuracy present in the first calculation this might not be true. If the correct result of the first computation happens to be in the range 1.27 to 1.30 (exclusive), then reporting that the first calculation is less than the second is false. About the only reasonable test is to see if the two values are within the *error* tolerance of one another. If so, treat the values as equal (so one wouldn't be considered less than or greater than the other). If you determine that the values are not equal to one another within the desired error tolerance, then you can compare them to see if one value is less than or greater than the other. This is known as a *miserly approach* to comparing for less than or greater than (that is, we try to find as few values that are less than or greater than as possible).

The other possibility is to use an *eager approach* to the comparison. An eager approach attempts to make the result of the comparison true as often as possible. Given two values that you want to compare, and an error tolerance you're interested in achieving, here's how you'd eagerly compare the two values for less than or greater than:

```
if( A < (B + error)) then Eager_A_lessthan_B;
if( A > (B - error)) then Eager_A_greaterthan_B;
```

Don't forget that calculations like (B + error) are subject to their own inaccuracies, depending on the relative magnitudes of the values B and error, and the inaccuracy of this calculation may very well affect the final result that you achieve in the comparison.

There are other problems that can occur when using floating-point values. This book can only point out some of the major problems and make you aware that you cannot treat floating-point arithmetic like real arithmetic — the inaccuracies present in limited-precision arithmetic can get you into trouble if you are not careful. A good text on numerical analysis or even scientific computing can help fill in the details that are beyond the scope of this book. If you are going to be working with floating-point arithmetic, *in any language*, you should take the time to study the effects of limited-precision arithmetic on your computations.

4.2   IEEE Floating-Point Formats

When Intel's 80x86 designers planned to introduce a floating-point unit (FPU) for its original 8086 microprocessor, they were smart enough to realize that the electrical engineers and solid-state physicists who design chips probably didn't have the necessary numerical analysis background to design a good floating-point representation. So Intel went out and hired the best numerical analyst it could find to design a floating-point format for its 8087 FPU. That person then hired two other experts in the field, and the three of them (Kahn, Coonan, and Stone) designed Intel's floating-point format. They did such a good job designing the KCS Floating-Point Standard that the IEEE organization used this format as the basis for the IEEE floating-point format.

To handle a wide range of performance and accuracy requirements, Intel actually introduced *three* floating-point formats: single precision, double precision, and extended precision. The single- and double-precision formats corresponded to C's `float` and `double` types or FORTRAN's `real` and `double`-precision types. Intel intended to use extended precision for long chains of computations. Extended precision contains 16 extra bits that the calculations can use as guard bits before rounding down to a double-precision value when storing the result.

4.2.1 Single-Precision Floating-Point Format

The single-precision format uses a 24-bit mantissa and an 8-bit exponent. The mantissa usually represents a value between 1.0 and just less than 2.0. The HO bit of the mantissa is always assumed to be one and represents a value just to the left of the binary point. The remaining 23 mantissa bits appear to the right of the binary point and represent the value:

```
1.mmmmmmm mmmmmmmm mmmmmmmm
```

The presence of the implied one bit is why the mantissa is always greater than or equal to one. Even if the other mantissa bits are all zero, the implied one bit always gives us the value one. Each position to the right of the binary point represents a value (zero or one) times a successive negative power of two, but even if we had an almost infinite number of one bits after the binary point, they still would not add up to two. So the mantissa can represent values in the range 1.0 to just less than 2.0.

Some examples would probably be useful here. Consider the decimal value 1.7997. Here are the steps we could go though to compute the binary mantissa for this value:

- Subtract 2^0 from 1.7997 to produce 0.7997 and %1.0000000000000000000000000.

- Subtract 2^{-1} ($^1/_2$) from 0.7997 to produce 0.2997 and %1.1000000000000000000000000.

- Subtract 2^{-2} ($^1/_4$) from 0.2997 to produce 0.0497 and %1.1100000000000000000000000.

- Subtract 2^{-5} ($^1/_{32}$) from 0.0497 to produce 0.0185 and %1.1100100000000000000000000.

- Subtract 2^{-6} ($^1/_{64}$) from 0.0185 to produce 0.00284 and %1.1100110000000000000000000.

- Subtract 2^{-9} ($^1/_{512}$) from 0.00284 to produce 0.000871 and %1.1100110010000000000000000.

- Subtract 2^{-10} ($^1/_{1,024}$) from 0.000871 to (approximately) produce zero and %1.1100110011000000000000000.

Although there is an infinite number of values between one and two, we can only represent eight million (2^{23}) of them because we use a 23-bit mantissa (the 24th bit is always one). This is the reason for inaccuracy in floating-point arithmetic — we only have 23 bits of precision in computations involving single-precision floating-point values.

The mantissa uses a *one's complement* format rather than two's complement. This means that the 24-bit value of the mantissa is simply an unsigned binary number, and the sign bit, in bit position 31, determines whether that value is positive or negative. One's complement numbers have the unusual property that there are two representations for zero (with the sign bit set or clear). Generally, this is important only to the person designing the floating-point software or hardware system. We will assume that the value zero always has the sign bit clear. The single-precision floating-point format takes the form shown in Figure 4-2.

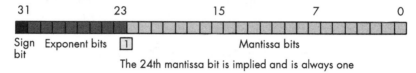

The 24th mantissa bit is implied and is always one

Figure 4-2: Single-precision (32-bit) floating-point format

To represent values outside the range 1.0 to just under 2.0, the exponent portion of the floating-point format comes into play. The floating-point format raises two to the power specified by the exponent and then multiplies the mantissa by this value. The exponent is eight bits and uses an *excess-127* format (sometimes called bias-127 exponents). In excess-127 format, the exponent 2^0 is represented by the value 127 ($7f). Therefore, to convert an exponent to excess-127 format, simply add 127 to the exponent value. For example, the single precision representation for 1.0 is $3f800000. The mantissa is 1.0 (including the implied bit) and the exponent is 2^0, or 127 ($7f) when you add in the excess-127 exponent value.

The use of excess-127 format for the exponent makes it easier to compare floating-point values. As it turns out, if we handle the sign bit (bit 31) separately, we can easily compare two floating-point numbers for less than or greater than by simply comparing them as though they were unsigned integers. To handle the sign bit, we simply note the signs of the two values. If the signs are not equal, then the positive value (the one with bit 31 set to zero) will be greater than the number that has the HO bit set to one.[2] If the sign bits are both zero, then we can use a straight unsigned binary comparison. If the signs are both one, then we do an unsigned comparison but invert the result (so if the sign bits are set, we treat less than as greater

---

[2] Actually, there are a couple of exceptions. As you'll see momentarily, the floating-point format has two representations for zero — one with the sign bit set and one with the sign bit clear; a floating-point comparison should treat these two values as equal. Likewise, there are a couple of special floating-point values that are incomparable, the comparison operation must consider those values as well.

than and vice versa). On some CPUs a 32-bit unsigned comparison is much faster than a 32-bit floating-point comparison. In such situations, it's probably worthwhile to do the comparison using integer arithmetic rather than floating-point arithmetic.

With a 24-bit mantissa, you will get approximately $6\frac{1}{2}$ decimal digits of precision (one half digit of precision means that the first six digits can all be in the range 0..9 but the seventh digit can only be in the range 0..x where x < 9 and is generally close to 5). With an 8-bit excess-127 exponent, the dynamic range of single-precision floating-point numbers is approximately $2^{\pm128}$ or about $10^{\pm38}$.

Although single-precision floating-point numbers are perfectly suitable for many applications, the dynamic range is somewhat limited and is unsuitable for many financial, scientific, and other applications. Furthermore, during long chains of computations, the limited accuracy of the single precision format may introduce serious error. For serious calculations, a floating-point format with more precision is necessary.

4.2.2   Double-Precision Floating-Point Format

The double-precision format helps overcome the problems of the single-precision floating-point. Using twice the space, the double-precision format has an 11-bit excess-1,023 exponent and a 53-bit mantissa (including an implied HO bit of one) plus a sign bit. This provides a dynamic range of about $10^{\pm308}$ and $14\frac{1}{2}$ digits of precision, which is sufficient for most applications. Double-precision floating-point values take the form shown in Figure 4-3.

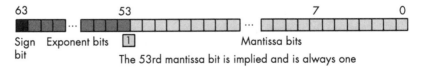

Figure 4-3: Double-precision (64-bit) floating-point format

4.2.3   Extended-Precision Floating-Point Format

In order to help ensure accuracy during long chains of computations involving double-precision floating-point numbers, Intel designed the extended-precision format. The extended-precision format uses 80 bits. Twelve of the additional 16 bits are appended to the mantissa, and 4 of the additional bits are appended to the exponent. Unlike the single- and double-precision values, the extended-precision format's mantissa does not have an implied HO bit that is always one. Therefore, the extended-precision format provides a 64-bit mantissa, a 15-bit excess-16,383 exponent, and a 1-bit sign. The format for the extended-precision floating-point value appears in Figure 4-4.

Sign   Exponent bits   Mantissa bits
bit

Figure 4-4: Extended-precision (80-bit) floating-point format

On the 80x86 FPUs, all computations are done using the extended-precision form. Whenever you load a single- or double-precision value, the FPU automatically converts it to an extended-precision value. Likewise, when you store a single or double precision value to memory, the FPU automatically rounds the value down to the appropriate size before storing it. By always working with the extended-precision format, Intel guarantees a large number of guard bits are present to ensure the accuracy of your computations. By performing all computations using 80 bits, Intel helps ensure (but not guarantee) that you will get full 32- or 64-bit accuracy in your computations. Because the FPUs do not provide a large number of guard bits in 80-bit computations, some error will inevitably creep into the LO bits of an extended-precision computation. However, if your computation is correct to 64 bits, the 80-bit computation will generally provide *at least* 64 accurate bits. Most of the time you will get even more. While you cannot assume that you get an accurate 80-bit computation, you can usually do better than 64 bits when using the extended-precision format.

Non-Intel CPUs that support floating-point arithmetic generally provide only the 32-bit and 64-bit formats. As such, calculations on those CPUs may produce less accurate results than the equivalent string of calculations on the 80x86 using 80-bit calculations.

4.3   Normalization and Denormalized Values

To maintain maximum precision during floating-point computations, most computations use *normalized* values. A normalized floating-point value is one whose HO mantissa bit contains one. Keeping floating-point numbers normalized is beneficial because it maintains the maximum number of bits of precision in a computation. If several HO bits of the mantissa are all zero, the mantissa has that many fewer bits of precision available for computation. Therefore, a floating-point computation will be more accurate if it involves only normalized values.

Almost any unnormalized value can be normalized by shifting the mantissa bits to the left and decrementing the exponent until a one appears in the HO bit of the mantissa.[3] Remember, the exponent is a binary exponent. Each time you increment the exponent, you multiply the floating-point value by two. Likewise, whenever you decrement the exponent, you divide the floating-point value by two. By the same token, shifting the mantissa to the

---

[3] In the rare case where you wind up with more than one bit to the left of the binary point, you can normalize the mantissa by shifting its bits to the right one position and incrementing the exponent.

left one bit position multiplies the floating-point value by two, and shifting the mantissa to the right divides the floating-point value by two. Therefore, shifting the mantissa to the left one position *and* decrementing the exponent does not change the value of the floating-point number (this is why, as you saw earlier, there are multiple representations for certain numbers in the floating-point format).

Here's an example of an unnormalized value:

0.100000×2^1

Shift the mantissa to the left one position and decrement the exponent to normalize it:

1.000000×2^0

There are two important cases in which a floating-point number cannot be normalized. Zero is one of these special cases. Obviously it cannot be normalized because the floating-point representation for zero contains no one bits. This, however, is not a problem because we can exactly represent the value zero with only a single bit. The IEEE floating-point formats use all zero bits in the exponent and mantissa fields to denote the value zero. Note that the IEEE floating-point format supports both +0 and −0 (depending on the value of the sign bit). Arithmetic calculations and comparisons treat positive and negative zero as equivalent, and software operating on floating-point values that represent zero can use the sign bit as a flag to indicate different things. For example, you could use the sign bit to indicate that the value is exactly zero (with the sign bit clear) or to indicate that it is actually nonzero but too small to represent with the current format (by setting the sign bit). Intel recommends using the sign bit to indicate that zero was produced via underflow of a negative value (with the sign bit set) or underflow of a positive number (with the sign bit clear). Presumably, their FPUs set the sign bit according to their recommendations when the FPUs produce a zero result. However, for the purposes of calculation, the floating-point formats ignore the sign bit when dealing with the value zero.

The second case in which we cannot normalize a floating-point number is when we have some HO bits in the mantissa that are zero but the biased exponent[4] is also zero (and we cannot decrement it to normalize the mantissa). Rather than disallow certain small values, whose HO mantissa bits and biased exponent are zero (the most negative exponent possible), the IEEE standard allows special *denormalized* values to represent these smaller values.[5] Although the use of denormalized values allows IEEE floating-point computations to produce better results than if underflow occurred, keep in mind that denormalized values offer fewer bits of precision.

---

[4] "Biased" means to add an offset to the value, e.g., an excess-127 exponent has a bias of 127.
[5] The alternative would be to underflow the values to zero.

4.4 Rounding

During a calculation, as you have seen, floating-point arithmetic functions may produce a result with greater precision than the floating-point format supports (the *guard bits* in the calculation maintain this extra precision). When the calculation is complete and the code needs to store the result back into a floating-point variable, something must be done about those extra bits of precision. How the system uses with those extra guard bits to affect the bits it does maintain is known as *rounding,* and how it is done can affect the accuracy of the computation. Traditionally, floating-point software and hardware use one of four different ways to round values: truncation, rounding up, rounding down, or rounding to nearest.

Truncation is easy, but it generates the least accurate results in a chain of computations. Few modern floating-point systems use truncation except as a means for converting floating-point values to integers (truncation is the standard conversion when coercing a floating-point value to an integer).

Rounding up is another function that is useful on occasion. Rounding up leaves the value alone if the guard bits are all zero, but if the current mantissa does not exactly fit into the destination bits, then rounding up sets the result to the smallest possible larger value in the floating-point format. Like truncation, this is not a normal rounding mode. It is, however, useful for implementing functions like *ceil* (which rounds a floating-point value to the smallest possible larger integer).

Rounding down is just like rounding up, except it rounds the result to the largest possible smaller value. This may sound like truncation, but there is a subtle difference between truncation and rounding down. Truncation always rounds towards zero. For positive numbers, truncation and rounding down do the same thing. However, for negative numbers, truncation simply uses the existing bits in the mantissa, whereas rounding down will actually add a one bit to the LO position if the result was negative. Like truncation, this is not a normal rounding mode. It is, however, useful for implementing functions like *floor* (which rounds a floating-point value to the largest possible smaller integer).

Rounding to nearest is probably the most intuitive way to process the guard bits. If the value of the guard bits is less than half the value of the LO bit of the mantissa, then rounding to nearest truncates the result to the largest possible smaller value (ignoring the sign). If the guard bits represent some value that is greater than half of the value of the LO mantissa bit, then rounding to nearest rounds the mantissa to the smallest possible greater value (ignoring the sign). If the guard bits represent a value that is exactly half the value of the LO bit of the mantissa, then the IEEE floating-point standard says that half the time it should round up and half the time it should round down. You do this by rounding the mantissa to the value that has a zero in the LO bit position. That is, if the current mantissa already has a zero in its LO bit, you use the current mantissa value; if the current mantissa value has a one in the LO mantissa position, then you add one to the mantissa to round it up to the smallest possible larger value with a zero in the LO bit. This scheme, mandated by the IEEE floating-point standard, produces the best possible result when loss of precision occurs.

Here are some examples of rounding, using 24-bit mantissas, with 4 guard bits (that is, these examples round 28-bit numbers to 24-bit numbers using the rounding to nearest algorithm):

```
1.000_0100_1010_0100_1001_0101_0001 -> 1.000_0100_1010_0100_1001_0101
1.000_0100_1010_0100_1001_0101_1100 -> 1.000_0100_1010_0100_1001_0110
1.000_0100_1010_0100_1001_0101_1000 -> 1.000_0100_1010_0100_1001_0110

1.000_0100_1010_0100_1001_0100_0001 -> 1.000_0100_1010_0100_1001_0100
1.000_0100_1010_0100_1001_0100_1100 -> 1.000_0100_1010_0100_1001_0101
1.000_0100_1010_0100_1001_0100_1000 -> 1.000_0100_1010_0100_1001_0100
```

4.5 Special Floating-Point Values

The IEEE floating-point format provides a special encoding for several special values. In this section we'll look these special values, their purpose and meaning, and their representation in the floating-point format.

Under normal circumstances, the exponent bits of a floating-point number do not contain all zeros or all ones. An exponent containing all one or zero bits indicates a special value.

If the exponent contains all ones and the mantissa is nonzero (discounting the implied bit), then the HO bit of the mantissa (again discounting the implied bit) determines whether the value represents a *quiet not-a-number* (QNaN) or a *signaling not-a-number* (SNaN) (see Table 4-1). These not-a-number (NaN) results tell the system that some serious miscalculation has taken place and that the result of the calculation is completely undefined. QNaNs represent indeterminate results, while SNaNs specify that an invalid operation has taken place. Any calculation involving a NaN produces an NaN result, regardless of the values of any other operand(s). Note that the sign bit is irrelevant for NaNs. The binary representations of NaNs are shown in Table 4-1.

Table 4-1: Binary Representations for NaN

NaN	FP Format	Value
SNaN	32 bits	%s_11111111_0xxxx...xx (The value of s value is irrelevant — at least one of the x bits must be nonzero.)
SNaN	64 bits	%s_1111111111_0xxxxx...x (The value of s is irrelevant — at least one of the x bits must be nonzero.)
SNaN	80 bits	%s_1111111111_0xxxxx...x (The value of s is irrelevant — at least one of the x bits must be nonzero.)

Table 4-1: Binary Representations for NaN (continued)

NaN	FP Format	Value
QNaN	32 bits	%s_11111111_1xxxx...xx (The value of s is irrelevant.)
QNaN	64 bits	%s_1111111111_1xxxxx...x (The value of s is irrelevant.)
QNaN	80 bits	%s_1111111111_1xxxxx...x (The value of s is irrelevant.)

Two other special values are represented when the exponent contains all one bits, and the mantissa contains all zeros. In such a case, the sign bit determines whether the result is the representation for +*infinity* or −*infinity*. Whenever a calculation involves infinity as one of the operands, the arithmetic operation will produce one of the (well-defined) values found in Table 4-2.

Table 4-2: Operations Involving Infinity

Operation	Result
n / ±infinity	0
±infinity × ±infinity	±infinity
±nonzero / 0	±infinity
infinity + infinity	infinity
n + infinity	infinity
n − infinity	−infinity
±0 / ±0	NaN
infinity − infinity	NaN
±infinity / ±infinity	NaN
±infinity × 0	NaN

Finally, if the exponent bits are all zero, the sign bit indicates which of the two special values, −0 or +0, the floating-point number represents. Because the floating-point format uses a one's complement notation, there are two separate representations for zero. Note that with respect to comparisons, arithmetic, and other operations, +0 is equal to −0.

4.6 Floating-Point Exceptions

The IEEE floating-point standard defines certain degenerate conditions under which the floating-point processor (or software-implemented floating-point code) should possibly notify the application software. These exceptional conditions include the following:

- Invalid operation
- Division by zero
- Denormalized operand

- Numeric overflow
- Numeric underflow
- Inexact result

Of these, inexact result is the least serious, because most floating calculations will produce an inexact result. A denormalized operand also isn't too serious (though this exception indicates that your calculation may be less accurate as a result of less available precision). The other exceptions indicate a more serious problem, and you shouldn't ignore them.

How the computer system notifies your application of these exceptions depends on the CPU/FPU, operating system, and programming language, so we can't really go into how one might handle these exceptions. Generally, though, you can use the exception-handling facilities in your programming language to trap these conditions as they occur in your particular environment. Note that most computer systems require that you explicitly tell them to generate a notification for these exceptional conditions; otherwise, the system will not notify you when one of the exceptional conditions exist.

4.7 Floating-Point Operations

Although most modern CPUs support a floating-point unit (FPU) that does floating-point arithmetic in hardware, it's worthwhile to actually develop a set of software floating-point arithmetic routines to get a solid feel for what's involved in floating-point arithmetic. Generally, when designing a software-based floating-point package, you would use assembly language to write the math functions because speed is a primary design goal for a floating-point package. However, in this chapter we're only writing this floating-point package to get a clearer picture of what's involved in floating-point arithmetic, so we'll opt for code that is easy to write, read, and understand. As it turns out, floating-point addition and subtraction are easy to do in a high-level language like C/C++ or Pascal, so we'll implement these functions in these languages. Floating-point multiplication and division actually turn out to be easier to do in assembly language than in a high-level language, so this book will write the floating-point multiplication and division routines using HLA.

4.7.1 Floating-Point Representation

For the purposes of the floating-point functions we're about to develop, this section will use the IEEE 32-bit single-precision floating-point format (shown earlier in Figure 4-2), which uses a one's complement representation for signed values. This means that the sign bit (bit 31) contains a one if the number is negative and a zero if the number is positive. The exponent is an 8-bit excess-127 exponent sitting in bits 23..30, and the mantissa is a 24-bit value with an implied HO bit of one. Because of the implied HO bit, this format does not support denormalized values.

4.7.2 Floating-Point Addition and Subtraction

Because the IEEE floating-point format supports signed real values, it turns out that addition and subtraction use essentially the same code. After all, computing X – Y is equivalent to computing X + (–Y). So if we can add a negative number with some other value, then we can also perform subtraction by first negating some number and then adding them. And because the IEEE floating-point format uses the one's complement representation, negating a value is trivial — we just invert the sign bit.

Because we're using the standard IEEE 32-bit single-precision floating-point format, we could theoretically get away with using the C/C++ float data type (assuming the underlying C/C++ compiler also uses this format, as most do on modern machines). However, you'll soon see that when doing floating-point calculations in software, we need to manipulate various fields within the floating-point format as bit strings and integer values. Therefore, it's more convenient to use a 32-bit unsigned integer type to hold the bit representation for our floating-point values. To avoid confusing our real values with actual integer values in a program, we'll define the following real data type (which assumes that unsigned longs are 32-bit values in your implementation of C/C++) and declare all our real variables using this type:

```
typedef long unsigned real;
```

One advantage of using the same floating-point format that C/C++ uses for float values is that we can assign floating-point literal constants to our real variables, and we can do other floating-point operations such as input and output using existing library routines. However, one potential problem is that C/C++ will attempt to automatically convert between integer and floating-point formats if we use a real variable in a floating-point expression (remember, as far as C/C++ is concerned, real is just a long unsigned integer value). This means that we need to tell the compiler to treat the bit patterns found in our real variables as though they were float objects.

A simple type coercion like (float) realVariable will not work. The C/C++ compiler will emit code to convert the integer it believes realVariable to contain into the equivalent floating-point value. However, the bit pattern in realVariable is a floating-point value, so no conversion is required. We want the C/C++ compiler to treat the bit pattern it finds in realVariable as a float without doing any conversion. The following C/C++ macro is a sneaky way to do this:

```
#define asreal(x) (*((float *) &x))
```

Note that this macro requires a single parameter that must be a real variable. The result of this macro is a variable that the compiler believes is a float variable.

Now that we have our `float` variable, we'll develop two C/C++ functions to compute floating-point addition and subtraction: `fpadd` and `fpsub`. These two functions will each take three parameters: the left and right operands of the operator and a pointer to a destination where these functions will store their result. The prototypes for these functions are the following:

```
void fpadd( real left, real right, real *dest );
void fpsub( real left, real right, real *dest );
```

The `fpsub` function is almost trivial. All it has to do is negate the right operand and call the `fpadd` function to do the real work. Here's the code for the `fpsub` function:

```
void fpsub( real left, real right, real *dest )
{
    right = right ^ 0x80000000;    // Invert the sign bit of the right operand.
    fpadd( left, right, dest );    // Let fpadd do the real work.
}
```

The `fpadd` function is where all the real work is done. To make `fpadd` a little easier to understand and maintain, we'll decompose the function into several different functions that help with various activities that take place. In an actual software floating-point library routine, you'd probably not do this decomposition because the extra subroutine calls would be a little slower; however, we're developing `fpadd` for educational purposes, not for actual use as part of a software floating-point library, and readability is a bit more important than performance in this particular instance. Besides, if you need high-performance floating-point addition, you'll probably use a hardware FPU rather than a software implementation.

The IEEE floating-point formats are good examples of packed data types. As you've seen in previous chapters, packed data types are great for reducing storage requirements for a data type, but they're not the best format when you need to use the packed fields in actual calculations. Therefore, one of the first things our floating-point functions will do is unpack the sign, exponent, and mantissa fields from the floating-point representation. The following C/C++ functions handle these simple tasks.

The first unpacking function is the `extractSign` function. This function extracts the sign bit (bit 31) from our packed floating-point representation and returns the value zero (for positive numbers) or one (for negative numbers).

```
inline int extractSign( real from )
{
    return( from >> 31);
}
```

This code could have also extracted the sign bit using this (possibly more efficient) expression:

```
(from & 0x80000000) != 0
```

However, shifting bit 31 down to bit 0 is, arguably, easier to understand.

The next utility function we'll look at unpacks the exponent from bits 23..30 in the packed real format. It does this by shifting the real value to the right by 23 bits, and then it masks out the sign bit. One other thing that this function will do is convert the excess-127 exponent to a two's complement format (this is easily achieved by subtracting 127 from the excess-127 exponent we extract). Here's the function that does this:

```
inline int extractExponent( real from )
{
    return ((from >> 23) & 0xff) - 127;
}
```

Extracting the mantissa is easy. All we have to do is mask out the exponent and sign bits and then insert the implied HO bit of one. The only catch is that we must return zero if the entire value is zero. Here's the function that extracts the mantissa from the real value:

```
inline int extractMantissa( real from )
{
    if( (from & 0x7fffffff) == 0 ) return 0;
    return ((from & 0x7FFFFF) | 0x800000 );
}
```

As you learned earlier, whenever adding or subtracting two values using scientific notation (and the IEEE floating-point format uses scientific notation), you must first adjust the two values so that they have the same exponent. For example, consider the addition of the following two decimal (base-10) numbers: 1.2345e3 + 8.7654e1.

To add these two numbers together, we must first adjust one or the other so that their exponents are the same. We can reduce the exponent of the first number by shifting the decimal point to the right. For example, the following values are all equivalent to 1.2345e3:

```
12.345e2 123.45e1 1234.5 12345e-1
```

Likewise, we can increase the value of an exponent by shifting the decimal point to the left. The following values are all equal to 8.7654e1:

```
0.87654e2 0.087654e3 0.0087654e4
```

For floating-point addition and subtraction involving binary numbers, we can make the binary exponents the same by shifting the mantissa one position to the left and decrementing the exponent, or by shifting the mantissa one position to the right and incrementing the exponent.

A problem with adjusting the exponent of one operand so that it matches the exponent of the other operand is that we only have so many bits to use to represent the mantissa. Shifting the mantissa bits to the right means that we reduce the precision of our number (because the bits wind up going off the LO end of the mantissa). To preserve as much accuracy as possible in our calculations, we shouldn't truncate the bits we shift out of the mantissa. As noted earlier, we should round the result to the nearest value we can represent with the remaining mantissa bits. These are the IEEE rules for rounding, in the following order:

- Truncate the result if the last bit shifted out was a zero.
- Bump the mantissa up by one if the last bit shifted out was a one and there was at least one bit set to one in all the other bits that were shifted out.[6]
- If the last we shifted out was a one, and all the other bits were zeros, then round the resulting mantissa up by one if the mantissa's LO bit contains a one.

Shifting the mantissa and rounding it is a relatively complex operation, and it will occur a couple of times in the floating-point addition code. Therefore, it's another candidate for a utility function. Here's the C/C++ code that implements this functionality:

```
// shiftAndRound:
//
// Shifts a mantissa to the right the number of bits specified.
// Rounds the result according to the IEEE rules for rounding,
//   which are:
//
// If the bits we shift out are a value that is greater than one-half the
//   value of the LO bit we are left with, then we need
//   to round the value up by adding one to the LO bit position.
// If the bits we shift out are a value that is less than one-half the value
//   of the LO bit we are left with (after denormalization), then we need
//   to round the value down (i.e., just leave the value alone).
// If the bits we shift out are exactly one-half the value of the LO bit
//   we are left with, then we need to round the value to the next larger
//   number that has a zero in the LO bit (round up if there's currently a one,
//   or leave the value unchanged if the LO bit contains a zero).

void shiftAndRound( int *valToShift, int bitsToShift )
```

---

[6] If the algorithm only shifts out a single bit, then you assume that "all the other bits" are zeros.

```
{
    // Masks is used to mask out bits to check for a "sticky" bit.

    static unsigned masks[24] =
    {
        0, 1, 3, 7, 0xf, 0x1f, 0x3f, 0x7f,
        0xff, 0x1ff, 0x3ff, 0x7ff, 0xfff, 0x1fff, 0x3fff, 0x7fff,
        0xffff, 0x1ffff, 0x3ffff, 0x7ffff, 0xfffff, 0x1fffff, 0x3fffff,
        0x7fffff
    };

    // HOmasks: Masks out the HO bit of the value masked by the masks entry.

    static unsigned HOmasks[24] =
    {
        0,
        1, 2, 4, 0x8, 0x10, 0x20, 0x40, 0x80,
        0x100, 0x200, 0x400, 0x800, 0x1000, 0x2000, 0x4000, 0x8000,
        0x10000, 0x20000, 0x40000, 0x80000, 0x100000, 0x200000, 0x400000
    };

    // shiftedOut: Holds the value that will be shifted out of a mantissa
    //   during the denormalization operation (used to round a denormalized
    //   value).

    int shiftedOut;

    assert( bitsToShift <= 23 );


    // Okay, first grab the bits we're going to shift out (so we can determine
    //   how to round this value after the shift).

    shiftedOut = *valToShift & masks[ bitsToShift ];

    // Shift the value to the right the specified number of bits.
    // Note: bit 31 is always zero, so it doesn't matter if the C
    //   compiler does a logical shift right or an arithmetic shift right.

    *valToShift = *valToShift >> bitsToShift;

    // If necessary, round the value:

    if( ( shiftedOut > HOmasks[ bitsToShift ] )
    {
        // If the bits we shifted out are greater than 1/2 the LO bit, then
        //   round the value up by one.
```

```
        *valToShift = *valToShift + 1;
    }
    else if( shiftedOut == HOmasks[ bitsToShift ] )
    {
        // If the bits we shifted out are exactly 1/2 of the LO bit's value,
        //  then round the value to the nearest number whose LO bit is zero.

        *valToShift = *valToShift + (*valToShift & 1);
    }
    // else
    // We round the value down to the previous value. The current
    //  value is already truncated (rounded down), so we don't have to do
    //  anything.
}
```

The "trick" in this code is that it uses a couple of lookup tables, *masks* and *HOmasks,* to extract those bits that the mantissa will use from the shift right operation. The masks table entries contain one bits (set bits) in the positions that will be lost during the shift. The HOmasks table entries contain a single set bit in the position specified by the index into the table; that is, the entry at index zero contains a one in bit position zero, the entry at index one contains a one in bit position one, and so on. This code selects an entry from each of these tables based on the number of mantissa bits it needs to shift to the right.

If the original mantissa value, logically ANDed with the appropriate entry in masks, is greater than the corresponding entry in HOmasks, then the shiftAndRound function rounds the shifted mantissa to the next greater value. If the ANDed mantissa value is equal to the corresponding HOmasks element, this code rounds the shifted mantissa value according to its LO bit (note that the expression (*valToShift & 1) produces one if the mantissa's LO bit is one, and it produces zero otherwise). Finally, if the ANDed mantissa value is less than the entry from the HOmasks table, then this code doesn't have to do anything because the mantissa is already rounded down.

Once we've adjusted one of the values so that the exponents of both operands are the same, the next step in the addition algorithm is to compare the signs of the values. If the signs of the two operands are both the same, we can simply add their mantissas (using a standard integer add operation). If the signs of the operands are different, we have to subtract, rather than add, the mantissas. Because floating-point values use one's complement representation, and standard integer arithmetic uses two's complement, we cannot simply subtract the negative value from the positive value. Instead, we have to subtract the smaller value from the larger value and determine the sign of the result based on the signs and magnitudes of the original operands. Table 4-3 describes how to accomplish this.

Table 4-3: Dealing with Operands That Have Different Signs

Left Sign	Right Sign	Left Mantissa > Right Mantissa?	Compute Mantissa As	Result Sign Is
−	+	Yes	LeftMantissa − RightMantissa	−
+	−	Yes	LeftMantissa − RightMantissa	+
−	+	No	RightMantissa − LeftMantissa	+
+	−	No	RightMantissa − LeftMantissa	−

Whenever adding or subtracting two 24-bit numbers, it is possible to produce a result that requires 25 bits (this, in fact, is a common result when dealing with normalized values). Immediately after an addition or subtraction, the floating-point code has to check the result for overflow. If this has happened, it needs to shift the mantissa right by one bit, round the result, and then increment the exponent. After completing this step, all that remains is to pack the resulting sign, exponent, and mantissa fields into the packed 32-bit IEEE floating-point format and the addition (or subtraction) is complete. The following packFP function is responsible for packing the *sign, exponent,* and *mantissa* fields into the 32-bit floating-point format:

```
// packFP:
//
// Packs the sign, exponent, and mantissa fields into a
// 32-bit "real" value. Works for normalized values, denormalized
//  values, and zero, but does not work for NaNs and infinities.

inline real packFP( int sign, int exponent, int mantissa )
{
   return
       (real)
       (
               (sign << 31)
           |   ((exponent + 127) << 23)
           |   (mantissa & 0x7fffff)
       );
}
```

With the utility routines out of the way, it's time to take a look at the fpadd function, which adds two floating-point values, producing a 32-bit real result:

```
// fpadd:
//
//    Computes:
//       dest = left + right
// where all three operands are "real" values (32-bit floats).
```

```
void fpadd( real left, real right, real *dest )
{
    // The following variables hold the fields associated with the
    //  left operand:

    int             Lexponent;
    long unsigned   Lmantissa;
    int             Lsign;

    // The following variables hold the fields associated with the
    //  right operand:

    int             Rexponent;
    long unsigned   Rmantissa;
    int             Rsign;

    // The following variables hold the separate fields of the result:

    int   Dexponent;
    long  unsigned Dmantissa;
    int   Dsign;


    // Extract the fields so that they're easy to work with:

    Lexponent = extractExponent( left );
    Lmantissa = extractMantissa( left );
    Lsign     = extractSign( left );

    Rexponent = extractExponent( right );
    Rmantissa = extractMantissa( right );
    Rsign     = extractSign( right );


    // Code to handle special operands (infinity and NaNs):

    if( Lexponent == 127 )
    {
        if( Lmantissa == 0 )
        {
            // If the left operand is infinity, then the result
            //  depends upon the value of the right operand.

            if( Rexponent == 127 )
            {
                // If the exponent is all one bits (127 after unbiasing)
                //  then the mantissa determines if we have an infinity value
                //  (zero mantissa), a QNaN (mantissa = 0x800000) or a SNaN
                //  (nonzero mantissa not equal to 0x800000).
```

```
                    if( Rmantissa == 0 )  // Do we have infinity?
                    {
                        // infinity + infinity = infinity
                        // -infinity - infinity = -infinity
                        // -infinity + infinity = NaN
                        // infinity - infinity = NaN

                        if( Lsign == Rsign )
                        {
                            *dest = right;
                        }
                        else
                        {
                            *dest = 0x7fC00000;  // +QNaN
                        }
                    }
                    else  // Rmantissa is nonzero, so it's a NaN
                    {
                        *dest = right;  // Right is a NaN, propagate it.
                    }
                }

        }
        else // Lmantissa is nonzero, Lexponent is all ones.
        {
            // If the left operand is some NaN, then the result will
            //  also be the same NaN.

            *dest = left;
        }

        // We've already calculated the result, so just return.

        return;

    }
    else if( Rexponent == 127 )
    {
        // Two case: right is either a NaN (in which case we need to
        //  propagate the NaN regardless of left's value) or it is
        //  +/- infinity. Because left is a "normal" number, we'll also
        //  wind up propagating the infinity because any normal number
        //  plus infinity is infinity.

        *dest = right;  // Right is a NaN, propagate it.
        return;
    }
```

```
// Okay, we've got two actual floating-point values. Let's add them
//   together. First, we have to "denormalize" one of the operands if
//   their exponents aren't the same (when adding or subtracting values,
//   the exponents must be the same).
//
// Algorithm: choose the value with the smaller exponent. Shift its
//   mantissa to the right the number of bits specified by the difference
//   between the two exponents.

Dexponent = Rexponent;
if( Rexponent > Lexponent )
{
    shiftAndRound( &Lmantissa, (Rexponent - Lexponent));
}
else if( Rexponent < Lexponent )
{
    shiftAndRound( &Rmantissa, (Lexponent - Rexponent));
    Dexponent = Lexponent;
}


// Okay, add the mantissas. There is one catch: if the signs are opposite
//   then we've actually got to subtract one value from the other (because
//   the FP format is one's complement, we'll subtract the larger mantissa
//   from the smaller and set the destination sign according to a
//   combination of the original sign values and the largest mantissa).

if( Rsign ^ Lsign )
{
    // Signs are different, must subtract one value from the other.

    if( Lmantissa > Rmantissa )
    {
        // The left value is greater, so the result inherits the
        //   sign of the left operand.

        Dmantissa = Lmantissa - Rmantissa;
        Dsign = Lsign;
    }
    else
    {
        // The right value is greater, so the result inherits the
        //   sign of the right operand.

        Dmantissa = Rmantissa - Lmantissa;
        Dsign = Rsign;
    }

}
else
{
```

```
        // Signs are the same, so add the values:

    Dsign = Lsign;
    Dmantissa = Lmantissa + Rmantissa;
}


// Normalize the result here.
//
// Note that during addition/subtraction, overflow of one bit is possible.
//   deal with that possibility here (if overflow occurred, shift the
//   mantissa to the right one position and adjust for this by incrementing
//   the exponent). Note that this code returns infinity if overflow occurs
//   when incrementing the exponent (infinity is a value with an exponent
//   of $FF);

if( Dmantissa >= 0x1000000 )
{
    // Never more than one extra bit when doing addition/subtraction.
    // Note that by virtue of the floating-point format we're using,
    //   the maximum value we can produce via addition or subtraction is
    //   a mantissa value of 0x1ffffe. Therefore, when we round this
    //   value it will not produce an overflow into the 25th bit.

    shiftAndRound( &Dmantissa, 1 ); // Move result into 24 bits.
    ++Dexponent;                    // Shift operation did a div by two,
                                    //   this counteracts the effect of
                                    //   the shift (incrementing exponent
                                    //   multiplies the value by two).

}
else
{
    // If the HO bit is clear, normalize the result
    //   by shifting bits up and simultaneously decrementing
    //   the exponent. We will treat zero as a special case
    //   because it's a common enough result.

    if( Dmantissa != 0 )
    {

        // The while loop multiplies the mantissa by two (via a shift
        //   left) and then divides the whole number by two (by
        //   decrementing the exponent. This continues until the HO bit of
        //   Dmantissa is set or the exponent becomes −127 (zero in the
        //   biased-127 form). If Dexponent drops down to −128, then we've
        //   got a denormalized number and we can stop.

        while( (Dmantissa < 0x800000) && (Dexponent > −127 ))
        {
            Dmantissa = Dmantissa << 1;
            --Dexponent;
```

```
                }

            }
            else
            {
                // If the mantissa went to zero, clear everything else, too.

                Dsign = 0;
                Dexponent = 0;
            }
        }

        // Reconstruct the result and store it away:

        *dest = packFP( Dsign, Dexponent, Dmantissa );

}
```

To conclude this discussion of the software implementation of the `fpadd` and `fsub` functions, here's a C main function that demonstrates the use of these functions:

```
// A simple main program that does some trivial tests on fpadd and fpsub.

int main( int argc, char **argv )
{
    real l, r, d;

    asreal(l) = 1.0;

    asreal(r) = 2.0;

    fpadd( l, r, &d );
    printf( "dest = %x\n", d );
    printf( "dest = %12E\n", asreal( d ));

    l = d;
    asreal(r) = 4.0;
    fpsub( l, r, &d );
    printf( "dest2 = %x\n", d );
    printf( "dest2 = %12E\n", asreal( d ));
}
```

4.7.3 Floating-Point Multiplication and Division

Most software floating-point libraries are actually written in hand-optimized assembly language, not in a high-level language. As the previous section shows, it's perfectly possible to write floating-point routines in a high-level language and, particularly in the case of single-precision floating-point addition and subtraction, you could actually write the code efficiently. Given the right library routines, it's also possible to write the floating-point multiplication and division routines in a high-level language. This section presents an HLA implementation of the single-precision floating-point multiplication and division algorithms, however, because it turns out that their implementation is actually easier in assembly language than in a high-level language like C/C++.

The HLA code in this section implements two functions, fpmul and fpdiv, that have the following prototypes:

```
procedure fpmul( left:real32; right:real32 );  @returns( "eax" );
procedure fpdiv( left:real32; right:real32 );  @returns( "eax" );
```

Beyond the fact that this code is written in assembly language rather than C, there are two main differences you should note between the code in this section and the code in the previous section. First, the HLA code uses the built-in real32 data type rather than creating a new data type for our real values. This code can do that because we can easily coerce any 32-bit memory object to real32 or dword in assembly language. Therefore, there is no reason to play games with the data types. The second thing you'll notice about these prototypes is that they only support two parameters; there is no destination parameter. These functions simply return the real32 result in the EAX register.[7]

4.7.3.1 Floating-Point Multiplication

Whenever you multiply two values in scientific notation, you compute the result sign, exponent, and mantissa as follows:

- The result sign is the exclusive-OR of the operand signs. That is, the result is positive if both operand signs were the same, and the result sign is negative if the operand signs were different.

- The result exponent is the sum of the operands' exponents.

- The result mantissa is the integer (fixed-point) product of the two operand mantissas.

Beyond these rules, there are a few additional rules that affect the floating-point multiplication algorithm that are a direct result of the IEEE floating-point format:

- If either, or both, of the operands are zero, the result is zero (this is a special case because the representation for zero is special).

- If either operand is infinity, the result is infinity.

- If either operand is a NaN, the result is that same NaN.

---

[7] Those who know a little 80x86 assembly language may wonder if it's legal to return a floating-point value in an integer register. Of course it is! EAX can hold any 32-bit value, not just integers. Presumably, if you're writing a software-based floating-point package, you don't have floating-point hardware available and, therefore, you can't pass floating-point values around in the floating-point registers.

The fpmul procedure begins by checking the operands to see if either of them is zero. If so, the function immediately returns a 0.0 result to the caller. Next, the fpmul code checks for NaN or infinity values in the left and right operands. If it finds one of these values, the fpmul procedure returns that same value to the caller.

If both of the fpmul operands are reasonable floating-point values, then the fpmul code extracts the sign, exponent, and mantissa fields of the packed floating-point value. Actually, "extract" isn't the correct term for fpmul; isolate is probably a better description of what this code does to the sign and exponent fields. Look at the code that isolates the sign bits of the two operands and computes the result sign:

```
mov( (type dword left), ebx );   // Result sign is the XOR of the
xor( (type dword right), ebx );  // operand signs.
and( $8000_0000, ebx );          // Keep only the sign bit.
```

This code exclusive-ORs the HO bits of the two operands (as well as all the other bits) and then masks out bits 0..30, leaving only the result sign value in bit 31 of the EBX register. This procedure doesn't bother moving the sign bit down to bit 0 (as you'd normally do when unpacking data) because it would just have to move this bit back to bit 31 when it repacks the floating-point value later.

The fpmul procedure uses the same trick when processing the exponent. It simply isolates bits 23..30 and operates on the exponent in place. When multiplying two values using scientific notation, you must add the values of the exponents together. Note, however, that the floating-point exponents use an excess-127 format; simply adding the exponents together creates a problem because the bias winds up being added twice. Therefore, the exponent-processing code must subtract 127 from the exponent's sum first. The following code isolates the exponent bits, adjusts for the extra bias, and adds the exponents together:

```
mov( (type dword left), ecx );    // Exponent goes into bits 23..30
and( $7f80_0000, ecx );           //  of ECX; mask these bits.
sub( 126 << 23, ecx );            // Eliminate the bias of 127.

mov( (type dword right), eax );
and( $7f80_0000, eax );

// For multiplication, we need to add the exponents:

add( eax, ecx );                  // Exponent value is now in bits
                                  //  23..30 of ECX.
```

First, you'll notice that this code subtracts 126 rather than 127 (the value you'd normally expect to have to subtract in order to eliminate the extra bias). The reason for this is that later on we will need to double the result of the multiplication of the mantissas. Subtracting 126 rather than 127 does this multiplication by two implicitly for us (saving an instruction later on).

If the sum of the exponents with add(eax, ecx), above, is too large to fit into eight bits, there will be a carry out of bit 30 into bit 31 of ECX, which will set the 80x86 overflow flag. If overflow occurs on a multiplication, our code will return infinity as the result.

If overflow does not occur, then the fpmul procedure needs to set the implied HO bit of the two mantissa values. The following code handles this chore, as well as stripping out all the exponent and sign bits from the mantissas. This code also left justifies the mantissa bits up against bit position 31 in EAX and EDX.

```
mov( (type dword left), eax );
mov( (type dword right), edx );

// If we don't have a zero value then set the implied HO bit of the mantissa:

if( eax <> 0 ) then

    or( $80_0000, eax );  // Set the implied bit to one.

endif;
shl( 8, eax );  // Moves mantissa to bits 8..31 and removes sign/exp.

// Repeat this for the right operand.

if( edx <> 0 ) then

    or( $80_0000, edx );

endif;
shl( 8, edx );
```

Once this code shifts the mantissas to bit 31 in EAX and EDX, it does the multiplication by using the 80x86 mul instruction:

```
mul( edx );
```

This instruction computes the 64-bit product of EAX and EDX, leaving the product in EDX:EAX (the HO double word is in EDX, and the LO double word is in EAX). Note that the product of any two n-bit integers produces a number that could require as many as $2*n$ bits. That's why the mul instruction computes EDX:EAX = EAX*EDX. Left justifying the mantissas in EAX and EDX before doing the multiplication is what ensures the mantissa of the product winds up in bits 7..30 of EDX (it would have been nice to have them wind up in bit positions 8..31 of EDX, but fixed-point multiplication winds up shifting the value down one bit in this case; that's why this code only subtracted 126 when adjusting for the excess-127 value). As these numbers were normalized prior to the multiplication, bit 30 of EDX will contain a one after the multiplication unless the result is zero. Note that the 32-bit IEEE real format does not support denormalized values, so we don't have to worry about this case when using 32-bit floating-point values.

Because the mantissas were actually 24 bits each, the product of the mantissas that the mul instruction produces could have as many as 48 significant bits. However, our result mantissa can only hold 24 bits, so we need to round the value to produce a 24-bit result (using, of course, the IEEE rounding algorithm — see Section 4.4, "Rounding"). Here's the code that rounds the value in EDX to 24 significant bits (in positions 8..31):

```
test( $80, edx );  // Clears zero flag if bit seven of EDX = 1.
if( @nz ) then

    add( $FFFF_FFFF, eax );  // Sets carry if EAX <> 0.
    adc( $7f, dl );          // Sets carry if DL:EAX > $80_0000_0000.
    if( @c ) then

        // If DL:EAX > $80_0000_0000 then round the mantissa
        //   up by adding one to bit position eight:

        add( 1 << 8, edx );

    else // DL:EAX = $80_0000_0000

        // We need to round to the value that has a zero
        //   in bit position zero of the mantissa (bit #8 of EDX):

        test( 8, edx );  // Clears zero flag if bit #8 contains a one.
        if( @nz ) then

            add( 1 << 8, edx );  // Adds a one starting at bit position eight.

            // If there was an overflow, renormalize:

            if( @c ) then

                rcr( 1, edx );  // Shift overflow (in carry) back into EDX.
                inc( ecx );     // Shift did a divide by two. Fix that.

        endif;

        endif;

    endif;

endif;
```

An interesting thing to note about this rounding code is that it may need to renormalize the number after rounding. If the mantissa contains all one bits and needs to be rounded up, this will produce an overflow out of the HO bit of the mantissa. The rcr and inc instructions at the end of this code sequence put the overflow bit back into the mantissa if overflow occurs.

The only thing left for fpmul to do after this is pack the destination sign, exponent, and mantissa into the 32-bit EAX register. The following code does this:

```
shr( 8, edx );           // Move mantissa into bits 0..23.
and( $7f_ffff, edx );    // Clear the implied bit.
lea( eax, [edx+ecx] );   // Merge mantissa and exponent into EAX.
or( ebx, eax );          // Merge in the sign.
```

The only tricky thing in this code is the use of the lea (load effective address) instruction to compute the sum of EDX (the mantissa) and ECX (the exponent) and move the result to EAX all with a single instruction.

4.7.3.2 Floating-Point Division

Floating-point division is a little bit more involved than multiplication because the IEEE floating-point standard says many things about degenerate conditions that can occur during division. We're not going to discuss all the code that handles those conditions here. Instead, see the discussion of the conditions for fpmul earlier, and check out the complete code listing for fdiv later in this section.

Assuming we have reasonable numbers to divide, the division algorithm first computes the result sign using the same algorithm (and code) as for multiplying. When dividing two values using scientific notation, we have to subtract their exponents. Unlike the multiplication algorithm, it's going to be more convenient to truly unpack the exponents for the two division operands and convert them from excess-127 to two's complement form. Here's the code that does this:

```
mov( (type dword left), ecx );   // Exponent comes from bits 23..30.
shr( 23, ecx );
and( $ff, ecx );                 // Mask out the sign bit (in bit 8).

mov( (type dword right), eax );
shr( 23, eax );
and( $ff, eax );

// Eliminate the bias from the exponents:

sub( 127, ecx );
sub( 127, eax );
```

```
// For division, we need to subtract the exponents:

sub( eax, ecx );                    // Leaves result exponent in ECX.
```

The 80x86 div instruction absolutely, positively requires the quotient to fit into 32 bits. If this condition is not true, the CPU may abort the operation with a divide exception. As long as the HO bit of the divisor contains a one and the HO two bits of the dividend contain %01, we will not get a division error. Here's the code the prepares the operands prior to the division operation:

```
mov (type dword left), edx );
if( edx <> 0 ) then

    or( $80_0000, edx );    // Set the implied bit to one in the left operand.
    shl( 8, edx );

endif;
mov( (type dword right), edi );
if( edi <> 0 ) then

    or( $80_0000 );         // Set the implied bit to one in the right operand.
    shl( 8, edi );

else

    // Division by zero error, here.

endif;
```

The next step is to actually do the division. As noted earlier, in order to prevent a division error, we have to shift the dividend one bit to the right (to set the HO two bits to %01). The code that does this shift and then the division is as follows:

```
xor( eax, eax );    // EAX := 0;
shr( 1, edx );      // Shift EDX:EAX to the right one bit to
rcr( 1, eax );      //   prevent a division error.
div( edi );         // Compute EAX = EDX:EAX / EDI.
```

Once the div instruction executes, the quotient is sitting in the HO 24 bits of EAX, and the remainder is in AL:EDX. We now need to normalize and round the result. Rounding is a little easier because AL:EDX contains the remainder after the division; it will contain a value less than $80:0000_0000 (that is, the 80x86 AL register contains $80 and EDX contains zero) if we need to round down, it will contain a value greater than $80:0000_0000 if we need to round up, and it will contain exactly $80:0000_0000 if we need to round to the nearest value.

Here's the code that does this:

```
test( $80, al );      // See if the bit just below the LO bit of the
if( @nz ) then        //   mantissa contains a zero or one.

    // Okay, the bit just below the LO bit of our mantissa contains a one.
    // If all other bits below the mantissa and this bit contain zeros,
    //   we have to round to the nearest mantissa value whose LO bit is zero.

    test( $7f, al );               // Clears zero flag if bits 0..6 <> 0.
    if( @nz || edx <> 0 ) then     // If bits 0..6 in AL are zero and EDX
                                   //   is zero.

        // We need to round up:

        add( $100, eax );  // Mantissa starts in bit #8 );
        if( @c ) then      // Carry set if mantissa overflows.

            // If there was an overflow, renormalize.

            rcr( 1, eax );
            inc( ecx );

        endif;

else

        // The bits below the mantissa are exactly 1/2 the value
        //   of the LO mantissa bit. So we need to round to the value
        //   that has a LO mantissa bit of zero:

        test( $100, eax );
        if( @nz ) then

            add( $100, eax );
            if( @c ) then

                // If there was an overflow, renormalize.

                rcr( 1, eax );  // Put overflow bit back into EAX.
                inc( ecx );     // Adjust exponent accordingly.

            endif;

        endif;

    endif;

endif;
```

The last step in fpdiv is to add the bias back into the exponent (and verify that overflow doesn't occur) and then pack the quotient's sign, exponent, and mantissa fields into the 32-bit floating-point format. Here's the code that does this:

```
if( (type int32 ecx) > 127 ) then

    mov( $ff–127, ecx );      // Set exponent value for infinity
    xor( eax, eax );          //  because we just had overflow.

elseif( (type int32 ecx) < –128 ) then

    mov( –127, ecx );         // Return zero for underflow (note that
    xor( eax, eax );          //  next we add 127 to ECX).

endif;
add( 127, ecx );              // Add the bias back in.
shl( 23, ecx );               // Move the exponent to bits 23..30.

// Okay, assemble the final real32 value:

shr( 8, eax );                // Move mantissa into bits 0..23.
and( $7f_ffff, eax );         // Clear the implied bit.
or( ecx, eax );               // Merge mantissa & exponent into EAX.
or( ebx, eax );               // Merge in the sign.
```

Whew! This has been a lot of code. However, it's worthwhile to go through all this just to see how floating-point operations work (so you can gain an appreciation of exactly what an FPU is doing for you).

4.8   For More Information

Donald Knuth's *The Art of Computer Programming, Volume Two: Seminumerical Algorithms,* provides an in-depth discussion of floating-point arithmetic and floating-point formats. This book is required reading for someone who wants to fully understand how floating-point arithmetic operates. Also, Intel's documentation on its Pentium processors explains its floating-point formats, exceptional conditions, and other issues related to the use of its FPU. Likewise, the manufacturer's literature for any CPU that supports floating-point arithmetic will explain the specifics for the use of that CPU's floating-point unit.

Those interested in trapping floating-point exceptions from a high-level language will need to check their language vendor's documentation to determine how this is done. Unfortunately, there are few standards around, so most compiler vendors use a proprietary scheme or a CPU- or

OS-dependent scheme to trap these exceptions. For general information about the effects of precision and accuracy in floating-point calculations, a good textbook on numerical analysis would be a reasonable place to start.

Finally, *The Art of Assembly Language* (No Starch Press) contains lots of additional information related to floating-point arithmetic including the implementation of various transcendental and other functions. The UCR Standard Library for 80x86 Assembly Language Programmers (a software package I've developed that is available at http://webster.cs.ucr.edu; check out the "Assembler Tools" link and look under MASM) contains a full software-based floating-point package in 16-bit 8086 assembly language. The HLA Standard Library includes source code for several FPU support routines, including floating-point I/O and conversion. Check out the Webster website for more details (look under "HLA" when following the "Assembler Tools" link).

5

CHARACTER REPRESENTATION

Although computers are famous for their "number-crunching" capabilities, the truth is that most computer systems process character data far more often than numbers. Given the importance of character manipulation in modern software, a thorough understanding of character and string data is necessary if you're going to write great code.

The term *character* refers to a human or machine-readable symbol that is typically a nonnumeric entity. In general, a character is any symbol that you can type on a keyboard or display on a video display. Note that in addition to alphabetic characters, character data includes punctuation symbols, numeric digits, spaces, tabs, carriage returns (the ENTER key), other control characters, and other special symbols.

This chapter looks at how we represent characters, strings, and character sets within a computer system. This chapter also discusses various operations on these data types.

5.1 Character Data

Most computer systems use a 1- or 2-byte binary sequence to encode the various characters. Windows and Linux certainly fall into this category, using the ASCII or Unicode character sets, whose members can all be represented using 1- or 2-byte binary sequences. The EBCDIC character set, in use on IBM mainframes and minicomputers, is another example of a single-byte character code.

I will discuss all three of these character sets, and their internal representations, in this chapter. I will also describe how to create your own *custom* character sets later in this chapter.

5.1.1 The ASCII Character Set

The ASCII (American Standard Code for Information Interchange) character set maps 128 characters to the unsigned integer values 0..127 ($0..$7F). Although the exact mapping of characters to numeric values is arbitrary and unimportant, a standardized mapping allows you to communicate between programs and peripheral devices. The standard ASCII codes are useful because nearly everyone uses them. Therefore, if you use the ASCII code 65 to represent the character *A*, then you know that some peripheral device (such as a printer) will correctly interpret this value as the character *A*.

Because the ASCII character set provides only 128 different characters, an interesting question arises: "What do we do with the additional 128 values ($80..$FF) that we can represent with a byte?" One answer is to ignore those extra values. That will be the primary approach of this book. Another possibility is to extend the ASCII character set by an additional 128 characters. Of course, unless you can get everyone to agree upon one particular extension of the character set,[1] the whole purpose of having a standardized character set will be defeated. And getting everyone to agree is a difficult task.

Despite some major shortcomings, ASCII data is *the* standard for data interchange across computer systems and programs. Most programs can accept ASCII data, and most programs can produce ASCII data. Because you will probably be dealing with ASCII characters in your programs, it would be wise to study the layout of the character set and memorize a few key ASCII codes (such as those for *0*, *A*, *a*, and so on). Table A-1 in Appendix A lists all the characters in the standard ASCII character set.

The ASCII character set is divided into four groups of 32 characters. The first 32 characters, ASCII codes $0 through $1F (0 through 31), form a special set of nonprinting characters called the *control characters*. We call them control characters because they perform various printer and display control operations rather than displaying actual symbols. Examples of control characters include *carriage return*, which positions the cursor at the

---

[1] Back before Windows became popular, IBM supported an extended 256-element character set on its text displays. Though this character set is "standard" even on modern PCs, few applications or peripheral devices continue to use the extended characters.

beginning of the current line of characters;[2] line feed, which moves the cursor down one line on the output device; and backspace, which moves the cursor back one position to the left. Unfortunately, different control characters perform different operations on different output devices. There is very little standardization among output devices. To find out exactly how a particular control character affects a particular device, you will need to consult its manual.

The second group of 32 ASCII character codes comprises various punctuation symbols, special characters, and the numeric digits. The most notable characters in this group include the space character (ASCII code $20) and the numeric digits (ASCII codes $30..$39).

The third group of 32 ASCII characters contains the uppercase alphabetic characters. The ASCII codes for the characters A through Z lie in the range $41..$5A. Because there are only 26 different alphabetic characters, the remaining six codes hold various special symbols.

The fourth and final group of 32 ASCII character codes represents the lowercase alphabetic symbols, five additional special symbols, and another control character (delete). Note that the lowercase character symbols use the ASCII codes $61..$7A. If you convert the codes for the upper- and lowercase characters to binary, you will notice that the uppercase symbols differ from their lowercase equivalents in exactly one bit position. For example, consider the character codes for E and e appearing in Figure 5-1.

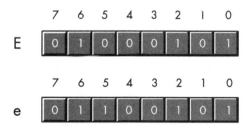

Figure 5-1: ASCII codes for E and e

The only place these two codes differ is in bit five. Uppercase alphabetic characters always contain a zero in bit five; lowercase alphabetic characters always contain a one in bit five. You can use this fact to quickly convert an alphabetic character between upper- and lowercase by simply inverting bit five. If you have an uppercase character, you can force it to lowercase by setting bit five to one. If you have a lowercase character and you wish to force it to uppercase, you can do so by setting bit five to zero.

Bits five and six determine the character's group (see Table 5-1). Therefore, you can convert any upper- or lowercase (or special) character to its corresponding control character by setting bits five and six to zero.

---

[2] Historically, carriage return refers to the *paper carriage* used on typewriters. A carriage return consisted of physically moving the carriage all the way to the right so that the next character typed would appear at the left-hand side of the paper.

Table 5-1: ASCII Character Groups Determined by Bits Five and Six

Bit 6	Bit 5	Group
0	0	Control characters
0	1	Digits and punctuation
1	0	Uppercase and special
1	1	Lowercase and special

Consider, for a moment, the ASCII codes of the numeric digit characters in Table 5-2. The decimal representations of these ASCII codes are not very enlightening. However, the hexadecimal representation of these ASCII codes reveals something very important — the LO nibble of the ASCII code is the binary equivalent of the represented number. By stripping away (setting to zero) the HO nibble of the ASCII code, you obtain the binary representation of that digit. Conversely, you can convert a binary value in the range 0..9 to its ASCII character representation by simply setting the HO nibble to %0011, or the decimal value 3. Note that you can use the logical AND operation to force the HO bits to zero; likewise, you can use the logical OR operation to force the HO bits to %0011 (decimal 3). For more information on string-to-numeric conversions, see Chapter 2.

Table 5-2: ASCII Codes for the Numeric Digits

Character	Decimal	Hexadecimal
0	48	$30
1	49	$31
2	50	$32
3	51	$33
4	52	$34
5	53	$35
6	54	$36
7	55	$37
8	56	$38
9	57	$39

Despite the fact that it is a "standard," simply encoding your data using ASCII characters does not guarantee compatibility across systems. While it's true that an *A* on one machine is most likely an *A* on another system, there is very little standardization across machines with respect to the use of the control characters. Indeed, of the 32 control codes in the first group of ASCII codes, plus the delete code in the last group, there are only 4 control codes commonly supported by most devices and applications — backspace (BS), tab, carriage return (CR), and line feed (LF). Worse still, different machines often use these "supported" control codes in different ways. End-of-line is a particularly troublesome example. Windows, MS-DOS, CP/M, and other systems mark end-of-line by the two-character sequence CR/LF. The Apple Macintosh, and many other systems, mark end-of-line by a single CR character. Linux, BeOS, and other Unix systems mark end-of-line with a single LF character.

Attempting to exchange simple text files between such different systems can be an experience in frustration. Even if you use standard ASCII characters in all your files on these systems, you will still need to convert the data when exchanging files between them. Fortunately, such conversions are rather simple, and many text editors automatically handle files with different line endings (there are also many available freeware utilities that will do this conversion for you). Even if you have to do this in your own software, all that the conversion involves is copying all characters except the end-of-line sequence from one file to another, and then emitting the new end-of-line sequence whenever you encounter an old end-of-line sequence in the input file.

5.1.2 The EBCDIC Character Set

Although the ASCII character set is, unquestionably, the most popular character representation, it is certainly not the only format available. For example, IBM uses the EBCDIC code on many of its mainframe and mini-computer lines. Because EBCDIC appears mainly on IBM's big iron and you'll rarely encounter it on personal computer systems, we'll only consider it briefly in this book.

EBCDIC (pronounced EB-suh-dic) is an acronym that stands for *Extended Binary Coded Decimal Interchange Code*. If you're wondering if there was an unextended version of this character code, the answer is yes. Earlier IBM systems and keypunch machines used a character set known as BCDIC *(Binary Coded Decimal Interchange Code)*. This was a character set based on punched cards and decimal representation (for IBM's older decimal machines).

The first thing to note about EBCDIC is that it is not a single character set; rather, it is a family of character sets. While the EBCDIC character sets have a common core (for example, the encodings for the alphabetic characters are usually the same), different versions of EBCDIC (known as *code pages*) have different encodings for punctuation and special characters. Because there are a limited number of encodings available in a single byte, different code pages reuse some of the character encodings for their own special set of characters. So, if you're given a file that contains EBCDIC characters and someone asks you to translate it to ASCII, you'll quickly discover that this is not a trivial task.

Before you ever look at the EBCDIC character set, you should first realize that the forerunner of EBCDIC (BCDIC) was in existence long before modern digital computers. BCDIC was born on old-fashioned IBM keypunches and tabulator machines. EBCDIC was simply an extension of that encoding to provide an extended character set for IBM's computers.

However, EBCDIC inherited several peculiarities from BCDIC that seem strange in the context of modern computers. For example, the encodings of the alphabetic characters are not contiguous. This is probably a direct result of the fact that the original character encodings really did use a decimal (BCD) encoding. Originally (in BCD/decimal), the alphabetic characters probably did have a sequential encoding. However, when IBM expanded the character set, they used some of the binary combinations that are not present in the BCD format (values like %1010..%1111). Such binary values appear between two otherwise sequential BCD values, which explains why certain character sequences (such as the alphabetic characters) do not use sequential binary codes in the EBCDIC encoding.

Unfortunately, because of the weirdness of the EBCDIC character set, many common algorithms that work well on ASCII characters simply don't work with EBCDIC. This chapter will not consider EBCDIC beyond a token mention here or there. However, keep in mind that EBCDIC functional equivalents exist for most ASCII characters. Check out the IBM literature for more details.

5.1.3   Double-Byte Character Sets

Because of the encoding limitations of an 8-bit byte (which has a maximum of 256 characters) and the need to represent more than 256 characters, some computer systems use special codes to indicate that a particular character consumes two bytes rather than a single byte. Such double-byte character sets (DBCSs) do not encode every character using 16 bits — instead, they use a single byte for most character encodings and use two-byte codes only for certain characters.

A typical double-byte character set utilizes the standard ASCII character set along with several additional characters in the range $80..$FF. Certain values in this range are extension codes that tell the software that a second byte immediately follows. Each extension byte allows the DBCS to support another 256 different character codes. With three extension values, for example, the DBCS can support up to 1,021 different characters. You get 256 characters with each of the extension bytes, and you get 253 (256 − 3) characters in the standard single-byte set (minus three because the three extension byte values each consume one of the 256 combinations, and they don't count as characters).

Back in the days when terminals and computers used memory-mapped character displays, double-byte character sets weren't very practical. Hardware character generators really want each character to be the same size, and they want to process a limited number of characters. However, as bitmapped displays with software character generators became prevalent (Windows, Macintosh, and Unix/XWindows machines), it became possible to process DBCSs.

Although DBCSs can compactly represent a large number of characters, they demand more computing resources in order to process text in a DBCS format. For example, if you have a zero-terminated string containing DBCS characters (typical in the C/C++ languages), then determining the number of characters in the string can be considerable work. The problem is that some characters in the string consume two bytes while most others consume only one byte. A string length function has to scan byte-by-byte through each character of the string to locate any extension values that indicate that a single character consumes two bytes. This extra comparison more than doubles the time a high-performance string length function takes to execute. Worse still, many common algorithms that people use to manipulate string data fail when they apply them to DBCSs. For example, a common C/C++ trick to step through characters in a string is to either increment or decrement a pointer to the string using expressions like ++ptrChar or --ptrChar. Unfortunately, these tricks don't work with DBCSs. While someone using a DBCS probably has a set of standard C library routines available that work properly on DBCSs, it's also quite likely that other useful character functions they've written (or that others have written) don't work properly with the extended characters in a DBCS. For this and other reasons, you're far better off using the Unicode character set if you need a standardized character set that supports more than 256 characters. For all the details, keep reading.

5.1.4   The Unicode Character Set

A while back, engineers at Apple Computer and Xerox realized that their new computer systems with bitmapped displays and user-selectable fonts could display far more than 256 different characters at one time. Although DBCSs were a possibility, those engineers quickly discovered the compatibility problems associated with double-byte character sets and sought a different route. The solution they came up with was the Unicode character set. Unicode has since become an international standard adopted and supported by nearly every major computer manufacturer and operating system provider (Mac OS, Windows, Linux, Unix, and many other operating systems support Unicode).

Unicode uses a 16-bit word to represent each character. Therefore, Unicode supports up to 65,536 different character codes. This is obviously a huge advance over the 256 possible codes we can represent with an 8-bit byte. Furthermore, Unicode is upward compatible from ASCII; if the HO 9 bits[3] of a Unicode character's binary representation contain zero, then the LO 7 bits use the standard ASCII code. If the HO 9 bits contain some nonzero value, then the 16 bits form an extended character code (extended from ASCII, that is). If you're wondering why so many different character codes are necessary, simply note that certain Asian character sets contain 4,096

---

[3] ASCII is a 7-bit code. If the HO 9 bits of a 16-bit Unicode value are all zero, the remaining 7 bits are an ASCII encoding for a character.

characters (at least, in their Unicode character subset). The Unicode character set even provides a set of codes you can use to create an application-defined character set. At the time of this writing, approximately half of the 65,536 possible character codes have been defined; the remaining character encodings are reserved for future expansion.

Today, many operating systems and language libraries provide excellent support for Unicode. Microsoft Windows, for example, uses Unicode internally.[4] So operating system calls will actually run faster if you pass them Unicode strings rather than ASCII strings. (When you pass an ASCII string to a modern version of Windows, the OS first converts the string from ASCII to Unicode and then proceeds with the OS API function.) Likewise, whenever Windows returns a string to an application, that string is in Unicode form; if the application needs it in ASCII form, then Windows must convert the string from Unicode to ASCII before returning.

There are two big disadvantages to Unicode, however. First, Unicode character data requires twice as much memory to represent as ASCII or other single-byte encodings do. Although machines have far more memory today (both in RAM and on disk where text files usually reside), doubling the size of text files, databases, and in-memory strings (such as those for a text editor or word processor) can have a significant impact on the system. Worse, because strings are now twice as long, it takes almost twice as many instructions to process a Unicode string as it does to process a string encoded with single-byte characters. This means that string functions may run at half the speed of those functions that process byte-sized character data.[5] The second disadvantage to Unicode is that most of the world's data files out there are in ASCII or EBCDIC form, so if you use Unicode within an application, you wind up spending considerable time converting between Unicode and those other character sets.

Although Unicode is a widely accepted standard, it still is not seeing widespread use (though it is becoming more popular every day). Quite soon, Unicode will hit "critical mass" and really take off. However, that point is still in the future, so most of the examples in this text will continue to use ASCII characters. Still, at some point in the not-too-distant future, it wouldn't be unreasonable to emphasize Unicode rather than ASCII in a book like this.

5.2 Character Strings

After integers, character strings are probably the most common type in use in modern programs. In general, a *character string* is a sequence of characters that possesses two main attributes: a *length* and the *character data.*

---

[4] The Windows CE variant only supports Unicode. You don't even have the option of passing ASCII strings to a Win CE function.

[5] Some might argue that it shouldn't take any longer to process a Unicode string using instructions that process words versus processing byte strings using machine instructions that manipulate bytes. However, high-performance string functions tend to process double words (or more) at one time. Such string functions can process half as many Unicode characters at one time, so they'll require twice as many machine instructions to do the same amount of work.

Character strings may also possess other attributes, such as the *maximum length* allowable for that particular variable or a *reference count* that specifies how many different string variables refer to the same character string. We'll look at these attributes and how programs can use them in the following sections, which describe various string formats and some of the possible string operations.

5.2.1   Character String Formats

Different languages use different data structures to represent strings. Some string formats use less memory, others allow faster processing, some are more convenient to use, and some provide additional functionality for the programmer and operating system. To better understand the reasoning behind the design of character strings, it is instructive to look at some common string representations popularized by various high-level languages.

5.2.1.1   Zero-Terminated Strings

Without question, *zero-terminated strings* are probably the most common string representation in use today, because this is the native string format for C, C++, Java, and several other languages. In addition, you'll find zero-terminated strings in use in programs written in languages that don't have a specific native string format, such as assembly language.

A zero-terminated ASCII string is a sequence containing zero or more 8-bit character codes ending with a byte containing zero (or, in the case of Unicode, a sequence containing zero or more 16-bit character codes ending with a 16-bit word containing zero). For example, in C/C++, the ASCII string "abc" requires four bytes: one byte for each of the three characters *a*, *b*, and *c*, followed by a zero byte.

Zero-terminated strings have a couple of advantages over other string formats:

- Zero-terminated strings can represent strings of any practical length with only one byte of overhead (two bytes in Unicode).

- Given the popularity of the C/C++ programming languages, high-performance string processing libraries are available that work well with zero-terminated strings.

- Zero-terminated strings are easy to implement. Indeed, except for dealing with string literal constants, the C/C++ programming languages don't provide native string support. As far as the C and C++ languages are concerned, strings are just arrays of characters. That's probably why C's designers chose this format in the first place — so they wouldn't have to clutter up the language with string operators.

- This format allows you to easily represent zero-terminated strings in any language that provides the ability to create an array of characters.

However, despite these advantages, zero-terminated strings also have disadvantages — they are not always the best choice for representing character string data. These disadvantages are as follows:

- String functions often aren't very efficient when operating on zero-terminated strings. Many string operations need to know the length of the string before working on the string data. The only reasonable way to compute the length of a zero-terminated string is to scan the string from the beginning to the end. The longer your strings are, the slower this function runs. Therefore, the zero-terminated string format isn't the best choice if you need to process long strings.

- Though this is a minor problem, with the zero-terminated string format you cannot easily represent any character whose character code is zero (such as the ASCII NUL character).

- With zero-terminated strings there is no information contained within the string data itself that tells you how long a string can grow beyond the terminating zero byte. Therefore, some string functions, like concatenation, can only extend the length of an existing string variable and check for overflow if the caller explicitly passes in the maximum length.

5.2.1.2   Length-Prefixed Strings

A second string format, *length-prefixed strings,* overcomes some of the problems with zero-terminated strings. Length-prefixed strings are common in languages like Pascal; they generally consist of a single byte that specifies the length of the string, followed by zero or more 8-bit character codes. In a length-prefixed scheme, the string "abc" would consist of four bytes: the length byte ($03), followed by *a*, *b*, and *c*.

Length-prefixed strings solve two of the problems associated with zero-terminated strings. First, it is possible to represent the NUL character in a length-prefixed string, and second, string operations are more efficient. Another advantage to length-prefixed strings is that the length is usually sitting at position zero in the string (when viewing the string as an array of characters), so the first character of the string begins at index one in the array representation of the string. For many string functions, having a one-based index into the character data is much more convenient than a zero-based index (which zero-terminated strings use).

Length-prefixed strings do suffer from their own drawbacks, the principal drawback being that they are limited to a maximum of 255 characters in length (assuming a 1-byte length prefix). One can remove this limitation by using a 2- or 4-byte length value, but doing so increases the amount of overhead data from one to two or four bytes.

5.2.1.3 Seven-Bit Strings

An interesting string format that works for 7-bit codes like ASCII involves using the HO bit to indicate the end of the string. All but the last character code in the string would have their HO bit clear (or set, your choice) and the last character in the string would have its HO bit set (or clear, if all the other HO bits are set).

This 7-bit string format has several disadvantages:

- You have to scan the entire string in order to determine the length of the string.
- You cannot have zero-length strings in this format.
- Few languages provide literal string constants for 7-bit strings.
- You are limited to a maximum of 128 character codes, though this is fine when using plain ASCII.

However, the big advantage of 7-bit strings is that they don't require any overhead bytes to encode the length. Assembly language (using a macro to create literal string constants) is probably the best language to use when dealing with 7-bit strings — because the advantage of 7-bit strings is their compactness, and assembly language programmers tend to be the ones who worry most about compactness, this is a good match. Here's an HLA macro that will convert a literal string constant to a 7-bit string:

```
#macro sbs( s );

    // Grab all but the last character of the string:

    (@substr( s, 0, @length(s) – 1) +

        // Concatenate the last character with its HO bit set:

        char( uns8( char( @substr( s, @length(s) – 1, 1))) | $80 ))

#endmacro
    . . .
byte sbs( "Hello World" );
```

5.2.1.4 HLA Strings

As long as you're not too concerned about a few extra bytes of overhead per string, it's quite possible to create a string format that combines the advantages of both length-prefixed and zero-terminated strings without their disadvantages. The HLA language has done this with its native string format.[6]

---

[6] Note that HLA is an assembly language, so it's perfectly possible, and easy in fact, to support any reasonable string format. HLA's native string format is the one it uses for literal string constants, and this is the format that most of the routines in the HLA standard library support.

The biggest drawback to the HLA character string format is the amount of overhead required for each string (which can be significant, percentage-wise, if you're in a memory-constrained environment and you process many small strings). HLA strings contain both a length prefix and a zero-terminating byte, as well as some other information, that costs nine bytes of overhead per string.[7]

The HLA string format uses a 4-byte length prefix, allowing character strings to be just over four billion characters long (obviously, this is far more than any practical application will use). HLA also sticks a zero byte at the end of the character string data, so HLA strings are upward compatible with string functions that reference (but do not change the length of) zero-terminated strings. The additional four bytes of overhead in an HLA string contain the maximum legal length for that string. Having this extra field allows HLA string functions to check for string overflow, if necessary. In memory, HLA strings take the form shown in Figure 5-2.

The four bytes immediately before the first character of the string contain the current string length. The four bytes preceding the current string length contain the maximum string length. Immediately following the character data is a zero byte. Finally, HLA always ensures that the string data structure's length is a multiple of four bytes long (for performance reasons), so there may be up to three additional bytes of padding at the end of the object in memory (note that the string appearing in Figure 5-2 requires only one byte of padding to ensure that the data structure is a multiple of four bytes in length).

Figure 5-2: HLA string format

HLA string variables are actually pointers that contain the byte address of the first character in the string. To access the length fields, you would load the value of the string pointer into a 32-bit register. You'd access the Length field at offset −4 from the base register and the MaxLength field at offset −8 from the base register. Here's an example:

```
static
        s :string := "Hello World";
            . . .
        mov( s, esi );          // Move the address of 'H' in "Hello World"
                                //  into esi.
        mov( [esi-4], ecx );    // Puts length of string (11 for "Hello World")
                                //  into ECX.
            . . .
```

---

[7] Actually, because of memory alignment restrictions, there can be up to 12 bytes of overhead, depending on the string.

```
            mov( s, esi );
            cmp( eax, [esi-8] );  // See if value in EAX exceeds the maximum
                                  //  string length.
            ja StringOverflow;
```

One nice thing about HLA string variables is that (as read-only objects) HLA strings are compatible with zero-terminated strings. For example, if you have a function written in C or some other language that's expecting you to pass it a zero-terminated string, you can call that function and pass it an HLA string variable, like this:

```
someCFunc( hlaStringVar );
```

The only catch is that the C function must not make any changes to the string that would affect its length (because the C code won't update the Length field of the HLA string). Of course, you can always call a C strlen function upon returning to update the length field yourself, but generally, it's best not to pass HLA strings to a function that modifies zero-terminated strings.

5.2.1.5 Descriptor-Based Strings

The string formats we've considered up to this point have kept the attribute information (the lengths and terminating bytes) for a string in memory along with the character data. Perhaps a slightly more flexible scheme is to maintain information like the maximum and current lengths of a string in a record structure that also contains a pointer to the character data. We call such records *descriptors*. Consider the following Pascal/Delphi/Kylix data structure:

```
type
    dString :record
        curLength  :integer;
        strData    :^char;
    end;
```

Note that this data structure does not hold the actual character data. Instead, the strData pointer contains the address of the first character of the string. The curLength field specifies the current length of the string. Of course, you could add any other fields you like to this record, like a maximum length field, though a maximum length isn't usually necessary because most string formats employing a descriptor are *dynamic* (as will be discussed in the next section). Most string formats employing a descriptor just maintain the length field.

An interesting attribute of a descriptor-based string system is that the actual character data associated with a string could be part of a larger string. Because there are no length or terminating bytes within the actual character data, it is possible to have the character data for two strings overlap. For example, take a look at Figure 5-3. In this example, there are two strings: one representing the string "Hello World" and the second representing "World." Notice that the two strings overlap. This can save memory and make certain functions (like substring) very efficient. Of course, when strings overlap as these ones do, you cannot modify the string data because that could wipe out part of some other string.

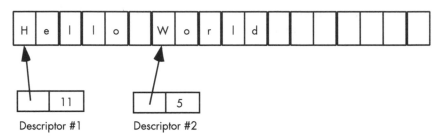

Descriptor #1   Descriptor #2

Figure 5-3: Overlapping strings using descriptors

5.2.2   Types of Strings: Static, Pseudo-Dynamic, and Dynamic

Based on the various string formats covered thus far, we can now define three string types according to when the system allocates storage for the string. There are static strings, pseudo-dynamic strings, and dynamic strings.

5.2.2.1   Static Strings

Pure *static strings* are those whose maximum size a programmer chooses when writing the program. Pascal (and Delphi "short" strings) fall into this category. Arrays of characters that you will use to hold zero-terminated strings in C/C++ also fall into this category. Consider the following declaration in Pascal:

```
(* Pascal static string example *)

var  pascalString :string(255);  // Max length will always be 255 characters.
```

And here's an example in C/C++:

```
// C/C++ static string example:

char cString[256];  // Max length will always be 255 characters
                    // (plus zero byte).
```

While the program is running, there is no way to increase the maximum sizes of these static strings. Nor is there any way to reduce the storage they will use. These string objects will consume 256 bytes at run time, period. One advantage to pure static strings is that the compiler can determine their maximum length at compile time and implicitly pass this information to a string function so it can test for bounds violations at run time.

5.2.2.2 Pseudo-Dynamic Strings

Pseudo-dynamic strings are those whose length the system sets at run time by calling a memory-management function like malloc to allocate storage for the string. However, once the system allocates storage for the string, the maximum length of the string is fixed. HLA strings generally operate in this manner.[8] An HLA programmer would typically call the stralloc function to allocate storage for a string variable. Once created via stralloc, however, that particular string object has a fixed length that cannot change.[9]

5.2.2.3 Dynamic Strings

Dynamic string systems, which typically use a descriptor-based format, will automatically allocate sufficient storage for a string object whenever you create a new string or otherwise do something that affects an existing string. Operations like string assignment and substring are relatively trivial in dynamic string systems — generally they only copy the string descriptor data, so such operations are fast. However, as the section on descriptor strings notes, when using strings this way, one cannot store data back into a string object, because it could modify data that is part of other string objects in the system.

The solution to this problem is to use a technique known as *copy on write*. Whenever a string function needs to change some characters in a dynamic string, the function first makes a copy of the string and then makes whatever modifications are necessary to the copy of the data. Research with typical programs suggests that copy-on-write semantics can improve the performance of many applications because operations like string assignment and substring are far more common than the modification of character data within strings. The only drawback to this mechanism is that after several modifications to string data in memory, there may be sections of the string heap area that contain character data that are no longer in use. To avoid a *memory leak,* dynamic string systems employing copy-on-write usually provide *garbage collection code* that scans through the string area looking for *stale* character data in order to recover that memory for other purposes. Unfortunately, depending on the algorithms in use, garbage collection can be slow.

5.2.3 Reference Counting for Strings

Consider the case where you have two string descriptors (or just pointers) pointing at the same string data in memory. Clearly, you cannot deallocate (that is, reuse for a different purpose) the storage associated with one of these pointers while the program is still using the other pointer to access the same data. One (alas, common) solution is to make the programmer responsible for keeping track of such details. Unfortunately, as applications become more complex, relying on the programmer to keep track of such

---

[8] Though, being assembly language, of course it's possible to create static strings and pure dynamic strings in HLA, as well.

[9] Actually, you could call strrealloc to change the size of an HLA string, but dynamic string systems generally do this automatically, something that the existing HLA string functions will not do for you if they detect a string overflow.

details often leads to dangling pointers, memory leaks, and other pointer-related problems in the software. A better solution is to allow the programmer to deallocate the storage for the character data in the string, and to have the deallocation process hold off on the actual deallocation until the programmer releases the last pointer referencing the character data for the string. To accomplish this, a string system can use *reference counters* to track the pointers and their associated data.

A *reference counter* is an integer that counts the number of pointers that reference a string's character data in memory. Every time you assign the address of the string to some pointer, you increment the reference counter by one. Likewise, whenever you wish to deallocate the storage associated with the character data for the string, you decrement the reference counter. Deallocation of the storage for the actual character data doesn't happen until the reference counter decrements to zero.

Reference counting works great when the language handles the details of string assignment automatically for you. If you try to implement reference counting manually, the only difficulty is ensuring that you always increment the reference counter when you assign a string pointer to some other pointer variable. The best way to do this is to never assign pointers directly but to handle all string assignments via some function (or macro) call that updates the reference counters in addition to copying the pointer data. If your code fails to update the reference counter properly, you'll wind up with dangling pointers or memory leaks.

5.2.4   Delphi/Kylix Strings

Although Delphi and Kylix provide a "short string" format that is compatible with the length-prefixed strings in earlier versions of Delphi, later versions of Delphi (4.0 and later) and Kylix use dynamic strings for their string data. Although this string format is unpublished (and, therefore, subject to change), experiments with Delphi at the time of this writing indicate that Delphi's string format is very similar to HLA's. Delphi uses a zero-terminated sequence of characters with a leading string length and a reference counter (rather than a maximum length as HLA uses). Figure 5-4 shows the layout of a Delphi string in memory.

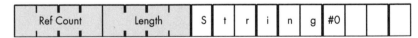

Figure 5-4: Delphi/Kylix string data format

Just like HLA, Delphi/Kylix string variables are pointers that point to the first character of the actual string data. To access the length and reference-counter fields, the Delphi/Kylix string routines use a negative offset of −4 and −8 from the character data's base address. However, because this string format is not published, applications should never access the length or reference counter fields directly. Delphi/Kylix provides a length function that extracts the string length for you, and there really is no need for your applications to access the reference counter field because the Delphi/Kylix string functions maintain this field automatically.

5.2.5   Creating Your Own String Formats

Typically, you will use the string format your language provides, unless you have special requirements. When you do have such requirements, you will find that most languages provide user-defined data-structuring capabilities that allow you to create your own custom string formats.

About the only problem you'll run into is that the language will probably insist on a single string format for literal string constants. However, you can usually write a short conversion function that will translate the literal strings in your language to whatever format you choose.

5.3   Character Sets

Like strings, character sets are another composite data type built upon the character data type. A *character set* is a mathematical set of characters. Membership in a set is a binary relation. A character is either in the set or it is not in the set; you cannot have multiple copies of the same character in a character set. Furthermore, the concept of sequence (whether one character comes before another, as in a string) is foreign to a character set. If two characters are members of a set, their order in the set is irrelevant.

Table 5-3 lists some of the more common character set functions to give you an idea of the types of operations applications typically perform on character sets.

Table 5-3: Common Character Set Functions

Function/Operator	Description
Membership (IN)	Checks to see if a character is a member of a character set (returns true/false).
Intersection	Returns the intersection of two character sets (that is, the set of characters that are members of both sets).
Union	Returns the union of two character sets (that is, all the characters that are members of either set or both sets).
Difference	Returns the difference of two sets (that is, those characters in one set that are not in the other).
Extraction	Extracts a single character from a set.
Subset	Returns true if one character set is a subset of another.
Proper subset	Returns true if one character set is a proper subset of another.
Superset	Returns true if one character set is a superset of another.
Proper superset	Returns true if one character set is a proper superset of another.
Equality	Returns true if one character set is equal to another.
Inequality	Returns true if one character set is not equal to another.

5.3.1   Powerset Representation of Character Sets

There are many different ways to represent character sets. Several languages implement character sets using an array of Boolean values (one Boolean value for each possible character code). Each Boolean value determines whether its corresponding character is or is not a member of the character set: true indicates that the specified character is a member of the set; false indicates that the corresponding character is not a member of the set. To conserve memory, most character set implementations allocate only a single bit for each character in the set; therefore, such character sets consume 16 bytes (128 bits) of memory when supporting 128 characters, or 32 bytes (256 bits) when supporting up to 256 possible characters. This representation of a character set is known as a *powerset*.

The HLA language uses an array of 16 bytes to represent the 128 possible ASCII characters. This array of 128 bits is organized in memory, as shown in Figure 5-5.

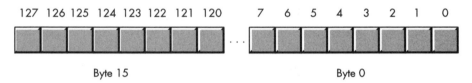

Byte 15   Byte 0

Figure 5-5: HLA character set representation

Bit zero of byte zero corresponds to ASCII code zero (the NUL character). If this bit is one, then the character set contains the NUL character; if this bit is zero, then the character set does not contain the NUL character. Likewise, bit one of byte eight corresponds to ASCII code 65, an uppercase *A*. Bit 65 will contain a one if *A* is a current member of the character set, it will contain zero if *A* is not a member of the set.

Pascal (for example, Delphi/Kylix) uses a similar scheme to represent character sets. Delphi allows up to 256 characters in a character set, so Delphi/Kylix character sets consume 256 bits (or 32 bytes) of memory.

While there are other possible ways to implement character sets, this bit vector (array) implementation has the advantage that it is very easy to implement set operations like union, intersection, difference comparison, and membership tests.

5.3.2   List Representation of Character Sets

Sometimes a powerset bitmap just isn't the right representation for a character set. For example, if your sets are always very small (no more than three or four members), using 16 or 32 bytes to represent such a set can be overkill. For very small sets, using a character string to represent a list of characters is probably the best way to go.[10] If you rarely have more than

---

[10] Though it is up to you to ensure that the character string maintains set semantics. That is, you never allow duplicate characters in such a string.

a few characters in a set, scanning through a string to locate a particular character is probably efficient enough for most applications.

On the other hand, if your character set has a large number of possible characters, then the powerset representation for the character set could become quite large (for example, Unicode character sets would require 8,192 bytes of memory to implement them as powersets). For these reasons (and more), the powerset representation isn't always the best. A list or character string representation could be more appropriate in such situations.

5.4 Designing Your Own Character Set

There is very little that is sacred about the ASCII, EBCDIC, and Unicode character sets. Their primary advantage is that they are international standards to which many systems adhere. If you stick with one of these standards, chances are good you'll be able to exchange information with other people. That is the whole purpose of these standardized codes.

However, these codes were not designed to make various character computations easy. ASCII and EBCDIC were designed with now-antiquated hardware in mind. In particular, the ASCII character set was designed to correspond to the mechanical teletypewriters' keyboards, and EBCDIC was designed with old punched-card systems in mind. Given that such equipment is mainly found in museums today, the layout of the codes in these character sets has almost no benefit in modern computer systems. If we could design our own character sets today, they'd probably be considerably different from ASCII or EBCDIC. They'd probably be based on modern keyboards (so they'd include codes for common keys, like LEFT ARROW, RIGHT ARROW, PGUP, and PGDN). The codes would also be laid out to make various common computations a whole lot easier.

Although the ASCII and EBCDIC character sets are not going away any time soon, there is nothing stopping you from defining your own application-specific character set. Of course, an application-specific character set is, well, application-specific, and you won't be able to share text files containing characters encoded in your custom character set with applications that are ignorant of your private encoding. But it is fairly easy to translate between different character sets using a lookup table, so you can convert between your application's internal character set and an external character set (like ASCII) when performing I/O operations. Assuming you pick a reasonable encoding that makes your programs more efficient overall, the loss of efficiency during I/O can be worthwhile. But how do you choose an encoding for your character set?

The first question you have to ask yourself is, "How many characters do you want to support in your character set?" Obviously, the number of characters you choose will directly affect the size of your character data. An easy choice is 256 possible characters, because bytes are the most common primitive data type that software uses to represent character data. Keep in mind, however, that if you don't really need 256 characters, you probably shouldn't try to define that many characters in your character set. For example, if you can get by with 128 characters or even 64 characters in your custom character set, then "text files" you create with such character sets will compress better. Likewise, data transmissions using your custom character set will be faster if you only have to transmit six or seven bits for each character instead of eight. If you need more than 256 characters, you'll have to weigh the advantages and disadvantages of using multiple code pages, double-byte character sets, or 16-bit characters. And keep in mind that Unicode provides for user-defined characters. So if you need more than 256 characters in your character set, you might consider using Unicode and the user-defined points (character sets) to remain "somewhat standard" with the rest of the world.

However, in this section, we'll define a character set containing 128 characters using an 8-bit byte. For the most part, we're going to simply rearrange the codes in the ASCII character set to make them more convenient for several calculations, and we're going to rename a few of the control codes so they make sense on modern systems instead of the old mainframes and teletypes for which they were created. However, we will add a few new characters beyond those defined by the ASCII standard. Again, the main purpose of this exercise is to make various computations more efficient, not create new characters. We'll call this character set the HyCode character set.

NOTE *The development of HyCode in this chapter is not an attempt to create some new character set standard. HyCode is simply a demonstration of how you can create a custom, application-specific, character set to improve your programs.*

5.4.1 Designing an Efficient Character Set

We should think about several things when designing a new character set. For example, do we need to be able to represent strings of characters using an existing string format? This can have a bearing on the encoding of our strings. For example, if you want to be able to use function libraries that operate on zero-terminated strings, then you need to reserve encoding zero in your custom character set for use as an end-of-string marker. Do keep in mind, however, that a fair number of string functions won't work with your new character set, no matter what you do. For example, functions like stricmp only work if you use the same representation for alphabetic characters as ASCII (or some other common character set). Therefore, you shouldn't feel hampered by the requirements of some particular string representation, because you're going to have to write many of your own string functions to process your custom characters. The HyCode character set doesn't reserve code zero for an end-of-string marker, and that's okay because, as we've seen, zero-terminated strings are not very efficient.

If you look at programs that make use of character functions, you'll see that certain functions occur frequently, such as these:

- Check a character to see if it is a digit.

- Convert a digit character to its numeric equivalent.

- Convert a numeric digit to its character equivalent.

- Check a character to see if it is alphabetic.

- Check a character to see if it is a lowercase character.

- Check a character to see if it is an uppercase character.

- Compare two characters (or strings) using a *case-insensitive* comparison.

- Sort a set of alphabetic strings (case-sensitive and case-insensitive sorting).

- Check a character to see if it is alphanumeric.

- Check a character to see if it is legal in an identifier.

- Check a character to see if it is a common arithmetic or logical operator.

- Check a character to see if it is a bracketing character (that is, one of *(,)*, *[,], {, }*, <, or >).

- Check a character to see if it is a punctuation character.

- Check a character to see if it is a *whitespace* character (such as a space, tab, or newline).

- Check a character to see if it is a cursor control character.

- Check a character to see if it is a scroll control key (such as PGUP, PGDN, HOME, and END).

- Check a character to see if it is a function key.

We'll design the HyCode character set to make these types of operations as efficient and as easy as possible. A huge improvement we can make over the ASCII character set is to assign contiguous character codes to characters belonging to the same type, such as alphabetic characters and control characters. This will allow us to do any of the tests above by using a pair of comparisons. For example, it would be nice if we could determine that a particular character is some sort of punctuation character by comparing against two values that represent upper and lower bounds of the entire range of such characters. While it's not possible to satisfy every conceivable range comparison this way, we can design our character set to accommodate the most common tests with as few comparisons as possible. Although ASCII does organize some of the character sequences in a reasonable fashion, we can do much better. For example, in ASCII, it is not possible to check for a punctuation character with a pair of comparisons because the punctuation characters are spread throughout the character set.

5.4.2 Grouping the Character Codes for Numeric Digits

Consider the first three functions in the previous list — we can achieve all three of these goals by reserving the character codes zero through nine for the characters *0* through *9*. First, by using a single unsigned comparison to check if a character code is less than or equal to nine, we can see if a character is a digit. Next, converting between characters and their numeric representations is trivial, because the character code and the numeric representation are one and the same.

5.4.3 Grouping Alphabetic Characters

Dealing with alphabetic characters is another common character/string problem. The ASCII character set, though nowhere near as bad as EBCDIC, just isn't well designed for dealing with alphabetic character tests and operations. Here are some problems with ASCII that we'll solve with HyCode:

- The alphabetic characters lie in two disjoint ranges. Tests for an alphabetic character, for example, require four comparisons.

- The lowercase characters have ASCII codes that are greater than the uppercase characters. For comparison purposes, if we're going to do a case-sensitive comparison, it's more intuitive to treat lowercase characters as being less than uppercase characters.

- All lowercase characters have a greater value than any individual uppercase character. This leads to counterintuitive results such as *a* being greater than *B* even though any school child who has learned their ABCs knows that this isn't the case.

HyCode solves these problems in a couple of interesting ways. First, HyCode uses encodings $4C through $7F to represent the 52 alphabetic characters. Because HyCode only uses 128 character codes ($00..$7F), the alphabetic codes consume the last 52 character codes. This means that if we want to test a character to see if it is alphabetic, we only need to compare whether the code is greater than or equal to $4C. In a high-level language, you'd write the comparison like this:

```
if( c >= 76) . . .
```

Or if your compiler supports the HyCode character set, like this:

```
if( c >= 'a') . . .
```

In assembly language, you could use a pair of instructions like the following:

```
        cmp( al, 76 );
        jnae NotAlphabetic;
```

```
        // Execute these statements if it's alphabetic

NotAlphabetic:
```

Another advantage of HyCode (and another big difference from other character sets) is that HyCode interleaves the lowercase and uppercase characters (that is, the sequential encodings are for the characters *a, A, b, B, c, C,* and so on). This makes sorting and comparing strings very easy, regardless of whether you're doing a case-sensitive or case-insensitive search. The interleaving uses the LO bit of the character code to determine whether the character code is lowercase (LO bit is zero) or uppercase (LO bit is one). HyCode uses the following encodings for alphabetic characters:

```
a:76, A:77, b:78, B:79, c:80, C:81, . . . y:124, Y:125, z:126, Z:127
```

Checking for an uppercase or lowercase alphabetic using HyCode is a little more work than checking whether a character is alphabetic, but when working in assembly it's still less work than you'll need for the equivalent ASCII comparison. To test a character to see if it's a member of a single case, you effectively need two comparisons; the first test is to see if it's alphabetic, and then you determine its case. In C/C++ you'd probably use statements like the following:

```
if( (c >= 76) && (c & 1))
{
    // execute this code if it's an uppercase character
}

if( (c >= 76) && !(c & 1))
{
    // execute this code if it's a lowercase character
}
```

Note that the subexpression (c & 1) evaluates true (1) if the LO bit of c is one, meaning we have an uppercase character if c is alphabetic. Likewise, !(c & 1) evaluates true if the LO bit of c is zero, meaning we have a lowercase character. If you're working in 80x86 assembly language, you can actually test a character to see if it is uppercase or lowercase by using three machine instructions:

```
// Note: ROR(1, AL) maps lowercase to the range $26..$3F (38..63)
//       and uppercase to $A6..$BF (166..191). Note that all other characters
//       get mapped to smaller values within these ranges.

        ror( 1, al );
        cmp( al, $26 );
```

```
        jnae NotLower;      // Note: must be an unsigned branch!

            // Code that deals with a lowercase character.

NotLower:

// For uppercase, note that the ROR creates codes in the range $A8..$BF which
//   are negative (8-bit) values. They also happen to be the *most* negative
//   numbers that ROR will produce from the HyCode character set.

        ror( 1, al );
        cmp( al, $a6 );
        jge NotUpper;      // Note: must be a signed branch!

            // Code that deals with an uppercase character.

NotUpper:
```

Unfortunately, very few languages provide the equivalent of an ror operation, and only a few languages allow you to (easily) treat character values as signed and unsigned within the same code sequence. Therefore, this sequence is probably limited to assembly language programs.

5.4.4 Comparing Alphabetic Characters

The HyCode grouping of alphabetic characters means that lexicographical ordering (i.e., "dictionary ordering") is almost free, no matter what language you're using. As long as you can live with the fact that lowercase characters are less than the corresponding uppercase characters, sorting your strings by comparing the HyCode character values will give you lexicographical order. This is because, unlike ASCII, HyCode defines the following relations on the alphabetic characters:

```
a < A < b < B < c < C < d < D < . . . < w < W < x < X < y < Y < z < Z
```

This is exactly the relationship you want for lexicographical ordering, and it's also the intuitive relationship most people would expect.

Case-insensitive comparisons only involve a tiny bit more work than straight case-sensitive comparisons (and far less work than doing case-insensitive comparisons using a character set like ASCII). When comparing two alphabetic characters, you simply mask out their LO bits (or force them both to one) and you automatically get a case-insensitive comparison.

To see the benefit of the HyCode character set when doing case-insensitive comparisons, let's first take a look at what the standard case-insensitive character comparison would look like in C/C++ for two ASCII characters:

```
if( toupper( c ) == toupper( d ))
{
```

```
        // do code that handles c==d using a case-insensitive comparison.
}
```

This code doesn't look too bad, but consider what the toupper function (or, usually, macro) expands to:[11]

```
#define toupper(ch) ((ch >= 'a' && ch <= 'z') ? ch & 0x5f : ch )
```

With this macro, you wind up with the following once the C preprocessor expands the former if statement:

```
if
(
        ((c >= 'a' && c <= 'z') ? c & 0x5f : c )
    == ((d >= 'a' && d <= 'z') ? d & 0x5f : d )
)
{
        // do code that handles c==d using a case-insensitive comparison.
}
```

This example expands to 80x86 code similar to this:

```
        // assume c is in cl and d is in dl.

        cmp( cl, 'a' );     // See if c is in the range 'a'..'z'
        jb NotLower;
        cmp( cl, 'z' );
        ja NotLower;
        and( $5f, cl );     // Convert lowercase char in cl to uppercase.
NotLower:

        cmp( dl, 'a' );     // See if d is in the range 'a'..'z'
        jb NotLower2;
        cmp( dl, 'z' );
        ja NotLower2;
        and( $5f, dl );     // Convert lowercase char in dl to uppercase.
NotLower2:

        cmp( cl, dl );      // Compare the (now uppercase if alphabetic)
                            //  chars.
        jne NotEqual;       // Skip the code that handles c==d if they're
                            //  not equal.

            // do code that handles c==d using a case-insensitive comparison.
NotEqual:
```

---

[11] Actually, it's worse than this because most C standard libraries use lookup tables to map ranges of characters, but we'll ignore that issue here.

When using HyCode, case-insensitive comparisons are much simpler. Here's what the HLA assembly code would look like:

```
// Check to see if CL is alphabetic. No need to check DL as the comparison
// will always fail if DL is non-alphabetic.

          cmp( cl, 76 );        // If CL < 76 ('a') then it's not alphabetic
          jb TestEqual;         //   and there is no way the two chars are equal
                                //   (even ignoring case).

          or( 1, cl );          // CL is alpha, force it to uppercase.
          or( 1, dl );          // DL may or may not be alpha. Force to
                                //   uppercase if it is.
TestEqual:
          cmp( cl, dl );        // Compare the uppercase versions of the chars.
          jne NotEqual;         // Bail out if they're not equal.

TheyreEqual:
          // do code that handles c==d using a case-insensitive comparison.

NotEqual:
```

As you can see, the HyCode sequence uses half the instructions for a case-insensitive comparison of two characters.

5.4.5 Other Character Groupings

Because alphabetic characters are at one end of the character-code range and numeric characters are at the other, it takes two comparisons to check a character to see if it's alphanumeric (which is still better than the four comparisons necessary when using ASCII). Here's the Pascal/Delphi/Kylix code you'd use to see if a character is alphanumeric:

```
if( ch < chr(10) or ch >= chr(76)) then . . .
```

Several programs (beyond compilers) need to efficiently process strings of characters that represent program identifiers. Most languages allow alphanumeric characters in identifiers, and, as you just saw, we can check a character to see if it's alphanumeric using only two comparisons.

Many languages also allow underscores within identifiers, and some languages, such as MASM and TASM, allow other characters like the at character (@) and dollar sign ($) to appear within identifiers. Therefore, by assigning the underscore character the value 75, and by assigning the $ and @ characters the codes 73 and 74, we can still test for an identifier character using only two comparisons.

For similar reasons, the HyCode character set groups several other classes of characters into contiguous character-code ranges. For example, HyCode groups the cursor control keys together, the whitespace characters, the bracketing characters (parentheses, brackets, braces, and angle brackets), the arithmetic operators, the punctuation characters, and so on. Table 5-4 lists the complete HyCode character set. If you study the numeric codes assigned to each of these characters, you'll discover that their code assignments allow efficient computation of most of the character operations described earlier.

Table 5-4: The HyCode Character Set

Binary	Hex	Decimal	Character	Binary	Hex	Decimal	Character
0000_0000	00	0	0	0001_1110	1E	30	End
0000_0001	01	1	1	0001_1111	1F	31	Home
0000_0010	02	2	2	0010_0000	20	32	PgDn
0000_0011	03	3	3	0010_0001	21	33	PgUp
0000_0100	04	4	4	0010_0010	22	34	left
0000_0101	05	5	5	0010_0011	23	35	right
0000_0110	06	6	6	0010_0100	24	36	up
0000_0111	07	7	7	0010_0101	25	37	down/ linefeed
0000_1000	08	8	8	0010_0110	26	38	nonbreaking space
0000_1001	09	9	9	0010_0111	27	39	paragraph
0000_1010	0A	10	keypad	0010_1000	28	40	carriage return
0000_1011	0B	11	cursor	0010_1001	29	41	newline/enter
0000_1100	0C	12	function	0010_1010	2A	42	tab
0000_1101	0D	13	alt	0010_1011	2B	43	space
0000_1110	0E	14	control	0010_1100	2C	44	(
0000_1111	0F	15	command	0010_1101	2D	45	)
0001_0000	10	16	len	0010_1110	2E	46	[
0001_0001	11	17	len128	0010_1111	2F	47	]
0001_0010	12	18	bin128	0011_0000	30	48	{
0001_0011	13	19	EOS	0011_0001	31	49	}
0001_0100	14	20	EOF	0011_0010	32	50	<
0001_0101	15	21	sentinel	0011_0011	33	51	>
0001_0110	16	22	break/ interrupt	0011_0100	34	52	=
0001_0111	17	23	escape/ cancel	0011_0101	35	53	^
0001_1000	18	24	pause	0011_0110	36	54		
0001_1001	19	25	bell	0011_0111	37	55	&
0001_1010	1A	26	back tab	0011_1000	38	56	-
0001_1011	1B	27	backspace	0011_1001	39	57	+
0001_1100	1C	28	delete				
0001_1101	1D	29	Insert				*(continued on the next page)*

Table 5-4: The HyCode Character Set (continued)

Binary	Hex	Decimal	Character	Binary	Hex	Decimal	Character
0011_1010	3A	58	*	0101_1101	5D	93	l
0011_1011	3B	59	/	0101_1110	5E	94	i
0011_1100	3C	60	%	0101_1111	5F	95	J
0011_1101	3D	61	~	0110_0000	60	96	k
0011_1110	3E	62	!	0110_0001	61	97	K
0011_1111	3F	63	?	0110_0010	62	98	l
0100_0000	40	64	,	0110_0011	63	99	L
0100_0001	41	65	.	0110_0100	64	100	m
0100_0010	42	66	:	0110_0101	65	101	M
0100_0011	43	67	;	0110_0110	66	102	n
0100_0100	44	68	"	0110_0111	67	103	N
0100_0101	45	69	'	0110_1000	68	104	o
0100_0110	46	70	`	0110_1001	69	105	O
0100_0111	47	71	\	0110_1010	6A	106	p
0100_1000	48	72	#	0110_1011	6B	107	P
0100_1001	49	73	$	0110_1100	6C	108	q
0100_1010	4A	74	@	0110_1101	6D	109	Q
0100_1011	4B	75	_	0110_1110	6E	110	r
0100_1100	4C	76	a	0110_1111	6F	111	R
0100_1101	4D	77	A	0111_0000	70	112	s
0100_1110	4E	78	b	0111_0001	71	113	S
0100_1111	4F	79	B	0111_0010	72	114	t
0101_0000	50	80	c	0111_0011	73	115	T
0101_0001	51	81	C	0111_0100	74	116	u
0101_0010	52	82	d	0111_0101	75	117	U
0101_0011	53	83	D	0111_0110	76	118	v
0101_0100	54	84	e	0111_0111	77	119	V
0101_0101	55	85	E	0111_1000	78	120	w
0101_0110	56	86	f	0111_1001	79	121	W
0101_0111	57	87	F	0111_1010	7A	122	x
0101_1000	58	88	g	0111_1011	7B	123	X
0101_1001	59	89	G	0111_1100	7C	124	y
0101_1010	5A	90	h	0111_1101	7D	125	Y
0101_1011	5B	91	H	0111_1110	7E	126	z
0101_1100	5C	92	i	0111_1111	7F	127	Z

5.5   For More Information

ASCII, EBCDIC, and Unicode are all international standards. You can find out more about the EBCDIC character set families on IBM's website (http://www.ibm.com). ASCII and Unicode are both ISO standards, and ISO provides reports for both character sets. Generally, those reports cost money, but you can also find out lots of information about the ASCII and Unicode character sets by searching for them by name on the Internet. You can also read about UNICODE at http://www.unicode.org.

Those who are interested in more information about character, string, and character set functions should consider reading references on the following languages:

- The Awk programming language
- The Perl programming language
- The SNOBOL4 programming language
- The Icon programming language
- The SETL programming language
- The High Level Assembly (HLA) language

In particular, the HLA programming language provides a wide set of character, string, character set, and pattern matching functions. Check out the HLA Standard Library Reference Manual, usually found at http://webster.cs.ucr.edu, for more details.

6

MEMORY ORGANIZATION
AND ACCESS

This chapter describes the basic components that make up a computer system: the CPU, memory, I/O, and the bus that connects them. Although you can write software without this knowledge, writing great, high-performance code requires an understanding of this material.

This chapter begins by discussing bus organization and memory organization. These two hardware components may have as large a performance impact on your software as the CPU's speed. Knowing about memory performance characteristics, data locality, and cache operation can help you design software that runs as fast as possible. Writing *great* code requires a strong knowledge of the computer's architecture.

6.1 The Basic System Components

The basic operational design of a computer system is called its *architecture.* John von Neumann, a pioneer in computer design, is given credit for the principal architecture in use today. For example, the 80x86 family uses the *von Neumann architecture* (VNA). A typical von Neumann system has three major components: the *central processing unit* (CPU), *memory,* and *input/output* (I/O), as shown in Figure 6-1.

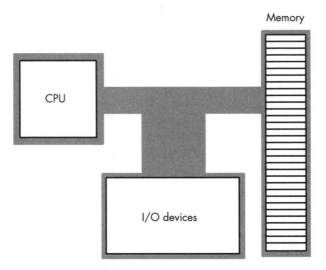

Figure 6-1: Typical von Neumann machine

In VNA machines, like the 80x86, the CPU is where all the action takes place. All computations occur within the CPU. Data and machine instructions reside in memory until the CPU requires them, at which point the system transfers the data into the CPU. To the CPU, most I/O devices look like memory; the major difference between memory and I/O devices is the fact that the latter are generally located in the outside world, whereas the former is located within the same machine.

6.1.1 The System Bus

The *system bus* connects the various components of a VNA machine. Most CPUs have three major buses: the *address* bus, the *data* bus, and the *control* bus. A bus is a collection of wires on which electrical signals pass between components of the system. These buses vary from processor to processor, but each bus carries comparable information on most processors. For example, the data buses on the Pentium and 80386 may have different implementations, but both variants carry data between the processor, I/O, and memory.

6.1.1.1 The Data Bus

CPUs use the *data bus* to shuffle data between the various components in a computer system. The size of this bus varies widely among CPUs. Indeed, bus size is one of the main attributes that defines the "size" of the processor.

Most modern, general-purpose CPUs employ a 32-bit-wide or 64-bit-wide data bus. Some processors use 8-bit or 16-bit data buses, there may well be some CPUs with 128-bit buses by the time you read this. For the most part, however, the CPUs in personal computers tend to use 32-bit or 64-bit data buses (and 64-bit data buses are the most prevalent).

You'll often hear a processor called an *8-, 16-, 32-, or 64-bit processor.* The smaller of the number of data lines on the processor and the size of the largest general-purpose integer register determines the processor size. For example, modern Intel 80x86 CPUs all have 64-bit buses, but only provide 32-bit general-purpose integer registers, so we'll classify these devices as 32-bit processors. The AMD x86-64 processors support 64-bit integer registers and a 64-bit bus, so they're 64-bit processors.

Although the 80x86 family members with 8-, 16-, 32-, and 64-bit data buses can process data blocks up to the bit width of the bus, they can also access smaller memory units of 8, 16, or 32 bits. Therefore, anything you can do with a small data bus can be done with a larger data bus as well; the larger data bus, however, may access memory faster and can access larger chunks of data in one memory operation. You'll read about the exact nature of these memory accesses a little later in this chapter.

6.1.2 The Address Bus

The data bus on an 80x86 family processor transfers information between a particular memory location or I/O device and the CPU. The only question is, "Which memory location or I/O device?" The address bus answers that question. To uniquely identify each memory location and I/O device, the system designer assigns a unique memory address to each. When the software wants to access a particular memory location or I/O device, it places the corresponding address on the address bus. Circuitry within the device checks this address and transfers data if there is an address match. All other memory locations ignore the request on the address bus.

With a single address bus line, a processor could access exactly two unique addresses: zero and one. With n address lines, the processor can access 2^n unique addresses (because there are 2^n unique values in an n-bit binary number). Therefore, the number of bits on the address bus will determine the *maximum* number of addressable memory and I/O locations. Early 80x86 processors, for example, provided only 20 lines on the address bus. Therefore, they could only access up to 1,048,576 (or 2^{20}) memory locations. Larger address buses can access more memory (see Table 6-1 on the next page).

Table 6-1: 80x86 Addressing Capabilities

Processor	Address Bus Size	Maximum Addressable Memory
8088, 8086, 80186, 80188	20	1,048,576 (1 megabyte)
80286, 80386sx	24	16,777,216 (16 megabytes)
80386dx	32	4,294,976,296 (4 gigabytes)
80486, Pentium	32	4,294,976,296 (4 gigabytes)
Pentium Pro, II, III, IV	36	68,719,476,736 (64 gigabytes)

Newer processors will support 40-, 48-, and 64-bit address buses. The time is coming when most programmers will consider 4 GB (gigabytes) of storage to be too small, just as we consider 1 MB (megabyte) insufficient today. (There was a time when 1 MB was considered far more than anyone would ever need!) Many other processors (such as SPARC and IA-64) already provide much larger addresses buses and, in fact, support addresses up to 64 bits in the software.

A 64-bit address range is truly infinite as far as memory is concerned. No one will ever put 2^{64} bytes of memory into a computer system and feel that they need more. Of course, people have made claims like this in the past. A few years ago, no one ever thought a computer would need 1 GB of memory, but computers with a gigabyte of memory or more are very common today. However, 2^{64} really is infinity for one simple reason—it's nearly physically impossible to build that much memory based on estimates of the current size of the universe (which estimate about 2^{76} different elementary particles in the universe). Keeping in mind that it takes about 4 billion DVDs to hold 2^{64} bytes of memory, it's unlikely you'll ever see a computer system with this much memory. Then again, maybe we really will use whole planets as computer systems one day, as Douglas Adams predicts in *The Hitchhiker's Guide to the Galaxy*. Who knows?

6.1.3 The Control Bus

The control bus is an eclectic collection of signals that control how the processor communicates with the rest of the system. To illustrate its importance, consider the data bus for a moment. The CPU uses the data bus to move data between itself and memory. This prompts the question, "How does the system know whether it is sending or receiving data?" Well, the system uses two lines on the control bus, *read* and *write*, to determine the data flow direction (CPU to memory, or memory to CPU). So when the CPU wants to write data to memory, it *asserts* (places a signal on) the write control line. When the CPU wants to read data from memory, it asserts the read control line.

Although the exact composition of the control bus varies among processors, some control lines are common to all processors and are worth a brief mention. Among these are the system clock lines, interrupt lines, byte enable lines, and status lines.

The *byte enable lines* appear on the control bus of some CPUs that support byte-addressable memory. These control lines allow 16-, 32-, and 64-bit processors to deal with smaller chunks of data by communicating the size of the accompanying data. Additional details appear later in the sections on 16-bit and 32-bit buses.

The control bus also contains a signal that helps distinguish between address spaces on the 80x86 family of processors. The 80x86 family, unlike many other processors, provides two distinct address spaces: one for memory and one for I/O. However, it does not have two separate physical address buses (for I/O and memory). Instead, the system shares the address bus for both I/O and memory addresses. Additional control lines decide whether the address is intended for memory or I/O. When such signals are active, the I/O devices use the address on the LO 16 bits of the address bus. When inactive, the I/O devices ignore the signals on the address bus, and the memory subsystem takes over at that point.

6.2 Physical Organization of Memory

A typical CPU addresses a maximum of 2^n different memory locations, where n is the number of bits on the address bus (most computer systems built around 80x86 family CPUs do not include the maximum addressable amount of memory). Of course, the first question you should ask is, "What exactly is a memory location?" The 80x86, as an example, supports *byte-addressable memory*. Therefore, the basic memory unit is a byte. With address buses containing 20, 24, 32, or 36 address lines, the 80x86 processors can address 1 MB, 16 MB, 4 GB, or 64 GB of memory, respectively. Some CPU families do not provide byte-addressable memory (commonly, they only address memory in double-word or even quad-word chunks). However, because of the vast amount of software written that assumes memory is byte-addressable (such as all those C/C++ programs out there), even CPUs that don't support byte-addressable memory in hardware still use byte addresses and simulate byte addressing in software. We'll return to this issue shortly.

Think of memory as an array of bytes. The address of the first byte is zero and the address of the last byte is 2^n-1. For a CPU with a 20-bit address bus, the following pseudo-Pascal array declaration is a good approximation of memory:

```
Memory: array [0..1048575] of byte; // One-megabyte address space (20 bits)
```

To execute the equivalent of the Pascal statement Memory [125] := 0; the CPU places the value zero on the data bus, the address 125 on the address bus, and asserts the write line on the control bus, as in Figure 6-2 on the next page.

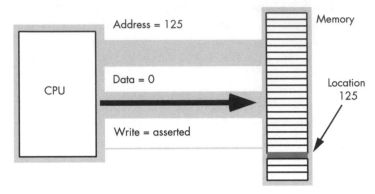

Figure 6-2: Memory write operation

To execute the equivalent of `CPU := Memory [125];` the CPU places the address 125 on the address bus, asserts the read line on the control bus, and then reads the resulting data from the data bus (see Figure 6-3).

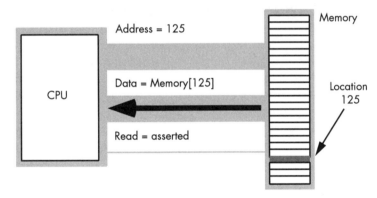

Figure 6-3: Memory read operation

This discussion applies *only* when accessing a single byte in memory. What happens when the processor accesses a word or a double word? Because memory consists of an array of bytes, how can we possibly deal with values larger than eight bits?

Different computer systems have different solutions to this problem. The 80x86 family stores the LO byte of a word at the address specified and the HO byte at the next location. Therefore, a word consumes two consecutive memory addresses (as you would expect, because a word consists of two bytes). Similarly, a double word consumes four consecutive memory locations.

The address for a word or a double word is the address of its LO byte. The remaining bytes follow this LO byte, with the HO byte appearing at the address of the word plus one or the address of the double word plus three (see Figure 6-4). Note that it is quite possible for byte, word, and double-word values to overlap in memory. For example, in Figure 6-4, you could have a word variable beginning at address 193, a byte variable at address 194, and a double-word value beginning at address 192. Bytes, words, and double words may begin at *any* valid address in memory. We will soon see, however, that starting larger objects at an arbitrary address is not a good idea.

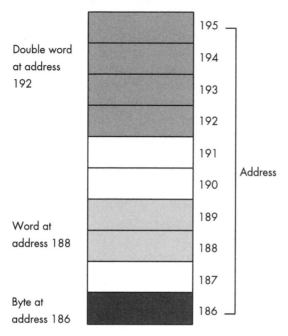

Figure 6-4: Byte, word, and double-word storage in memory (on an 80x86)

6.2.1 8-Bit Data Buses

A processor with an 8-bit bus (like the old 8088 CPU) can transfer 8 bits of data at a time. Because each memory address corresponds to an 8-bit byte, an 8-bit bus turns out to be the most convenient architecture (from the hardware perspective), as Figure 6-5 shows.

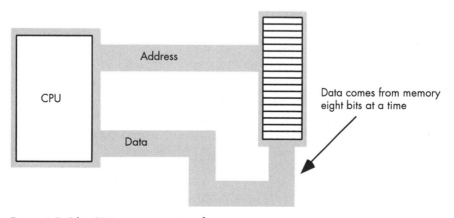

Figure 6-5: 8-bit CPU <-> memory interface

The term *byte-addressable memory array* means that the CPU can address memory in chunks as small as a single byte. It also means that this is the *smallest* unit of memory you can access at once with the processor. That is, if the processor wants to access a 4-bit value, it must read eight bits and then ignore the extra four bits.

It is also important to realize that byte addressability does not imply that the CPU can access eight bits starting at any arbitrary bit boundary. When you specify address 125 in memory, you get the entire eight bits at that address — nothing less, nothing more. Addresses are integers; you cannot specify, for example, address 125.5 to fetch fewer than eight bits or to fetch a byte straddling 2-byte addresses.

Although CPUs with an 8-bit data bus conveniently manipulate byte values, they can also manipulate word and double-word values. However, this requires multiple memory operations because these processors can only move eight bits of data at once. To load a word requires two memory operations; to load a double word requires four memory operations.

6.2.2 16-Bit Data Buses

Some CPUs (such as the 8086, the 80286, and variants of the ARM/StrongARM processor family) have a 16-bit data bus. This allows these processors to access twice as much memory in the same amount of time as their 8-bit counterparts. These processors organize memory into two *banks*: an "even" bank and an "odd" bank (see Figure 6-6).

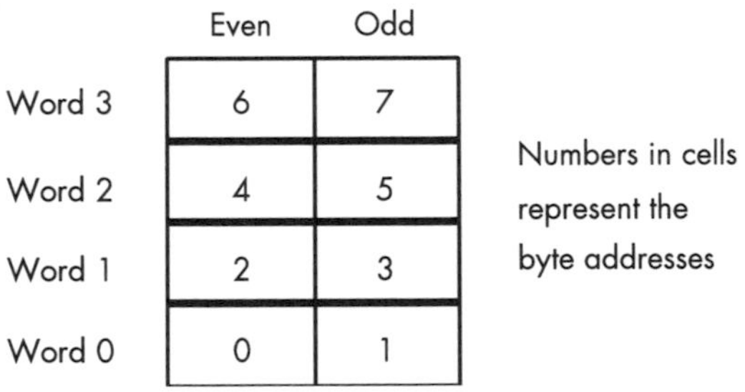

	Even	Odd
Word 3	6	7
Word 2	4	5
Word 1	2	3
Word 0	0	1

Numbers in cells represent the byte addresses

Figure 6-6: Byte addressing in word memory

Figure 6-7 illustrates the data bus connection to the CPU. In this figure, the data bus lines D0 through D7 transfer the LO byte of the word, while bus lines D8 through D15 transfer the HO byte of the word.

The 16-bit members of the 80x86 family can load a word from any arbitrary address. As mentioned earlier, the processor fetches the LO byte of the value from the address specified and the HO byte from the next consecutive address. However, this creates a subtle problem if you look closely at Figure 6-7. What happens when you access a word that begins on an odd address? Suppose you want to read a word from location 125. The LO byte of the word comes from location 125 and the HO byte of the word comes from location 126. It turns out that there are two problems with this approach.

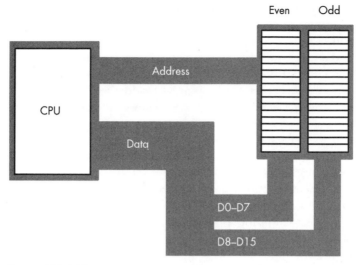

Even   Odd

CPU

Address

Data

D0–D7

D8–D15

Figure 6-7: 16-bit processor memory organization (e.g., 80286)

As you can see in Figure 6-7, data bus lines 8 through 15 (the HO byte) connect to the odd bank, and data bus lines 0 through 7 (the LO byte) connect to the even bank. Accessing memory location 125 will transfer data to the CPU on lines D8 through D15 of the data bus, placing the data in the HO byte; yet we need this in the LO byte! Fortunately, the 80x86 CPUs automatically recognize and handle this situation.

The second problem is even more obscure. When accessing words, we're really accessing two separate bytes, each of which has a separate byte address. So the question arises, "What address appears on the address bus?" The 16-bit 80x86 CPUs always place even addresses on the bus. Bytes at even addresses always appear on data lines D0 through D7, and the bytes at odd addresses always appear on data lines D8 through D15. If you access a word at an even address, the CPU can bring in the entire 16-bit chunk in one memory operation. Likewise, if you access a single byte, the CPU activates the appropriate bank (using a *byte-enable* control line) and transfers that byte on the appropriate data lines for its address.

So, what happens when the CPU accesses a word at an odd address, like the example given earlier? The CPU cannot place the address 125 on the address bus and read the 16 bits from memory. There are no odd addresses coming out of a 16-bit 80x86 CPU — the addresses are always even. Therefore, if you try to put 125 on the address bus, 124 will actually appear on the bus. Were you to read the 16 bits at this address, you would get the word at addresses 124 (LO byte) and 125 (HO byte) — not what you'd expect. Accessing a word at an odd address requires two memory operations. First, the CPU must read the byte at address 125, and then it needs to read the byte at address 126. Finally, it needs to swap the positions of these bytes internally because both entered the CPU on the wrong half of the data bus.

Fortunately, the 16-bit 80x86 CPUs hide these details from you. Your programs can access words at *any* address and the CPU will properly access and swap (if necessary) the data in memory. However, accessing a word at an odd address will require two memory operations (just as with the 8-bit bus on the 8088/80188), so accessing words at odd addresses on a 16-bit processor is slower than accessing words at even addresses. *By carefully arranging how you use memory, you can improve the speed of your programs on these CPUs.*

6.2.3   32-Bit Data Buses

Accessing 32-bit quantities always takes at least two memory operations on the 16-bit processors. If you access a 32-bit quantity at an odd address, a 16-bit processor may require three memory operations to access the data.

The 80x86 processors with a 32-bit data bus (such as the 80386 and 80486) use four banks of memory connected to the 32-bit data bus (see Figure 6-8).

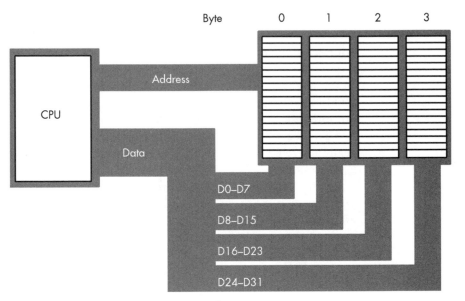

Figure 6-8: 32-bit processor memory interface

With a 32-bit memory interface, the 80x86 CPU can access any single byte with one memory operation. With a 16-bit memory interface the address placed on the address bus is always an even number, and similarly with a 32-bit memory interface, the address placed on the address bus is always some multiple of four. Using various *byte-enable* control lines, the CPU can select which of the four bytes at that address the software wants to access. As with the 16-bit processor, the CPU will automatically rearrange bytes as necessary.

A 32-bit CPU can also access a word at most memory addresses using a single memory operation, though word accesses at certain addresses will take two memory operations (see Figure 6-9). This is the same problem encountered with the 16-bit processor attempting to retrieve a word with an odd LO byte address, except it occurs half as often — only when the LO byte address divided by four leaves a remainder of three.

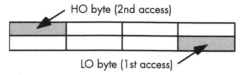

Figure 6-9: Accessing a word on a 32-bit processor at (address mod 4) = 3

A 32-bit CPU can access a double word in a single memory operation *only if* the address of that value is evenly divisible by four. If not, the CPU may require two memory operations.

Once again, the 80x86 CPU handles all this automatically. However, there is a performance benefit to proper data alignment. Generally, the LO byte of word values should always be placed at even addresses, and the LO byte of double-word values should always be placed at addresses that are evenly divisible by four.

6.2.4   64-Bit Buses

The Pentium and later processors provide a 64-bit data bus and special cache memory that reduces the impact of nonaligned data access. Although there may still be a penalty for accessing data at an inappropriate address, modern x86 CPUs suffer from the problem less frequently than the earlier CPUs. The discussion in Section 6.4.3, "Cache Memory," will look at the details.

6.2.5   Small Accesses on Non-80x86 Processors

Although the 80x86 processor is not the only processor around that will let you access a byte, word, or double-word object at an arbitrary byte address, most processors created in the past 30 years do *not* allow this. For example, the 68000 processor found in the original Apple Macintosh system will allow you to access a byte at any address, but will raise an exception if you attempt to access a word at an odd address.[1] Many processors require that you access an object at an address that is an even multiple of the object's size or the CPU will raise an exception.

Most RISC processors, including those found in modern Power Macintosh systems, do not allow you to access byte and word objects at all. Most RISC CPUs require that all data accesses be the same size as the data bus (or general-purpose integer register size, whichever is smaller). This is generally a double-word (32-bit) access. If you want to access a byte or a word on such a machine, you have to treat bytes and words as packed fields and

---

[1] 680x0 series processors starting with the 68020, found in later Macintosh systems, corrected this and allowed data access of words and double words at arbitrary addresses.

use the shift and mask techniques to extract or insert byte and word data in a double word. Although it is nearly impossible to avoid byte accesses in software that does any character and string processing, if you expect your software to run on various modern RISC CPUs, you should avoid word data types in favor of double words if you don't want to pay a performance penalty for the word accesses.

6.3 Big Endian Versus Little Endian Organization

Earlier, you read that the 80x86 CPU family stores the LO byte of a word or double-word value at a particular address in memory and the successive HO bytes at successively higher addresses. There was also a vague statement to the effect that "different processors handle this in different ways." Well, now is the time to learn how different processors store multi-byte objects in byte-addressable memory.

Almost every CPU you'll use whose "bit size" is some power of two (8, 16, 32, 64, and so on) will number the bits and nibbles as shown in the previous chapters. There are some exceptions, but they are rare, and most of the time they represent a notational change, not a functional change (meaning you can safely ignore the difference). Once you start dealing with objects larger than eight bits, however, life becomes more complicated. Different CPUs organize the bytes in a multibyte object differently.

Consider the layout of the bytes in a double word on an 80x86 CPU (see Figure 6-10). The LO byte, which contributes the smallest component of a binary number, sits in bit positions zero through seven and appears at the lowest address in memory. It seems reasonable that the bits that contribute the least would be located at the lowest address in memory.

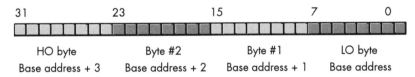

HO byte	Byte #2	Byte #1	LO byte
Base address + 3	Base address + 2	Base address + 1	Base address

Figure 6-10: Byte layout in a double word on the 80x86 processor

Unfortunately, this is not the only organization that is possible. Some CPUs, for example, reverse the memory addresses of all the bytes in a double word, using the organization shown in Figure 6-11.

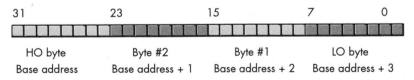

HO byte	Byte #2	Byte #1	LO byte
Base address	Base address + 1	Base address + 2	Base address + 3

Figure 6-11: Alternate byte layout in a double word

The Apple Macintosh and most non-80x86 Unix boxes use the data organization appearing in Figure 6-11. Therefore, this isn't some rare and esoteric convention; it's quite common. Furthermore, even on 80x86 systems, certain protocols (such as network transmissions) specify the data organization for double words as shown in Figure 6-11. So this isn't something you can ignore if you work on PCs.

The byte organization that Intel uses is whimsically known as the *little endian byte organization*. The alternate form is known as *big endian byte organization*. If you're wondering, these terms come from Jonathan Swift's *Gulliver's Travels*; the Lilliputians were arguing over whether one should open an egg by cracking it on the little end or the big end, a parody of the arguments the Catholics and Protestants were having over their respective doctrines when Swift was writing.

The time for arguing over which format is better was back before there were several different CPUs created using different *byte genders*. (Many programmers refer to this as byte sex. Byte gender is a little less offensive, hence the use of that term in this book.) Today, we have to deal with the fact that different CPUs sport different byte genders, and we have to take care when writing software if we want that software to run on both types of processors. Arguing over whether one format is better than another is irrelevant at this point; regardless of which format is better or worse, we may have to put extra code in our programs to deal with both formats (including the worse of the two, whichever that is).

The big endian versus little endian problem occurs when we try to pass binary data between two computers. For example, the double-word binary representation of 256 on a little endian machine has the following byte values:

LO byte:	0
Byte #1:	1
Byte #2:	0
HO byte:	0

If you assemble these four bytes on a little endian machine, their layout takes this form:

Byte:	3	2	1	0	
256:	0	0	1	0	(each digit represents an 8-bit value)

On a big endian machine, however, the layout takes the following form:

Byte:	3	2	1	0	
256:	0	1	0	0	(each digit represents an 8-bit value)

This means that if you take a 32-bit value from one of these machines and attempt to use it on the other machine (whose byte gender is not the same), you won't get correct results. For example, if you take a big endian version of the value 256, you'll discover that it has the bit value one in bit position 16 in the little endian format. If you try to use this value on a little endian machine, that machine will think that the value is actually 65,536 (that is, %1_0000_0000_0000_0000). Therefore, when exchanging data between two different machines, the best solution is to convert your values to some canonical form and then, if necessary, convert the canonical form back to the local format if the local and canonical formats are not the same. Exactly what constitutes a "canonical" format depends, usually, on the transmission medium. For example, when transmitting data across networks, the canonical form is usually big endian because TCP/IP and some other network protocols use the big endian format. This does not suggest that big endian is always the canonical form. For example, when transmitting data across the Universal Serial Bus (USB), the canonical format is little endian. Of course, if you control the software on both ends, the choice of canonical form is arbitrary; still, you should attempt to use the appropriate form for the transmission medium to avoid confusion down the road.

To convert between the endian forms, you must do a *mirror-image swap* of the bytes in the object. To cause a mirror-image swap, you must swap the bytes at opposite ends of the binary number, and then work your way towards the middle of the object swapping pairs of bytes as you go along. For example, to convert between the big endian and little endian format within a double word, you'd first swap bytes zero and three, then you'd swap bytes one and two (see Figure 6-12).

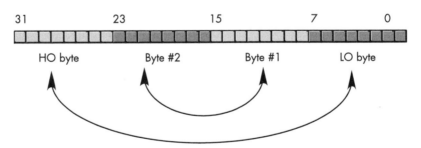

Figure 6-12: Endian conversion in a double word

For word values, all you need to do is swap the HO and LO bytes to change the byte gender. For quad-word values, you need to swap bytes zero and seven, one and six, two and five, and three and four. Because very little software deals with 128-bit integers, you'll probably not need to worry about long-word gender conversion, but the concept is the same if you do.

Note that the byte gender conversion process is reflexive. That is, the same algorithm that converts big endian to little endian also converts little endian to big endian. If you run the algorithm twice, you wind up with the data in the original format.

Even if you're not writing software that exchanges data between two computers, the issue of byte gender may arise. To illustrate this point, consider that some programs assemble larger objects from discrete bytes by assigning those bytes to specific positions within the larger value. If the software puts the LO byte into bit positions zero through seven (little endian format) on a big endian machine, the program will not produce correct results. Therefore, if the software needs to run on different CPUs that have different byte organizations, the software will have to determine the byte gender of the machine it's running on and adjust how it assembles larger objects from bytes accordingly.

To illustrate how to build larger objects from discrete bytes, perhaps the best place to start is with a short example that first demonstrates how one could assemble a 32-bit object from four individual bytes. The most common way to do this is to create a discriminant union structure that contains a 32-bit object and a 4-byte array:

NOTE *Many languages, but not all, support the discriminant union data type. For example, in Pascal, you would instead use a case variant record. See your language reference manual for details.*

For those who are not familiar with unions, they are a data structure similar to records or structs except the compiler allocates the storage for each field of the union at the same address in memory. Consider the following two declarations from the C programming language:

```
struct
{
    short unsigned i;    // Assume shorts require 16 bits.
    short unsigned u;
    long unsigned r;     // Assume longs require 32 bits.
} RECORDvar;

union
{
    short unsigned i;
    short unsigned u;
    long unsigned r;
} UNIONvar;
```

As Figure 6-13 on the next page shows, the RECORDvar object consumes eight bytes in memory, and the fields do not share their memory with any other fields (that is, each field starts at a different offset from the base address of the record). The UNIONvar variable, on the other hand, overlays all the fields in the union in the same memory locations. Therefore, writing a value to the i field of the union also overwrites the value of the u field as well as two bytes of the r field (whether they are the LO or HO bytes depends entirely on the byte gender of the CPU).

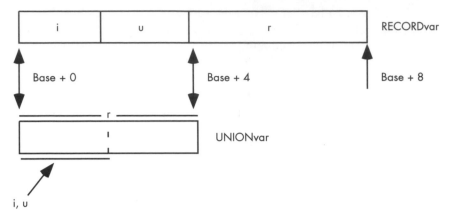

Figure 6-13: Layout of a union versus a record (struct) in memory

In the C programming language, you can use this behavior of a union to gain access to the individual bytes of a 32-bit object. Consider the following union declaration in C:

```
union
{
    unsigned long bits32; /* This assumes that C uses 32 bits for
                             unsigned long */
    unsigned char bytes[4];
} theValue;
```

This creates the data type shown in Figure 6-14 on a little endian machine and the structure shown in Figure 6-15 on a big endian machine.

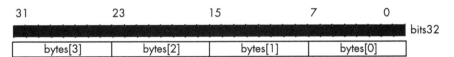

Figure 6-14: A C union on a little endian machine

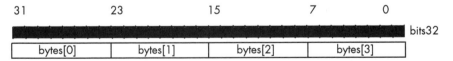

Figure 6-15: A C union on a big endian machine

To assemble a 32-bit object from four discrete bytes on a little endian machine, you'd use code like the following:

```
theValue.bytes[0] = byte0;
theValue.bytes[1] = byte1;
theValue.bytes[2] = byte2;
theValue.bytes[3] = byte3;
```

This code functions properly because C allocates the first byte of an array at the lowest address in memory (corresponding to bits 0..7 in the theValue.bits32 object on a little endian machine), the second byte of the array follows (bits 8..15), then the third (bits 16..23), and finally the HO byte (occupying the highest address in memory, corresponding to bits 24..31).

However, on a big endian machine, this code won't work properly because theValue.bytes[0] corresponds to bits 24..31 of the 32-bit value rather than bits 0..7. To assemble this 32-bit value properly on a big endian system, you'd need to use code like the following:

```
theValue.bytes[0] = byte3;
theValue.bytes[1] = byte2;
theValue.bytes[2] = byte1;
theValue.bytes[3] = byte0;
```

The only question remaining is, "How do you determine if your code is running on a little endian or big endian machine?" This is actually an easy task to accomplish. Consider the following C code:

```
theValue.bytes[0] = 0;
theValue.bytes[1] = 1;
theValue.bytes[2] = 0;
theValue.bytes[3] = 0;
isLittleEndian = theValue.bits32 == 256;
```

On a big endian machine, this code sequence will store the value one into bit 16, producing a 32-bit value that is definitely not equal to 256, whereas on a little endian machine this code will store the value one into bit 8, producing a 32-bit value equal to 256. Therefore, you can test the isLittleEndian variable to determine whether the current machine is little endian (true) or big endian (false).

6.4 The System Clock

Although modern computers are quite fast and getting faster all the time, they still require a finite amount of time to accomplish even the smallest tasks. On von Neumann machines, most operations are *serialized*, which means that the computer executes commands in a prescribed order. It wouldn't do, in the following code sequence for example, to execute the Pascal statement I := I * 5 + 2; before the statement I := J; finishes:

```
I := J;
I := I * 5 + 2;
```

On real computer systems, operations do not occur instantaneously. Moving a copy of J into I takes a certain amount of time. Likewise, multiplying I by five and then adding two and storing the result back into I takes time.

A natural question to ask is, "How does the processor execute statements in the proper order?" The answer is, "The system clock."

The system clock serves as the timing standard within the system, so to understand why certain operations take longer than others, you must first understand the function of the system clock.

The *system clock* is an electrical signal on the control bus that alternates between zero and one at a periodic rate (see Figure 6-16). All activity within the CPU is synchronized with the edges (rising or falling) of this clock signal.

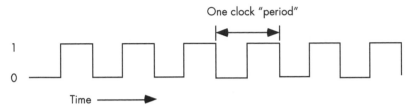

Figure 6-16: The system clock

The frequency with which the system clock alternates between zero and one is the *system clock frequency* and the time it takes for the system clock to switch from zero to one and back to zero is the *clock period*. One full period is also called a *clock cycle*. On most modern systems, the system clock switches between zero and one at rates exceeding several billion times per second. A typical Pentium IV chip, circa 2004, runs at speeds of three billion cycles per second or faster. *Hertz* (Hz) is the unit corresponding to one cycle per second, so the aforementioned Pentium chip runs at between 3,000 and 4,000 million hertz, or 3,000–4,000 megahertz (MHz), also known as 3–4 gigahertz (GHz). Typical frequencies for 80x86 parts range from 5 MHz up to several gigahertz and beyond.

As you may have noticed, the clock period is the reciprocal of the clock frequency. For example, a 1-MHz clock would have a clock period of one microsecond (one millionth of a second). A CPU running at 1 GHz would have a clock period of one nanosecond (ns), or one billionth of a second. We usually express clock periods in millionths or billionths of a second.

To ensure synchronization, most CPUs start an operation on either the *falling edge* (when the clock goes from one to zero) or the *rising edge* (when the clock goes from zero to one). The system clock spends most of its time at either zero or one and very little time switching between the two. Therefore, a clock edge is the perfect synchronization point.

Because all CPU operations are synchronized with the clock, the CPU cannot perform tasks any faster than the clock runs. However, just because a CPU is running at some clock frequency doesn't mean that it executes that many operations each second. Many operations take multiple clock cycles to complete, so the CPU often performs operations at a significantly slower rate.

6.4.1 Memory Access and the System Clock

Memory access is an operation that is synchronized with the system clock. That is, memory access occurs no more often than once every clock cycle. Indeed, on some older processors, it takes several clock cycles to access a memory location. The *memory access time* is the number of clock cycles between a memory request (read or write) and when the memory operation completes. This is an important value, because longer memory access times result in lower performance.

Modern CPUs are much faster than memory devices, so systems built around these CPUs often use a second clock, the bus clock, which is some fraction of the CPU speed. For example, typical processors in the 100-MHz-to-4-GHz range can use 800-MHz, 500-MHz, 400-MHz, 133-MHz, 100-MHz, or 66-MHz bus clocks (a given CPU generally supports several different bus speeds, and the exact range the CPU supports depends upon that CPU).

When reading from memory, the memory access time is the time between when the CPU places an address on the address bus and the time when the CPU takes the data off the data bus. On typical 80x86 CPUs with a one cycle memory access time, the timing of a read operation looks something like that shown in Figure 6-17. The timing of writing data to memory is similar (sec Figure 6-18).

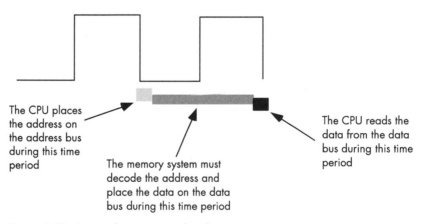

The CPU places the address on the address bus during this time period

The memory system must decode the address and place the data on the data bus during this time period

The CPU reads the data from the data bus during this time period

Figure 6-17: A typical memory read cycle

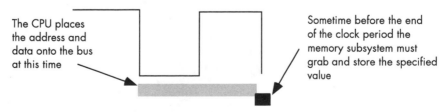

The CPU places the address and data onto the bus at this time

Sometime before the end of the clock period the memory subsystem must grab and store the specified value

Figure 6-18: A typical memory write cycle

Note that the CPU doesn't wait for memory. The access time is specified by the bus clock frequency. If the memory subsystem doesn't work fast enough to keep up with the CPU's expected access time, the CPU will read garbage data on a memory read operation and will not properly store the data on a memory write. This will surely cause the system to fail.

Memory devices have various ratings, but the two major ones are capacity and speed. Typical dynamic RAM (random access memory) devices have capacities of 512 MB (or more) and speeds of 0.25–100 ns. A typical 3-GHz Pentium system uses 2.0-ns (500-MHz) memory devices.

Wait just a second here! Earlier we saw that the memory speed must match the bus speed or the system would fail. At 3 GHz the clock period is roughly 0.33 ns. How can a system designer get away with using 2.0 ns memory? The answer is wait states.

6.4.2 Wait States

A *wait state* is an extra clock cycle that gives a device additional time to respond to the CPU. For example, a 100-MHz Pentium system has a 10-ns clock period, implying that you need 10-ns memory. In fact, the implication is that you need even faster memory devices because in most computer systems there is additional decoding and buffering logic between the CPU and memory. This circuitry introduces its own delays. In Figure 6-19, you can see that buffering and decoding costs the system an additional 10 ns. If the CPU needs the data back in 10 ns, the memory must respond in 0 ns (which is impossible).

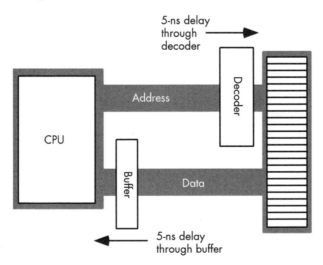

Figure 6-19: Decoding and buffer delays

If cost-effective memory won't work with a fast processor, how do companies manage to sell fast PCs? One part of the answer is the wait state. For example, if you have a 100-MHz processor with a memory cycle time of 10 ns and you lose 2 ns to buffering and decoding, you'll need 8-ns memory. What if your system can only support 20-ns memory, though? By adding wait states to extend the memory cycle to 20 ns, you can solve this problem.

Almost every general-purpose CPU in existence provides a pin (whose signal appears on the control bus) that allows the insertion of wait states. If necessary, the memory address decoding circuitry asserts this signal to give the memory sufficient access time (see Figure 6-20).

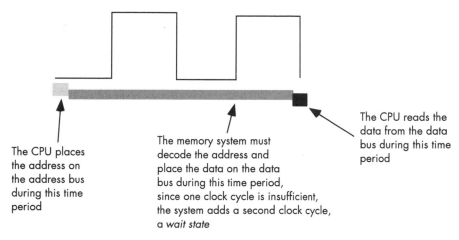

The CPU places the address on the address bus during this time period

The memory system must decode the address and place the data on the data bus during this time period, since one clock cycle is insufficient, the system adds a second clock cycle, a *wait state*

The CPU reads the data from the data bus during this time period

Figure 6-20: Inserting a wait state into a memory read operation

Needless to say, from the system-performance point of view, wait states are *not* a good thing. While the CPU is waiting for data from memory, it cannot operate on that data. Adding a wait state typically *doubles* the amount of time required to access memory. Running with a wait state on every memory access is almost like cutting the processor clock frequency in half. You're going to get less work done in the same amount of time.

However, we're not doomed to slow execution because of added wait states. There are several tricks hardware designers can employ to achieve zero wait states *most* of the time. The most common of these is the use of *cache* (pronounced "cash") memory.

6.4.3   Cache Memory

If you look at a typical program, you'll discover that it tends to access the same memory locations repeatedly. Furthermore, you'll also discover that a program often accesses adjacent memory locations. The technical names given to these phenomena are *temporal locality of reference* and *spatial locality of reference*. When exhibiting spatial locality, a program accesses neighboring memory locations within a short period after the initial memory access.

When displaying temporal locality of reference, a program accesses the same memory location repeatedly during a short time. Both forms of locality occur in the following Pascal code segment:

```
for i := 0 to 10 do
        A [i] := 0;
```

There are two occurrences each of spatial and temporal locality of reference within this loop. Let's consider the obvious ones first.

In this Pascal code, the program references the variable i several times. The for loop compares i against 10 to see if the loop is complete. It also increments i by one at the bottom of the loop. The assignment statement also uses i as an array index. This shows temporal locality of reference in action because the CPU accesses i at three points in a short time period.

This program also exhibits spatial locality of reference. The loop itself zeros out the elements of array A by writing a zero to the first location in A, then to the second location in A, and so on. Because Pascal stores the elements of A in consecutive memory locations, each loop iteration accesses adjacent memory locations.

There is an additional example of temporal and spatial locality of reference in this Pascal example. Machine instructions also reside in memory, and the CPU fetches these instructions sequentially from memory and executes these instructions repeatedly, once for each loop iteration.

If you look at the execution profile of a typical program, you'll discover that the program typically executes less than half the statements. Generally, a program might only use 10 to 20 percent of the memory allotted to it. At any one given time, a 1-MB program might only access 4–8 KB of data and code. So if you paid an outrageous sum of money for expensive zero-wait-state RAM, you would only be using a tiny fraction of it at any one given time. Wouldn't it be nice if you could buy a small amount of fast RAM and dynamically reassign its addresses as the program executes?

This is exactly what cache memory does for you. Cache memory sits between the CPU and main memory. It is a small amount of very fast memory. Unlike normal memory, the bytes appearing within a cache do not have fixed addresses. Instead, cache memory can dynamically reassign addresses. This allows the system to keep recently accessed values in the cache. Addresses that the CPU has never accessed or hasn't accessed in some time remain in main (slow) memory. Because most memory accesses are to recently accessed variables (or to locations near a recently accessed location), the data generally appears in cache memory.

A cache *hit* occurs whenever the CPU accesses memory and finds the data in the cache. In such a case, the CPU can usually access data with zero wait states. A cache *miss* occurs if the data cannot be found in the cache. In that case, the CPU has to read the data from main memory, incurring a performance loss. To take advantage of temporal locality of reference, the CPU copies data into the cache whenever it accesses an address not present in the cache. Because it is likely the system will access that same location shortly, the system will save wait states on future accesses by having that data in the cache.

Cache memory does not eliminate the need for wait states. Although a program may spend considerable time executing code in one area of memory, eventually it will call a procedure or wander off to some section of code outside cache memory. When that happens, the CPU has to go to main memory to fetch the data. Because main memory is slow, this will require the insertion of wait states. However, once the CPU accesses the data, it is now available in the cache for future use.

We've discussed how cache memory handles the temporal aspects of memory access, but not the spatial aspects. Caching memory locations *when you access them* won't speed up the program if you constantly access consecutive locations that you've never before accessed. To solve this problem, when a cache miss occurs most caching systems will read several consecutive bytes of main memory (engineers call this block of data a *cache line*). 80x86 CPUs, for example, read between 16 and 64 bytes upon a cache miss. But this brings up an important question. If you read 16 bytes, why read the bytes in blocks rather than as you need them? As it turns out, most memory chips available today have special modes that let you quickly access several consecutive memory locations on the chip. The cache exploits this capability to reduce the average number of wait states needed to access sequential memory locations. Although reading 16 bytes on each cache miss is expensive if you only access a few bytes in the corresponding cache line, cache memory systems work quite well in the average case.

It should come as no surprise that the ratio of cache hits to misses increases with the size (in bytes) of the cache memory subsystem. The 80486 CPU, for example, has 8,192 bytes of on-chip cache. Intel claims to get an 80–95 percent hit rate with this cache (meaning 80–95 percent of the time the CPU finds the data in the cache). This sounds very impressive. However, if you play around with the numbers a little bit, you'll discover it's not all *that* impressive. Suppose we pick the 80 percent figure. This means that one out of every five memory accesses, on the average, will not be in the cache. If you have a 50-MHz processor and a 90-ns memory access time, four out of five memory accesses require only one clock cycle (because they are in the cache) and the fifth will require about ten wait states. Ten wait states were computed as follows: five clock cycles to read the first four bytes (10 + 20 + 20 + 20 + 20 = 90). However, the cache always reads 16 consecutive bytes. Most 80486-era memory subsystems let you read consecutive addresses in about 40 ns after accessing the first location. Therefore, the 80486 will require an additional 6 clock cycles to read the remaining three double words. The total is 11 clock cycles or 10 wait states.

Altogether, the system will require 15 clock cycles to access five memory locations, or 3 clock cycles per access, on the average. That's equivalent to two wait states added to every memory access. Doesn't sound so impressive, does it? It gets even worse as you move up to faster processors and the difference in speed between the CPU and memory increases.

There are a couple of ways to improve the situation. First, you can add more cache memory. Alas, you can't pull an 80486 chip apart and solder more cache onto the chip. However, modern Pentium CPUs have a significantly larger cache than the 80486 and operate with fewer average wait states. This improves the cache hit ratio, reducing the number of wait states. For example, increasing the hit ratio from 80 percent to 90 percent lets you access 10 memory locations in 20 cycles. This reduces the average number of wait states per memory access to one wait state, a substantial improvement.

Another way to improve performance is to build a *two-level* caching system. Many Pentium systems work in this fashion. The first level is the on-chip 8,192-byte cache. The next level, between the on-chip cache and main memory, is a secondary cache often built on the computer system circuit board (see Figure 6-21). However, on newer processors, the first- and second-level caches generally appear in the same packaging as the CPU. This allows the CPU designers to build a higher performance CPU/memory interface, allowing the CPU to move data between caches and the CPU (as well as main memory) much more rapidly.

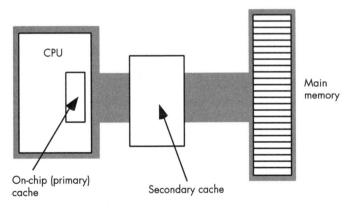

Figure 6-21: A two-level caching system

A typical secondary cache contains anywhere from 32,768 bytes to over 1 MB of memory. Common sizes on PC subsystems are 256 KB, 512 KB, and 1,024 KB (1 MB) of cache.

You might ask, "Why bother with a two-level cache? Why not use a 262,144-byte cache to begin with?" It turns out that the secondary cache generally does not operate at zero wait states. The circuitry to support 262,144 bytes of fast memory would be *very* expensive, so most system designers use slower memory, which requires one or two wait states. This is still *much* faster than main memory. Combined with the existing on-chip level-one cache, you can get better performance from the system with a two-level caching system.

Today, you'll find that some systems incorporate an off-CPU *third-level cache*. Though the performance improvement afforded by a third-level cache is nowhere near what you get with a first- or second-level cache subsystem, third-level cache subsystems can be quite large (usually several megabytes) and work well for large systems with gigabytes of main memory. For programs that manipulate considerable data, yet exhibit locality of reference, a third-level caching subsystem can be very effective.

6.5   CPU Memory Access

Most CPUs have two or three different ways to access memory. The most common *memory addressing modes* modern CPUs support are *direct, indirect,* and *indexed.* A few CPUs (like the 80x86) support additional addressing modes like *scaled indexed,* while some RISC CPUs only support indirect access to memory. Having additional memory addressing modes makes memory access more flexible. Sometimes a particular addressing mode can allow you to access data in a complex data structure with a single instruction, where two or more instructions would be required on a CPU without that addressing mode. Therefore, having a wide variety of ways to access memory is generally good as these complex addressing modes allow you to use fewer instructions.

It would seem that the 80x86 processor family (with many different types of mcmory addressing modes) would be more efficient than a RISC processor that only supports a small number of addressing modes. In many respects, this is absolutely true; those RISC processors can often take three to five instructions to do what a single 80x86 instruction does. However, this does not mean that an 80x86 program will run three to five times faster. Don't forget that access to memory is very slow, usually requiring wait states. Whereas the 80x86 frequently accesses memory, RISC processors rarely do. Therefore, that RISC processor can probably execute the first four instructions, which do not access memory at all, while the single 80x86 instruction, which accesses memory, is spinning on some wait states. In the fifth instruction the RISC CPU might access memory and will incur wait states of its own. If both processors execute an average of one instruction per clock cycle and have to insert 30 wait states for a main memory access, we're talking about a difference of 31 clock cycles (80x86) versus 35 clock cycles (RISC), only about a 12 percent difference.

If an application must access slow memory, then choosing an appropriate addressing mode will often allow that application to compute the same result with fewer instructions and with fewer memory accesses, thus improving performance. Therefore, understanding how an application can use the different addressing modes a CPU provides is important if you want to write fast and compact code.

6.5.1 The Direct Memory Addressing Mode

The direct addressing mode encodes a variable's memory address as part of the actual machine instruction that accesses the variable. On the 80x86 for example, direct addresses are 32-bit values appended to the instruction's encoding. Generally, a program uses the direct addressing mode to access global static variables. Here's an example of the direct addressing mode in HLA assembly language:

```
static
    i:dword;
        . . .
    mov( eax, i ); // Store EAX's value into the i variable.
```

When accessing variables whose memory address is known prior to the execution of the program, the direct addressing mode is ideal. With a single instruction you can reference the memory location associated with the variable. On those CPUs that don't support a direct addressing mode, you may need an extra instruction (or more) to load a register with the variable's memory address prior to accessing that variable.

6.5.2 The Indirect Addressing Mode

The indirect addressing mode typically uses a register to hold a memory address (there are a few CPUs that use memory locations to hold the indirect address, but this form of indirect addressing is rare in modern CPUs).

There are a couple of advantages of the indirect addressing mode over the direct addressing mode. First, you can modify the value of an indirect address (the value being held in a register) at run time. Second, encoding which register specifies the indirect address takes far fewer bits than encoding a 32-bit (or 64-bit) direct address, so the instructions are smaller. One disadvantage of the indirect addressing mode is that it may take one or more instructions to load a register with an address before you can access that address.

Here is a typical example of a sequence in HLA assembly language that uses an 80x86 indirect addressing mode (brackets around the register name denote the use of indirect addressing):

```
static
    byteArray: byte[16];
        . . .
    lea( ebx, byteArray );  // Loads EBX register with the address
                            //  of byteArray.
    mov( [ebx], al );       // Loads byteArray[0] into AL.
    inc( ebx );             // Point EBX at the next byte in memory
                            //  (byteArray[1]).
    mov( [ebx], ah );       // Loads byteArray[1] into AH.
```

The indirect addressing mode is useful for many operations, such as accessing objects referenced by a pointer variable.

6.5.3 The Indexed Addressing Mode

The indexed addressing mode combines the direct and indirect addressing modes into a single addressing mode. Specifically, the machine instructions using this addressing mode encode both an offset (direct address) and a register in the bits that make up the instruction. At run time, the CPU computes the sum of these two address components to create an *effective address*. This addressing mode is great for accessing array elements and for indirect access to objects like structures and records. Though the instruction encoding is usually larger than for the indirect addressing mode, the indexed addressing mode offers the advantage that you can specify an address directly within an instruction without having to use a separate instruction to load the address into a register.

Here is a typical example of a sequence in HLA that uses an 80x86 indexed addressing mode:

```
static
    byteArray: byte[16];
      . . .
    mov( 0, ebx );                    // Initialize an index into the array.
    while( ebx < 16 ) do

        mov( 0, byteArray[ebx] );     // Zeros out byteArray[ebx].
        inc( ebx );                   // EBX := EBX +1, move on to the
                                      //   next array element.

    endwhile;
```

The byteArray[ebx] instruction in this short program demonstrates the indexed addressing mode. The effective address is the address of the byteArray variable plus the current value in the EBX register.

To avoid wasting space encoding a 32-bit or 64-bit address into every instruction that uses an indexed addressing mode, many CPUs provide a shorter form that encodes an 8-bit or 16-bit offset as part of the instruction. When using this smaller form, the register provides the base address of the object in memory, and the offset provides a fixed displacement into that data structure in memory. This is useful, for example, when accessing fields of a record or structure in memory via a pointer to that structure. The earlier HLA example encodes the address of byteArray using a 4-byte address. Compare this with the following use of the indexed addressing mode:

```
lea( ebx, byteArray ); // Loads the address of byteArray into EBX.
   . . .
mov( al, [ebx+2] );    // Stores al into byteArray[2]
```

This last instruction encodes the displacement value using a single byte (rather than four bytes), hence the instruction is shorter and more efficient.

6.5.4   The Scaled Indexed Addressing Modes

The scaled indexed addressing mode, available on several CPUs, provides two facilities above and beyond the indexed addressing mode:

- The ability to use two registers (plus an offset) to compute the effective address

- The ability to multiply one of those two registers' values by a common constant (typically 1, 2, 4, or 8) prior to computing the effective address.

This addressing mode is especially useful for accessing elements of arrays whose element sizes match one of the scaling constants (see the discussion of arrays in the next chapter for the reasons).

The 80x86 provides a scaled index addressing mode that takes one of several forms, as shown in the following HLA statements:

```
mov( [ebx+ecx*1], al );             // EBX is base address, ecx is index.
mov( wordArray[ecx*2], ax );        // wordArray is base address, ecx is index.
mov( dwordArray[ebx+ecx*4], eax );  // Effective address is combination
                                    //  of offset(dwordArray)+ebx+(ecx*4).
```

6.6   For More Information

This chapter has spent considerable time discussing how the CPU organizes memory and how the CPU accesses memory. There are a couple of good sources of additional information on this subject.

My book *The Art of Assembly Language* (No Starch Press), or nearly any other textbook on assembly language programming, will provide additional information about CPU addressing modes, allocating and accessing local (automatic) variables, and manipulating parameters at the machine code level. Any decent textbook on programming language design or compiler design will have lots to say about the run-time organization of memory for typical compiled languages.

A good computer architecture textbook is another place you'll find information on system organization. Patterson and Hennessy's architecture books *Computer Organization & Design: The Hardware/Software Interface* and *Computer Architecture: A Quantitative Approach* are well-regarded textbooks you might consider reading to gain a more in-depth perspective on CPU and system design.

Chapter 11 in this book also provides additional information about cache memory and memory architecture.

7

COMPOSITE DATA TYPES AND MEMORY OBJECTS

Composite data types are types that are composed of other, more primitive, types. Examples of composite data types commonly found in applications include pointers, arrays, records or structures, and unions. Many high-level languages provide syntactical abstractions for these composite data types that make them easy to declare and use, all the time hiding their underlying complexities.

Though the cost of using these composite data types is not terrible, it is very easy for a programmer to introduce inefficiencies into an application by using these data types without understanding the underlying costs. Great programmers, therefore, are cognizant of the costs associated with using composite data types so they can use them in an appropriate manner. This chapter discusses the costs associated with these composite data types to better enable you to write great code.

7.1   Pointer Types

A *pointer* is a variable whose value refers to some other object. Now you've probably experienced pointers firsthand in Pascal, C/C++, or some other programming language, and you may be feeling a little anxious right now. Well, fear not! Pointers are actually *easy* to deal with.

Probably the best place to start is with the definition of a pointer. High-level languages like Pascal and C/C++ hide the simplicity of pointers behind a wall of abstraction. This added complexity tends to frighten programmers because *they don't understand what's going on behind the scenes.* However, a little knowledge can erase all your fears of pointers.

Let's just ignore pointers for a moment and work with something that's easier to understand: an array. Consider the following array declaration in Pascal:

```
M: array [0..1023] of integer;
```

Even if you don't know Pascal, the concept here is easy to understand. M is an array with 1,024 integers in it, indexed from M[0] to M[1023]. Each one of these array elements can hold an integer value that is independent of the others. In other words, this array gives you 1,024 different integer variables each of which you access via an array index rather than by name.

If you have a program with the statement M[0]:=100; it probably wouldn't take you any time to figure out what this statement is doing. It stores the value 100 into the first element of the array M. Now consider the following two statements:

```
i := 0; (* assume i is an integer variable *)
M [i] := 100;
```

You should agree, without too much hesitation, that these two statements do the same thing as M[0]:=100;. Indeed, you're probably willing to agree that you can use any integer expression in the range 0..1,023 as an index of this array. The following statements *still* perform the same operation as our earlier statement:

```
i := 5;       (* assume all variables are integers*)
j := 10;
k := 50;
m [i * j - k] := 100;
```

Okay, how about the following:

```
M [1] := 0;
M [ M [1] ] := 100;
```

Whoa! Now that takes a few moments to digest. However, if you take it slowly, it makes sense and you'll discover that these two instructions perform the same operation as before. The first statement stores zero into array element M[1]. The second statement fetches the value of M[1], which is zero, and uses that value to determine where it stores the value 100.

If you're willing to accept this example as reasonable — perhaps bizarre, but usable nonetheless — then you'll have no problems with pointers, *because M[1] is a pointer!* Well, not really, but if you were to change "M" to "memory" and treat each element of this array as a separate memory location, then this *is* the definition of a pointer: a pointer is a memory variable whose value is the address of some other memory object.

7.1.1 Pointer Implementation

Although most languages implement pointers using memory addresses, a pointer is actually an abstraction of a memory address, and therefore a language could define a pointer using any mechanism that maps the value of the pointer to the address of some object in memory. Some implementations of Pascal, for example, use offsets from some fixed memory address as pointer values. Some languages (such as dynamic languages like LISP) might actually implement pointers by using double indirection. That is, the pointer object contains the address of some memory variable whose value is the address of the object to be accessed. This double indirection may seem somewhat convoluted, but it does offer certain advantages when using a complex memory management system. However, this chapter will assume that a pointer is a variable whose value is the address of some other object in memory.

As you've seen in examples from previous chapters, you can indirectly access an object using a pointer with two 80x86 machine instructions (or with a similar sequence on other CPUs), as follows:

```
mov( PointerVariable, ebx );    // Load the pointer variable into a register.
mov( [ebx], eax );              // Use register indirect mode to access data.
```

Now consider the double-indirect pointer implementation described earlier. Access to data via double indirection is less efficient than the straight pointer implementation because it takes an extra machine instruction to fetch the data from memory. This isn't obvious in a high-level language like C/C++ or Pascal, where you'd use double indirection as follows (it looks very similar to single indirection):

```
i = **cDblPtr;         // C/C++
i := ^^pDblPtr;        (* Pascal *)
```

In assembly language, however, you'll see the extra work involved:

```
mov( hDblPtr, ebx );   // Get the pointer to a pointer.
mov( [ebx], ebx );     // Get the pointer to the value.
mov( [ebx], eax );     // Get the value.
```

Contrast this with the two assembly instructions (shown earlier) needed to access an object using single indirection. Because double indirection requires 50 percent more code than single indirection, you can see why many languages implement pointers using single indirection.

7.1.2   Pointers and Dynamic Memory Allocation

Pointers typically reference anonymous variables that you allocate on the *heap* (a region in memory reserved for dynamic storage allocation) using memory allocation/deallocation functions in different languages like *malloc/free* (C), *new/dispose* (Pascal), and *new/delete* (C++). Objects you allocate on the heap are known as *anonymous variables* because you refer to them by their address, and you do not associate a name with them. And because the allocation functions return the address of an object on the heap, you would typically store the function's return result into a pointer variable. True, the pointer variable may have a name, but that name applies to the pointer's data (an address), not the name of the object referenced by this address.

7.1.3   Pointer Operations and Pointer Arithmetic

Most languages that provide the pointer data type let you assign addresses to pointer variables, compare pointer values for equality or inequality, and indirectly reference an object via a pointer. Some languages allow additional operations; we're going to look at the possibilities in this section.

Many languages provide the ability to do limited arithmetic with pointers. At the very least, these languages will provide the ability to add an integer constant to a pointer, or subtract an integer constant from a pointer. To understand the purpose of these two arithmetic operations, note the syntax of the malloc function in the C standard library:

```
ptrVar = malloc( bytes_to_allocate );
```

The parameter you pass malloc specifies the number of bytes of storage to allocate. A good C programmer will generally supply an expression like sizeof(int) as the parameter to malloc. The sizeof function returns the number of bytes needed by its single parameter. Therefore, sizeof(int) tells malloc to allocate at least enough storage for an int variable. Now consider the following call to malloc:

```
ptrVar = malloc( sizeof( int ) * 8 );
```

If the size of an integer is 4 bytes, this call to malloc will allocate storage for 32 bytes. The malloc function allocates these 32 bytes at consecutive addresses in memory (see Figure 7-1).

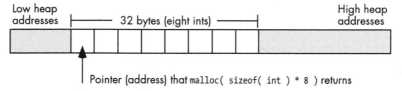

Figure 7-1: Memory allocation with malloc(sizeof(int) * 8)

The pointer that malloc returns contains the address of the first integer in this set, so the C program will only be able to directly access the very first of these eight integers. To access the individual addresses of the other seven integers, you will need to add an integer offset to the *base* address. On machines that support byte-addressable memory (such as the 80x86), the address of each successive integer in memory is the address of the previous integer plus the size of an integer. For example, if a call to the C standard library malloc routine returns the memory address $0300_1000, then the eight 4-byte integers that malloc allocates will lie at the following memory addresses:

Integer	Memory Addresses
0	$0300_1000..$0300_1003
1	$0300_1004..$0300_1007
2	$0300_1008..$0300_100b
3	$0300_100c..$0300_100f
4	$0300_1010..$0300_1013
5	$0300_1014..$0300_1017
6	$0300_1018..$0300_101b
7	$0300_101c..$0300_101f

7.1.3.1 Adding an Integer to a Pointer

Because these integers described in the preceding section are exactly four bytes apart, we need only add four to the address of the first integer to obtain the address of the second integer; likewise, the address of the third integer is the address of the second integer plus four, and so on. In assembly language, we could access these eight integers using code like the following:

```
malloc( @size( int32 ) * 8 );   // Returns storage for eight int32 objects.
                                 // EAX points at this storage.
mov( 0, ecx );
mov( ecx, [eax] );              // Zero out the 32 bytes (four bytes
mov( ecx, [eax+4] );            //  at a time).
```

```
mov( ecx, [eax+8] );
mov( ecx, [eax+12] );
mov( ecx, [eax+16] );
mov( ecx, [eax+20] );
mov( ecx, [eax+24] );
mov( ecx, [eax+28] );
```

Notice the use of the 80x86 indexed addressing mode to access the eight integers that malloc allocates. The EAX register maintains the base address (first address) of the eight integers that this code allocates, and the constant appearing in the addressing mode of the mov instructions selects the offset of the specific integer from this base address.

Most CPUs use byte addresses for memory objects. Therefore, when allocating multiple copies of some n-byte object in memory, the objects will not begin at consecutive memory addresses; instead, they will appear in memory at addresses that are n bytes apart. Some machines, however, do not allow a program to access memory at an arbitrary address in memory; they require that applications access data on address boundaries that are a multiple of a word, a double word, or even a quad word. Any attempt to access memory on some other boundary will raise an exception and (possibly) halt the application. If a high-level language supports pointer arithmetic, it must take this fact into consideration and provide a generic pointer arithmetic scheme that is portable across many different CPU architectures. The most common solution that high-level languages use when adding an integer offset to a pointer is to multiply that offset by the size of the object that the pointer references. That is, if you've got a pointer p to a 16-byte object in memory, then p + 1 points 16 bytes beyond where p points. Likewise, p + 2 points 32 bytes beyond the address contained in the pointer p. As long as the size of the data object is a multiple of the required alignment size (which the compiler can enforce by adding padding bytes, if necessary), this scheme avoids problems on those architectures that require aligned data access.

An important thing to realize is that the addition operator only makes sense between a pointer and an integer value. For example, in the C/C++ language you can indirectly access objects in memory using an expression like *(p + i) (where p is a pointer to an object and i is an integer value). It doesn't make any sense to add two pointers together. Similarly, it isn't reasonable to add other data types with a pointer. For example, adding a floating-point value to a pointer makes no sense. What would it mean to reference the data at some base address plus 1.5612? Operations on pointers involving strings, characters, and other data types don't make much sense, either. Integers (signed and unsigned) are the only reasonable values to add to a pointer.

On the other hand, not only can you add an integer to a pointer, you can also add a pointer to an integer and the result is still pointer (both p + i and i + p are legal). This is because addition is commutative.

7.1.3.2 Subtracting an Integer from a Pointer

Another reasonable pointer arithmetic operation is subtraction. Subtracting an integer from a pointer references a memory location immediately before the address held in the pointer. However, subtraction is not commutative and subtracting a pointer from an integer is not a legal operation (p − i is legal, but i − p is not).

In C/C++ *(p − i) accesses the ith object immediately before the object at which p points. In 80x86 assembly language, as in assembly on many processors, you can also specify a negative constant offset when using an indexed addressing mode, e.g.,

```
mov( [ebx−4], eax );
```

Keep in mind, that 80x86 assembly language uses byte offsets, not object offsets (as C/C++ does). Therefore, this statement loads into EAX the double word in memory immediately preceding the memory address in EBX.

7.1.3.3 Subtracting a Pointer from a Pointer

Unlike addition, it actually makes sense to subtract the value of one pointer variable from another. Consider the following C/C++ code that marches through a string of characters looking for the first *e* character that follows the first *a* that it finds:

```
int distance;
char *aPtr;
char *ePtr;
    . . .
aPtr = someString;  // Get ptr to start of string in aPtr.

// While we're not at the end of the string and the current
//   char isn't 'a':

while( *aPtr != '\0' && *aPtr != 'a' )
{
    aPtr = aPtr + 1;  // Move on to the next character pointed
                      //   at by aPtr.
}

// While we're not at the end of the string and the current
//   character isn't 'e':
ePtr = aPtr;         // Start at the 'a' char (or end of string
                     //   if no 'a').
while( *ePtr != '\0' && *ePtr != 'a' )
{
    ePtr = ePtr + 1;  // Move on to the next character pointed at by aPtr.
}
```

```
// Now compute the number of characters between the 'a' and the 'e'
//   (counting the 'a' but not counting the 'e'):

distance = (ePtr - aPtr);
```

The subtraction of these two pointers produces the number of data objects that exist between the two pointers (in this case, ePtr and aPtr point at characters, so the subtraction result produces the number of characters, or bytes, between the two pointers).

The subtraction of two pointer values only makes sense if the two pointers reference the same data structure in memory (for example, pointing at characters within the same string, as in this C/C++ example). Although C/C++ (and certainly assembly language) will allow you to subtract two pointers that point at completely different objects in memory, their difference will probably have very little meaning.

When using pointer subtraction in C/C++, the base types of the two pointers must be identical (that is, the two pointers must contain the addresses of two objects whose types are identical). This restriction exists because pointer subtraction in C/C++ produces the number of objects between the two pointers, not the number of bytes. It wouldn't make any sense to compute the number of objects between a byte in memory and a double word in memory; would you be counting the number of bytes or the number of double words in this case? Of course, in assembly language you can get away with this (and the result is always the number of bytes between the two pointers), but it still doesn't make much sense semantically.

Note that the subtraction of two pointers could return a negative number if the left pointer operand is at a lower memory address than the right pointer operand. Depending on your language and its implementation, you may need to take the absolute value of the result if you're only interested in the distance between the two pointers and you don't care which pointer contains the greater address.

7.1.3.4 Comparing Pointers

Comparisons are another set of operations that make sense for pointers. Almost every language that supports pointers will let you compare two pointers to see if they are equal or not equal. Such a comparison will tell you whether the pointers reference the same object in memory. Some languages (such as assembly and C/C++) will also let you compare two pointers to see if one pointer is less than or greater than another. This only makes sense, however, if the pointers have the same base type and both pointers contain the address of some object within the same data structure (such as an array, string, or record). If the comparison of two pointers suggests that the value of one pointer is less than the other, then this tells you that the first pointer references an object within the data structure appearing before the object referenced by the second pointer. The converse is equally true for the greater than comparison.

7.2   Arrays

After strings, arrays are probably the most common *composite data type* (a complex data type built up from smaller data objects). Yet few beginning programmers fully understand how arrays operate and know about their efficiency trade-offs. It's surprising how many novice programmers view arrays from a completely different perspective once they understand how arrays operate at the machine level.

Abstractly, an array is an aggregate data type whose members (elements) are all of the same type. A member is selected from the array by specifying the member's array index with an integer (or with some value whose underlying representation is an integer, such as character, enumerated, and Boolean types). This chapter assumes that all of the integer indexes of an array are numerically contiguous (though this is not required). That is, if both x and y are valid indexes of the array, and if x < y, then all i such that x < i < y are also valid indexes. In this book, we will assume that array elements occupy contiguous locations in memory. An array with five elements will appear in memory as shown in Figure 7-2.

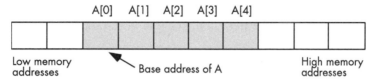

Figure 7-2: Array layout in memory

The *base address* of an array is the address of the first element of the array and is at the lowest memory location. The second array element directly follows the first in memory, the third element follows the second, and so on. Note that there is no requirement that the indexes start at zero. They may start with any number as long as they are contiguous. However, for the purposes of this discussion, it's easier to discuss array access if the first index is zero. We'll generally begin most arrays at index zero unless there is a good reason to do otherwise.

Whenever you apply the indexing operator to an array, the result is the unique array element specified by that index. For example, A[i] chooses the ith element from array A.

7.2.1   Array Declarations

Array declarations are very similar across many high-level languages. We'll look at some examples in many of these languages within this section.

C, C++, and Java all let you declare an array by specifying the total number of elements in an array. The syntax for an array declaration in these languages is as follows:

```
data_type  array_name [ number_of_elements ];
```

Here are some sample C/C++ array declarations:

```
char CharArray[ 128 ];
int intArray[ 8 ];
unsigned char ByteArray[ 10 ];
int *PtrArray[ 4 ];
```

If these arrays are declared as automatic variables, then C/C++ "initializes" them with whatever bit patterns happen to be present in memory. If, on the other hand, you declare these arrays as static objects, then C/C++ zeros out each array element. If you want to initialize an array yourself, then you can use the following C/C++ syntax:

```
data_type array_name[ number_of_elements ] = {element_list};
```

Here's a typical example:

```
int intArray[8] = {0,1,2,3,4,5,6,7};
```

HLA's array declaration syntax takes the following form, which is semantically equivalent to the C/C++ declaration:

```
array_name : data_type [ number_of_elements ];
```

Here are some examples of HLA array declarations, which all allocate storage for uninitialized arrays (the second example assumes that you have defined the integer data type in a type section of the HLA program):

```
static

    CharArray: char[128];       // Character array with elements
                                // 0..127.
    IntArray: integer[ 8 ];     // Integer array with elements 0..7.
    ByteArray: byte[10];        // Byte array with elements 0..9.
    PtrArray: dword[4];         // Double-word array with elements 0..3.
```

You can also initialize the array elements using declarations like the following:

```
RealArray: real32[8] := [ 0.0, 1.0, 2.0, 3.0, 4.0, 5.0, 6.0, 7.0 ];
IntegerAry: integer[8] := [ 8, 9, 10, 11, 12, 13, 14, 15 ];
```

Both of these definitions create arrays with eight elements. The first definition initializes each 4-byte real32 array element with one of the values in the range 0.0..7.0. The second declaration initializes each integer array element with one of the values in the range 8..15.

Pascal/Delphi/Kylix uses the following syntax to declare an array:

```
array_name : array[ lower_bound..upper_bound ] of data_type;
```

As in the previous examples, *array_name* is the identifier and *data_type* is the type of each element in this array. Unlike C/C++, Java, and HLA, in Pascal/Delphi/Kylix you specify the upper and lower bounds of the array rather than the array's size. The following are typical array declarations in Pascal:

```
type
    ptrToChar = ^char;
var
    CharArray: array[0..127] of char;          // 128 elements
    IntArray: array[ 0..7 ] of integer;        // 8 elements
    ByteArray: array[0..9] of char;            // 10 elements
    PtrArray: array[0..3] of ptrToChar;        // 4 elements
```

Although these Pascal examples start their indexes at zero, Pascal does not require a starting index of zero. The following is a perfectly valid array declaration in Pascal:

```
var
    ProfitsByYear : array[ 1998..2009 ] of real;  // 12 elements
```

The program that declares this array would use indexes 1998 through 2009 when accessing elements of this array, not 0 through 11.

Many Pascal compilers provide an extra feature to help you locate defects in your programs. Whenever you access an element of an array, these compilers will automatically insert code that will verify that the array index is within the bounds specified by the declaration. This extra code will stop the program if the index is out of range. For example, if an index into ProfitsByYear is outside the range 1998..2009, the program would abort with an error. This is a very useful feature that helps verify the correctness of your program.[1]

Generally, array indexes are integer values, though some languages allow other *ordinal types* (those data types that use an underlying integer representation). For example, Pascal allows char and boolean array indexes. In Pascal, it's perfectly reasonable and useful to declare an array as follows:

```
alphaCnt : array[ 'A'..'Z' ] of integer;
```

---

[1] Many Pascal compilers provide an option to turn off this array index range checking once your program is fully tested. Turning off the bounds checking improves the efficiency of the resulting program.

You access elements of alphaCnt using a character expression as the array index. For example, consider the following Pascal code that initializes each element of alphaCnt to zero:

```
for ch := 'A' to 'Z' do
    alphaCnt[ ch ] := 0;
```

Assembly language and C/C++ treat most ordinal values as special instances of integer values, so they are certainly legal array indexes. Most implementations of BASIC will allow a floating-point number as an array index, though BASIC always truncates the value to an integer before using it as an index.[2]

7.2.2 Array Representation in Memory

Abstractly, an array is a collection of variables that you access using an index. Semantically, we can define an array any way we please as long as it maps distinct indexes to distinct objects in memory and always maps the same index to the same object. In practice, however, most languages utilize a few common algorithms that provide efficient access to the array data.

The number of bytes of storage an array will consume is the product of the number of elements multiplied by the number of bytes per element in the array. Many languages also add a few additional bytes of padding at the end of the array so that the total length of the array is an even multiple of a nice value like four (on a 32-bit machine, a compiler may add bytes to the end of the array in order to extend its length to some multiple of four bytes). However, a program must *not* access these extra padding bytes because they may or may not be present. Some compilers will put them in, some will not, and some will only put them in depending on the type of object that immediately follows the array in memory.

Many optimizing compilers will attempt to place an array starting at a memory address that is an even multiple of some common size like two, four, or eight bytes. This effectively adds padding bytes before the beginning of the array or, if you prefer to think of it this way, it adds padding bytes to the end of the previous object in memory (see Figure 7-3).

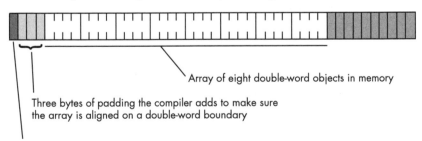

Array of eight double-word objects in memory

Three bytes of padding the compiler adds to make sure
the array is aligned on a double-word boundary

Single-byte object at an address that is an even multiple of four in memory

Figure 7-3: Adding padding bytes before an array

---

[2] BASIC allows you to use floating-point values as array indexes because the original BASIC language did not provide support for integer expressions; it only provided real values and string values.

On those machines that do not support byte-addressable memory, those compilers that attempt to place the first element of an array on an easily accessed boundary will allocate storage for an array on whatever boundary the machine supports. If the size of each array element is less than the minimum size memory object the CPU supports, the compiler implementer has two options:

- Allocate the smallest accessible memory object for each element of the array
- Pack multiple array elements into a single memory cell

The first option has the advantage of being fast, but it wastes memory because each array element carries along some extra storage that it doesn't need. The second option is compact, but it requires extra instructions to pack and unpack data when accessing array elements, which means that accessing elements is slower. Compilers on such machines often provide an option that lets you specify whether you want the data packed or unpacked so you can make the choice between space and speed.

If you're working on a byte-addressable machine (like the 80x86) then you probably don't have to worry about this issue. However, if you're using a high-level language and your code might wind up running on a different machine at some point in the future, you should choose an array organization that is efficient on all machines.

7.2.3 Accessing Elements of an Array

If you allocate all the storage for an array in contiguous memory locations, and the first index of the array is zero, then accessing an element of a one-dimensional array is simple. You can compute the address of any given element of an array using the following formula:

```
Element_Address = Base_Address + index * Element_Size
```

The Element_Size item is the number of bytes that each array element occupies. Thus, if the array contains elements of type byte, the Element_Size field is one and the computation is very simple. If each element of the array is a word (or another two-byte type) then Element_Size is two. And so on.

Consider the following Pascal array declaration:

```
var  SixteenInts : array[ 0..15] of integer;
```

To access an element of the SixteenInts on a byte-addressable machine, assuming 4-byte integers, you'd use this calculation:

```
Element_Address = AddressOf( SixteenInts) + index*4
```

In assembly language (where you would actually have to do this calculation manually rather than having the compiler do the work for you), you'd use code like the following to access array element SixteenInts[index]:

```
mov( index, ebx );
mov( SixteenInts[ ebx*4 ], eax );
```

7.2.4 Multidimensional Arrays

Most CPUs can easily handle one-dimensional arrays. Unfortunately, there is no magic addressing mode that lets you easily access elements of multi-dimensional arrays. That's going to take some work and several machine instructions.

Before discussing how to declare or access multidimensional arrays, it would be a good idea to look at how to implement them in memory. The first problem is to figure out how to store a multidimensional object in a one-dimensional memory space.

Consider for a moment a Pascal array of the following form:

```
A:array[0..3,0..3] of char;
```

This array contains 16 bytes organized as four rows of four characters. Somehow you have to draw a correspondence between each of the 16 bytes in this array and each of the 16 contiguous bytes in main memory. Figure 7-4 shows one way to do this.

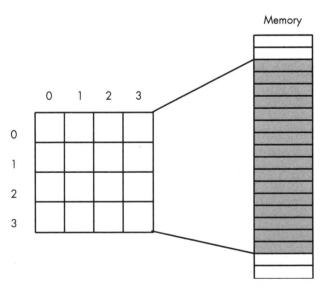

Figure 7-4: Mapping a 4x4 array to sequential memory locations

The actual mapping is not important as long as two things occur:

- No two entries in the array occupy the same memory location(s)
- Each element in the array always maps to the same memory location

Therefore, what you really need is a function with two input parameters — one for a row and one for a column value — that produces an offset into a contiguous block of 16 memory locations.

Any old function that satisfies these two constraints will work fine. However, what you really want is a mapping function that is efficient to compute at run time and that works for arrays with any number of dimensions and any bounds on those dimensions. While there are a large number of possible functions that fit this bill, there are two functions that most high-level languages use: *row-major ordering* and *column-major ordering*.

7.2.4.1   Row-Major Ordering

Row-major ordering assigns array elements to successive memory locations by moving across the rows and then down the columns. Figure 7-5 demonstrates this mapping.

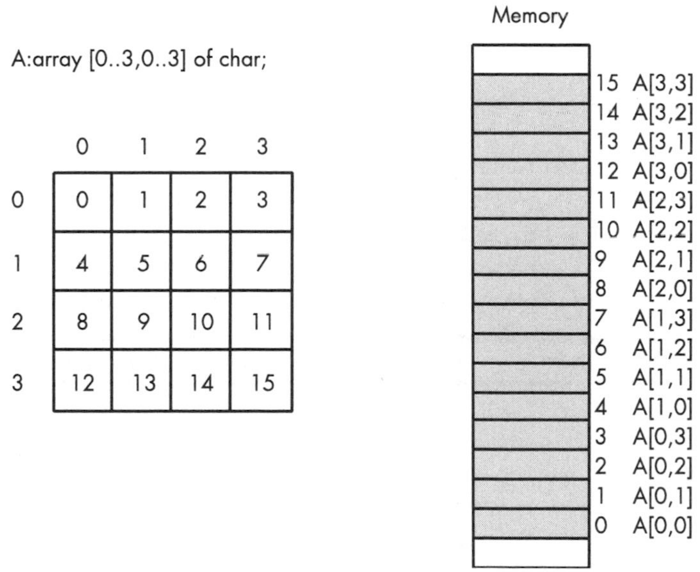

A:array [0..3,0..3] of char;

	0	1	2	3
0	0	1	2	3
1	4	5	6	7
2	8	9	10	11
3	12	13	14	15

Memory

15	A[3,3]
14	A[3,2]
13	A[3,1]
12	A[3,0]
11	A[2,3]
10	A[2,2]
9	A[2,1]
8	A[2,0]
7	A[1,3]
6	A[1,2]
5	A[1,1]
4	A[1,0]
3	A[0,3]
2	A[0,2]
1	A[0,1]
0	A[0,0]

Figure 7-5: Row-major array element ordering

Row-major ordering is the method employed by most high-level programming languages including Pascal, C/C++, Java, Ada, and Modula-2. It is very easy to implement and is easy to use in machine language. The conversion from a two-dimensional structure to a linear sequence is very intuitive. Figure 7-6 on the next page provides another view of the ordering of a 4×4 array.

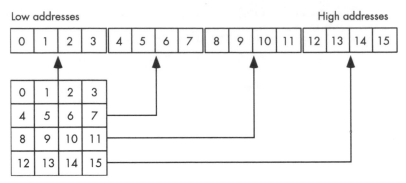

Figure 7-6: Another view of row-major ordering for a 4x4 array

The actual function that converts the set of multidimensional array indexes into a single offset is a slight modification of the formula for computing the address of an element of a one-dimensional array. The formula to compute the offset for a 4×4 two-dimensional row-major ordered array given an access of this form:

```
A[ colindex][ rowindex ]
```

... is as follows:

```
Element_Address = Base_Address + (colindex * row_size + rowindex) * Element_Size
```

As usual, `Base_Address` is the address of the first element of the array (`A[0][0]` in this case) and `Element_Size` is the size of an individual element of the array, in bytes. `Row_size` is the number of elements in one row of the array (four, in this case, because each row has four elements). Assuming `Element_Size` is one, this formula computes the following offsets from the base address:

Column Index	Row Index	Offset into Array
0	0	0
0	1	1
0	2	2
0	3	3
1	0	4
1	1	5
1	2	6
1	3	7
2	0	8
2	1	9
2	2	10
2	3	11

(continued)

Column Index	Row Index	Offset into Array
3	0	12
3	1	13
3	2	14
3	3	15

For a three-dimensional array, the formula to compute the offset into memory is only slightly more complex. Consider a C/C++ array declaration given as follows:

```
someType A[depth_size][col_size][row_size];
```

If you have an array access similar to A[depth_index][col_index][row_index] then the computation that yields the offset into memory is the following:

```
Address =
Base + ((depth_index * col_size + col_index)*row_size + row_index) * Element_Size

Element_size is the size, in bytes, of a single array element.
```

For a four-dimensional array, declared in C/C++ as:

```
type A[bounds0][bounds1][bounds2][bounds3];
```

. . . the formula for computing the address of an array element when accessing element A[i][j][k][m] is as follows:

```
Address =
    Base + (((i * bounds1 + j) * bounds2 + k) * bounds3 + m) * Element_Size
```

If you've got an n-dimensional array declared in C/C++ as follows:

```
dataType A[b_{n-1}][b_{n-2}]...[b_0];
```

. . . and you wish to access the following element of this array:

```
A[a_{n-1}][a_{n-2}]...[a_1][a_0]
```

. . . then you can compute the address of a particular array element using the following algorithm:

```
Address := a_{n-1}
for i := n-2 downto 0 do
    Address := Address * b_i + a_i
Address := Base_Address + Address*Element_Size
```

7.2.4.2 Column-Major Ordering

Column-major ordering is the other common array element address function. FORTRAN and various dialects of BASIC (such as older versions of Microsoft BASIC) use this scheme to index arrays. Pictorially, a column-major ordered array is organized as shown in Figure 7-7.

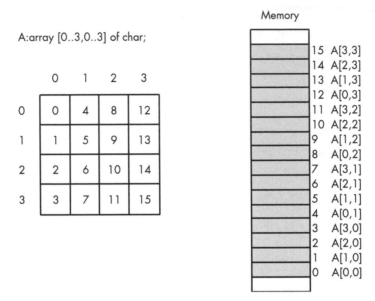

Figure 7-7: Column-major array element ordering

The formula for computing the address of an array element when using column-major ordering is very similar to that for row-major ordering. The difference is that you reverse the order of the index and size variables in the computation. That is, rather than working from the leftmost index to the rightmost, you operate on the indexes from the rightmost towards the leftmost.

For a two-dimensional column-major array, the formula is as follows:

```
Element_Address =
    Base_Address + (rowindex * col_size + colindex) * Element_Size
```

The formula for a three-dimensional column-major array is the following:

```
Element_Address =
    Base_Address +
        ((rowindex*col_size+colindex) * depth_size + depthindex) * Element_Size
```

And so on. Other than using these new formulas, accessing elements of an array using column-major ordering is identical to accessing arrays using row-major ordering.

7.2.4.3 Declaring Multidimensional Arrays

If you have an $m \times n$ array, it will have m × n elements and will require
m × n × Element_Size bytes of storage. To allocate storage for an array
you must reserve this amount of memory. With one-dimensional arrays,
the syntax that the different high-level languages employ is very similar.
However, their syntax starts to diverge when you consider multidimensional
arrays.

In C, C++, and Java, you use the following syntax to declare a multidimensional array:

```
data_type array_name [dim₁][dim₂] . . . [dimₙ];
```

Here is a concrete example of a three-dimensional array declaration in
C/C++:

```
int threeDInts[ 4 ][ 2 ][ 8 ];
```

This example creates an array with 64 elements organized with a depth of
four by two rows by eight columns. Assuming each int object requires 4 bytes,
this array consumes 256 bytes of storage.

Pascal's syntax actually supports two equivalent ways of declaring multidimensional arrays. The following example demonstrates both of these
forms:

```
var
        threeDInts  : array[0..3] of array[0..1] of array[0..7] of integer;
        threeDInts2 : array[0..3, 0..1, 0..7] of integer;
```

Semantically, there are only two major differences that exist among different
languages. The first difference is whether the array declaration specifies the
overall size of each array dimension or whether it specifies the upper and
lower bounds. The second difference is whether the starting index is zero,
one, or a user-specified value.

7.2.4.4 Accessing Elements of a Multidimensional Array

Accessing an element of a multidimensional array in a high-level language
is so easy that a typical programmer will do so without considering the associated cost. In this section, we'll look at some of the assembly language
sequences you'll need to access elements of a multidimension array to give
you a clearer picture of these costs.

Consider again, the C/C++ declaration of the ThreeDInts array from the
previous section:

```
int ThreeDInts[ 4 ][ 2 ][ 8 ];
```

In C/C++, if you wanted to set element [i][j][k] of this array to the value of n, you'd probably use a statement similar to the following:

```
ThreeDInts[i][j][k] = n;
```

This statement, however, hides a great deal of complexity. Recall the formula needed to access an element of a three-dimensional array:

```
Element_Address =
    Base_Address +
        ((rowindex * col_size + colindex) * depth_size + depthindex) *
            Element_Size
```

The ThreeDInts example does not avoid this calculation, it only hides it from you. The machine code that the C/C++ compiler generates is similar to the following:

```
intmul( 2, i, ebx );     // EBX = 2 * i
add( j, ebx );           // EBX = 2 * i + j
intmul( 8, ebx );        // EBX = (2 * i + j) * 8
add( k, ebx );           // EBX = (2 * i + j) * 8 + k
mov( n, eax );
mov( eax, ThreeDInts[ebx*4] );   // ThreeDInts[i][j][k] = n
```

Actually, ThreeDInts is special. The sizes of all the array dimensions are nice powers of two. This means that the CPU can use shifts instead of multiplication instructions to multiply EBX by two and by four in this example. Because shifts are often faster than multiplication, a decent C/C++ compiler will generate the following code:

```
mov( i, ebx );
shl( 1, ebx );           // EBX = 2 * i
add( j, ebx );           // EBX = 2 * i + j
shl( 3, ebx );           // EBX = (2 * i + j) * 8
add( k, ebx );           // EBX = (2 * i + j) * 8 + k
mov( n, eax );
mov( eax, ThreeDInts[ebx*4] );   // ThreeDInts[i][j][k] = n
```

Note that a compiler can only use this faster code if an array dimension is a power of two. This is the reason many programmers attempt to declare arrays whose dimension sizes are some power of two. Of course, if you must declare extra elements in the array to achieve this goal, you may wind up wasting space (especially with higher-dimensional arrays) to achieve a small increase in speed.

For example, if you need a 10×10 array and you're using row-major ordering, you could create a 10×16 array to allow the use of a shift (by four) instruction rather than a multiply (by 10) instruction. When using column-major ordering, you'd probably want to declare a 16×10 array to achieve the same effect, since row-major calculation doesn't use the size of the first dimension when calculating an offset into an array, and column-major calculation doesn't use the size of the second dimension when calculating an offset. In either case, however, the array would wind up having 160 elements instead of 100 elements. Only you can decide if this extra space is worth the small increase in speed you'll gain.

7.3 Records/Structures

Another major composite data structure is the Pascal *record* or C/C++ *structure*. The Pascal terminology is probably better, as it avoids confusion with the term *data structure*. Therefore, we'll adopt the term *record* here.

An array is homogeneous, meaning that its elements are all of the same type. A record, on the other hand, is heterogeneous and its elements can have differing types. The purpose of a record is to let you encapsulate logically related values into a single object.

Arrays let you select a particular element via an integer index. With records, you must select an element, known as a *field*, by the field's name. Each of the field names within the record must be unique. That is, the same field name may not appear two or more times in the same record. However, all field names are local to their record, and you may reuse those names elsewhere in the program.

7.3.1 Records in Pascal/Delphi

Here's a typical record declaration for a Student data type in Pascal/Delphi:

```
type
    Student =
        record
            Name:      string [64];
            Major:     smallint;    // 2-byte integer in Delphi
            SSN:       string[11];
            Mid1:      smallint;
            Midt:      smallint;
            Final:     smallint;
            Homework:  smallint;
            Projects:  smallint;
        end;
```

Many Pascal compilers allocate all of the fields in contiguous memory locations. This means that Pascal will reserve the first 65 bytes for the name,[3] the next 2 bytes hold the major code, the next 12 bytes the Social Security number, and so on.

---

[3] Pascal strings usually require an extra byte, in addition to all the characters in the string, to encode the length.

7.3.2   Records in C/C++

Here's the same declaration in C/C++:

```
typedef
    struct
    {
        char Name[65]; // Room for a 64-character zero-terminated string.
        short Major;   // Typically a 2-byte integer in C/C++
        char SSN[12];  // Room for an 11-character zero-terminated string.
        short Mid1;
        short Mid2;
        short Final;
        short Homework;
        short Projects
    } Student;
```

7.3.3   Records in HLA

In HLA, you can also create structure types using the record/endrecord declaration. In HLA, you would encode the record from the previous sections as follows:

```
type
    Student:
        record
            Name:      char[65];    // Room for a 64-character
                                    //   zero-terminated string.

            Major:     int16;
            SSN:       char[12];    // Room for an 11-character
                                    //   zero-terminated string.

            Mid1:      int16;
            Mid2:      int16;
            Final:     int16;
            Homework:  int16;
            Projects:  int16;
        endrecord;
```

As you can see, the HLA declaration is very similar to the Pascal declaration. Note that to stay consistent with the Pascal declaration, this example uses character arrays rather than strings for the Name and SSN (Social Security number) fields. In a typical HLA record declaration, you'd probably use a string type for at least the Name field (keeping in mind that a string variable is a four-byte pointer).

7.3.4 Memory Storage of Records

The following Pascal example demonstrates a typical Student variable declaration:

```
var
    John: Student;
```

Given the earlier declaration for the Pascal Student data type, this allocates 81 bytes of storage laid out in memory as shown in Figure 7-8.

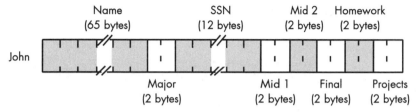

Figure 7-8: Student data structure storage in memory

If the label John corresponds to the *base address* of this record, then the Name field is at offset John + 0, the Major field is at offset John + 65, the SSN field is at offset John + 67, and so on.

Most programming languages let you refer to a record field by its name rather than by its numeric offset into the record. The typical syntax for field access uses the *dot operator* to select a field from a record variable. Given the variable John from the previous example, here's how you could access various fields in this record:

```
John.Mid1 = 80;              // C/C++ example
John.Final := 93;            (* Pascal Example *)
mov( 75, John.Projects );    // HLA example
```

Figure 7-8 suggests that all fields of a record appear in memory in the order of their declaration. In theory, a compiler can freely place the fields anywhere in memory that it chooses. In practice, though, almost every compiler places the fields in memory in the same order they appear within the record declaration. The first field usually appears at the lowest address in the record, the second field appears at the next highest address, the third field follows the second field in memory, and so on.

Figure 7-8 also suggests that compilers pack the fields into adjacent memory locations with no gaps between the fields. While this is true for many languages, this certainly isn't the most common memory organization for a record. For performance reasons, most compilers will actually align the fields of a record on appropriate memory boundaries. The exact details vary by language, compiler implementation, and CPU, but a typical compiler will place fields at an offset within the record's storage area that is "natural" for that particular field's data type. On the 80x86, for example, compilers that follow the Intel ABI (application binary interface) will allocate one-byte objects at any offset within the record, words only at even offsets, and double-word or larger objects on double-word boundaries. Although not all 80x86 compilers support the Intel ABI, most do, which allows records to be shared among functions and procedures written in different languages on the 80x86. Other CPU manufacturers provide their own ABI for their processors and programs that adhere to an ABI can share binary data at run time with other programs that adhere to the same ABI.

In addition to aligning the fields of a record at reasonable offset boundaries, most compilers will also ensure that the length of the entire record is a multiple of two, four, or eight bytes. They accomplish this by adding padding bytes at the end of the record to fill out the record's size. The reason that compilers pad the size of a record is to ensure that the record's length is an even multiple of the size of the largest scalar (non-composite data type) object in the record or the CPU's optimal alignment size, whichever is smaller. For example, if a record has fields whose lengths are one, two, four, eight, and ten bytes long, then an 80x86 compiler will generally pad the record's length so that it is an even multiple of eight. This allows you to create an array of records and be assured that each record in the array starts at a reasonable address in memory.

Although some CPUs don't allow access to objects in memory at misaligned addresses, many compilers allow you to disable the automatic alignment of fields within a record. Generally, the compiler will have an option you can use to globally disable this feature. Many of these compilers also provide a *pragma* or a packed keyword of some sort that lets you turn off field alignment on a record-by-record basis. Disabling the automatic field alignment feature may allow you to save some memory by eliminating the padding bytes between the fields (and at the end of the record), provided that field misalignment is acceptable on your CPU. The cost, of course, is that the program may run a little bit slower when it needs to access misaligned values in memory.

One reason to use a packed record is to gain manual control over the alignment of the fields within the record. For example, suppose you have a couple of functions written in two different languages and both of these functions need to access some data in a record. Further, suppose that the two compilers for these functions do not use the same field alignment algorithm. A record declaration like the following (in Pascal) may not be compatible with the way both functions access the record data:

```
type
    aRecord: record
        bField : byte;  (* assume Pascal compiler supports a byte type *)
        wField : word;  (* assume Pascal compiler supports a word type *)
```

```
      dField : dword; (* assume Pascal compiler supports a double-word type *)
   end; (* record *)
```

The problem here is that the first compiler could use the offsets zero, two, and four for the bField, wField, and dField fields, respectively, while the second compiler might use offsets zero, four, and eight.

Suppose however, that the first compiler allows you to specify the packed keyword before the record keyword, causing the compiler to store each field immediately following the previous one. Although using the packed keyword will not make the records compatible with both functions, it will allow you to manually add padding fields to the record declaration, as follows:

```
type
   aRecord: packed record
      bField   :byte;
      padding0 :array[0..2] of byte;  (* add padding to dword align wField *)
      wField   :word;
      padding1 :word;                 (* add padding to dword align dField *)
      dField   :dword;
   end; (* record *)
```

Maintaining code where you've handled the padding in a manual fashion can be a real chore. However, if incompatible compilers need to share data, this is a trick worth knowing because it can make data sharing possible. For the exact details concerning packed records, you'll have to consult your language's reference manual.

7.4 Discriminant Unions

A discriminant union (or just *union*) is very similar to a record. Like records, unions have fields and you access those fields using dot notation. In fact, in many languages, about the only syntactical difference between records and unions is the use of the keyword union rather than record. Semantically, however, there is a big difference between a record and a union. In a record, each field has its own offset from the base address of the record, and the fields do not overlap. In a union, however, all fields have the same offset, zero, and all the fields of the union overlap. As a result, the size of a record is the sum of the sizes of all the fields (plus, possibly, some padding bytes), whereas a union's size is the size of its largest field (plus, possibly, some padding bytes at the end).

Because the fields of a union overlap, you might think that a union has little use in a real-world program. After all, if the fields all overlap, then changing the value of one field changes the values of all the other fields as well. This generally means that the use of a union's field is *mutually exclusive* — that is, you can only use one field at any given time. This observation is generally correct, but although this means that unions aren't as generally applicable as records, they still have many uses.

7.4.1 Unions in C/C++

Here's an example of a union declaration in C/C++:

```
typedef union
{
    unsigned int   i;
    float          r;
    unsigned char  c[4];

} unionType;
```

Assuming the C/C++ compiler in use allocates four bytes for unsigned integers, the size of a `unionType` object will be four bytes (because all three fields are 4-byte objects).

7.4.2 Unions in Pascal/Delphi/Kylix

Pascal/Delphi/Kylix use *case variant records* to create a discriminant union. The syntax for a case variant record is the following:

```
type
    typeName =
        record
            <<non-variant/union record fields go here>>

            case tag of
                const1:( field_declaration );
                const2:( field_declaration );
                    .
                    .
                    .
                constn:( field_declaration )   (* no semicolon follows
                                                    the last field *)

        end;
```

In this example, tag is either a type identifier (such as Boolean, char, or some user-defined type) or it can be a field declaration of the form `identifier:type`. If the tag item takes this latter form, then `identifier` becomes another field of the record (and not a member of the *variant section* — those declarations following the case) and has the specified type. When using this second form, the Pascal compiler could generate code that raises an exception whenever the application attempts to access any of the variant fields except the one specified by the value of the tag field. In practice, though, almost no Pascal compilers do this. Still, keep in mind that the Pascal language standard suggests that compilers should do this, so some compilers out there might actually do this check.

Here's an example of two different case variant record declarations in Pascal:

```
type
    noTagRecord=
        record
            someField: integer;
            case boolean of
                true:( i:integer );
                false:( b:array[0..3] of char)
        end; (* record *)

    hasTagRecord=
        record
            case which:(0..2) of
                0:( i:integer );
                1:( r:real );
                2:( c:array[0..3] of char )
        end; (* record *)
```

As you can see in the hasTagRecord union, a Pascal case-variant record does not require any normal record fields. This is true even if you do not have a tag field.

7.4.3 Unions in HLA

HLA supports unions as well. Here's a typical union declaration in HLA:

```
type
    unionType:
        union
            i: int32;
            r: real32;
            c: char[4];
        endunion;
```

7.4.4 Memory Storage of Unions

The big difference between a union and a record is the fact that records allocate storage for each field at different offsets, whereas unions overlay each of the fields at the same offset in memory. For example, consider the following HLA record and union declarations:

```
type
    numericRec:
        record
            i: int32;
            u: uns32;
            r: real64;
        endrecord;
```

```
numericUnion:
    union
        i: int32;
        u: uns32;
        r: real64;
    endunion;
```

If you declare a variable, n, of type numericRec, you access the fields as n.i,
n.u, and n.r, exactly as though you had declared the n variable to be type
numericUnion. However, the size of a numericRec object is 16 bytes because the
record contains two double-word fields and a quad-word (real64) field. The
size of a numericUnion variable, however, is eight bytes. Figure 7-9 shows the
memory arrangement of the i, u, and r fields in both the record and union.

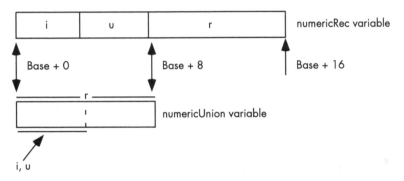

Figure 7-9: Layout of a union versus a record variable

7.4.5   Other Uses of Unions

In addition to conserving memory, programmers often use unions to create
aliases in their code. As you may recall, an alias is a second name for some
memory object. Although aliases are often a source of confusion in a
program, and should be used sparingly, using an alias can sometimes be
convenient. For example, in some section of your program you might need
to constantly use type coercion to refer to a particular object. One way to
avoid this is to use a union variable with each field representing one of the
different types you want to use for the object. As an example, consider the
following HLA code fragment:

```
type
    CharOrUns:
        union
            c:char;
            u:uns32;
        endunion;

static
    v:CharOrUns;
```

With a declaration like this one, you can manipulate an uns32 object by accessing v.u. If, at some point, you need to treat the LO byte of this uns32 variable as a character, you can do so by simply accessing the v.c variable, as follows:

```
mov( eax, v.u );
stdout.put( "v, as a character, is '", v.c, "'" nl );
```

Another common practice is to use unions to disassemble a larger object into its constituent bytes. Consider the following C/C++ code fragment:

```
typedef union
{
    unsigned int u;
    unsigned char bytes[4];
} asBytes;

asBytes composite;
        .
        .
        .
    composite.u = 1234576890;
    printf
    (
        "HO byte of composite.u is %u, LO byte is %u\n",
        composite.u[3],
        composite.u[0]
    );
```

Although composing and decomposing data types using unions is a useful trick every now and then, be aware that this code is not portable. Remember, the HO and LO bytes of a multibyte object appear at different addresses on big endian versus little endian machines. This code fragment works fine on little endian machines, but fails to display the right bytes on big endian CPUs. Any time you use unions to decompose larger objects, you should be aware that the code might not be portable across different machines. Still, disassembling larger values into the corresponding bytes, or assembling a larger value from bytes, is usually much more efficient than using shift lefts, shift rights, and AND operations. Therefore, you'll see this trick used quite a bit.

7.5 For More Information

This chapter has dealt with the low-level implementation of common data structures you'll find in various languages. For more information on data types, you can head off in two directions at this point — lower or higher.

To learn more about the low-level implementation of various data types, you'll probably want to start learning and mastering assembly language. My book *The Art of Assembly Language* (No Starch Press) is a good place to begin that journey.

Higher-level data-structure information is available in just about any decent college textbook on data structures and algorithm design. There are literally hundreds of these books available covering a wide range of subjects.

For those interested in a combination of low-level and high-level concepts, a good choice is Donald Knuth's *The Art of Computer Programming, Volume I: Fundamental Algorithms*. This text is available in nearly every bookstore that carries technical books.

8

BOOLEAN LOGIC
AND DIGITAL DESIGN

Boolean logic is the basis of computation in modern computer systems. You can represent any algorithm, or any electronic computer circuit, using a system of Boolean equations. To fully understand how software operates you need to understand basic Boolean logic and digital design.

This material is especially important to those who want to design electronic circuits or write software that controls electronic circuits. Even if you never plan to do this, you can use your knowledge of Boolean logic to optimize your software. However, there is one other reason for studying Boolean functions, even if you never intend to do either of these two things. Many high-level languages process Boolean expressions, such as those that control an if statement or while loop. By optimizing your Boolean expressions, it is often possible to improve the performance of high-level language code. Therefore, studying Boolean functions is important even if you never intend to design an electronic circuit. It can help you write better code in a traditional programming language.

8.1 Boolean Algebra

Boolean algebra is a deductive mathematical system. A *binary operator* "°" accepts a pair of Boolean inputs and produces a single Boolean value. For example, the Boolean AND operator accepts two Boolean inputs and produces a single Boolean output (the logical AND of the two inputs).

8.1.1 The Boolean Operators

For our purposes, we will base Boolean algebra on the following set of operators and values:

- The two possible values in the Boolean system are zero and one. Often we will call these values *false* and *true*, respectively.

- The symbol "•" represents the logical AND operation. For example, $A \cdot B$ is the result of logically ANDing the Boolean values A and B. When using single letter variable names, this text will drop the "•" symbol; therefore, AB also represents the logical AND of the variables A and B, which we will also call the product of A and B.

- The symbol "+" represents the logical OR operation. For example, $A + B$ is the result of logically ORing the Boolean values A and B. We will also call this the sum of A and B.

- Logical complement, logical negation, and NOT, are all names for the same unary operator. This chapter will use the ($'$) symbol to denote logical negation. For example, A' denotes the logical NOT of A.

8.1.2 Boolean Postulates

Every algebraic system follows a certain set of initial assumptions, or *postulates*. You can deduce additional rules, theorems, and other properties of the system from this basic set of postulates. Boolean algebra systems are no different, and usually employ the following postulates:

- *Closure.* A Boolean system is *closed* with respect to a particular binary operator if, for every pair of Boolean values, it only produces a Boolean result.

- *Commutativity.* A binary operator "°" is said to be commutative if $A ° B = B ° A$ for all possible Boolean values A and B.

- *Associativity.* A binary operator "°" is said to be associative if $(A ° B) ° C = A ° (B ° C)$ for all Boolean values A, B, and C.

- *Distribution.* Two binary operators "°" and "%" are distributive if $A ° (B \% C) = (A ° B) \% (A ° C)$ for all Boolean values A, B, and C.

- *Identity.* A Boolean value I is said to be the *identity element* with respect to some binary operator "°" if $A ° I = A$ for all Boolean values A.

- *Inverse.* A Boolean value I is said to be the *inverse element* with respect to some binary operator "°" if $A ° I = B$ and $B \neq A$ (i.e., B is the opposite value of A in a Boolean system) for all Boolean values A and B.

When applied to the Boolean operators, the preceding postulates produce the following set of *Boolean postulates*:

- P1: Boolean algebra is closed under the AND, OR, and NOT operations.
- P2: The identity element of AND (•) is one, and the identity element of OR (+) is zero. There is no identity element with respect to logical NOT (').
- P3: The • and + operators are commutative.
- P4: • and + are distributive with respect to one another. That is, $A • (B + C) = (A • B) + (A • C)$ and $A + (B • C) = (A + B) • (A + C)$.
- P5: • and + are both associative. That is, $(A • B) • C = A • (B • C)$ and $(A + B) + C = A + (B + C)$.
- P6: For every value A there exists a value A' such that $A • A' = 0$ and $A + A' = 1$. This value is the logical complement (or NOT) of A.

You can prove all other theorems in Boolean algebra using this set of Boolean postulates. This chapter will not go into the formal proofs of the following theorems, but familiarity with some important theorems in Boolean algebra will be useful. Here are some of the important theorems:

Th1: $A + A = A$

Th2: $A • A = A$

Th3: $A + 0 = A$

Th4: $A • 1 = A$

Th5: $A • 0 = 0$

Th6: $A + 1 = 1$

Th7: $(A + B)' = A' • B'$

Th8: $(A • B)' = A' + B'$

Th9: $A + A • B = A$

Th10: $A • (A + B) = A$

Th11: $A + A'B = A + B$

Th12: $A' • (A + B') = A'B'$

Th13: $AB + AB' = A$

Th14: $(A' + B') • (A' + B) = A'$

Th15: $A + A' = 1$

Th16: $A • A' = 0$

Theorems seven and eight are called DeMorgan's Theorems *after the mathematician who discovered them.*

An important principle in the Boolean algebra system is that of *duality*. Each pair, theorems 1 and 2, theorems 3 and 4, and so on, forms a *dual*. Any valid expression you can create using the postulates and theorems of Boolean algebra remains valid if you interchange the operators and constants appearing in the expression. Specifically, if you exchange the • and + operators and swap the 0 and 1 values in an expression, the resulting expression will obey all the rules of Boolean algebra. *This does not mean the dual expression computes the same values;* it only means that both expressions are legal in the Boolean algebra system.

8.1.3   Boolean Operator Precedence

If several different Boolean operators appear within a single Boolean expression, the result of the expression depends on the *precedence* of the operators. The following Boolean operators are ordered from highest precedence to lowest:

- parentheses
- logical NOT
- logical AND
- logical OR

The logical AND and OR operators are *left associative*. This means that if two operators with the same precedence appear between three operands, you must evaluate the expressions from left to right. The logical NOT operation is right associative, although it would produce the same result using either left or right associativity because it is a unary operator having only a single operand.

8.2   Boolean Functions and Truth Tables

A Boolean *expression* is a sequence of zeros, ones, and *literals* separated by Boolean operators. A Boolean literal is a primed (negated) or unprimed variable name, and all variable names will be a single alphabetic character. A Boolean function is a specific Boolean expression; we will generally give Boolean functions the name *F* with a possible subscript. For example, consider the following Boolean function:

$$F_0 = AB + C$$

This function computes the logical AND of A and B and then logically ORs this result with C. If $A = 1$, $B = 0$, and $C = 1$, then F_0 returns the value one ($1 \bullet 0 + 1 = 1$).

You can also represent a Boolean function with a *truth table*. The truth tables for the logical AND and OR functions are shown in Table 8-1 and Table 8-2.

Table 8-1: AND truth table

AND	0	1
0	0	0
1	0	1

Table 8-2: OR truth table

OR	0	1
0	0	1
1	1	1

For binary operators and two input variables, this form of a truth table is very natural and convenient. However, for functions involving more than two variables, these truth-table forms don't work well.

Table 8-3 shows another way to represent truth tables. This form has several advantages — it is easier to fill in the table, it supports three or more variables, and it provides a compact representation for two or more functions. The example in Table 8-3 demonstrates how to create a truth table for three different functions of three input variables.

Table 8-3: Truth Table Format for a Function of Three Variables

C	B	A	F = ABC	F = AB + C	F = A+BC
0	0	0	0	0	0
0	0	1	0	0	1
0	1	0	0	0	0
0	1	1	0	1	1
1	0	0	0	1	0
1	0	1	0	1	1
1	1	0	0	1	1
1	1	1	1	1	1

Although you can create an infinite variety of Boolean functions, they are not all unique. For example, $F = A$ and $F = AA$ are two different functions. By theorem two, however, it is easy to show that these two functions produce exactly the same result no matter what input value you supply for *A*. As it turns out, if you fix the number of input variables you're going to allow, there are a finite number of unique Boolean functions possible. For example, there are only 16 unique Boolean functions with two input variables and there are only 256 possible Boolean functions with three input variables. Given *n* input variables, there are 2^{2^n} unique Boolean functions (two raised to two raised to the *nth* power). With two input variables there are $2^{2^2} = 2^4$ or 16 different functions. With three input variables there are $2^{2^3} = 2^8$ or 256 possible functions. Four input variables have 2^{2^4} or 2^{16}, or 65,536 unique Boolean functions.

When working with only 16 Boolean functions (two input variables), we can name each unique function. Table 8-4 lists common names for these functions.

Table 8-4: Common Names for Boolean Functions of Two Variables

Function Number[1]	Function Name	Description
0	Zero (clear)	Always returns zero regardless of A and B input values
1	Logical NOR	(NOT (A OR B)) = (A + B)'
2	Inhibition (AB')	Inhibition = AB' (A AND not B). Also equivalent to A > B or B < A
3	NOT B	Ignores A and returns B'
4	Inhibition (BA')	Inhibition = BA' (B AND not A). Also equivalent to B > A or A < B
5	NOT A	Returns A' and ignores B
6	Exclusive-or (XOR)	A ⊕ B. Also equivalent to A ≠ B
7	Logical NAND	(NOT (A AND B)) = (A • B)'
8	Logical AND	A • B = (A AND B)
9	Equivalence (exclusive-NOR)	(A = B). Also known as exclusive-NOR (not exclusive-OR)
10	A	Copy A. Returns the value of A and ignores B's value
11	Implication, B implies A	A + B'. (If B then A). Also equivalent to B ≥ A
12	B	Copy B. Returns the value of B and ignores A's value
13	Implication, A implies B	B + A'. (If A then B). Also equivalent to A ≥ B
14	Logical OR	A + B. Returns A OR B
15	One (set)	Always returns one regardless of A and B input values

[1] See the discussion of function numbers in the next section.

8.3 Function Numbers

Beyond two input variables, there are too many functions to provide a specific name for each. Therefore, even when we are referring to functions with two input variables, we will refer to the function's number rather than the function's name. For example, F_8 denotes the logical AND of A and B for a two-input function and F_{14} denotes the logical OR operation. Of course, for functions with more than two input variables, the question is, "How do we determine a function's number?" For example, what is the corresponding function number for the function $F = AB + C$? Computing the answer is easily done by looking at the truth table for the function. If we treat the values for A, B, and C as bits in a binary number with C being the HO bit and A being the LO bit, they produce the binary strings that correspond to numbers in the range zero through seven. Associated with each of these binary strings is the function result, either zero or one. If we construct a binary number by placing the function result of each combination of the A, B, and C input values into the bit position specified by the binary string of the A, B, and C bits, the resulting binary number will be the corresponding function number. If this doesn't make sense, an example will help clear it up. Consider the truth table for $F = AB + C$ (see Table 8-5).

Table 8-5: Truth table for F = AB + C

C	B	A	F = AB + C
0	0	0	0
0	0	1	0
0	1	0	0
0	1	1	1
1	0	0	1
1	0	1	1
1	1	0	1
1	1	1	1

Note how the input variables C, B, and A combine to form binary number sequences in the range %000..%111 (0..7). If we use these values to denote bit numbers in an 8-bit value (CBA = %111 specifies bit seven, CBA = %110 specifies bit six, and so on), we can determine the function number by placing at each of these bit positions the result of F = AB + C, for the corresponding combination of C, B, and A values:

```
CBA:           7   6   5   4   3   2   1   0
F = AB + C:    1   1   1   1   1   0   0   0
```

Now, if we treat this bit string as a binary number, it produces the function number \$F8 or 248. We will usually denote function numbers in decimal. This also provides insight into why there are 2^{2^n} different functions given n input variables: if you have n input variables, there are 2^n different variable value combinations, and thus 2^n bits in the function's binary number. If you have m bits, there are 2^m different possible arrangements of those bits. Therefore, for n input variables there are $m = 2^n$ possible bits and 2^m or 2^{2^n} possible functions.

8.4 Algebraic Manipulation of Boolean Expressions

You can transform one Boolean expression into an equivalent expression by applying the postulates and theorems of Boolean algebra. This is important if you want to convert a given expression to a *canonical form* (a standardized form) or if you want to minimize the number of literals or terms in an expression. (A *literal* is a primed or unprimed variable, and a *term* is a variable or a product [logical AND] of several different literals.) Minimizing the number of literals and terms can be important because electrical circuits often consist of individual components that implement each literal or term. Minimizing the number of literals and terms in an expression allows a circuit designer to use fewer electrical components and, therefore, to reduce the monetary cost of the system.

Unfortunately, there are no fixed rules you can apply to optimize a given expression. Much like constructing mathematical proofs, an individual's ability to easily do these transformations is usually a function of experience. Nevertheless, a few examples can show the possibilities:

ab + ab' + a'b	= a(b + b') + a'b	By P4
	= a • 1 + a'b	By P5
	= a + a'b	By Th4
	= a + b	By Th11
(a'b + a'b' + b')`	= (a'(b + b') + b')'	By P4
	= (a'• 1 + b')'	By P5
	= (a' + b')	By Th4
	= ((ab)')'	By Th8
	= ab	By definition of not
b(a + c) + ab' + bc' + c	= ba + bc + ab' + bc' + c	By P4
	= a(b + b') + b(c + c') + c	By P4
	= a • 1 + b • 1 + c	By P5
	= a + b + c	By Th4

8.5 Canonical Forms

Because there is a finite number of unique Boolean functions with n input variables, yet an infinite number of possible logic expressions you can construct from a finite number of functions, there is an infinite number of equivalent logic expressions. To help eliminate confusion, logic designers generally specify a Boolean function using a *canonical*, or standardized, form. For each different Boolean function, we can choose a single canonical representation of that function.

There are several possible ways to define a set of canonical representations for all the possible Boolean functions of n variables. Within each canonical set, there is a single expression that describes each Boolean function in the system, so as long as you only utilize functions from a single canonical set, all of the functions in the set will be unique. We will discuss only two canonical systems in this chapter and employ only the first of the two. The first is the so-called *sum of minterms* and the second is the *product of maxterms*. Using the duality principle we can convert between these two.

As mentioned earlier, a *term* is either a single literal or a product (logical AND) of several different literals. For example, if you have two variables, A and B, there are eight possible terms: A, B, A', B', $A'B'$, $A'B$, AB', and AB. For three variables we have 26 different terms: A, B, C, A', B', C', $A'B'$, $A'B$, AB', AB, $A'C'$, A', AC', AC, $B'C'$, $B'C$, BC', BC, $A'B'C'$, $AB'C'$, ABC', ABC', $A'B'C$, $AB'C$, $A'BC$, and ABC. As you can see, as the number of variables increases, the number of terms increases dramatically. A *minterm* is a product containing exactly n literals, where n is the number of input variables. For example, the minterms for the two variables A and B are $A'B'$, AB', $A'B$, and AB. Likewise, the minterms for three variables A, B, and C are $A'B'C'$, $AB'C'$, $A'BC'$, ABC', $A'B'C$, $AB'C$, $A'BC$, and ABC. In general, there are 2^n minterms for n variables. The set of possible minterms is very easy to generate because they correspond to the sequence of binary numbers (see Table 8-6).

Table 8-6: Generating Minterms from Binary Numbers

Binary Equivalent (CBA)	Minterm
000	A'B'C'
001	AB'C'
010	A'BC'
011	ABC'
100	A'B'C
101	AB'C
110	A'BC
111	ABC

We can derive the canonical form for *any* Boolean function using a sum (logical OR) of minterms. Given $F_{248} = AB + C$ the equivalent canonical form is $ABC + A'BC + AB'C + A'B'C + ABC'$. Algebraically, we can show that the canonical form is equivalent to $AB + C$ as follows:

ABC + A'BC + AB'C + A'B'C + ABC'	=	BC(A + A') + B'C(A + A') + ABC'	By P4
	=	BC • 1 + B'C • 1 + ABC'	By Th15
	=	C(B + B') + ABC'	By P4
	=	C + ABC'	By Th15 & Th4
	=	C + AB	By Th11

Obviously, the canonical form is not the optimal form. On the other hand, there is a big advantage to using the sum of minterms canonical form: it is very easy to generate the truth table for a function from this canonical form. It is also very easy to generate the sum of minterms canonical form equation from the truth table.

8.5.1   Sum of Minterms Canonical Form and Truth Tables

To build the truth table from the sum of minterms canonical form, follow these steps:

1. Convert minterms to binary equivalents by substituting a *1* for unprimed variables and a *0* for primed variables:

$$F_{248} = CBA + CBA' + CB'A + CB'A' + C'BA$$
$$= 111 + 110 + 101 + 100 + 011$$

2. Place the number *1* in the function column for the appropriate minterm entries:

C	B	A	F = AB + C
0	0	0	
0	0	1	
0	1	0	
0	1	1	1
1	0	0	1
1	0	1	1
1	1	0	1
1	1	1	1

3. Finally, place the number *0* in the function column for the remaining entries:

C	B	A	F = AB + C
0	0	0	0
0	0	1	0
0	1	0	0
0	1	1	1
1	0	0	1
1	0	1	1
1	1	0	1
1	1	1	1

Going in the other direction, generating a logic function from a truth table, is almost as easy. Follow these steps:

1. Locate all the entries in the truth table with a function result of one. In this table, these are the last five entries. The number of table entries containing ones determines the number of minterms in the canonical equation.

2. Generate the individual minterms by substituting A, B, or C for ones and A', B', or C' for zeros. In this example, the result of F_{248} is one when CBA equals 111, 110, 101, 100, or 011. Therefore, $F_{248} = CBA + CBA' + CB'A + CB'A' + C'AB$. The last entry in the table contains all ones, so we generate the minterm CBA. The second-to-last entry contains 110, so we generate the minterm CBA'. Likewise, 101 produces $CB'A$, 100 produces $CB'A'$, and 011 produces $C'BA$.

3. The logical OR and logical AND operations are both commutative, so we can rearrange the terms within the minterms as we please, and we can rearrange the minterms within the overall function as we see fit.

This process works equally well for any number of variables, as with the truth table in Table 8-7 for the function $F_{53,504} = ABCD + A'BCD + A'B'CD + A'B'C'D$.

Table 8-7: Truth table for $F_{53,504}$

D	C	B	A	F = ABCD + A'BCD + A'B'CD + A'B'C'D
0	0	0	0	0
0	0	0	1	0
0	0	1	0	0
0	0	1	1	0
0	1	0	0	0
0	1	0	1	0
0	1	1	0	0
0	1	1	1	0

(continued on the next page)

Table 8-7: Truth table for $F_{53,504}$ (continued)

D	C	B	A	F = ABCD + A'BCD + A'B'CD + A'B'C'D
1	0	0	0	1
1	0	0	1	0
1	0	1	0	0
1	0	1	1	0
1	1	0	0	1
1	1	0	1	0
1	1	1	0	1
1	1	1	1	1

Perhaps the easiest way to generate the canonical form of a Boolean function is to first generate the truth table for that function and then build the canonical form from the truth table. In fact, we'll use this technique when converting between the two canonical forms.

8.5.2 Deriving the Sum of Minterms Canonical Form Algebraically

It is also a simple matter to generate the sum of minterms canonical form algebraically. Using the distributive law and theorem 15 ($A + A' = 1$) makes this task easy. Consider $F_{248} = AB + C$. This function contains two terms, AB and C, but they are not minterms. We can convert the first term to a sum of minterms as follows:

```
AB    = AB • 1            By Th4
      = AB • (C + C')     By Th 15
      = ABC + ABC'        By distributive law
      = CBA + C'BA        By associative law
```

Similarly, we can convert the second term in F_{248} to a sum of minterms as follows:

```
C     = C • 1                          By Th4
      = C • (A + A')                   By Th15
      = CA + CA'                       By distributive law
      = CA • 1 + CA' • 1               By Th4
      = CA • (B + B') + CA' • (B + B') By Th15
      = CAB + CAB' + CA'B + CA'B'      By distributive law
      = CBA + CBA' + CB'A + CB'A'      By associative law
```

The last step (rearranging the terms) in these two conversions is optional. To obtain the final canonical form for F_{248} we need only sum the results from these two conversions:

$$F_{248} = (CBA + C'BA) + (CBA + CBA' + CB'A + CB'A')$$
$$= CBA + CBA' + CB'A + CB'A' + C'BA$$

8.5.3 Product of Maxterms Canonical Form

Another canonical form is the *products of maxterms*. A maxterm is the sum (logical OR) of all input variables, primed or unprimed. For example, consider the following logic function *G* of three variables in products of maxterms form:

$$G = (A + B + C) \bullet (A' + B + C) \bullet (A + B' + C)$$

Like the sum of minterms form, there is exactly one product of maxterms for each possible logic function. Of course, for every product of maxterms form, there is an equivalent sum of minterms form. In fact, the function *G* in this example is equivalent to the earlier sum of minterms form of F_{248}:

$$F_{248} = CBA + CBA' + CB'A + CB'A' + C'BA = AB + C$$

Generating a truth table from the product of maxterms is no more difficult than building it from the sum of minterms. You use the duality principle to accomplish this. Remember, the duality principle says to swap AND for OR and zeros for ones (and vice versa). Therefore, to build the truth table, you would first swap primed and non-primed literals. In *G*, this would yield:

$$G = (A' + B' + C') \bullet (A + B' + C') \bullet (A' + B + C')$$

The next step is to swap the logical OR and logical AND operators. This produces the following:

$$G = A'B'C' + AB'C' + A'BC'$$

Finally, you need to swap all zeros and ones. This means that for each of the maxterms listed above, you need to store zeros into the function column of the truth table, and then fill in the rest of the truth table's function column with ones. This will place a zero in rows zero, one, and two in the truth table. Filling the remaining entries with ones produces F_{248}.

You can easily convert between these two canonical forms by generating the truth table for one form and working backward from the truth table to produce the other form. Consider the function of two variables, $F_7 = A + B$. The sum of minterms form is $F_7 = A'B + AB' + AB$. The truth table takes the form shown in Table 8-8.

Table 8-8: OR truth table for two variables

A	B	F_7
0	0	0
1	0	1
0	1	1
1	1	1

Working backward to get the product of maxterms, we first locate all entries in the truth table that have a zero result. The entry with A and B both equal to zero is the only entry with a zero result. This gives us the first step of $G = A'B'$. However, we still need to invert all the variables to obtain $G = AB$. By the duality principle, we also need to swap the logical OR and logical AND operators, obtaining $G = A + B$. This is the canonical *product of maxterms* form.

8.6   Simplification of Boolean Functions

Because there is an infinite variety of Boolean functions of n variables, but only a finite number of them are unique, you might wonder if there is some method that will simplify a given Boolean function to produce the optimal form. Of course, you can always use algebraic transformations to attempt to produce this optimal form, but you are not guaranteed to arrive at the best result. On the other hand, there are two methods that will *always* reduce a given Boolean function to its optimal form: the map method and the prime implicants method. In this book, we will only cover the map method.

Because an optimal form must exist for any logic function, you may wonder why we don't use the optimal form for the canonical form. There are two reasons. First, although it is easy to convert between the truth table forms and the canonical form, it is not as easy to generate the optimal form from a truth table. Second, there may be several optimal forms for a single function.

Using the map method to manually optimize Boolean functions is practical only for functions of two, three, or four variables. With care, you can use it for functions of five or six variables, but the map method is cumbersome to use at that point. For more than six variables, attempting map simplifications by hand would not be wise although it's probably quite reasonable to write a *program* that uses the map method for seven or more variables.

The first step in using the map method is to build a special two-dimensional truth table for the function (see Figure 8-1). *Take a careful look at these truth tables.* They do not use the same forms appearing earlier in this chapter. In particular, the progression of the 2-bit values is 00, 01, 11, 10, not 00, 01, 10, 11. This is very important! If you organize the truth tables in a binary sequence, the mapping optimization method will not work properly. We will call this a *truth map* to distinguish it from the standard truth table.

B \ A	0	1
0	B'A'	B'A
1	BA'	BA

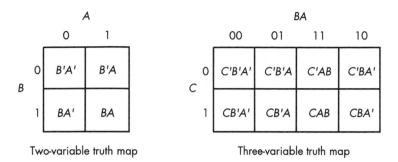

Two-variable truth map

C \ BA	00	01	11	10
0	C'B'A'	C'B'A	C'AB	C'BA'
1	CB'A'	CB'A	CAB	CBA'

Three-variable truth map

DC \ BA	00	01	11	10
00	D'C'B'A'	D'C'B'A	D'C'AB	D'C'BA'
01	D'CB'A'	D'CB'A	D'CAB	D'CBA'
11	DCB'A'	DCB'A	DCAB	DCBA'
10	DC'B'A'	DC'B'A	DC'AB	DC'BA'

Four-variable truth map

Figure 8-1: Two-, three-, and four-variable truth maps

Assuming your Boolean function is already in sum of minterms canonical form, insert ones for each of the truth map cells corresponding to one of the minterms in the function. Place zeros everywhere else. For example, consider the function of three variables *F* = *C'B'A* + *C'BA'* + *C'BA* + *CB'A'* + *CB'A* + *CBA'* + *CBA*. Figure 8-2 shows the truth map for this function.

C \ BA	00	01	11	10
0	0	1	1	1
1	1	1	1	1

Figure 8-2: A truth map for F = C'B'A + C'BA' + C'BA + CB'A' + CB'A + CBA' + CBA

The next step is to draw outlines around rectangular groups of ones. The rectangles you enclose must have sides whose lengths are powers of two. For functions with three variables, the rectangles can have sides whose lengths are one, two, and four. The set of rectangles you draw must surround all cells containing ones in the truth map. The trick is to draw all possible rectangles unless a rectangle would be completely enclosed within another, but at the same time to draw the fewest number of rectangles. Note that the rectangles may overlap as long as one rectangle does not completely enclose the other. In the truth map in Figure 8-3, there are three such rectangles.

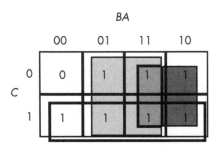

Three possible rectangles whose lengths
and widths are powers of two

Figure 8-3: Surrounding rectangular groups of ones in a truth map

Each rectangle represents a term in the simplified Boolean function. Therefore, the simplified Boolean function will contain only three terms. You build each term using the process of elimination — eliminate any variables whose primed and unprimed forms both appear within the rectangle. Consider the long skinny rectangle in Figure 8-3 that is sitting in the row where *C = 1*. This rectangle contains both *A* and *B* in primed and unprimed forms. Therefore, we can eliminate both *A* and *B* from the term. Because the rectangle sits in the *C = 1* region, this rectangle represents the single literal *C*.

Now consider the light gray square in Figure 8-3. This rectangle includes *C, C', B, B',* and *A*. Therefore, it represents the single term *A*. Likewise, the dark gray square in Figure 8-3 contains *C, C', A, A',* and *B*. Therefore, it represents the single term *B*.

The final, optimal, function is the sum (logical OR) of the terms represented by the three squares, or *F = A + B + C*. You do not have to consider the remaining squares containing zeros.

When enclosing groups of ones in the truth map, you must consider the fact that a truth map forms a *torus* (a doughnut shape). The right edge of the map *wraps around* to the left edge (and vice versa). Likewise, the top edge *wraps around* to the bottom edge. This introduces additional possibilities when drawing rectangles around groups of ones in a map. Consider the Boolean function *F = C'B'A' + C'BA' + CB'A' + CBA'*. Figure 8-4 shows the truth map for this function.

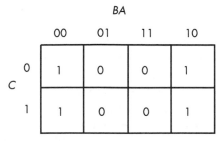

Figure 8-4: Truth map for F = C'B'A' + C'BA' + CB'A + CBA'

At first glance, you would think that the minimum number of rectangles is two, as shown in Figure 8-5.

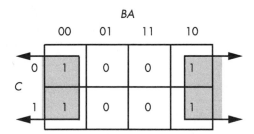

Figure 8-5: First attempt at surrounding rectangles formed by ones

However, because the truth map is a continuous object with the right side and left sides connected, we can actually form a single, square rectangle, as Figure 8-6 shows.

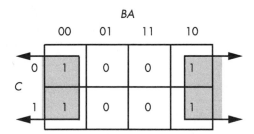

Figure 8-6: Correct rectangle for the function

Why do we care if we have one rectangle or two in the truth map? The answer is that the larger the rectangles are, the more terms they will eliminate. The fewer rectangles that we have, the fewer terms will appear in the final Boolean function.

The example in Figure 8-5 with two rectangles generates a function with two terms. The rectangle on the left eliminates the C variable, leaving $A'B'$ as its term. The rectangle on the right also eliminates the C variable, leaving the term BA'. Therefore, this truth map would produce the equation $F = A'B' + A'B$. We know this is not optimal (see theorem 13).

Now consider the truth map in Figure 8-6. Here we have a single rectangle, so our Boolean function will only have a single term. Obviously, this is better than an equation with two terms. Because this rectangle includes both C and C', and also B and B', the only term left is A'. This Boolean function, therefore, reduces to $F = A'$.

There are only two types of truth maps that the map method cannot handle properly: a truth map that contains all zeros or a truth map that contains all ones. These two cases correspond to the Boolean functions $F = 0$ and $F = 1$ (that is, the function number is zero or $2^n - 1$). When you see either of these truth maps, you will know how to optimally represent the function.

An important thing to remember when optimizing Boolean functions using the mapping method is that you always want to pick the largest rectangles whose sides' lengths are powers of two. You must do this even for overlapping rectangles (unless one rectangle encloses another). Consider the Boolean function $F = C'B'A' + C'BA' + CB'A' + C'AB + CBA' + CBA$. This produces the truth map appearing in Figure 8-7.

BA

	00	01	11	10
C 0	1	0	1	1
1	1	0	1	1

Figure 8-7: Truth map for $F = C'B'A' + C'BA' + CB'A' + C'AB + CBA' + CBA$

The initial temptation is to create one of the sets of rectangles found in Figure 8-8. However, the correct mapping appears in Figure 8-9.

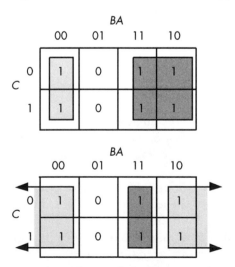

Figure 8-8: Obvious choices for rectangles

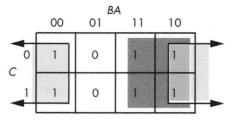

Figure 8-9: Correct set of rectangles for F = C'B'A' + C'BA' + CB'A' + C'AB + CBA' + CBA

All three mappings will produce a Boolean function with two terms. However, the first two will produce the expressions $F = B + A'B'$ and $F = AB + A'$. The third form produces $F = B + A'$. Obviously, this last form is the optimized one (see theorems 11 and 12).

For functions of three variables, the size of the rectangle determines the number of terms it represents:

- A rectangle enclosing a single square represents a minterm. The associated term will have three literals.
- A rectangle surrounding two squares containing ones represents a term containing two literals.
- A rectangle surrounding four squares containing ones represents a term containing a single literal.
- A rectangle surrounding eight squares represents the function $F = 1$.

Truth maps you create for functions of four variables are even trickier. This is because there are many places rectangles can hide from you along the edges. Figure 8-10 shows some possible places rectangles can hide.

This list of patterns doesn't even begin to cover all of them! For example, the diagrams in Figure 8-10 show none of the 1×2 rectangles. You must exercise care when working with four variable maps to ensure you select the largest possible rectangles, especially when overlap occurs. This is particularly important when you have a rectangle next to an edge of the truth map.

As with functions of three variables, the size of the rectangle in a four-variable truth map controls the number of terms it represents.

- A rectangle enclosing a single square represents a minterm. The associated term will have four literals.
- A rectangle surrounding two squares containing ones represents a term containing three literals.
- A rectangle surrounding four squares containing ones represents a term containing two literals.
- A rectangle surrounding eight squares containing ones represents a term containing a single literal.
- A rectangle surrounding 16 squares represents the function $F = 1$.

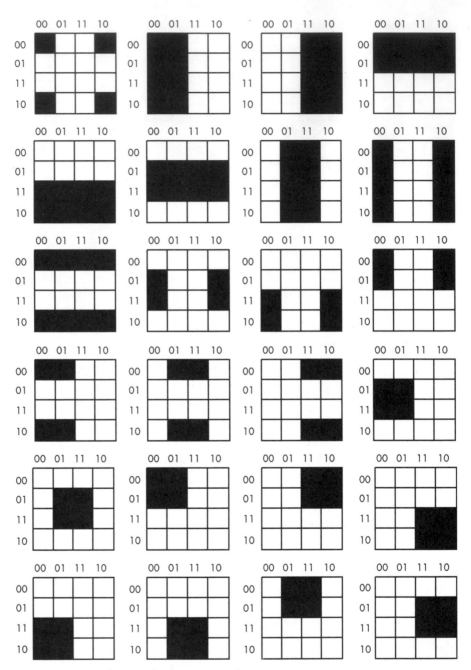

Figure 8-10: Partial pattern list for a 4×4 truth map

One final example will demonstrate the optimization of a function containing four variables. The function is $F = D'C'B'A' + D'C'B'A + D'C'BA + D'C'BA' + D'CB'A + D'CBA + DCB'A + DCBA + DC'B'A' + DC'BA'$, and the truth map appears in Figure 8-11.

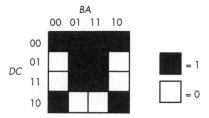

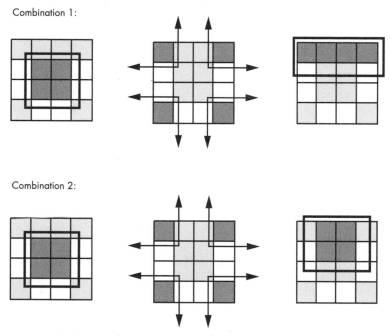

Figure 8-11: Truth map for F = D'C'B'A' + D'C'B'A + D'C'BA + D'C'BA' + D'CB'A + D'CBA + DCB'A + DCBA + DC'B'A' + DC'BA'

Here are two possible sets of maximal rectangles for this function, each producing three terms (see Figure 8-12). Both functions are equivalent; both are optimal (remember, there is no guarantee that there is a unique optimal solution). Either will suffice for our purposes.

Combination 1:

Combination 2:

Figure 8-12: Two combinations yielding three terms

First, let's consider the term represented by the rectangle formed by the four corners. This rectangle contains B, B', D, and D', so we can eliminate those terms. The remaining terms contained within these rectangles are C' and A', so this rectangle represents the term C'A'.

The second rectangle, common to both maps in Figure 8-12, is the rectangle formed by the middle four squares. This rectangle includes the terms A, B, B', C, D, and D'. Eliminating B, B', D, and D', we obtain CA as the term for this rectangle.

The uppermost of the two combinations in Figure 8-12 has a third term represented by the top row. This term includes the variables A, A', B, B', C' and D'. Because it contains A, A', B, and B', we can eliminate these terms.

This leaves the term $C'D'$. Therefore, the function represented by the upper truth map is $F = C'A' + CA + C'D'$.

The lower of the two combinations in Figure 8-12 has a third term represented by the top/middle four squares. This rectangle subsumes the variables A, B, B', C, C', and D'. We can eliminate B, B', C, and C' leaving the term AD. Therefore, the function represented by the lower truth map is $F = C'A' + CA + AD'$.

8.7   What Does This Have to Do with Computers, Anyway?

Although the connection between computer systems and Boolean logic in programming languages like C or Pascal may seem tenuous, it is actually much stronger than it first appears. There is a one-to-one relationship between the set of all Boolean functions and the set of all electronic circuits. Electrical engineers, who design CPUs and other computer-related circuits, have to be intimately familiar with this stuff.

Although the implementation of an algorithm in hardware is well beyond the scope of this book, one important point must be made with respect to such circuitry: Any algorithm you can implement in software, you can also implement directly in hardware. This means that any program you can write, you can also specify as a sequence of Boolean equations.

Of course, it is much easier to specify a solution to a programming problem using languages like Pascal, C, or even assembly language than it is to specify the solution using Boolean equations. Therefore, it is unlikely that you would ever implement an entire program using a set of state machines and other logic circuitry. Nevertheless, there are times when a hardware implementation is better. A hardware solution can be one, two, three, or more orders of magnitude faster than an equivalent software solution. Therefore, some time-critical operations may require a hardware solution.

A more interesting fact is that it is also possible to implement all hardware functions in software. This is important because many operations you would normally implement in hardware are much cheaper to implement using software on a microprocessor. Indeed, one of the primary uses of assembly language on modern systems is to inexpensively replace a complex electronic circuit. It is often possible to replace many tens or hundreds of dollars of electronic components with a single $5 microcomputer chip. The whole field of embedded systems deals with this very problem. Embedded systems are computer systems embedded in other products. For example, most microwave ovens, TV sets, video games, CD players, and other consumer devices contain one or more complete computer systems whose sole purpose is to replace a complex hardware design. Engineers use computers for this purpose because they are less expensive and easier to design with than traditional electronic circuitry.

You can easily design software that reads switches (input variables) and turns on motors, LEDs, or lights, or that locks or unlocks a door. To write such software, you will need an understanding of Boolean functions and of how to implement such functions in software.

8.7.1 Correspondence Between Electronic Circuits and Boolean Functions

For any Boolean function, you can design an equivalent electronic circuit and vice versa. Because Boolean functions only use the AND, OR, and NOT Boolean operators (these are the only operators that appear within canonical forms), we can construct any electronic circuit using only these three operations. The Boolean AND, OR, and NOT functions correspond to the AND, OR, and inverter (NOT) electronic circuit gates (see Figure 8-13). These symbols are standard electronic symbols appearing in *schematic diagrams.* (interested readers wanted to learn more about electronic schematic diagrams should check out any book on electronic design).

The lines to the left of each item in Figure 8-13, with the *A* and *B* labels, correspond to a logic function input; the line leaving each diagram corresponds to the function's output.

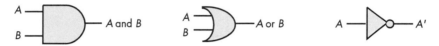

Figure 8-13: AND, OR, and inverter (NOT) gates

However, you actually need only a single gate type to implement *any* electronic circuit. This gate is the NAND (not AND) gate, shown in Figure 8-14. The NAND gate tests its two inputs (*A* and *B*) and presents a false on the output pin if both inputs are true, it places true on the output pin if both inputs are not true.

Figure 8-14: The NAND gate

To prove that we can construct any Boolean function using only NAND gates, we must show how to build an inverter (NOT), an AND gate, and an OR gate. Building an inverter is easy; just connect the two inputs together (see Figure 8-15).

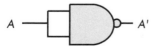

Figure 8-15: Inverter built from a NAND gate

Once we can build an inverter, building an AND gate is easy — just invert the output of a NAND gate. After all, NOT (NOT (*A* AND *B*)) is equivalent to *A* AND *B* (see Figure 8-16). Of course, this takes two NAND gates to construct a single AND gate, but no one said that circuits constructed only with NAND gates would be optimal, only that they would be possible.

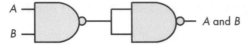

Figure 8-16: Constructing an AND gate from two NAND gates

The remaining gate we need to synthesize is the logical-OR gate. We can easily construct an OR gate from NAND gates by applying DeMorgan's Theorems.

(A or B)'	=	A' and B'	DeMorgan's Theorem.
A or B	=	(A' and B')'	Invert both sides of the equation.
A or B	=	A' nand B'	Definition of NAND operation.

By applying these transformations, you get the circuit in Figure 8-17.

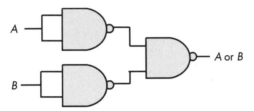

Figure 8-17: Constructing an OR gate from NAND gates

You might be wondering why we would even bother with this. After all, why not just use logical AND, OR, and inverter gates directly? There are two reasons. First, NAND gates are generally less expensive to build than other gates. Second, it is also much easier to build up complex integrated circuits from the same basic building blocks than it is to construct an integrated circuit using different basic gates.

8.7.2   Combinatorial Circuits

A computer's CPU is built from combinatorial circuits. A *combinatorial circuit* is a system containing basic Boolean operations (AND, OR, NOT), some inputs, and a set of outputs. A combinatorial circuit often implements several different Boolean functions, with each output corresponding to an individual logic function. It is very important that you remember that *each output represents a different Boolean function.*

8.7.2.1   Addition Circuits

You can implement addition using Boolean functions. Suppose you have two 1-bit numbers, *A* and *B*. You can produce the 1-bit sum and the 1-bit carry of this addition using these two Boolean functions:

```
S  =  AB' + A'B          Sum of A and B.
C  =  AB                 Carry from addition of A and B.
```

These two Boolean functions implement a *half adder*. Electrical engineers call it a half adder because it adds two bits together but cannot add in a carry from a previous operation. A *full adder* adds three 1-bit inputs (two bits plus a carry from a previous addition) and produces two outputs: the sum and the carry. These are the two logic equations for a full adder:

$$S = A'B'C_{in} + A'BC_{in}' + AB'C_{in}' + ABC_{in}$$
$$C_{out} = AB + AC_{in} + BC_{in}$$

Although these equations only produce a single bit result (plus a carry), it is easy to construct an *n*-bit sum by combining adder circuits (see Figure 8-18).

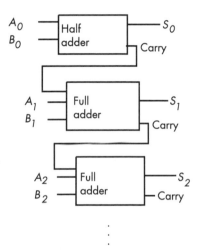

Figure 8-18: Building an n-bit adder using half and full adders

8.7.2.2 Seven-Segment LED Decoders

Another common combinatorial circuit is the *seven-segment decoder*. Decoder circuits are among the more important circuits in computer system design — they provide the ability to recognize (or *decode*) a string of bits.

 The seven-segment decoder circuit accepts an input of four bits and determines which segments to illuminate on a seven-segment LED display. Because a seven-segment display contains seven output values (one for each segment), there will be seven logic functions associated with it (segments zero through six). See Figure 8-19 for the segment assignments. Figure 8-20 shows the active segments for each of the ten decimal values.

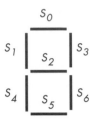

Figure 8-19: Seven-segment display

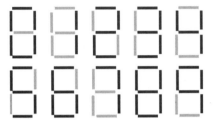

Figure 8-20: Seven-segment values for "0" through "9"

The four inputs to each of these seven Boolean functions are the four bits from a binary number in the range 0..9. Let D be the HO bit of this number and A be the LO bit. Each segment's logic function should produce a one (segment on) for all binary number inputs that have that segment illuminated in Figure 8-20. For example, S_4 (segment four) should be illuminated for numbers zero, two, six, and eight, which correspond to the binary values 0000, 0010, 0110, and 1000. For each of the binary values that illuminates a segment, you will have one minterm in the logic equation:

S_4 = D'C'B'A' + D'C'BA' + D'CBA' + DC'B'A'

S_0 (*segment zero*), as a second example, is on for the numbers zero, two, three, five, six, seven, eight, and nine, which correspond to the binary values 0000, 0010, 0011, 0101, 0110, 0111, 1000, and 1001. Therefore, the logic function for S_0 is as follows:

S_0 = D'C'B'A' + D'C'BA' + D'C'BA + D'CB'A + D'CBA' + D'CBA + DC'B'A' + DC'B'A

8.7.2.3 Decoding Memory Addresses

A decoder is also commonly used in memory expansion. For example, suppose a system designer wishes to install four (identical) 256-MB memory modules in a system to bring the total to 1 GB of RAM. Each of these 256-MB memory modules has 28 address lines ($A_0..A_{27}$), assuming each memory module is eight bits wide ($2^{28} \times 8$ bits is 256 MB).[1]

---

[1] Actually, most memory modules are wider than eight bits, so a real 256-MB memory module will have fewer than 28 address lines, but we will ignore this technicality in this example.

Unfortunately, if the system designer hooked up those four memory modules to the CPU's address bus, each of the modules would respond to the same addresses on the bus. Pandemonium would result. To correct this problem, each memory module needs to respond to a different set of addresses appearing on the address bus. By adding a chip-select line to each of the memory modules, and using a two-input, four-output decoder circuit, we can easily do this. See Figure 8-21 for the details.

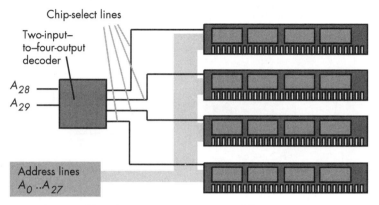

Figure 8-21: Adding four 256-MB memory modules to a system

The two-line–to–four-line decoder circuit in Figure 8-21 actually incorporates four different logic functions: one function for each of the outputs. Assuming the inputs are A and B ($A = A_{28}$ and $B = A_{29}$), then the four output functions are as follows:

Q_0 = A'B'
Q_1 = AB'
Q_2 = A'B
Q_3 = AB

Following standard electronic circuit notation, these equations use Q to denote an output. Also note that most circuit designers use *active low logic* for decoders and chip enables. This means that they enable a circuit when a low-input value (zero) is supplied and disable the circuit when a high-input value (one) is supplied. In a similar fashion, all the output lines of a decoder chip are normally high, and when the input values A and B select one particular output line, that line goes low. This means that these equations really need to be inverted for real-world examples. We have ignored this issue here and have used positive (or active high) logic.

8.7.2.4 Decoding Machine Instructions

Decoding circuits are also used to decode machine instructions. We'll cover this subject in much greater depth in Chapters 9 and 10, but a simple example is in order here.

Most modern computer systems represent machine instructions using binary values in memory. To execute an instruction, the CPU fetches the instruction's binary value from memory, decodes that value using decoder circuitry, and then does the appropriate work. To see how this is done, let's create a very simple CPU with a very simple instruction set. Figure 8-22 provides the instruction format (all the numeric codes that correspond to the various instructions) for our simple CPU.

WARNING *Do not conclude that the instruction format used in this example applies to any particular CPU's instruction set. The instruction format here is highly simplified to demonstrate instruction decoding.*

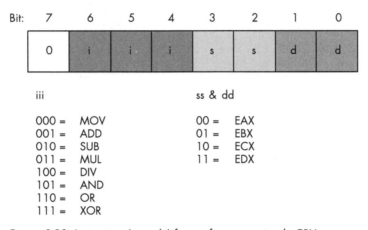

Figure 8-22: Instruction (opcode) format for a very simple CPU

To determine the 8-bit operation code (opcode) for a given instruction, the first thing you do is choose the instruction you want to encode. Let's pick mov(eax,ebx); as our simple example. To convert this instruction to its numeric equivalent, we follow these steps:

1. Look up the value for mov in the iii table in Figure 8-22. The corresponding value is 000, so we must substitute 000 for iii in the opcode byte.

2. Look up our source operand. The source operand is EAX, whose encoding in the source operand table (ss & dd) is 00. Therefore, we substitute 00 for ss in the instruction opcode.

3. Convert the destination operand to its numeric equivalent. The destination is in EBX, so we look up the value for this operand in the ss & dd table. Its value is 01, and we substitute 01 for dd in our opcode byte.

4. Assemble these three fields into the opcode byte (a packed data type), to obtain the bit value: %00000001.

Therefore, the numeric value $1 is the value for the mov(eax, ebx); instruction (see Figure 8-23).

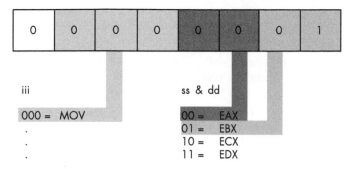

Figure 8-23: Encoding the MOV(EAX, EBX); instruction

Of course, in this example we were actually *encoding* the instructions. However, the real purpose of this exercise is to discover how the CPU can use a decoder circuit to decode the binary values for machine instructions and execute them at run time. A typical decoder circuit for this example appears in Figure 8-24.

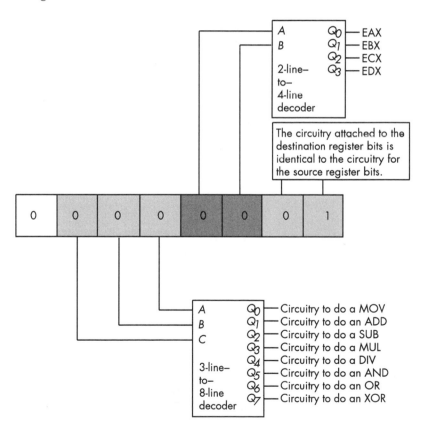

Figure 8-24: Decoding simple machine instructions

Notice how the circuit in Figure 8-24 uses three separate decoders to decode the individual fields of the opcode. This is much less complex than creating a single 7-line–to–128-line decoder to decode the entire opcode. Of course, all that the circuit in Figure 8-24 will do is tell you which instruction and what operands a given opcode specifies. To actually execute this instruction, you must supply additional circuitry to select the source and destination operands from an array of registers and act accordingly upon those operands. Such circuitry is beyond the scope of this chapter, so we'll save the juicy details for later.

8.7.3   Sequential and Clocked Logic

One major problem with combinatorial logic is that it is *memoryless*. In theory, all logic function outputs depend only on the current inputs. Any change in the input values immediately appears on the outputs.[2] Unfortunately, computers need the ability to *remember* the results of past computations. This is the domain of sequential, or clocked, logic.

8.7.3.1   The Set/Reset Flip-Flop

A *memory cell* is an electronic circuit that remembers an input value after the removal of that input value. The most basic memory unit is the *set/reset flip-flop* (S/R flip-flop). You can construct an *S/R flip-flop* memory cell using two NAND gates, as shown in Figure 8-25. In this diagram, you'll notice that the outputs of the two NAND gates are recirculated back to one of the inputs of the other NAND gate.

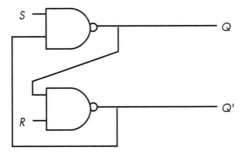

Figure 8-25: Set/reset flip flop constructed from NAND gates

The S and R inputs are normally high, or one. If you toggle the S input by *temporarily* setting its value to zero and then bringing it back to one, the Q output is set to one. Likewise, if you toggle the R input from one to zero and back to one, this sets the Q output to zero.

Notice that if both S and R are one, then the Q output depends upon the original value of Q itself. That is, whatever Q happens to be, the top NAND gate continues to output that same value. If Q was originally one, then the bottom NAND gate receives two inputs of one (both Q and R), and the

---

[2] In practice, there is a short *propagation delay* between a change in the inputs and the corresponding outputs in any electronic implementation of a Boolean function.

bottom NAND gate produces an output of zero (Q'). As a result, the two inputs to the top NAND gate are zero and one, and the top NAND gate produces an output of one, matching the original value for Q.

On the other hand, if the original value of Q was zero, then the inputs to the bottom NAND gate are $Q = 0$ and $R = 1$, and the output of this bottom NAND gate is one. As a result, the inputs to the top NAND gate are $S = 1$ and $Q' = 1$. This produces a zero output, the original value of Q.

Now suppose Q is zero, S is zero, and R is one. This sets the two inputs to the top NAND gate to one and zero, forcing the output (Q) to one. Returning S to the high state does not change the output at all, because the value of Q' is one. You will obtain this same result if Q is one, S is zero, and R is one. Again, this produces a Q output value of one, and again this value remains one even when S switches from zero to one. To overcome this and produce a Q output of one, you must toggle the S input. The same idea applies to the R input, except that toggling it forces the Q output to zero rather than to one.

There is one catch to this circuit. It does not operate properly if you set both the S and R inputs to zero simultaneously. This forces both the Q and Q' outputs to one (which is logically inconsistent). Whichever input remains zero the longest determines the final state of the flip-flop. A flip-flop operating in this mode is said to be *unstable*.

Table 8-9 lists all the output configurations for an S/R flip-flop based on the current inputs and the previous output values.

Table 8-9: S/R Flip-Flop Output States Based on Current Inputs and Previous Outputs

Previous Q	Previous Q'	S Input	R Input	Q Output	Q' Output
x[1]	x	0 (1 → 0 → 1)	1	1	0
x	x	1	0 (1 → 0 → 1)	0	1
x	x	0	0	1	1[2]
0	1	1	1	0	1
1	0	1	1	1	0

[1] x = *don't care,* implying that the value may be zero or one and it won't affect the outputs.
[2] This is an *unstable* configuration and will change once S or R are set to one.

8.7.3.2   The D Flip-Flop

The only problem with the S/R flip-flop is that to be able to remember either a zero or a one value, you must have two different inputs. A memory cell would be more valuable to us if we could specify the data value to remember with one input value and supply a second *clock input* value to *latch* the data input value.[3] This type of flip-flop, the D flip-flop (*D* stands for *data*) uses the circuit in Figure 8-26.

---

[3] "Latch" simply means to *remember* the value. That is, a D flip-flop is the basic memory element because it can remember one data bit appearing on its D input.

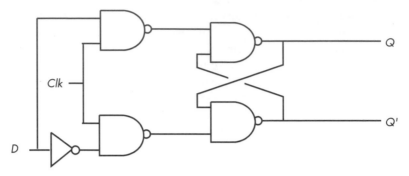

Figure 8-26: Implementing a D flip-flop with NAND gates

Assuming you fix the Q and Q' outputs to either 0/1 or 1/0, sending a *clock pulse* that goes from zero to one and back to zero will copy the D input to the Q output (and set Q' to the inverse of Q). To see how this works, just note that the right half of the circuit diagram in Figure 8-26 is an S/R flip-flop. If the data input is one while the clock line is high, this places a zero on the S input of the S/R flip-flop (and a one on the R input). Conversely, if the data input is zero while the clock line is high, this places a zero on the R input (and a one on the S input) of the S/R flip-flop, thus clearing the S/R flip-flop's output. Whenever the clock input is low, both the S and R input are high, and the outputs of the S/R flip-flop do not change.

Although remembering a single bit is often important, in most computer systems you will want to remember a group of bits. You can do this by combining several D flip-flops in parallel. Concatenating flip-flops to store an *n*-bit value forms a *register*. The electronic schematic in Figure 8-27 shows how to build an 8-bit register from a set of D flip-flops.

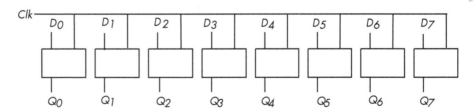

Figure 8-27: An 8-bit register implemented with eight D flip-flops

Note that the eight D flip-flops in Figure 8-27 use a common clock line. This diagram does not show the Q' outputs on the flip-flops because they are rarely required in a register.

D flip-flops are useful for building many sequential circuits beyond simple registers. For example, you can build a *shift register* that shifts the bits one position to the left on each clock pulse. A 4-bit shift register appears in Figure 8-28.

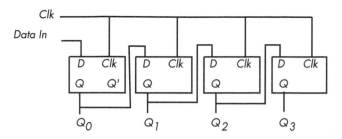

Figure 8-28: A 4-bit shift register built from D flip-flops

You can even build a *counter* that counts the number of times the clock toggles from one to zero and back to one using flip-flops. The circuit in Figure 8-29 implements a four bit counter using D flip-flops.

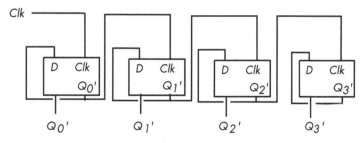

Figure 8-29: A 4-bit counter built from D flip-flops

Surprisingly, you can build an entire CPU with combinatorial circuits and only a few additional sequential circuits. For example, you can build a simple state machine known as a sequencer by combining a counter and a decoder, as shown in Figure 8-30.

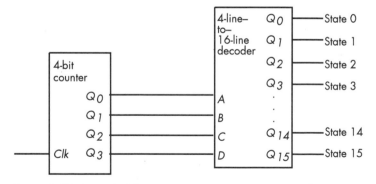

Figure 8-30: A simple 16-state sequencer

For each cycle of the clock in Figure 8-30, this sequencer activates one of its output lines. Those lines, in turn, may control other circuits. By "firing" those other circuits on each of the 16 output lines of the decoder, we can control the order in which the circuits accomplish their tasks. This is essential in a CPU, as we often need to control the sequence of various operations. For example, it wouldn't be a good thing if the add(eax,ebx); instruction stored the result into EBX before fetching the source operand from EAX (or EBX). A simple sequencer such as this one can tell the CPU when to fetch the first operand, when to fetch the second operand, when to add them together, and when to store the result away. However, we're getting a little ahead of ourselves; we'll discuss this in detail in the next two chapters.

8.8 For More Information

A good understanding of Boolean algebra and digital design is necessary for anyone who wants to understand the internal operation of a CPU. As an added bonus, programmers who understand digital design can write better programs. Although a detailed knowledge of Boolean algebra and digital circuit design isn't necessary if you simply want to write typical programs, this knowledge will help explain why CPU manufacturers have chosen to implement instructions in certain ways. These questions will undoubtedly arise as we begin to look at the low-level implementation of the CPU.

This chapter is not, by any means, a complete treatment of this subject. If you're interested in learning more about Boolean algebra and digital circuit design, there are dozens and dozens of books on this subject.

9

CPU ARCHITECTURE

Great code is aware of the underlying
hardware on which it executes. Without
question, the design of the central processing unit (CPU) has the greatest impact
on the performance of your software. This
chapter, and the next, discuss the design of CPUs and
their instruction sets — information that is absolutely
crucial for writing high-performance software.

9.1 Basic CPU Design

A CPU is capable of executing a set of commands (or machine instructions),
each of which accomplishes some small task. To execute a particular instruction,
a CPU requires a certain amount of electronic circuitry specific to that
instruction. Therefore, as you increase the number of instructions the CPU
can support, you also increase the complexity of the CPU and you increase the
amount of circuitry (logic gates) needed to support those instructions. To keep

the number of logic gates on the CPU reasonably small (thus lowering the CPU's cost), CPU designers must restrict the number and complexity of the instructions that the CPU is capable of executing. This small set of instructions is the CPU's *instruction set*.

Programs in early computer systems were often "hardwired" into the circuitry. That is, the computer's wiring determined exactly what algorithm the computer would execute. One had to rewire the computer in order to use the computer to solve a different problem. This was a difficult task, something that only electrical engineers were able to do. The next advance in computer design was the programmable computer system, one that allowed a computer operator to easily "rewire" the computer system using sockets and plug wires (a *patch board* system). A computer program consisted of rows of sockets, with each row representing one operation during the execution of the program. The programmer could determine which of several instructions would be executed by plugging a wire into the particular socket for the desired instruction (see Figure 9-1).

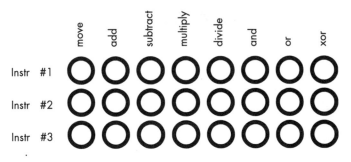

Figure 9-1: Patch board programming

Of course, a major problem with this scheme was that the number of possible instructions was severely limited by the number of sockets one could physically place on each row. CPU designers quickly discovered that with a small amount of additional logic circuitry, they could reduce the number of sockets required for specifying n different instructions from n sockets to $\log_2(n)$ sockets. They did this by assigning a unique numeric code to each instruction and then representing each code as a binary number (for example, Figure 9-2 shows how to represent eight instructions using only three bits).

The example in Figure 9-2 requires eight logic functions to decode the A, B, and C bits on the patch board, but the extra circuitry (a single three-line–to–eight-line decoder) is worth the cost because it reduces the total number of sockets from eight to three for each instruction.

Of course, many CPU instructions do not stand alone. For example, a move instruction is a command that moves data from one location in the computer to another, such as from one register to another. The move instruction requires two operands: a source operand and a destination operand. The CPU's designer usually encodes the source and destination operands as part of the machine instruction, with certain sockets corresponding to the source and certain sockets corresponding to the destination.

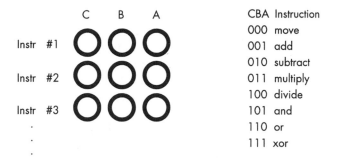

CBA	Instruction
000	move
001	add
010	subtract
011	multiply
100	divide
101	and
110	or
111	xor

Figure 9-2: Encoding instructions

Figure 9-3 shows one possible combination of sockets that would handle this. The move instruction would move data from the source register to the destination register, the add instruction would add the value of the source register to the destination register, and so on. This scheme allows the encoding of 128 different instructions with just seven sockets per instruction.

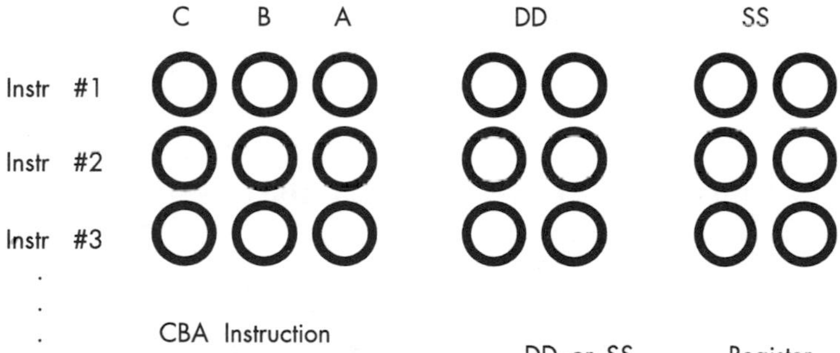

CBA	Instruction
000	move
001	add
010	subtract
011	multiply
100	divide
101	and
110	or
111	xor

DD -or- SS	Register
00	AX
01	BX
10	CX
11	DX

Figure 9-3: Encoding instructions with source and destination fields

One of the primary advances in computer design was the invention of the *stored program computer*. A big problem with patch-board programming was that the number of machine instructions in a program was limited by the number of rows of sockets available on the machine. Early computer designers recognized a relationship between the sockets on the patch board and bits in memory. They figured they could store the numeric equivalent of a machine instruction in main memory, fetch the instruction's numeric equivalent from memory when the CPU wanted to execute the instruction, and then load that binary number into a special register to decode the instruction.

The trick was to add additional circuitry, called the control unit (CU), to the CPU. The control unit uses a special register, the instruction pointer, that holds the address of an instruction's numeric code (also known as an *operation code* or *opcode*). The control unit fetches this instruction's opcode from memory and places it in the instruction decoding register for execution. After executing the instruction, the control unit increments the instruction pointer and fetches the next instruction from memory for execution. This process repeats for each instruction the program executes.

The goal of the CPU's designer is to assign an appropriate number of bits to the opcode's instruction field and to its operand fields. Choosing more bits for the instruction field lets the opcode encode more instructions, just as choosing more bits for the operand fields lets the opcode specify a larger number of operands (often memory locations or registers). However, some instructions have only one operand, while others don't have any operands at all. Rather than waste the bits associated with these operand fields for instructions that don't have the maximum number of operands, the CPU designers often reuse these fields to encode additional opcodes, once again with some additional circuitry. The Intel 80x86 CPU family is a good example of this, with machine instructions ranging from 1 to almost 15 bytes long.[1]

9.2 Decoding and Executing Instructions: Random Logic Versus Microcode

Once the control unit fetches an instruction from memory, you may wonder, "Exactly how does the CPU execute this instruction?" In traditional CPU design there have been two common approaches used: hardwired logic and emulation (microcode). The 80x86 family, for example, uses both of these techniques.

A hardwired, or *random logic*,[2] approach uses decoders, latches, counters, and other hardware logic devices to operate on the opcode data. The microcode approach involves a very fast but simple internal processor that uses the CPU's opcodes as indexes into a table of operations called the *microcode*, and then executes a sequence of *microinstructions* that do the work of the *macroinstruction* they are emulating.

---

[1] Though this is, by no means, the most complex instruction set. The VAX, for example, has instructions up to 150 bytes long!

[2] There is actually nothing random about this logic at all. This design technique gets its name from the fact that if you view a photomicrograph of a CPU die that uses microcode, the microcode section looks very regular; the same photograph of a CPU that utilizes random logic contains no such easily discernible patterns.

The random-logic approach has the advantage of decreasing the amount of time it takes to execute an opcode's instruction, provided that typical CPU speeds are faster than memory speeds, a situation that has been true for quite some time. The drawback to the random-logic approach is that it is difficult to design the necessary circuitry for CPUs with large and complex instruction sets. The hardware logic that executes the instructions winds up requiring a large percentage of the chip's real estate, and it becomes difficult to properly lay out the logic so that related circuits are close to one another in the two-dimensional space of the chip.

CPUs based on microcode contain a small, very fast *execution unit* (circuitry in the CPU that is responsible for executing a particular function) that uses the binary opcode to select a set of instructions from the microcode bank. This microcode executes one microinstruction per clock cycle, and the sequence of microinstructions executes all the steps to do whatever calculations are necessary for that instruction.

The microcode approach may appear to be substantially slower than the random-logic approach because of all the steps involved. But this isn't necessarily true. Keep in mind that with a random-logic approach to instruction execution, a sequencer that steps through several states (one state per clock cycle) often makes up part of the random logic. Whether you use up clock cycles executing microinstructions or stepping through a random-logic state machine, you're still burning up time.

However, microcode does suffer from one disadvantage compared to random logic: the speed at which the processor runs can be limited by the speed of the internal microcode execution unit. Although this *micro-engine* itself is usually quite fast, the micro-engine must fetch its instructions from the microcode ROM (read-only memory). Therefore, if memory technology is slower than the execution logic, the system will have to introduce wait states into the microcode ROM access, thus slowing the micro-engine down. However, micro-engines generally don't support the use of wait states, so this means that the micro-engine must run at the same speed as the microcode ROM, which effectively limits the speed at which the micro-engine, and therefore the CPU, can run.

Which approach is better for CPU design? That depends entirely on the current state of memory technology. If memory technology is faster than CPU technology, the microcode approach tends to make more sense. If memory technology is slower than CPU technology, random logic tends to produce faster execution of machine instructions.

9.3 Executing Instructions, Step by Step

To be able to write great code, you need to understand how a CPU executes individual machine instructions. To that end, let's consider four representative 80x86 instructions: mov, add, loop, and jnz (jump if not zero). By understanding these four instructions, you can get a good feel for how a CPU executes all the instructions in the instruction set.

The mov instruction copies the data from the source operand to the destination operand. The add instruction adds the value of its source operand to its destination operand. The loop and jnz instructions are *conditional-jump* instructions — they test some condition and then jump to some other instruction in memory if the condition is true, or continue with the next instruction if the condition is false. The jnz instruction tests a Boolean variable within the CPU known as the *zero flag* and either transfers control to the target instruction if the zero flag contains zero, or continues with the next instruction if the zero flag contains one. The program specifies the address of the target instruction (the instruction to jump to) by specifying the distance, in bytes, from the jnz instruction to the target instruction in memory.

The loop instruction decrements the value of the ECX register and transfers control to a target instruction if ECX does not contain zero (after the decrement). This is a good example of a *Complex Instruction Set Computer* (CISC) instruction because it does multiple operations:

1. It subtracts one from ECX.
2. It does a conditional jump if ECX does not contain zero.

That is, loop is roughly equivalent to the following instruction sequence:

```
sub( 1, ecx ); // On the 80x86, the sub instruction sets the zero flag
jnz SomeLabel; // the result of the subtraction is zero.
```

To execute the mov, add, jnz, and loop instructions, the CPU has to execute a number of different steps. Although each 80x86 CPU is different and doesn't necessarily execute the exact same steps, these CPUs do execute a similar sequence of operations. Each operation requires a finite amount of time to execute, and the time required to execute the entire instruction generally amounts to one clock cycle per operation or stage (as we usually refer to each of these steps) that the CPU executes. Obviously, the more steps needed for an instruction, the slower it will run. Complex instructions generally run slower than simple instructions, because complex instructions usually have many execution stages.

9.3.1 The mov Instruction

Although each CPU is different and may run different steps when executing instructions, the 80x86 mov(*srcReg,destReg*); instruction could use the following execution steps:

1. Fetch the instruction's opcode from memory.
2. Update the EIP (extended instruction pointer) register with the address of the byte following the opcode.
3. Decode the instruction's opcode to see what instruction it specifies.

4. Fetch the data from the source register (srcReg).

5. Store the fetched value into the destination register (destReg).

The mov(srcReg,destMem); instruction could use the following execution steps:

1. Fetch the instruction's opcode from memory.

2. Update the EIP register with the address of the byte following the opcode.

3. Decode the instruction's opcode to see what instruction it specifies.

4. Fetch the displacement associated with the memory operand from the memory location immediately following the opcode.

5. Update EIP to point at the first byte beyond the operand that follows the opcode.

6. If the mov instruction uses a complex addressing mode (for example, the indexed addressing mode), compute the effective address of the destination memory location.

7. Fetch the data from srcReg.

8. Store the fetched value into the destination memory location.

Note that a mov(srcMem,destReg); instruction is very similar, simply swapping the register access for the memory access in these steps.

The mov(constant,destReg); instruction could use the following execution steps:

1. Fetch the instruction's opcode from memory.

2. Update the EIP register with the address of the byte following the opcode.

3. Decode the instruction's opcode to see what instruction it specifies.

4. Fetch the constant associated with the source operand from the memory location immediately following the opcode.

5. Update EIP to point at the first byte beyond the constant that follows the opcode.

6. Store the constant value into the destination register.

Assuming each step requires one clock cycle for execution, this sequence will require six clock cycles to execute.

The mov(constant,destMem); instruction could use the following execution steps:

1. Fetch the instruction's opcode from memory.

2. Update the EIP register with the address of the byte following the opcode.

3. Decode the instruction's opcode to see what instruction it specifies.

4. Fetch the displacement associated with the memory operand from the memory location immediately following the opcode.

5. Update EIP to point at the first byte beyond the operand that follows the opcode.

6. Fetch the constant operand's value from the memory location immediately following the displacement associated with the memory operand.

7. Update EIP to point at the first byte beyond the constant.

8. If the mov instruction uses a complex addressing mode (for example, the indexed addressing mode), compute the effective address of the destination memory location.

9. Store the constant value into the destination memory location.

9.3.2 The add Instruction

The add instruction is a little more complex. Here's a typical set of operations that the add(srcReg,destReg); instruction must complete:

1. Fetch the instruction's opcode from memory.

2. Update the EIP register with the address of the byte following the opcode.

3. Decode the instruction's opcode to see what instruction it specifies.

4. Fetch the value of the source register and send it to the arithmetic logical unit (ALU), which handles arithmetic on the CPU.

5. Fetch the value of the destination register operand and send it to the ALU.

6. Instruct the ALU to add the values.

7. Store the result back into the destination register operand.

8. Update the flags register with the result of the addition operation.

NOTE *The flags register, also known as the condition-codes register or program-status word, is an array of Boolean variables in the CPU that tracks whether the previous instruction produced an overflow, a zero result, a negative result, or other such condition.*

If the source operand is a memory location instead of a register, and the add instruction takes the form add(srcMem,destReg); then the operation is slightly more complicated:

1. Fetch the instruction's opcode from memory.

2. Update the EIP register with the address of the byte following the opcode.

3. Decode the instruction's opcode to see what instruction it specifies.

4. Fetch the displacement associated with the memory operand from the memory location immediately following the opcode.

5. Update EIP to point at the first byte beyond the operand that follows the opcode.

6. If the add instruction uses a complex addressing mode (for example, the indexed addressing mode), compute the effective address of the source memory location.

7. Fetch the source operand's data from memory and send it to the ALU.

8. Fetch the value of the destination register operand and send it to the ALU.

9. Instruct the ALU to add the values.

10. Store the result back into the destination register operand.

11. Update the flags register with the result of the addition operation.

If the source operand is a constant and the destination operand is a register, the add instruction takes the form add(constant,destReg); and here is how the CPU might deal with it:

1. Fetch the instruction's opcode from memory.

2. Update the EIP register with the address of the byte following the opcode.

3. Decode the instruction's opcode to see what instruction it specifies.

4. Fetch the constant operand that immediately follows the opcode in memory and send it to the ALU.

5. Update EIP to point at the first byte beyond the constant that follows the opcode.

6. Fetch the value of the destination register operand and send it to the ALU.

7. Instruct the ALU to add the values.

8. Store the result back into the destination register operand.

9. Update the flags register with the result of the addition operation.

This instruction sequence requires nine cycles to complete.

If the source operand is a constant, and the destination operand is a memory location, then the add instruction takes the form add(constant, destMem); and the operation is slightly more complicated:

1. Fetch the instruction's opcode from memory.

2. Update the EIP register with the address of the byte following the opcode.

3. Decode the instruction's opcode to see what instruction it specifies.

4. Fetch the displacement associated with the memory operand from memory immediately following the opcode.

5. Update EIP to point at the first byte beyond the operand that follows the opcode.

6. If the add instruction uses a complex addressing mode (for example, the indexed addressing mode), compute the effective address of the destination memory location.

7. Fetch the constant operand that immediately follows the memory operand's displacement value and send it to the ALU.

8. Fetch the destination operand's data from memory and send it to the ALU.

9. Update EIP to point at the first byte beyond the constant that follows the memory operand.

10. Instruct the ALU to add the values.

11. Store the result back into the destination memory operand.

12. Update the flags register with the result of the addition operation.

This instruction sequence requires 11 or 12 cycles to complete, depending on whether the effective address computation is necessary.

9.3.3 The jnz Instruction

Because the 80x86 jnz instruction does not allow different types of operands, there is only one sequence of steps needed for this instruction. The jnz label; instruction might use the following sequence of steps:

1. Fetch the instruction's opcode from memory.

2. Update the EIP register with the address of the displacement value following the instruction.

3. Decode the opcode to see what instruction it specifies.

4. Fetch the displacement value (the jump distance) and send it to the ALU.

5. Update the EIP register to hold the address of the instruction following the displacement operand.

6. Test the zero flag to see if it is clear (that is, if it contains zero).

7. If the zero flag was clear, copy the value in EIP to the ALU.

8. If the zero flag was clear, instruct the ALU to add the displacement and EIP values.

9. If the zero flag was clear, copy the result of the addition back to the EIP.

Notice how the jnz instruction requires fewer steps, and thus runs in fewer clock cycles, if the jump is not taken. This is very typical for conditional-jump instructions.

9.3.4 The loop Instruction

Because the 80x86 loop instruction does not allow different types of operands, there is only one sequence of steps needed for this instruction. The 80x86 loop instruction might use an execution sequence like the following:

1. Fetch the instruction's opcode from memory.
2. Update the EIP register with the address of the displacement operand following the opcode.
3. Decode the opcode to see what instruction it specifies.
4. Fetch the value of the ECX register and send it to the ALU.
5. Instruct the ALU to decrement this value.
6. Send the result back to the ECX register. Set a special internal flag if this result is nonzero.
7. Fetch the displacement value (the jump distance) following the opcode in memory and send it to the ALU.
8. Update the EIP register with the address of the instruction following the displacement operand.
9. Test the special internal flag to see if ECX was nonzero.
10. If the flag was set (that is, it contains one), copy the value in EIP to the ALU.
11. If the flag was set, instruct the ALU to add the displacement and EIP values.
12. If the flag was set, copy the result of the addition back to the EIP register.

As with the jnz instruction, you'll note that the loop instruction executes more rapidly if the branch is not taken and the CPU continues execution with the instruction that immediately follows the loop instruction.

9.4 Parallelism — The Key to Faster Processing

If we can reduce the amount of time it takes for a CPU to execute the individual instructions appearing in that CPU's instruction set, it should be fairly clear that an application containing a sequence of those instructions will also run faster (compared with executing that sequence on a CPU whose individual instructions have not been sped up). Though the steps associated with a particular instruction's execution are usually beyond the control of a software engineer, understanding those steps and why the CPU designer chose an particular implementation for an instruction can help you pick more appropriate instruction sequences that execute faster.

An early goal of the *Reduced Instruction Set Computer* (RISC) processors was to execute one instruction per clock cycle, on the average. However, even if a RISC instruction is simplified, the actual execution of the instruction still requires multiple steps. So how could they achieve the goal? The answer is parallelism.

Consider the following steps for a mov(srcReg,destReg); instruction:

1. Fetch the instruction's opcode from memory.
2. Update the EIP register with the address of the byte following the opcode.

3. Decode the instruction's opcode to see what instruction it specifies.

4. Fetch the data from srcReg.

5. Store the fetched value into the destination register (destReg).

There are five stages in the execution of this instruction, with certain dependencies existing between most of the stages. For example, the CPU must fetch the instruction's opcode from memory before it updates the EIP register instruction with the address of the byte beyond the opcode. Likewise, the CPU won't know that it needs to fetch the value of the source register until it decodes the instruction's opcode. Finally, the CPU must fetch the value of the source register before it can store the fetched value in the destination register.

All but one of the stages in the execution of this mov instruction are *serial*. That is, the CPU must execute one stage before proceeding to the next. The one exception is step 2, updating the EIP register. Although this stage must follow the first stage, none of the following stages in the instruction depend upon this step. Therefore, this could be the third, forth, or fifth step in the calculation and it wouldn't affect the outcome of the instruction. Further, we could execute this step concurrently with any of the other steps, and it wouldn't affect the operation of the mov instruction. By doing two of the stages in parallel, we can reduce the execution time of this instruction by one clock cycle. The following list of steps illustrates one possible concurrent execution:

1. Fetch the instruction's opcode from memory.

2. Decode the instruction's opcode to see what instruction it specifies.

3. Fetch the data from srcReg *and* update the EIP register with the address of the byte following the opcode.

4. Store the fetched value into the destination register (destReg).

Although the remaining stages in the mov(*reg,reg*); instruction must remain serialized, other forms of the mov instruction offer similar opportunities to save cycles by overlapping stages of their execution. For example, consider the 80x86 mov([ebx+*disp*],eax); instruction:

1. Fetch the instruction's opcode from memory.

2. Update the EIP register with the address of the byte following the opcode.

3. Decode the instruction's opcode to see what instruction it specifies.

4. Fetch the displacement value for use in calculating the effective address of the source operand.

5. Update EIP to point at the first byte after the displacement value in memory.

6. Compute the effective address of the source operand.

7. Fetch the value of the source operand's data from memory.

8. Store the result into the destination register operand.

Once again, there is the opportunity to overlap the execution of several stages in this instruction. In the following example, we reduce the number of execution steps from eight to six by overlapping both updates of EIP with two other operations:

1. Fetch the instruction's opcode from memory.

2. Decode the instruction's opcode to see what instruction it specifies, *and* update the EIP register with the address of the byte following the opcode.

3. Fetch the displacement value for use in calculating the effective address of the source operand.

4. Compute the effective address of the source operand, *and* update EIP to point at the first byte after the displacement value in memory.

5. Fetch the value of the source operand's data from memory.

6. Store the result into the destination register operand.

As a last example, consider the add(*constant*,[ebx+*disp*]); instruction (the instruction with the largest number of steps we've considered thus far). It's non-overlapped execution looks like this:

1. Fetch the instruction's opcode from memory.

2. Update the EIP register with the address of the byte following the opcode.

3. Decode the instruction's opcode to see what instruction it specifies.

4. Fetch the displacement value from the memory location immediately following the opcode.

5. Update EIP to point at the first byte beyond the displacement operand that follows the opcode.

6. Compute the effective address of the second operand.

7. Fetch the constant operand that immediately follows the displacement value in memory and send it to the ALU.

8. Fetch the destination operand's data from memory and send it to the ALU.

9. Update EIP to point at the first byte beyond the constant that follows the displacement operand.

10. Instruct the ALU to add the values.

11. Store the result back into the destination (second) operand.

12. Update the flags register with the result of the addition operation.

We can overlap several steps in this instruction by noting that certain stages don't depend on the result of their immediate predecessor:

1. Fetch the instruction's opcode from memory.

2. Decode the instruction's opcode to see what instruction it specifies *and* update the EIP register with the address of the byte following the opcode.

3. Fetch the displacement value from the memory location immediately following the opcode.

4. Update EIP to point at the first byte beyond the displacement operand that follows the opcode *and* compute the effective address of the memory operand (EBX+disp).

5. Fetch the constant operand that immediately follows the displacement value and send it to the ALU.

6. Fetch the destination operand's data from memory and send it to the ALU.

7. Instruct the ALU to add the values *and* update EIP to point at the first byte beyond the constant value

8. Store the result back into the second operand *and* update the flags register with the result of the addition operation.

Although it might seem possible to fetch the constant and the memory operand in the same step because their values do not depend upon one another, the CPU can't actually do this (yet!) because it has only a single data bus, and both values are coming from memory. However, in the next section you'll see how we can overcome this problem.

By overlapping various stages in the execution of these instructions, we've been able to substantially reduce the number of steps, and consequently the number of clock cycles, that the instructions need to complete execution. This process of executing various steps of the instruction in parallel with other steps is a major key to improving CPU performance without cranking up the clock speed on the chip. However, there's only so much to be gained from this approach alone, because instruction execution is still serialized. Starting with the next section we'll start to see how to overlap the execution of adjacent instructions in order to save additional cycles.

9.4.1 The Prefetch Queue

The key to improving the speed of a processor is to perform operations in parallel. If we were able to do two operations on each clock cycle, the CPU would execute instructions twice as fast when running at the same clock speed. However, simply deciding to execute two operations per clock cycle doesn't make accomplishing it easy.

As you have seen, the steps of the add instruction that involve adding two values and then storing their sum cannot be done concurrently, because you cannot store the sum until after you've computed it. Furthermore, there are some resources that the CPU cannot share between steps in an instruction.

There is only one data bus, and the CPU cannot fetch an instruction's opcode while it is trying to store some data to memory. In addition, many of the steps that make up the execution of an instruction share *functional units* in the CPU. Functional units are groups of logic that perform a common operation, such as the *arithmetic logical unit* (ALU) and the *control unit* (CU). A functional unit is only capable of one operation at a time. You cannot do two operations concurrently that use the same functional unit. To design a CPU that executes several steps in parallel, one must arrange those steps to reduce potential conflicts, or add additional logic so the two (or more) operations can occur simultaneously by executing in different functional units.

Consider again the steps a mov(srcMem, destReg); instruction might require:

1. Fetch the instruction's opcode from memory.
2. Update the EIP register to hold the address of the displacement value following the opcode.
3. Decode the instruction's opcode to see what instruction it specifies.
4. Fetch the displacement value from memory to compute the source operand's effective address.
5. Update the EIP register to hold the address of the byte beyond the displacement value.
6. Compute the effective address of the source operand.
7. Fetch the value of the source operand.
8. Store the fetched value into the destination register.

The first operation uses the value of the EIP register, so we cannot overlap it with the subsequent step, which adjusts the value in EIP. In addition, the first operation uses the bus to fetch the instruction opcode from memory, and because every step that follows this one depends upon this opcode, it is unlikely we will be able to overlap this first step with any other.

The second and third operations do not share any functional units, and the third operation doesn't depend upon the value of the EIP register, which is modified in the second step. Therefore, we can easily modify the control unit so that it combines these steps, adjusting the EIP register at the same time that it decodes the instruction. This will shave one cycle off the execution of the mov instruction.

The third and fourth steps, which decode the instruction's opcode and fetch the displacement value, do not look like they can be done in parallel because you must decode the instruction's opcode to determine whether the CPU needs to fetch a displacement operand from memory. However, we can design the CPU to go ahead and fetch the displacement anyway, so that it's available if we need it.

Of course, there is no way to overlap the execution of steps 7 and 8 in the mov instruction because it must surely fetch the value before storing it away.

By combining all the steps that are possible, we might obtain the following for a mov instruction:

1. Fetch the instruction's opcode from memory.
2. Decode the instruction's opcode to see what instruction it specifies, *and* update the EIP register to hold the address of the displacement value following the opcode.
3. Fetch the displacement value from memory to compute the source operand's effective address, *and* update the EIP register to hold the address of the byte beyond the displacement value.
4. Compute the effective address of the source operand.
5. Fetch the value of the source operand from memory.
6. Store the fetched value into the destination register.

By adding a small amount of logic to the CPU, we've shaved one or two cycles off the execution of the mov instruction. This simple optimization works with most of the other instructions as well.

9.4.1.1 Saving Fetched Bytes

Now that we've looked at some simple optimization techniques, consider what happens when the mov instruction executes on a CPU with a 32-bit data bus. If the mov instruction fetches an 8-bit displacement value from memory, the CPU may actually wind up fetching an additional three bytes along with the displacement value (the 32-bit data bus lets us fetch four bytes in a single bus cycle). The second byte on the data bus is actually the opcode of the next instruction. If we could save this opcode until the execution of the next instruction, we could shave a cycle off its execution time because it would not have to fetch the same opcode byte again.

9.4.1.2 Using Unused Bus Cycles

Can we make any more improvements? The answer is yes. Note that during the execution of the mov instruction, the CPU is not accessing memory on every clock cycle. For example, while storing the data into the destination register, the bus is idle. When the bus is idle, we can prefetch and save the instruction opcode and operands of the next instruction.

The hardware that does this is the prefetch queue. Figure 9-4 shows the internal organization of a CPU with a prefetch queue. The Bus Interface Unit (BIU), as its name implies, is responsible for controlling access to the address and data buses. The BIU acts as a "traffic cop" and handles simultaneous requests for bus access by different modules, such as the execution unit and the prefetch queue. Whenever some component inside the CPU wishes to access main memory, it sends this request to the BIU.

Whenever the execution unit is not using the BIU, the BIU can fetch additional bytes from the memory that holds the machine instructions and store them in the prefetch queue. Then, whenever the CPU needs an instruction opcode or operand value, it grabs *the next available byte* from the prefetch queue. Because the BIU grabs multiple bytes at a time from memory, and because, per clock cycle, it generally consumes fewer bytes from the prefetch queue than are in the queue, instructions will normally be sitting in the prefetch queue for the CPU's use.

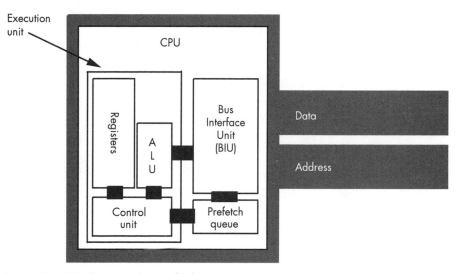

Figure 9-4: CPU design with a prefetch queue

Note, however, that we're not guaranteed that all instructions and operands will be sitting in the prefetch queue when we need them. For example, consider the 80x86 jnz Label; instruction. If the 2-byte form of the instruction appears at locations 400 and 401 in memory, the prefetch queue may contain the bytes at addresses 402, 403, 404, 405, 406, 407, and so on. Now consider what happens if jnz transfers control to Label. If the target address of the jnz instruction is 480, the bytes at addresses 402, 403, 404, and so on, won't be of any use to the CPU. The system will have to pause for a moment to fetch the data at address 480 before it can go on. Most of the time the CPU fetches sequential values from memory, though, so having the data in the prefetch queue saves time.

9.4.1.3 Overlapping Instructions

Another improvement we can make is to overlap decoding of the next instruction's opcode with the execution of the last step of the previous instruction. After the CPU processes the operand, the next available byte in the prefetch queue is an opcode, and the CPU can decode it in anticipation of its execution, because the instruction decoder is idle while the CPU executes the steps of the current instruction. Of course, if the current instruction modifies the EIP register, any time spent decoding the next instruction goes to waste, but as this decoding of the next instruction occurs in parallel with other operations of the current instruction, it does not slow down the system (though it does require extra circuitry to do this).

9.4.1.4 Summary of Background Prefetch Events

Our instruction execution sequence now assumes that the following CPU prefetch events are occurring in the background (and concurrently):

- If the prefetch queue is not full (generally it can hold between 8 and 32 bytes, depending on the processor) and the BIU is idle on the current clock cycle, fetch the next double word located at the address found in the EIP register at the beginning of the clock cycle.

- If the instruction decoder is idle and the current instruction does not require an instruction operand, the CPU should begin decoding the opcode at the front of the prefetch queue. If the current instruction requires an instruction operand, then the CPU begins decoding the byte just beyond that operand in the prefetch queue.

Now let's reconsider our mov(*srcreg,destreg*); instruction from Section 9.4, "Parallelism — The Key to Faster Processing." Because we've added the prefetch queue and the BIU, fetching and decoding opcode bytes and updating the EIP register takes place in parallel with the execution of specific stages of the previous instruction. Without the BIU and the prefetch queue, the mov(*reg,reg*); instruction would require the following steps:

1. Fetch the instruction's opcode from memory.
2. Decode the instruction's opcode to see what instruction it specifies.
3. Fetch the source register and update the EIP register with the address of the next instruction.
4. Store the fetched value into the destination register.

However, now that we can overlap the fetch and decode stages of this instruction with specific stages of the previous instruction, we get the following steps:

1. Fetch and decode the instruction — this is overlapped with the previous instruction.
2. Fetch the source register and update the EIP register with the address of the next instruction.
3. Store the fetched value into the destination register.

The instruction execution timings in this last example make a couple of optimistic assumptions — namely that the opcode is already present in the prefetch queue and that the CPU has already decoded it. If either is not true, additional cycles will be necessary to fetch the opcode from memory and decode the instruction.

9.4.2 Conditions That Hinder the Performance of the Prefetch Queue

Because they invalidate the prefetch queue, jump and conditional-jump instructions are slower than other instructions when the jump instructions actually transfer control to the target location. The CPU cannot overlap fetching and decoding of the opcode for the next instruction with the execution of a jump instruction that transfers control. Therefore, it may take several cycles after the execution of one of these jump instructions for the prefetch queue to recover. *If you want to write fast code, avoid jumping around in your program as much as possible.*

Note that the conditional-jump instructions only invalidate the prefetch queue if they actually transfer control to the target location. If the jump condition is false, then execution continues with the next instruction and the values in the prefetch queue remain valid. Therefore, if you can determine, while writing the program, which jump condition occurs most frequently, you should arrange your program so that the most common condition causes the program to continue with the next instruction rather than jump to a separate location.

In addition, instruction size in bytes can affect the performance of the prefetch queue. The larger the instruction, the faster the CPU will empty the prefetch queue. Instructions involving constants and memory operands tend to be the largest. If you execute a sequence of these instructions in a row, the CPU may wind up having to wait because it is removing instructions from the prefetch queue faster than the BIU is copying data to the prefetch queue. Therefore, you should attempt to use shorter instructions whenever possible because they will improve the performance of the prefetch queue.

Finally, prefetch queues work best when you have a wide data bus. The 16-bit 8086 processor runs much faster than the 8-bit 8088 because it can keep the prefetch queue full with fewer bus accesses. Don't forget, the CPU needs to use the bus for other purposes. Instructions that access memory compete with the prefetch queue for access to the bus. If you have a sequence of instructions that all access memory, the prefetch queue may quickly become empty if there are only a few bus cycles available for filling the prefetch queue during the execution of these instructions. Of course, once the prefetch queue is empty, the CPU must wait for the BIU to fetch new opcodes from memory before it can continue executing instructions.

9.4.3 Pipelining — Overlapping the Execution of Multiple Instructions

Executing instructions in parallel using a BIU and an execution unit is a special case of pipelining. Most modern processors incorporate pipelining to improve performance. With just a few exceptions, we'll see that pipelining allows us to execute one instruction per clock cycle.

The advantage of the prefetch queue is that it lets the CPU overlap fetching and decoding the instruction opcode with the execution of other instructions. That is, while one instruction is executing, the BIU is fetching and decoding the next instruction. Assuming you're willing to add hardware, you can execute almost all operations in parallel. That is the idea behind pipelining.

Pipelined operation improves the average performance of an application by executing several instructions concurrently. However, as you saw with the prefetch queue, certain instructions and certain combinations of instructions fare better than others in a pipelined system. By understanding how pipelined operation works, you can organize your applications to run faster.

9.4.3.1 A Typical Pipeline

Consider the steps necessary to do a generic operation:

1. Fetch the instruction's opcode from memory.
2. Decode the opcode *and*, if required, prefetch a displacement operand, a constant operand, or both.
3. If required, compute the effective address for a memory operand (e.g., [ebx+*disp*]).
4. If required, fetch the value of any memory operand and/or register.
5. Compute the result.
6. Store the result into the destination register.

Each of the steps in this sequence uses a separate tick of the system clock (Time = 1, Time = 2, Time = 3, and so on, represent consecutive ticks of the clock).

Assuming you're willing to pay for some extra silicon, you can build a little *miniprocessor* to handle each of these steps. The organization would look something like Figure 9-5.

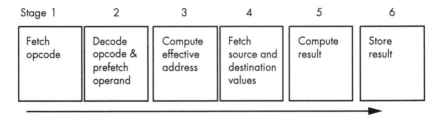

Figure 9-5: A pipelined implementation of instruction execution

Note the stages we've combined. For example, in stage 4 of Figure 9-5 the CPU fetches both the source and destination operands in the same step. You can do this by putting multiple data paths inside the CPU (such as from the registers to the ALU) and ensuring that no two operands ever compete for simultaneous use of the data bus (that is, there are no memory-to-memory operations).

If you design a separate piece of hardware for each stage in the pipeline in Figure 9-5, almost all these steps can take place in parallel. Of course, you cannot fetch and decode the opcode for more than one instruction at the same time, but you can fetch the opcode of the next instruction while decoding the current instruction's opcode. If you have an *n*-stage pipeline, you will usually have *n* instructions executing concurrently. Figure 9-6 shows pipelining in operation. T1, T2, T3, and so on, represent consecutive "ticks" (Time = 1, Time = 2, and so on) of the system clock.

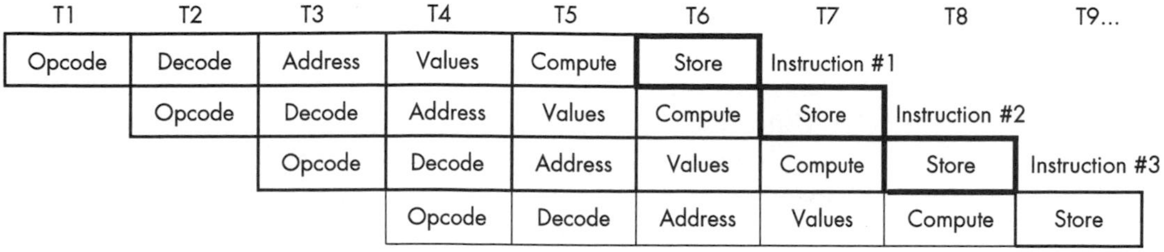

T1	T2	T3	T4	T5	T6	T7	T8	T9...
Opcode	Decode	Address	Values	Compute	Store	Instruction #1		
	Opcode	Decode	Address	Values	Compute	Store	Instruction #2	
		Opcode	Decode	Address	Values	Compute	Store	Instruction #3
			Opcode	Decode	Address	Values	Compute	Store

Figure 9-6: Instruction execution in a pipeline

At time T = T1, the CPU fetches the opcode byte for the first instruction. At T = T2, the CPU begins decoding the opcode for the first instruction, and, in parallel, it fetches a block of bytes from the prefetch queue in the event that the first instruction has an operand. Also in parallel with the decoding of the first instruction, the CPU instructs the BIU to fetch the opcode of the second instruction because the first instruction no longer needs that circuitry. Note that there is a minor conflict here. The CPU is attempting to fetch the next byte from the prefetch queue for use as an operand; at the same time it is fetching operand data from the prefetch queue for use as an opcode. How can it do both at once? You'll see the solution shortly.

At time T = T3, the CPU computes the address of any memory operand if the first instruction accesses memory. If the first instruction does not use an addressing mode requiring such computation, the CPU does nothing. During T3, the CPU also decodes the opcode of the second instruction and fetches any operands the second instruction has. Finally, the CPU also fetches the opcode for the third instruction. With each advancing tick of the clock, another step in the execution of each instruction in the pipeline completes, and the CPU fetches the opcode of yet another instruction from memory.

This process continues until at T = T6 the CPU completes the execution of the first instruction, computes the result for the second, and fetches the opcode for the sixth instruction in the pipeline. The important thing to see is that after T = T5, the CPU completes an instruction on every clock cycle. Once the CPU fills the pipeline, it completes one instruction on each cycle. This is true even if there are complex addressing modes to be computed, memory operands to fetch, or other operations that consume cycles on a nonpipelined processor. All you need to do is add more stages to the pipeline, and you can still effectively process each instruction in one clock cycle.

Now back to the small conflict in the pipeline organization I mentioned earlier. At T = T2, for example, the CPU attempts to prefetch a block of bytes containing any operands of the first instruction, and at the same time it fetches the opcode of the second instruction. Until the CPU decodes the first instruction, it doesn't know how many operands the instruction requires nor does it know their length. Moreover, the CPU doesn't know what byte to fetch as the opcode of the second instruction until it determines the length of any operands the first instruction requires. So how can the pipeline fetch the opcode of the next instruction in parallel with any address operands of the current instruction?

One solution is to disallow this simultaneous operation in order to avoid the potential *data hazard* (more about data hazards later). If an instruction has an address or constant operand, we can simply delay the start of the next instruction. Unfortunately, many instructions have these additional operands, so this approach will have a substantial negative impact on the execution speed of the CPU.

The second solution is to throw a lot more hardware at the problem. Operand and constant sizes usually come in 1-, 2-, and 4-byte lengths. Therefore, if we actually fetch the bytes in memory that are located at offsets one, three, and five bytes beyond the current opcode we are decoding, one of these three bytes will probably contain the opcode of the next instruction. Once we are through decoding the current instruction, we know how many bytes it consumes, and, therefore, we know the offset of the next opcode. We can use a simple data selector circuit to choose which of the three candidate opcode bytes we want to use.

In practice, we actually have to select the next opcode byte from more than three candidates because 80x86 instructions come in many different lengths. For example, a mov instruction that copies a 32-bit constant to a memory location can be 10 or more bytes long. Moreover, instructions vary in length from 1 to 15 bytes. And some opcodes on the 80x86 are longer than 1 byte, so the CPU may have to fetch multiple bytes in order to properly decode the current instruction. However, by throwing more hardware at the problem we can decode the current opcode at the same time we're fetching the next.

9.4.3.2 Stalls in a Pipeline

Unfortunately, the scenario presented in the previous section is a little too simplistic. There are two problems that our simple pipeline ignores: competition between instructions for access to the bus (known as *bus contention*), and nonsequential instruction execution. Both problems may increase the average execution time of the instructions in the pipeline. By understanding how the pipeline works, you can write your software to avoid problems in the pipeline and improve the performance of your applications.

Bus contention can occur whenever an instruction needs to access an item in memory. For example, if a mov(reg,mem); instruction needs to store data in memory and a mov(mem,reg); instruction is reading data from memory, contention for the address and data bus may develop because the CPU will be trying to fetch data from memory and write data to memory simultaneously.

One simplistic way to handle bus contention is through a *pipeline stall*. The CPU, when faced with contention for the bus, gives priority to the instruction farthest along in the pipeline. This causes the later instruction in the pipeline to *stall*, and it takes two cycles to execute that instruction (see Figure 9-7).

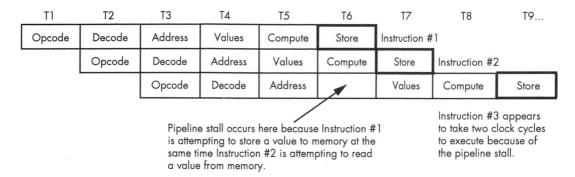

T1	T2	T3	T4	T5	T6	T7	T8	T9...
Opcode	Decode	Address	Values	Compute	Store	Instruction #1		
	Opcode	Decode	Address	Values	Compute	Store	Instruction #2	
		Opcode	Decode	Address		Values	Compute	Store

Pipeline stall occurs here because Instruction #1 is attempting to store a value to memory at the same time Instruction #2 is attempting to read a value from memory.

Instruction #3 appears to take two clock cycles to execute because of the pipeline stall.

Figure 9-7: A pipeline stall

There are many other cases of bus contention. For example, fetching operands for an instruction requires access to the prefetch queue at the same time that the CPU needs to access the queue to fetch the opcode of the next instruction. Given the simple pipelining scheme that we've outlined so far, it's unlikely that most instructions would execute at one clock (cycle) per instruction (CPI).

As another example of a pipeline stall, consider what happens when an instruction *modifies* the value in the EIP register? For example, the jnz instruction might change the value in the EIP register if it conditionally transfers control to its target label. This, of course, implies that the next set of instructions to be executed does not immediately follow the instruction that modifies EIP. By the time the instruction jnz label; completes execution (assuming the zero flag is clear, so that the branch is taken), we've already started five other instructions and we're only one clock cycle away from the completion of the first of these. Obviously, the CPU must not execute those instructions, or it will compute improper results.

The only reasonable solution is to *flush* the entire pipeline and begin fetching opcodes anew. However, doing so causes a severe execution-time penalty. It will take the length of the pipeline (six cycles in our example) before the next instruction completes execution. The longer the pipeline is, the more you can accomplish per cycle in the system, but the slower a program will run if it jumps around quite a bit. Unfortunately, you cannot control the number of stages in the pipeline,[3] but you can control the number of transfer instructions that appear in your programs. Obviously, you should keep these to a minimum in a pipelined system.

9.4.4 Instruction Caches — Providing Multiple Paths to Memory

System designers can resolve many problems with bus contention through the intelligent use of the prefetch queue and the cache memory subsystem. As you have seen, they can design the prefetch queue to buffer data from the instruction stream. However, they can also use a separate *instruction cache*

---

[3] Note, by the way, that the number of stages in an instruction pipeline varies among CPUs.

(apart from the data cache) to hold machine instructions. Though, as a programmer, you have no control over the cache organization of your CPU, knowing how the instruction cache operates on your particular CPU may allow you to use certain instruction sequences that would otherwise create stalls.

Suppose, for a moment, that the CPU has two separate memory spaces, one for instructions and one for data, each with its own bus. This is called the *Harvard architecture* because the first such machine was built at Harvard. On a Harvard machine there would be no contention for the bus. The BIU could continue to fetch opcodes on the instruction bus while accessing memory on the data/memory bus (see Figure 9-8).

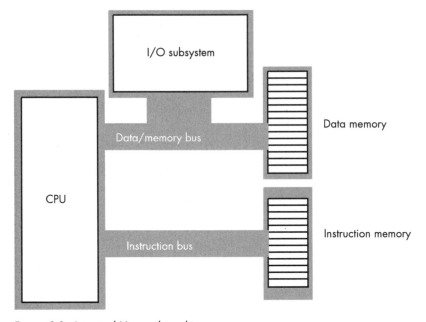

Figure 9-8: A typical Harvard machine

In the real world, there are very few true Harvard machines. The extra pins needed on the processor to support two physically separate buses increase the cost of the processor and introduce many other engineering problems. However, microprocessor designers have discovered that they can obtain many benefits of the Harvard architecture with few of the disadvantages by using separate on-chip caches for data and instructions. Advanced CPUs use an internal Harvard architecture and an external von Neumann architecture. Figure 9-9 shows the structure of the 80x86 with separate data and instruction caches.

Each path between the sections inside the CPU represents an independent bus, and data can flow on all paths concurrently. This means that the prefetch queue can be pulling instruction opcodes from the instruction cache while the execution unit is writing data to the data cache. However, it is not always possible, even with a cache, to avoid bus contention.

In the arrangement with two separate caches, the BIU still has to use the data/address bus to fetch opcodes from memory whenever they are not located in the instruction cache. Likewise, the data cache still has to buffer data from memory occasionally.

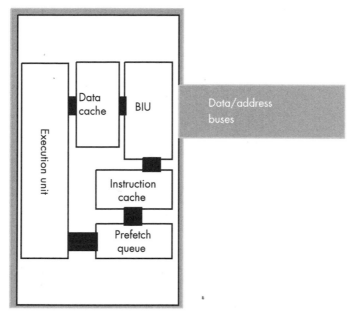

Figure 9-9: Using separate code and data caches

Although you cannot control the presence, size, or type of cache on a CPU, you must be aware of how the cache operates in order to write the best programs. On-chip level-one instruction caches are generally quite small (between 4 KB and 64 KB on typical CPUs) compared to the size of main memory. Therefore, the shorter your instructions, the more of them will fit in the cache (getting tired of "shorter instructions" yet?). The more instructions you have in the cache, the less often bus contention will occur. Likewise, using registers to hold temporary results places less strain on the data cache, so it doesn't need to flush data to memory or retrieve data from memory quite so often.

9.4.5 Pipeline Hazards

There is another problem with using a pipeline: hazards. There are two types of hazards: control hazards and data hazards. We've actually discussed control hazards already, although we did not refer to them by that name. A control hazard occurs whenever the CPU branches to some new location in memory and consequently has to flush from the pipeline the instructions that are in various stages of execution. The system resources used to begin the execution of the instructions the CPU flushes from the pipeline could have been put to more productive use, had the programmer organized the application to minimize the number of these instructions. So by understanding the effects of hazards on your code, you can write faster applications.

Let's take a look at data hazards using the execution profile for the following instruction sequence:

```
mov( SomeVar, ebx );
mov( [ebx], eax );
```

When these two instructions execute, the pipeline will look something like what is shown in Figure 9-10.

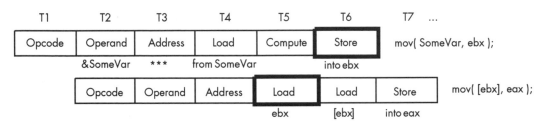

Figure 9-10: A data hazard

These two instructions attempt to fetch the 32-bit value whose address is held in the SomeVar pointer variable. *However, this sequence of instructions won't work properly!* Unfortunately, the second instruction has already accessed the value in EBX before the first instruction copies the address of memory location SomeVar into EBX (T5 and T6 in Figure 9-10).

CISC processors, like the 80x86, handle hazards automatically. (Some RISC chips do not, and if you tried this sequence on certain RISC chips you would store an incorrect value in EAX.) In order to handle the data hazard in this example, CISC processors stall the pipeline to synchronize the two instructions. The actual execution would look something like what is shown in Figure 9-11.

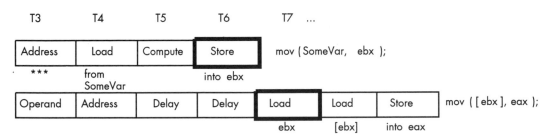

Figure 9-11: How a CISC CPU handles a data hazard

By delaying the second instruction by two clock cycles, the CPU guarantees that the load instruction will load EAX with the value at the proper address. Unfortunately, the mov([ebx],eax); instruction now executes in three clock cycles rather than one. However, requiring two extra clock cycles is better than producing incorrect results.

Fortunately, you (or your compiler) can reduce the impact that hazards have on program execution speed within your software. Note that a data hazard occurs when the source operand of one instruction was a destination operand of a previous instruction. There is nothing wrong with loading EBX from SomeVar and then loading EAX from [EBX]] (that is, the double-word memory location pointed at by EBX), *as long as they don't occur one right after the other.* Suppose the code sequence had been:

```
mov( 2000, ecx );
mov( SomeVar, ebx );
mov( [ebx], eax );
```

We could reduce the effect of the hazard in this code sequence by simply *rearranging the instructions.* Let's do that to obtain the following:

```
mov( SomeVar, ebx );
mov( 2000, ecx );
mov( [ebx], eax );
```

Now the mov([ebx],eax); instruction requires only one additional clock cycle rather than two. By inserting yet another instruction between the mov(SomeVar,ebx); and the mov([ebx],eax); instructions, you can eliminate the effects of the hazard altogether (of course, the inserted instruction must not modify the values in the EAX and EBX registers).

On a pipelined processor, the order of instructions in a program may dramatically affect the performance of that program. If you are writing assembly code, always look for possible hazards in your instruction sequences. Eliminate them wherever possible by rearranging the instructions. If you are using a compiler, choose a good compiler that properly handles instruction ordering.

9.4.6   Superscalar Operation — Executing Instructions in Parallel

With the pipelined architecture shown so far, we could achieve, at best, execution times of one CPI (clock per instruction). Is it possible to execute instructions faster than this? At first glance you might think, "Of course not, we can do at most one operation per clock cycle. So there is no way we can execute more than one instruction per clock cycle." Keep in mind, however, that a single instruction is *not* a single operation. In the examples presented earlier, each instruction has taken between six and eight operations to complete. By adding seven or eight separate units to the CPU, we could effectively execute these eight operations in one clock cycle, yielding one CPI. If we add more hardware and execute, say, 16 operations at once, can we achieve 0.5 CPI? The answer is a qualified yes. A CPU that includes this additional hardware is a *superscalar* CPU, and it can execute more than one instruction during a single clock cycle. The 80x86 family began supporting superscalar execution with the introduction of the Pentium processor.

A superscalar CPU has several execution units (see Figure 9-12). If it encounters in the prefetch queue two or more instructions that can execute independently, it will do so.

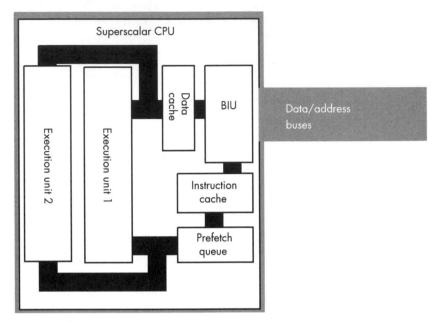

Figure 9-12: A CPU that supports superscalar operation

There are a couple of advantages to going superscalar. Suppose you have the following instructions in the instruction stream:

```
mov( 1000, eax );
mov( 2000, ebx );
```

If there are no other problems or hazards in the surrounding code, and all six bytes for these two instructions are currently in the prefetch queue, there is no reason why the CPU cannot fetch and execute both instructions in parallel. All it takes is extra silicon on the CPU chip to implement two execution units.

Besides speeding up independent instructions, a superscalar CPU can also speed up program sequences that have hazards. One limitation of normal CPUs is that once a hazard occurs, the offending instruction will completely stall the pipeline. Every instruction that follows the stalled instruction will also have to wait for the CPU to synchronize the execution of the offending instructions. With a superscalar CPU, however, instructions following the hazard may continue execution through the pipeline as long as they don't have hazards of their own. This alleviates (though it does not eliminate) some of the need for careful instruction scheduling.

The way you write software for a superscalar CPU can dramatically affect its performance. First and foremost is that rule you're probably sick of by now: *use short instructions*. The shorter your instructions are, the more instructions the CPU can fetch in a single operation and, therefore, the more likely the CPU will execute faster than one CPI. Most superscalar CPUs do not completely duplicate the execution unit. There might be multiple ALUs, floating-point units, and so on, which means that certain instruction sequences can execute very quickly, while others won't. You have to study the exact composition of your CPU to decide which instruction sequences produce the best performance.

9.4.7 Out-of-Order Execution

In a standard superscalar CPU, it is the programmer's (or compiler's) responsibility to schedule (arrange) the instructions to avoid hazards and pipeline stalls. Fancier CPUs can actually remove some of this burden and improve performance by automatically rescheduling instructions while the program executes. To understand how this is possible, consider the following instruction sequence:

```
mov( SomeVar, ebx );
mov( [ebx], eax );
mov( 2000, ecx );
```

A data hazard exists between the first and second instructions. The second instruction must delay until the first instruction completes execution. This introduces a pipeline stall and increases the running time of the program. Typically, the stall affects every instruction that follows. However, note that the third instruction's execution does not depend on the result from either of the first two instructions. Therefore, there is no reason to stall the execution of the mov(2000,ecx); instruction. It may continue executing while the second instruction waits for the first to complete. This technique is called *out-of-order execution* because the CPU can execute instructions prior to the completion of instructions appearing previously in the code stream.

Clearly, the CPU may only execute instructions out of sequence if doing so produces exactly the same results as in-order execution. While there are many little technical issues that make this problem more difficult than it seems, it is possible to implement this feature with enough engineering effort.

9.4.8 Register Renaming

One problem that hampers the effectiveness of superscalar operation on the 80x86 CPU is the 80x86's limited number of general-purpose registers. Suppose, for example, that the CPU had four different pipelines and, therefore, was capable of executing four instructions simultaneously. Presuming no conflicts existed among these instructions and they could all execute simultaneously, it would still be very difficult to actually achieve four instructions per clock cycle because most instructions operate on two register operands. For four instructions to execute concurrently, you'd need eight different registers: four destination registers and four source registers (none of the destination registers could double as source registers of other instructions). CPUs that have lots of registers can handle this task quite easily, but the limited register set of the 80x86 makes this difficult. Fortunately, there is a way to alleviate part of the problem through *register renaming*.

Register renaming is a sneaky way to give a CPU more registers than it actually has. Programmers will not have direct access to these extra registers, but the CPU can use them to prevent hazards in certain cases. For example, consider the following short instruction sequence:

```
mov( 0, eax );
mov( eax, i );
mov( 50, eax );
mov( eax, j );
```

Clearly, a data hazard exists between the first and second instructions and, likewise, a data hazard exists between the third and fourth instructions. Out-of-order execution in a superscalar CPU would normally allow the first and third instructions to execute concurrently, and then the second and fourth instructions could execute concurrently. However, a data hazard of sorts also exists between the first and third instructions because they use the same register. The programmer could have easily solved this problem by using a different register (say, EBX) for the third and fourth instructions. However, let's assume that the programmer was unable to do this because all the other registers were all holding important values. Is this sequence doomed to executing in four cycles on a superscalar CPU that should only require two?

One advanced trick a CPU can employ is to create a bank of registers for each of the general-purpose registers on the CPU. That is, rather than having a single EAX register, the CPU could support an array of EAX registers; let's call these registers EAX[0], EAX[1], EAX[2], and so on. Similarly, you could have an array of each of the other registers, so we could also have EBX[0]..EBX[n], ECX[0]..ECX[n], and so on. The instruction set does not give the programmer the ability to select one of these specific register array elements for a given instruction, but the CPU can automatically choose among the register array elements if doing so would not change the overall computation and could speed up the execution of the program. For example, consider the following sequence (with register array elements automatically chosen by the CPU):

```
mov( 0, eax[0] );
mov( eax[0], i );
mov( 50, eax[1] );
mov( eax[1], j );
```

Because EAX[0] and EAX[1] are different registers, the CPU can execute the first and third instructions concurrently. Likewise, the CPU can execute the second and fourth instructions concurrently.

This code provides an example of *register renaming*. Although this is a simple example, and different CPUs implement register renaming in many different ways, this example does demonstrate how the CPU can improve performance in certain instances using this technique.

9.4.9   Very Long Instruction Word (VLIW) Architecture

Superscalar operation attempts to schedule, in hardware, the execution of multiple instructions simultaneously. Another technique, which Intel is using in its IA-64 architecture, involves very long instruction words, or VLIW. In a VLIW computer system, the CPU fetches a large block of bytes (41 bits in the case of the IA-64 Itanium CPU) and decodes and executes this block all at once. This block of bytes usually contains two or more instructions (three in the case of the IA-64). VLIW computing requires the programmer or compiler to properly schedule the instructions in each block so that there are no hazards or other conflicts, but if properly scheduled, the CPU can execute three or more instructions per clock cycle.

The Intel IA-64 architecture is not the only computer system to employ a VLIW architecture. Transmeta's Crusoe processor family also uses a VLIW architecture. The Crusoe processor is different from the IA-64 architecture, insofar as it does not support native execution of IA-32 instructions. Instead, the Crusoe processor dynamically translates 80x86 instructions to Crusoe's VLIW instructions. This "code morphing" technology results in code running about 50 percent slower than native code, though the Crusoe processor has other advantages.

We will not consider VLIW computing any further here because the technology is just becoming available (and it's difficult to predict how it will impact system designs). Nevertheless, Intel and some other semiconductor manufacturers feel that it's the wave of the future, so keep your eye on it.

9.4.10   Parallel Processing

Most techniques for improving CPU performance via architectural advances involve the parallel execution of instructions. The techniques up to this point in this chapter can be treated as if they were transparent to the programmer. That is, the programmer does not have to do anything special to take minimal advantage of pipeline and superscalar operation. As you have seen, if programmers are aware of the underlying architecture, they can write code that runs faster, but these architectural advances often improve performance significantly even if programmers do not write special code to take advantage of them.

The only problem with ignoring the underlying architecture is that there is only so much the hardware can do to parallelize a program that requires sequential execution for proper operation. To truly produce a parallel program, the programmer must specifically write parallel code, though, of course, this does require architectural support from the CPU. This section and the next touch on the types of support a CPU can provide.

Common CPUs use what is known as the *Single Instruction, Single Data* (SISD) model. This means that the CPU executes one instruction at a time, and that instruction operates on a single piece of data.[4] Two common parallel models are the so-called *Single Instruction, Multiple Data* (SIMD) and *Multiple Instruction, Multiple Data* (MIMD) models. As it turns out, many modern CPUs, including the 80x86, also include limited support for these latter two parallel-execution models, providing a hybrid SISD/SIMD/MIMD architecture.

In the SIMD model, the CPU executes a single instruction stream, just like the pure SISD model. However, in the SIMD model, the CPU operates on multiple pieces of data concurrently rather than on a single data object. For example, consider the 80x86 add instruction. This is a SISD instruction that operates on (that is, produces) a single piece of data. True, the instruction fetches values from two source operands, but the end result is that the add instruction will store a sum into only a single destination operand. An SIMD version of add, on the other hand, would compute the sum of several values simultaneously. The Pentium III's MMX and SIMD instruction extensions, and the PowerPC's AltaVec instructions, operate in exactly this fashion. With the paddb MMX instruction, for example, you can add up to eight separate pairs of values with the execution of a single instruction. Here's an example of this instruction:

```
paddb( mm0, mm1 );
```

Although this instruction appears to have only two operands (like a typical SISD add instruction on the 80x86), the MMX registers (MM0 and MM1) actually hold eight independent byte values (the MMX registers are 64 bits wide but are treated as eight 8-bit values rather than as a single 64-bit value).

Note that SIMD instructions are only useful in specialized situations. Unless you have an algorithm that can take advantage of SIMD instructions, they're not that useful. Fortunately, high-speed 3-D graphics and multimedia applications benefit greatly from these SIMD (and MMX) instructions, so their inclusion in the 80x86 CPU offers a huge performance boost for these important applications.

The MIMD model uses multiple instructions, operating on multiple pieces of data (usually with one instruction per data object, though one of these instructions could also operate on multiple data items). These multiple instructions execute independently of one another, so it's very rare that a single program (or, more specifically, a single thread of execution) would use the MIMD model. However, if you have a multiprogramming environment with multiple programs attempting to execute concurrently, the MIMD model does allow each of those programs to execute their own code stream simultaneously. This type of parallel system is called a multiprocessor system.

---

[4] We will ignore the parallelism provided by pipelining and superscalar operation in this discussion.

9.4.11 Multiprocessing

Pipelining, superscalar operation, out-of-order execution, and VLIW designs are techniques that CPU designers use in order to execute several operations in parallel. These techniques support *fine-grained parallelism* and are useful for speeding up adjacent instructions in a computer system. If adding more functional units increases parallelism, you might wonder what would happen if you added another CPU to the system. This technique, known as *multiprocessing*, can improve system performance, though not as uniformly as other techniques.

Multiprocessing doesn't help a program's performance unless that program is specifically written for use on a multiprocessor system. If you build a system with two CPUs, those CPUs cannot trade off executing alternate instructions within a single program. In fact, it is very expensive, time-wise, to switch the execution of a program's instructions from one processor to another. Therefore, multiprocessor systems are only effective with an operating system that executes multiple processes or threads concurrently. To differentiate this type of parallelism from that afforded by pipelining and superscalar operation, we'll call this kind of parallelism *coarse-grained parallelism*.

Adding multiple processors to a system is not as simple as wiring two or more processors to the motherboard. To understand why this is so, consider two separate programs running on separate processors in a multiprocessor system. Suppose also that these two processors communicate with one another by writing to a block of shared physical memory. Unfortunately, when CPU 1 attempts to writes to this block of memory it caches the data (locally on the CPU) and might not actually write the data to physical memory for some time. If CPU 2 attempts to simultaneously read this block of shared memory, it winds up reading the old data out of main memory (or its local cache) rather than reading the updated data that CPU 1 wrote to its local cache. This is known as the *cache-coherency* problem. In order for these two functions to operate properly, the two CPUs must notify each other whenever they make changes to shared objects, so the other CPU can update its local, cached copy.

One area where the RISC CPUs have a big advantage over Intel's CPUs is in the support for multiple processors in a system. While Intel 80x86 systems reach a point of diminishing returns at around 16 processors, Sun SPARC and other RISC processors easily support 64-CPU systems (with more arriving, it seems, every day). This is why large databases and large Web server systems tend to use expensive Unix-based RISC systems rather than 80x86 systems.

Newer versions of the Pentium IV and Xeon processors support a hybrid form of multiprocessing known as *hyperthreading*. The idea behind hyperthreading is deceptively simple — in a typical superscalar processor it is rare for an instruction sequence to utilize all the CPU's functional units on each clock cycle. Rather than allow those functional units to go unused, the CPU can run two separate threads of execution concurrently and keep all the CPU's functional units occupied. This allows a single CPU to, effectively, do the work of 1.5 CPUs in a typical multiprocessor system.

9.5 For More Information

The in-depth study of computer architecture could very well be considered a "follow-on course" to the material this chapter presents. There are many college and professional texts on computer architecture available today. Patterson and Hennessy's *Computer Architecture: A Quantitative Approach* is one of the better regarded texts on this subject (though it is a bit heavily biased towards RISC architectures).

One subject missing from this chapter is the design of the CPU's actual instruction set. That is the subject of the next chapter in this book.

10

INSTRUCTION SET ARCHITECTURE

This chapter discusses the implementation of a CPU's instruction set. Although the choice of a given instruction set (for example, the 80x86 instruction set) is usually beyond the control of a software engineer, understanding the choices a hardware design engineer has to make when designing a CPU's instruction set can definitely help you write better code.

CPU instruction sets contain several trade-offs based on assumptions that computer architects make concerning the way software engineers write code. If the machine instructions you choose match the assumptions the CPU's designers have made, then your code will probably run faster and require fewer machine resources. Conversely, if your code violates the assumptions the hardware engineers have made, chances are pretty good it will not perform as well as it otherwise could.

Although studying the instruction set may seem like a task suited only to assembly language programmers, even high-level language programmers should understand the design of their CPU's instruction set. After all, every high-level language statement maps to some sequence of machine instructions. Indeed, studying generic instruction set design is probably more important to high-level language programmers than it is to assembly programmers (who should study the specific instruction set they are using), as the general concepts are portable across architectures. Therefore, even if you don't ever intend to write software using assembly language, it's important to understand how the underlying machine instructions work and how they were designed in the first place.

10.1   The Importance of the Design of the Instruction Set

The design of the CPU's instruction set is one of the most interesting and important aspects of CPU design. The instruction set architecture (ISA) is something that a designer must get correct from the start of the design cycle. Features like caches, pipelining, superscalar implementation, and so on, can all be grafted on o a CPU long after the original design is obsolete. However, it is very difficult to change the instruction set once a CPU is in production and people are writing software using those instructions. Therefore, instruction set design requires very careful consideration.

You might be tempted to think that the kitchen sink approach to instruction set design (as in "everything, including the kitchen sink"), in which you include every instruction you can dream up, is best. This approach fails for several reasons, as you'll soon see. Instruction set design is the epitome of compromise management. Good instruction set design involves selecting what to throw out rather than what to keep. It's easy enough to say, "Let's include everything." The hard part is deciding what to leave out once it becomes clear that you can't have every instruction on the chip. Why can't we have it all? Well, in the real world some *nasty realities* prevent this:

Nasty reality 1: Silicon real estate   The first problem with "putting it all on the chip" is that each feature requires some number of transistors on the CPU's silicon die (chip). CPU designers work with a "silicon budget" and are given a finite number of transistors to work with. This means that there aren't enough transistors to support "putting every possible feature" on a CPU. The original 8086 processor, for example, had a transistor budget of fewer than 30 thousand transistors. The Pentium III processor had a budget of over 8 million transistors. These two budgets reflect the differences in semiconductor technology in 1978 versus 1998.

Nasty reality 2: Cost   Although it is possible to use millions of transistors on a CPU today, the more transistors that are used the more expensive the CPU becomes. For example, at the beginning of 2004, Pentium IV processors using millions of transistors cost hundreds of dollars. Contemporary CPUs with 30,000 transistors cost only a few dollars.

Nasty reality 3: Expandability   One problem with the kitchen sink approach is that it's very difficult to anticipate all the features people will want. For example, Intel's MMX and SIMD instruction enhancements were added to make multimedia programming more practical on the Pentium processor. Back in 1978, when Intel created the first 8086 processor, very few people could have possibly anticipated the need for these instructions. Therefore, a CPU designer needs to allow for making extensions to the instruction set in future members of the CPU family to handle unanticipated needs.

Nasty reality 4: Legacy support   This is almost the opposite of expandability. Often, an instruction that the CPU designer feels is important turns out to be less useful than anticipated. For example, the loop instruction on the 80x86 CPU sees very little use in modern high-performance programs. The 80x86 enter instruction is another good example. When designing a CPU using the kitchen sink approach, it is common to discover that most programs never use some of the instructions. Unfortunately, removing instructions from later versions of a processor will break existing programs that use those instructions. Generally, once an instruction is added to the instruction set, it will have to be supported in all future members of the processor. Unless very few programs use the instruction, and CPU designers are willing to let them break, removing instructions is a difficult thing to do.

Nasty reality 5: Complexity   The popularity of a new processor is easily measured by how much software people write for that processor. Most CPU designs die a quick death because no one writes software specific to that CPU. Therefore, a CPU designer must consider the assembly programmers and compiler writers who will be using the chip upon introduction. While a kitchen sink approach might seem to appeal to such programmers, the truth is that no one wants to learn an overly complex system. A CPU that does everything under the sun appeals mostly to someone who is already familiar with the CPU. However, pity the poor soul who doesn't know the chip and has to learn it all at once.

These problems with the kitchen sink approach all have a common solution: design a simple instruction set for the first version of the CPU, and leave room for later expansion. This is one of the main reasons the 80x86 has proven to be so popular and long-lived. Intel started with a relatively simple CPU and figured out how to extend the instruction set over the years to accommodate new features.

10.2   Basic Instruction Design Goals

The efficiency of your programs largely depends upon the instructions that they use. Short instructions use very little memory and often execute rapidly — nice attributes to have when writing great code. On the other hand, larger instructions can often handle more complex tasks, with a single instruction often doing the work of several less-complex instructions. To enable software engineers to write the best possible code, computer architects must strike a careful compromise between overly simplistic instructions (which are short and efficient, but don't do very much work) and overly complex instructions that consume excessive memory or require too many machine cycles to execute.

In a typical CPU, the computer encodes instructions as numeric values (operation codes or *opcodes*) and stores them in memory. The encoding of these instructions is one of the major tasks in instruction set design, requiring careful thought. Each instruction must have a unique opcode (clearly, two different instructions cannot share the same opcode or the CPU will not be able to differentiate them). With an n-bit number, there are 2^n different possible opcodes, so to encode m instructions requires at least $\log_2(m)$ bits. The main point to keep in mind is that the size of individual CPU instructions is dependent on the total number of instructions that the CPU supports.

Encoding opcodes is a little more involved than assigning a unique numeric value to each instruction. Remember, decoding each instruction and executing the specified task requires actual circuitry. Suppose we have a 7-bit opcode. With an opcode of this size, we could encode 128 different instructions. To decode each of these 128 instructions requires a 7-line to 128-line decoder — an expensive piece of circuitry. However, assuming that the instruction opcodes contain certain (binary) patterns, a single large decoder can often be replaced by several smaller, less expensive decoders.

If an instruction set contains 128 unrelated instructions, there's little one can do other than decode the entire bit string for each instruction. However, in most architectures the instructions fall into related groups. On the 80x86 CPUs, for example, the mov(eax,ebx); and mov(ecx,edx); instructions have different opcodes because the instructions are different. However, these two instructions are obviously related in that they both move data from one register to another. The only differences between the two are their source and destination operands. This suggests that CPU designers could encode instructions like mov with a sub-opcode, and then they could encode the instruction's operands using other bit fields within the opcode.

For example, given an instruction set with only eight instructions, each with two operands, and each operand having only one of four possible values, the instructions could be encoded using three packed fields containing three, two, and two bits, respectively (see Figure 10-1). This encoding only needs three simple decoders to determine what the CPU should do. While this is a simple case, it does demonstrate one very important facet of instruction set design — it is important to make opcodes easy to decode and the easiest way to do this is to construct the opcode using several different bit fields. The smaller these bit fields are, the easier it will be for the hardware to decode and execute the instruction.

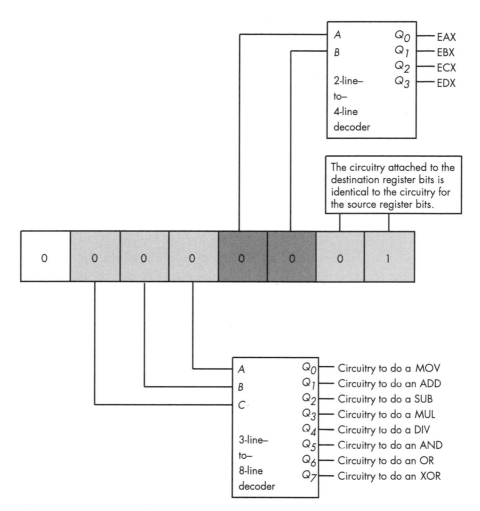

Figure 10-1: Separating an opcode into several fields to ease decoding

It would seem that when encoding 2^n different instructions using n bits, there would be very little leeway in choosing the size of the instruction. It's going to take n bits to encode those 2^n instructions; you can't do it with any fewer. It is possible, however, to use more than n bits; and believe it or not, that's the secret to reducing the average instruction size.

10.2.1   Choosing Opcode Length

Before discussing how it is possible to use larger instructions to generate shorter programs, a quick digression is necessary. The first thing to know is that the opcode length isn't arbitrary. Assuming that a CPU is capable of reading bytes from memory, the opcode will probably have to be some even multiple of eight bits long. If the CPU is not capable of reading bytes from memory (most RISC CPUs read memory only in 32- or 64-bit chunks), then the opcode is going to be the same size as the smallest object the CPU can read from memory at one time. Any attempt to shrink the opcode size below this limit is futile. In this chapter, we'll work with opcodes that must have a length that is a multiple of eight bits.

Another point to consider here is the size of an instruction's operands. Some CPU designers include all operands in their opcode. Other CPU designers do not count operands like immediate constants or address displacements as part of the opcode. We will take the latter approach here and not count either of these as part of the actual opcode.

An 8-bit opcode can encode only 256 different instructions. Even if we don't count instruction operands as part of the opcode, having only 256 different instructions is a stringent limit. Though CPUs with 8-bit opcodes exist, modern processors tend to have far more than 256 different instructions. Because opcodes must have a length that is a multiple of 8 bits, the next smallest possible opcode size is 16 bits. A 2-byte opcode can encode up to 65,536 different instructions, though the opcode size has doubled from 8 to 16 bits (meaning that the instructions will be larger).

When reducing instruction size is an important design goal, CPU designers often employ data compression theory to reduce the average instruction size. The first step is to analyze programs written for a typical CPU and count the number of occurrences of each instruction over a large number of applications. The second step is to create a list of these instructions, sorted by their frequency of use. Next, the most frequently used instructions are assigned 1-byte opcodes; 2-byte opcodes are assigned to the next most frequently used instructions, and opcodes of three or more bytes are assigned to the rarely used instructions. Although this scheme requires opcodes with a maximum size of three or more bytes, most of the actual instructions appearing in a program will use one or two byte opcodes. The average opcode length will be somewhere between one and two bytes (let's call it 1.5 bytes), and a typical program will be shorter than had all instructions employed a 2-byte opcode (see Figure 10-2).

Although using variable-length instructions allows one to create smaller programs, it comes at a price. First, decoding variable-length instructions is a bit more complicated than decoding fixed-length instructions. Before decoding a particular instruction field, the CPU must first decode the instruction's size. This extra step consumes time and may affect the overall performance of the CPU by introducing delays in the decoding step and, thereby, limiting the maximum clock speed of the CPU (because those delays stretch out a single clock period, thus reducing the CPU's clock frequency). Another problem with having variable-length instructions is that it makes decoding multiple instructions in a pipeline difficult, because the CPU cannot easily determine the instruction boundaries in the prefetch queue.

These reasons, along with some others, explain why most popular RISC architectures avoid variable-length instructions. However, in this chapter, we'll study a variable-length approach because saving memory is an admirable goal.

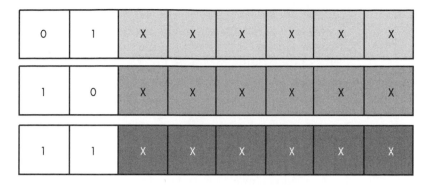

If the HO two bits of the first opcode byte are not both zero, then the whole opcode is one byte long, and the remaining six bits let us encode 64 1-byte instructions. Because there are a total of three opcode bytes of this form, we can encode up to 192 different 1-byte instructions.

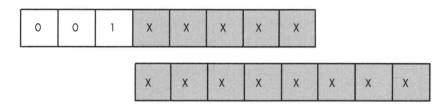

If the HO three bits of our first opcode byte contain %001, then the opcode is two bytes long, and the remaining 13 bits let us encode 8,192 different instructions.

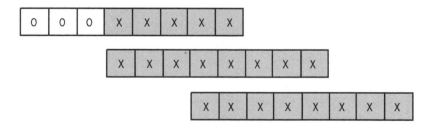

If the HO three bits of our first opcode byte contain all zeros, then the opcode is three bytes long, and the remaining 21 bits let us encode two million (2^{21}) different instructions.

Figure 10-2: Encoding instructions using a variable-length opcode

10.2.2 Planning for the Future

Before actually choosing the instructions to implement in a CPU, designers must plan for the future. The need for new instructions will undoubtedly appear after the initial design, so reserving some opcodes specifically for expansion purposes is a good idea. Given the instruction opcode format appearing in Figure 10-2, it might not be a bad idea to reserve one block of 64 1-byte opcodes, half (4,096) of the 2-byte opcodes, and half (1,048,576) of the 3-byte opcodes for future use. Giving up 64 of the very valuable 1-byte opcodes may seem extravagant, but history suggests that such foresight is rewarded.

10.2.3   Choosing Instructions

The next step is to choose the instructions to implement. Even if nearly half the instructions have been reserved for future expansion, that doesn't mean that all the remaining opcodes must be used to implement instructions. A designer can leave a good number of these instructions unimplemented, effectively reserving them for the future as well. The right approach is not to use up the opcodes as quickly as possible, but rather to produce a consistent and complete instruction set given the design compromises. The main point to keep in mind here is that it's much easier to add an instruction later than it is to remove an instruction later. So, for the first go-around, it's generally better to go with a simpler design rather than a more complex design.

The first step is to choose some generic instruction types. Early in the design process it is important to limit the choice to very common instructions. Instruction sets of other processors are probably the best place to look for suggestions when choosing these instructions. For example, most processors will have instructions like the following:

- Data movement instructions (such as mov)
- Arithmetic and logical instructions (such as add, sub, and, or, not)
- Comparison instructions
- A set of conditional jump instructions (generally used after the comparison instructions)
- Input/output instructions
- Other miscellaneous instructions

The designer of the CPU's initial instruction set should have the goal of choosing a reasonable set of instructions that will allow programmers to write efficient programs without adding so many instructions that the instruction set design exceeds the silicon budget or violates other design constraints. This requires strategic decisions, which CPU designers should make based on careful research, experimentation, and simulation.

10.2.4   Assigning Opcodes to Instructions

Once the initial instructions have been chosen, the next step is to assign opcodes to them. The first step is to group the instructions into sets according to the characteristics they share. For example, an add instruction is probably going to support the exact same set of operands as the sub instruction. Therefore, it makes sense to put these two instructions into the same group. On the other hand, the not instruction generally requires only a single operand, as does a neg instruction. Therefore, it makes sense to put these two instructions in the same group, but in a different group from the one with add and sub.

Once all the instructions are grouped, the next step is to encode them. A typical encoding scheme will use some bits to select the group the instruction falls into, some bits to select a particular instruction from that group, and some bits to encode the operand types (such as registers, memory locations, and constants). The number of bits needed to encode all this information can have a direct impact on the instruction's size, regardless of the instruction's usage frequency. For example, suppose two bits are needed to select an instruction's group, four bits to select the instruction within that group, and six bits to specify the instruction's operand types. In this case, the instructions are not going to fit into an 8-bit opcode. On the other hand, if all that's needed is to push one of eight different registers onto the stack, four bits will be enough to specify the push instruction group, and three bits will be enough to specify the register.

Encoding instruction operands with a minimal amount of space is always a problem, because many instructions allow a large number of operands. For example, the generic 80x86 mov instruction allows two operands and requires a 2-byte opcode.[1] However, Intel noticed that the mov(*disp*,eax); and mov(eax,*disp*); instructions occur frequently in programs. Therefore, they created a special 1-byte version of these instructions to reduce their size and, consequently, the size of programs that use these instructions. Note that Intel did not remove the 2-byte versions of these instructions. There are two different instructions that will store EAX into memory and two different instructions that will load EAX from memory. A compiler or assembler would always emit the shorter versions of each of these pairs of instructions.

Notice an important trade-off Intel made with the mov instruction: *it gave up an extra opcode in order to provide a shorter version of one variant of each instruction.* Actually, Intel uses this trick all over the place to create shorter and easier-to-decode instructions. Back in 1978, creating redundant instructions to reduce program size was a good compromise given the cost of memory. Today, however, a CPU designer would probably use those redundant opcodes for different purposes.

10.3 The Y86 Hypothetical Processor

Because of enhancements made to the 80x86 processor family over the years, Intel's design goals in 1978, and advances in computer architecture over the years, the encoding of 80x86 instructions is very complex and somewhat

---

[1] Actually, Intel claims it's a 1-byte opcode plus a 1-byte *mod-reg-r/m* byte. For our purposes, we'll treat the *mod-reg-r/m* byte as part of the opcode.

illogical. The 80x86 is not a good example to use when introducing the design of an instruction set. Therefore, to further our discussion, we will discuss instruction set design in two stages: first, we will develop a simple (trivial) instruction set for a hypothetical processor that is a small subset of the 80x86, and then we will expand our discussion to the full 80x86 instruction set. Our hypothetical processor is not a true 80x86 CPU, so we will call it the Y86 processor to avoid any accidental association with the Intel x86 family.

10.3.1 Y86 Limitations

The hypothetical Y86 processor is a *very* stripped down version of the 80x86 CPUs. Before we begin, let's lay out the restrictions we've placed on our Y86 instruction set design:

- The Y86 only supports one operand size — 16 bits. This simplification frees us from having to encode the size of the operand as part of the opcode (thereby reducing the total number of opcodes we will need).

- The Y86 processor only supports four 16-bit registers: AX, BX, CX, and DX. This lets us encode register operands with only two bits (versus the three bits the 80x86 family requires to encode eight registers).

- The Y86 only supports a 16-bit address bus with a maximum of 65,536 bytes of addressable memory.

These simplifications, plus a very limited instruction set, will allow us to encode all Y86 instructions using a one-byte opcode and a 2-byte displacement/offset when applicable.

10.3.2 Y86 Instructions

Including both forms of the mov instruction, the Y86 CPU still provides only 18 basic instructions. Seven of these instructions have two operands, eight of these instructions have one operand, and five instructions have no operands at all. The instructions are mov (two forms), add, sub, cmp, and, or, not, je, jne, jb, jbe, ja, jae, jmp, get, put, and halt.

10.3.2.1 The mov Instruction

The mov instruction is actually two instructions merged into the same instruction class. These are the two forms of the mov instruction:

```
mov( reg/memory/constant, reg );
mov( reg, memory );
```

In these forms, *reg* is either AX, BX, CX, or DX; *constant* is a numeric constant using hexadecimal notation, and *memory* is an operand specifying a memory location. The *reg/memory/constant* operand tells you that this particular operand may be either a register, a memory location, or a constant.

10.3.2.2 Arithmetic and Logical Instructions

The arithmetic and logical instructions take the following forms:

```
add( reg/memory/constant, reg );
sub( reg/memory/constant, reg );
cmp( reg/memory/constant, reg );
and( reg/memory/constant, reg );
or( reg/memory/constant, reg );

not( reg/memory );
```

The add instruction adds the value of the first operand to the value of the second operand, storing the sum in the second operand. The sub instruction subtracts the value of the first operand from the value of the second, storing the difference in the second operand. The cmp instruction compares the value of the first operand against the value of the second and saves the result of the comparison for use by the conditional jump instructions (described in the next section). The and and or instructions compute bitwise logical operations between their two operands and store the result of the operation in the second operand. The not instruction appears separately because it only supports a single operand. not is the bitwise logical operation that inverts the bits of its single memory or register operand.

10.3.2.3 Control Transfer Instructions

The *control transfer instructions* interrupt the execution of instructions stored in sequential memory locations and transfer control to instructions stored at some other point in memory. They do this either unconditionally, or conditionally, using the result from a cmp instruction. These are the control transfer instructions:

```
ja   dest;  // Jump if above (i.e., greater than)
jae  dest;  // Jump if above or equal (i.e., greater than or equal to)
jb   dest;  // Jump if below (i.e., less than)
jbe  dest;  // Jump if below or equal (i.e., less than or equal to)
je   dest;  // Jump if equal
jne  dest;  // Jump if not equal

jmp  dest;  // Unconditional jump
```

The first six instructions (ja, jae, jb, jbe, je, and jne) let you check the result of the previous cmp instruction, that is the result of the comparison of that instruction's first and second operands.[2] For example, if you compare the AX and BX registers with a cmp(ax,bx); instruction and execute the ja instruction, the Y86 CPU will jump to the specified destination location if AX is greater than BX. If AX is not greater than BX, control will fall through to the next instruction in the program. In contrast to the first six instructions,

---

[2] The Y86 processor only performs *unsigned* comparisons.

the jmp instruction unconditionally transfers control to the instruction at the destination address.

10.3.2.4 Miscellaneous Instructions

The Y86 supports three instructions that do not have any operands. The get and put instructions let you read and write integer values: get will stop and prompt the user for a hexadecimal value and then store that value into the AX register; put displays the value of the AX register in hexadecimal format. The halt instruction terminates program execution.

10.3.3 Addressing Modes on the Y86

Before assigning opcodes, we have to take a look at the operands these instructions support. As you've seen, the 18 Y86 instructions use five different operand types: registers, constants, and three memory-addressing modes (the *indirect* addressing mode, the *indexed* addressing mode, and the *direct* addressing mode). The following paragraphs explain these operand types.

Register operands are the easiest to understand. Consider the following forms of the mov instruction:

```
mov( ax, ax );
mov( bx, ax );
mov( cx, ax );
mov( dx, ax );
```

The first instruction accomplishes absolutely nothing. It copies the value from the AX register back into the AX register. The remaining three instructions copy the values of BX, CX, and DX into AX. Note that these instructions leave BX, CX, and DX unchanged. The second operand, the destination operand, is not limited to AX; you can move values to and from any of these registers.

Constants are also easy to understand. The following instructions load their respective registers with the specified constant (all numeric constants in Y86 assembly language are given in hexadecimal, so the "$" prefix is not necessary):

```
mov( 25, ax );
mov( 195, bx );
mov( 2056, cx );
mov( 1000, dx );
```

As mentioned, the Y86 instruction set uses three addressing modes to access data in memory. The following instructions demonstrate the use of these three addressing modes:

```
mov( [1000], ax );
mov( [bx], ax );
mov( [1000+bx], ax );
```

The first instruction uses the *direct addressing mode* to load AX with the 16-bit value stored in memory starting at location $1000.

The mov([bx],ax); instruction loads AX with the value at the memory location specified by the contents of the BX register, rather than simply storing BX's value into AX. This is the *indirect addressing mode*. Note that mov([1000],ax); is equivalent to the following two instructions:

```
mov( 1000, bx );
mov( [bx], ax );
```

The third of the addressing mode examples above, mov([1000+bx], ax);, provides an example of the *indexed addressing mode*. This instruction adds the value of the BX register with the value $1000 and uses this sum as the effective memory address. Then it loads the value at this effective memory address into the AX register. This instruction is useful for accessing elements of arrays, records, and other data structures.

10.3.4 Encoding Y86 Instructions

Because a real CPU uses logic circuitry to decode the opcodes and act appropriately on them, we have seen that it is not a very good idea to arbitrarily assign opcodes to machine instructions. A typical CPU opcode uses a certain number of bits in the opcode to denote the instruction class (such as mov, add, sub), and a certain number of bits to encode each of the operands.

A typical Y86 instruction takes the form shown in Figure 10-3. The basic instruction is either one or three bytes long, and the instruction opcode consists of a single byte that contains three fields. The first field, consisting of the HO three bits, defines the instruction, and these three bits provide eight possible combinations. As there are 18 different Y86 instructions, we'll have to pull some tricks to handle the remaining 10 instructions.

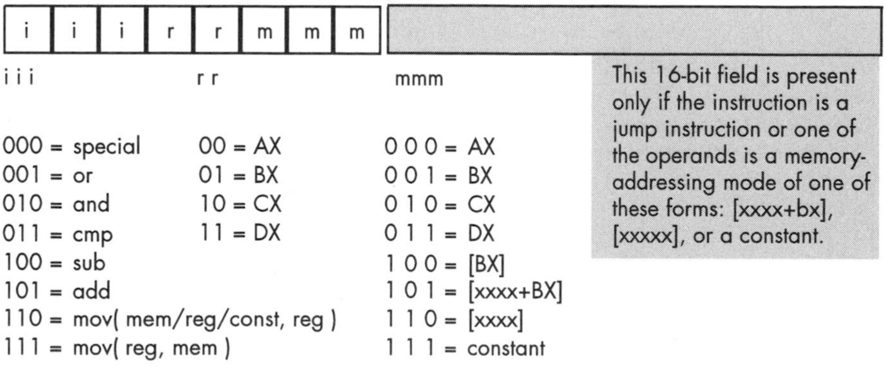

i	i	i	r	r	m	m	m	

i i i	r r	m m m	This 16-bit field is present only if the instruction is a jump instruction or one of the operands is a memory-addressing mode of one of these forms: [xxxx+bx], [xxxxx], or a constant.
000 = special	00 = AX	0 0 0 = AX	
001 = or	01 = BX	0 0 1 = BX	
010 = and	10 = CX	0 1 0 = CX	
011 = cmp	11 = DX	0 1 1 = DX	
100 = sub		1 0 0 = [BX]	
101 = add		1 0 1 = [xxxx+BX]	
110 = mov(mem/reg/const, reg)		1 1 0 = [xxxx]	
111 = mov(reg, mem)		1 1 1 = constant	

Figure 10-3: Basic Y86 instruction encoding

10.3.4.1 Eight Generic Y86 Instructions

As you can see in Figure 10-3, seven of the eight basic opcodes encode the or, and, cmp, sub, and add instructions, as well as both versions of the mov instruction. The eighth basic opcode is a special *expansion opcode*. This special instruction class provides a mechanism that allows us to expand the number of available instruction classes, which we will return to shortly.

To determine the full opcode for a particular instruction, you need only select the appropriate bits for the *iii*, *rr*, and *mmm* fields (identified in Figure 10-3). The *rr* field contains the destination register (except for the version of the mov instruction whose *iii* field is %111), and the *mmm* field encodes the source operand. For example, to encode the mov(bx,ax); instruction you would select *iii* = 110 (mov(*reg*,*reg*);), *rr* = 00 (AX), and *mmm* = 001 (BX). This produces the 1-byte instruction %11000001 or $C0.

Some Y86 instructions are larger than one byte. To illustrate why this is necessary, take, for example, the instruction mov([1000],ax);, which loads the AX register with the value stored at memory location $1000. The encoding for the opcode is %11000110 or $C6. However, the encoding for the mov([2000],ax); instruction is also $C6. Clearly these two instructions do different things: one loads the AX register from memory location $1000, while the other loads the AX register from memory location $2000.

In order to differentiate between instructions that encode an address using the [*xxxx*] or [*xxxx*+bx] addressing modes, or to encode a constant using the immediate addressing mode, you must append the 16-bit address or constant after the instruction's opcode. Within this 16-bit address or constant, the LO byte must follow the opcode in memory and the HO byte must follow the LO byte. So, the three byte encoding for mov([1000],ax); would be $C6, $00, $10, and the three byte encoding for mov([2000],ax); would be $C6, $00, $20.

10.3.4.2 Using the Special Expansion Opcode

The *special* opcode in Figure 10-3 allows the Y86 CPU to expand the set of available instructions that can be encoded using a single byte. This opcode handles several zero- and one-operand instructions, as shown in Figures 10-4 and 10-5.

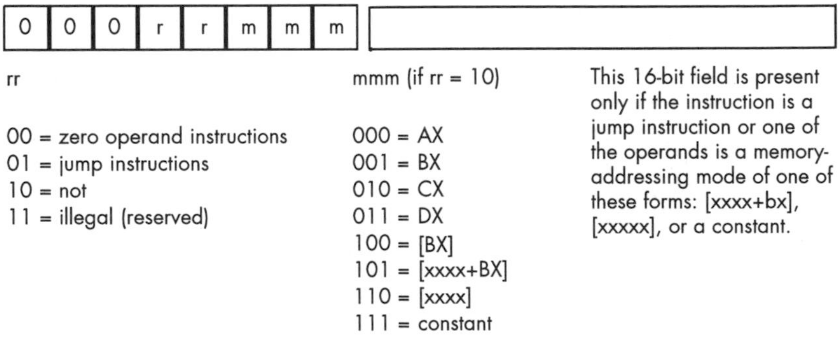

0	0	0	r	r	m	m	m			

rr

00 = zero operand instructions
01 = jump instructions
10 = not
11 = illegal (reserved)

mmm (if rr = 10)

000 = AX
001 = BX
010 = CX
011 = DX
100 = [BX]
101 = [xxxx+BX]
110 = [xxxx]
111 = constant

This 16-bit field is present only if the instruction is a jump instruction or one of the operands is a memory-addressing mode of one of these forms: [xxxx+bx], [xxxxx], or a constant.

Figure 10-4: Single-operand instruction encodings (iii = %000)

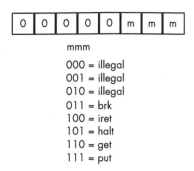

mmm

000 = illegal
001 = illegal
010 = illegal
011 = brk
100 = iret
101 = halt
110 = get
111 = put

Figure 10-5: Zero-operand instruction encodings (iii = %000 and rr = %00)

There are four one-operand instruction classes whose encodings are shown in Figure 10-4. The first 2-bit encoding for the *rr* field, %00, further expands the instruction set by providing a way to encode the zero-operand instructions shown Figure 10-5. Five of these instructions are illegal instruction opcodes; the three valid opcodes are the halt instruction, which terminates program execution, the get instruction, which reads a hexadecimal value from the user and stores this value in the AX register, and the put instruction, which outputs the value in the AX register.

The second 2-bit encoding for the *rr* field, %01, is also part of an expansion opcode that provides all the Y86 *jump* instructions (see Figure 10-6). The third *rr* field encoding, %10, is for the not instruction. The fourth *rr* field encoding is currently unassigned. Any attempt to execute an opcode with an *iii* field encoding of %000 and an *rr* field encoding of %11 will halt the processor with an illegal instruction error. CPU designers often reserve unassigned opcodes like this one to allow themselves to extend the instruction set at a future date (as Intel did when moving from the 80286 processor to the 80386).

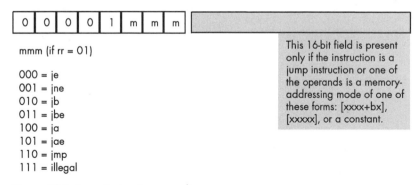

mmm (if rr = 01)

000 = je
001 = jne
010 = jb
011 = jbe
100 = ja
101 = jae
110 = jmp
111 = illegal

This 16-bit field is present only if the instruction is a jump instruction or one of the operands is a memory-addressing mode of one of these forms: [xxxx+bx], [xxxxx], or a constant.

Figure 10-6: Jump instruction encodings

As shown in Figure 10-6, there are seven jump instructions in the Y86 instruction set and they all take the following form: j*xx address*;. The jmp instruction copies the 16-bit address value that follows the opcode into the instruction pointer register, causing the CPU to fetch the next instruction from the target address of the jmp.

The jmp instruction is an example of an unconditional jump instruction. It always transfers control to the target address. The remaining six instructions — ja, jae, jb, jbe, je, and jne — are conditional jump instructions. They test some condition and only jump to the instruction's destination address if the condition is true; if the condition is false, these six instructions fall through to the next program instruction in memory. You would normally execute these conditional jump instructions immediately after a cmp instruction, as the cmp instruction sets the less than and equality flags that the conditional jump instructions test. Note that there are eight possible jump opcodes, but the Y86 uses only seven of them. The eighth opcode, %00001111, is another illegal opcode.

10.3.5 Examples of Encoding Y86 Instructions

Keep in mind that the Y86 processor fetches instructions as bit patterns from memory. It then decodes and executes those bit patterns. The processor does not execute instructions as strings of characters that are readable by humans, such as mov(ax,bx);. Instead, it executes the bit pattern $C1 in memory. Instructions like mov(ax,bx); and add(5,cx); are human-readable representations of instructions that must first be converted into binary representation, or *machine code*. In this section, we will explore this conversion.

10.3.5.1 The add Instruction

The first step in converting instructions to machine code is to choose an instruction to convert. We'll start with a very simple example, the add(cx,dx); instruction. Once you've chosen the instruction, you look up the instruction in one of the opcode figures from the previous section. The add instruction is in the first group (see Figure 10-3) and has an *iii* field of %101. The source operand is CX, so the *mmm* field is %010 and the destination operand is DX so the *rr* field is %11. Merging these bits produces the opcode %10111010 or $BA (see Figure 10-7).

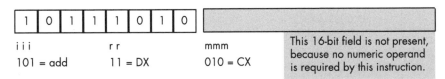

Figure 10-7: Encoding the add(cx, dx); instruction

Now consider the add(5,ax); instruction. Because this instruction has an immediate source operand (a constant), the *mmm* field will be %111 (see Figure 10-3). The destination register operand is AX (%00), and the instruction class field is %101, so the full opcode becomes $10100111 or $A7. However, this does not complete the encoding of the instruction. We also have to include the 16-bit constant $0005 as part of the instruction. The binary encoding of the constant must immediately follow the opcode in memory, with the LO byte of the constant following the opcode, and the HO byte of the constant following its LO byte, because the bytes are arranged in little endian order. So the sequence of bytes in memory, from lowest address to highest address, is $A7, $05, $00 (see Figure 10-8).

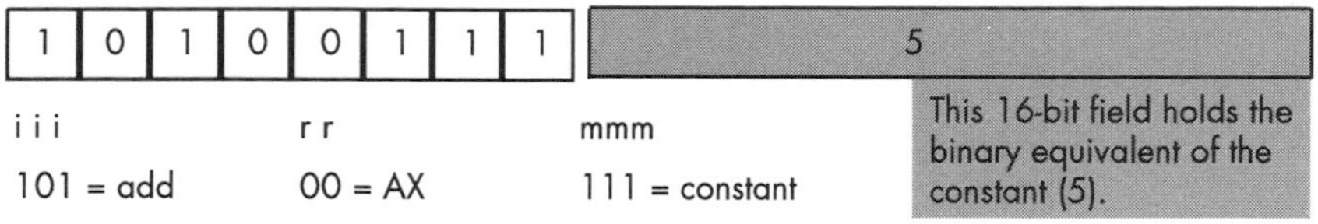

1	0	1	0	0	1	1	1		5

iii   rr   mmm   This 16-bit field holds the binary equivalent of the

101 = add   00 = AX   111 = constant   constant (5).

Figure 10-8: Encoding the add(5, ax); instruction

The add([2ff+bx],cx); instruction also contains a 16-bit constant that is the displacement portion of the indexed addressing mode. To encode this instruction, we use the following field values: iii = %101, rr = %10, and mmm = %101. This produces the opcode byte %10110101 or $B5. The complete instruction also requires the constant $2FF so the full instruction is the 3-byte sequence $B5, $FF, $02 (see Figure 10-9).

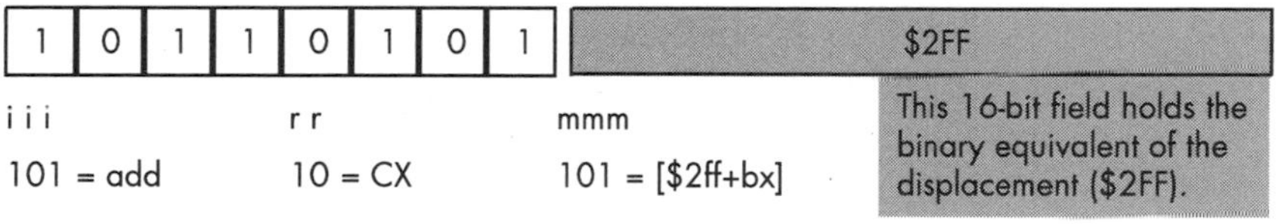

1	0	1	1	0	1	0	1		$2FF

iii   rr   mmm   This 16-bit field holds the binary equivalent of the

101 = add   10 = CX   101 = [$2ff+bx]   displacement ($2FF).

Figure 10-9: Encoding the add([$2ff+bx], cx); instruction

Now consider the add([1000],ax); instruction. This instruction adds the 16-bit contents of memory locations $1000 and $1001 to the value in the AX register. Once again, iii = %101 for the add instruction. The destination register is AX so rr = %00. Finally, the addressing mode is the displacement-only addressing mode, so mmm = %110. This forms the opcode %10100110, or $A6. The complete instruction is three bytes long because it must also encode the displacement (address) of the memory location in the two bytes following the opcode. Therefore, the complete 3-byte sequence is $A6, $00, $10 (see Figure 10-10).

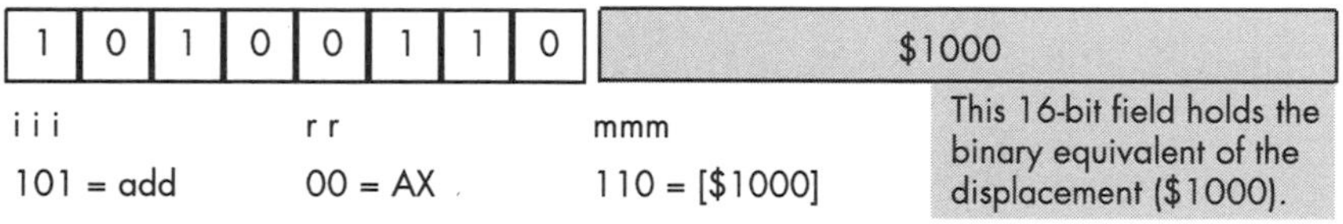

1	0	1	0	0	1	1	0		$1000

iii   rr   mmm   This 16-bit field holds the binary equivalent of the

101 = add   00 = AX   110 = [$1000]   displacement ($1000).

Figure 10-10: Encoding the add ([1000], ax); instruction

The last addressing mode to consider is the register indirect addressing mode, [bx]. The add([bx],bx); instruction uses the following encoded values: mmm = %101, rr = %01 (bx), and mmm = %100 ([bx]). Because the value in the BX register completely specifies the memory address, there is no need to attach a displacement field to the instruction's encoding. Hence, this instruction is only one byte long (see Figure 10-11).

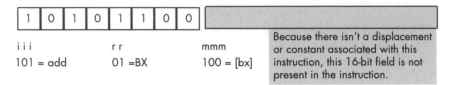

iii	rr	mmm	Because there isn't a displacement or constant associated with this instruction, this 16-bit field is not present in the instruction.
101 = add	01 = BX	100 = [bx]	

Figure 10-11: Encoding the add ([bx], bx); instruction

You use a similar approach to encode the sub, cmp, and, and or instructions. The only difference between encoding these instructions and the add instruction is the value you use for the *iii* field in the opcode.

10.3.5.2   The mov Instruction

The Y86 mov instruction is special, because it comes in two forms. The only difference between the encoding of the add instruction and the encoding of the mov instruction's first form (*iii* = %110) is the *iii* field. This first form of mov copies either a constant or data from the register or memory address specified by the *mmm* field into the destination register specified by the *rr* field.

The second form of the mov instruction (*iii* = %111) copies data from the source register specified by the *rr* field to a destination memory location that the *mmm* field specifies. In this second form of the mov instruction, the source and destination meanings of the *rr* and *mmm* fields are reversed so that *rr* is the source field and *mmm* is the destination field. Another difference between the two forms of mov is that in its second form, the *mmm* field may only contain the values %100 ([bx]), %101 ([disp+bx]), and %110 ([disp]). The destination values cannot be any of the registers encoded by *mmm* field values in the range %000..%011 or a constant encoded by an *mmm* field of %111. These encodings are illegal because the first form of the mov handles cases with a register destination, and because storing data into a constant doesn't make any sense.

10.3.5.3   The not Instruction

The not instruction is the only instruction with a single memory/register operand that the Y86 processor supports. The not instruction has the following syntax:

not(*reg*);

or

not(*address*);

. . . where *address* represents one of the memory addressing modes ([bx], [disp+bx], or [disp]). You may not specify a constant operand for the not instruction.

Because the not instruction has only a single operand, it needs only the *mmm* field to encode this operand. An *iii* field of %000 along with an *rr* field of %10 identifies the not instruction. In fact, whenever the *iii* field contains zero, the CPU knows that decoding beyond the *iii* field is necessary to identify the instruction. In this case, the *rr* field specifies whether we have encoded the not instruction or one of the other specially encoded instructions.

To encode an instruction like not(ax);, you would simply specify %000 for the *iii* field and %10 for the *rr* field. Then you would encode the *mmm* field the same way you would encode it for the add instruction. Because *mmm* = %000 for AX, the encoding of not(ax); would be %00010000 or $10 (see Figure 10-12).

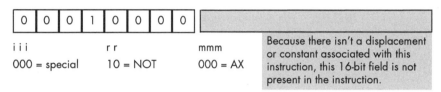

0	0	0	1	0	0	0	0

iii   r r   mmm
000 = special   10 = NOT   000 = AX

Because there isn't a displacement or constant associated with this instruction, this 16-bit field is not present in the instruction.

Figure 10-12: Encoding the not(AX); instruction

The not instruction does not allow an immediate, or constant, operand, so the opcode %00010111 ($17) is an illegal opcode.

10.3.5.4 The Jump Instructions

The Y86 jump instructions also use the *special* encoding, meaning that the *iii* field for jump instructions is always %000. These instructions are always three bytes long. The first byte, the opcode, specifies which jump instruction to execute and the next two bytes specify the address in memory to which the CPU transfers control (if the condition is met, in the case of the conditional jumps). There are seven different Y86 jump instructions, six conditional jumps, and one unconditional jump, jmp. All seven of these instructions set *iii* = %000 and *rr* = %01, and therefore only differ according to their *mmm* fields. The eighth possible opcode, with an *mmm* field value of %111, is an illegal opcode (see Figure 10-6).

Encoding these instructions is relatively straightforward. Picking the instruction you want to encode completely determines the opcode. The opcode values fall in the range $08..$0E ($0F is the illegal opcode).

The only field that requires some thought is the 16-bit operand that follows the opcode. This field holds the address of the target instruction to which the unconditional jump always transfers, and to which the conditional jumps transfer if the transfer condition is true. To properly encode this 16-bit operand you must know the address of the opcode byte of the target instruction. If you've already converted the target instruction to binary form and stored it into memory, you're all set — just specify the target instruction's address as the sole operand of the jump instruction. On the other hand, if you haven't yet written, converted, and placed the target instruction into memory, knowing its address would seem to require a bit of divination. Fortunately, you can figure out the target address by computing the lengths of all the instructions between the current jump instruction you're encoding and the target instruction. Unfortunately, this is an arduous task.

The best way to go about calculating the distance is to write all your instructions down on paper, compute their lengths (which is easy, because all instructions are either one or three bytes long depending on whether they have a 16-bit operand), and then assign an appropriate address to each instruction. Once you've done this, you'll know the starting address for each instruction, and you can put target address operands into your jump instructions as you encode them.

10.3.5.5 The Zero-Operand Instructions

The remaining instructions, the zero-operand instructions, are the easiest to encode. Because they have no operands they are always one byte long. These instructions always have iii = %000 and rr = %00, and mmm specifies the particular instruction opcode (see Figure 10-5). Note that the Y86 CPU leaves five of these instructions undefined (so we can use these opcodes for future expansion).

10.3.6 Extending the Y86 Instruction Set

The Y86 CPU is a trivial CPU, suitable only for demonstrating how to encode machine instructions. However, like any good CPU, the Y86 design does provide the capability for expansion. Therefore, if you wanted to improve the CPU by adding new instructions, the Y86's instruction set will allow you to do it.

You can increase the number of instructions in a CPU's instruction set by using either undefined or illegal opcodes on the CPU. Because the Y86 CPU has several illegal and undefined opcodes, we can use them to expand the instruction set.

Using undefined opcodes to define new instructions works best when there are undefined bit patterns within an opcode group, and the new instruction you want to add falls into that same group. For example, the opcode %00011mmm falls into the same group as the not instruction, which also has an iii field value of %000. If you decided that you really needed a neg (negate) instruction, using the %00011mmm opcode makes sense because you'd probably expect the neg instruction to use the same syntax as the not instruction. Likewise, if you want to add a zero-operand instruction to the instruction set, there are five undefined zero-operand instructions in the Y86 instruction set for you to choose from (%0000000..%00000100, see Figure 10-5). You'd just appropriate one of these opcodes and assign your instruction to it.

Unfortunately, the Y86 CPU doesn't have many illegal opcodes available. For example, if you wanted to add the shl (shift left), shr (shift right), rol (rotate left), and ror (rotate right) instructions as single-operand instructions, there is insufficient space within the group of single-operand instruction opcodes to add these instructions (only %00011*mmm* is currently open). Likewise, there are no two-operand opcodes open, so if you wanted to add an xor (exclusive OR) instruction or some other two-operand instruction, you'd be out of luck.

A common way to handle this dilemma, and one the Intel designers have employed, is to use one of the undefined opcodes as a prefix opcode byte. For example, the opcode $FF is illegal (it corresponds to a mov(dx,const); instruction), but we can use this byte as a special prefix byte to further expand the instruction set (see Figure 10-13).[3]

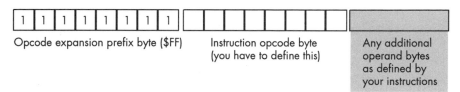

Opcode expansion prefix byte ($FF)   Instruction opcode byte (you have to define this)   Any additional operand bytes as defined by your instructions

Figure 10-13: Using a prefix byte to extend the instruction set

Whenever the CPU encounters a prefix byte in memory, it reads and decodes the next byte in memory as the actual opcode. However, it does not treat the second byte as it would a standard opcode that did not come after a prefix byte. Instead, it allows the CPU designer to create a completely new opcode scheme, independent of the original instruction set. A single-expansion opcode byte allows the CPU designer to add up to 256 additional instructions to the instruction set. If the CPU designer wishes to add even more instructions, that designer can use additional illegal opcode bytes (in the original instruction set) to add yet more expansion opcodes, each with their own independent instruction sets, or the CPU designer can follow the opcode expansion prefix byte with a 2-byte opcode (yielding up to 65,536 new instructions) or any other scheme the CPU designer can dream up.

Of course, one big drawback to this opcode expansion scheme is that it increases the size of the new instructions by one byte, because each instruction now requires the prefix byte as part of the opcode. This also increases the cost of the circuitry (decoding prefix bytes and multiple instruction sets is fairly complex), so you don't want to use this scheme for the basic instruction set. Nevertheless, it does provide a good mechanism for expanding the instruction set when you've run out of opcodes.

10.4   Encoding 80x86 Instructions

The Y86 processor is simple to understand; it is easy to encode instructions by hand for this processor, and it is a great vehicle for learning how to assign opcodes. It's also a purely hypothetical device intended only as a teaching

---

[3] We could also have used values $F7, $EF, and $E7 as they also correspond to an attempt to store a register into a constant. However, $FF is easier to decode. On the other hand, if you need even more prefix bytes for instruction expansion, you can use these three values as well.

tool. It's time to take a look at the machine instruction format for a real CPU — the 80x86. After all, the programs you're going to write will run on a real CPU, like the 80x86, so to fully appreciate what your compilers are doing with your code (so you can choose the best statements and data structures when writing that code), you need to understand how real instructions are encoded. Even if you're using a different CPU, studying the 80x86 instruction encoding is a good exercise, because it is one of the more complex instruction sets in common use today and will provide a good insight into the operation of other real-world CPUs.

They don't call the 80x86 a *Complex* Instruction Set Computer (CISC) chip for nothing. Although more complex instruction encodings do exist, no one is going to challenge the assertion that the 80x86 has a complex instruction encoding. The generic 80x86 instruction takes the form shown in Figure 10-14. Although this diagram seems to imply that instructions can be up to 16 bytes long, instructions cannot actually be greater than 15 bytes in length.

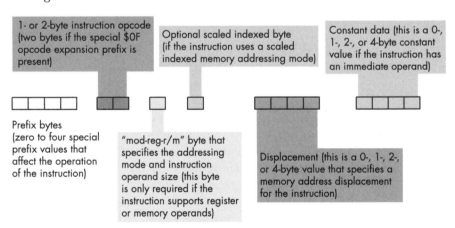

Figure 10-14: 80x86 instruction encoding

The prefix bytes are not the same as the opcode expansion prefix byte that we discussed in the previous section. Instead, the 80x86 prefix bytes modify the behavior of existing instructions. An instruction may have a maximum of four prefix bytes attached to it, but the 80x86 certainly supports more than four different prefix values. Also note that the behaviors of many prefix bytes are mutually exclusive, and the instruction's results will be undefined if you put a pair of mutually exclusive prefix bytes in front of an instruction. We'll take a look at a couple of these prefix bytes in a moment.

The 80x86 supports two basic opcode sizes: a standard 1-byte opcode and a 2-byte opcode consisting of a $0F opcode expansion prefix byte and a second byte specifying the actual instruction. One way to think of this opcode expansion prefix byte is as an 8-bit extension of the *iii* field in the Y86 encoding. This enables the encoding of up to 512 different instruction classes, although the 80x86 does not yet use them all. In reality, various instruction classes use certain bits in this opcode expansion prefix byte for decidedly non-instruction-class purposes. For example, consider the add instruction opcode. It takes the form shown in Figure 10-15.

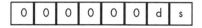

add opcode

d = 0 if adding from register to memory
d = 1 if adding from memory to register

s = 0 if adding 8-bit operands
s = 1 if adding 16-bit or 32-bit operands

Figure 10-15: 80x86 add opcode

Bit 1 (d) specifies the direction of the transfer. If this bit is zero, then the destination operand is a memory location, such as in add(al,[ebx]);. If this bit is one, the destination operand is a register, as in add([ebx],al);.

Note that bit 0 (s) specifies the size of the operands the add instruction operates upon. There is a problem here, however. The 80x86 family supports up to three different operand sizes: 8-bit operands, 16-bit operands, and 32-bit operands. With a single size bit, the instruction can only encode two of these three different sizes. In modern (32-bit) operating systems, the vast majority of operands are either 8 bits or 32 bits, so the 80x86 CPU uses the size bit in the opcode to encode 8-bit or 32-bit sizes. For 16-bit operands, which occur less frequently than 8-bit or 32-bit operands, Intel uses a special opcode prefix byte to specify the size. As long as instructions that have 16-bit operands occur less than one out of every eight instructions (and this is generally true), this is more compact than adding another bit to the instruction's size. Using a size prefix byte allowed Intel's designers to extend the number of operand sizes without having to change the instruction encoding inherited from the original 16-bit processors in this CPU family.

10.4.1 Encoding Instruction Operands

The *mod-reg-r/m* byte (see Figure 10-14) provides the encoding for instruction operands by specifying the base addressing mode used to access the operands and the instruction operand size. This byte contains the fields shown in Figure 10-16.

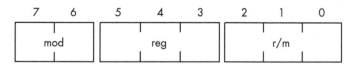

Figure 10-16: mod-reg-r/m byte

The *reg* field almost always specifies an 80x86 register. However, depending on the instruction, the register specified by *reg* can be either the source or the destination operand. To distinguish between the two possibilities, many instructions have the *d* (direction) field in their opcode that contains a value of zero when *reg* is the source and a value of one when *reg* is the destination operand.

This field uses the 3-bit register encodings found in Table 10-1. As you just learned, the size bit in the instruction's opcode specifies whether the *reg* field specifies an 8- or 32-bit register (when operating under a modern, 32-bit operating system). To make the *reg* field specify a 16-bit register requires setting the size bit in the opcode to one, as well as adding an additional prefix byte.

Table 10-1: *reg* Field Encodings

reg Value	Register If Data Size Is 8 Bits	Register If Data Size Is 16 Bits	Register If Data Size Is 32 Bits
%000	al	ax	eax
%001	cl	cx	ecx
%010	dl	dx	edx
%011	bl	bx	ebx
%100	ah	sp	esp
%101	ch	bp	ebp
%110	dh	si	esi
%111	bh	di	edi

With the *d* bit in the opcode of a two-operand instruction determining whether the *reg* field contains the source operand or the destination operand, the *mod* and *r/m* fields combine to specify the other of the two operands. In the case of a single-operand instruction like not or neg, the *reg* field will contain an opcode extension and *mod* and *r/m* will combine to specify the only operand. The *mod* and *r/m* fields together specify the operand addressing modes listed in Tables 10-2 and 10-3.

Table 10-2: *mod* Field Encodings

mod	Description
%00	Specifies register indirect addressing mode (with two exceptions: scaled indexed [*sib*] addressing modes with no displacement operand when *r/m* = %100; and displacement-only addressing mode when *r/m* = %101).
%01	Specifies that a 1-byte signed displacement follows the addressing mode byte(s).
%10	Specifies that a 1-byte signed displacement follows the addressing mode byte(s).
%11	Specifies direct register access.

Table 10-3: *mod-r/m* Encodings

mod	r/m	Addressing Mode
%00	%000	[eax]
%01	%000	[eax+$disp_8$]
%10	%000	[eax+$disp_{32}$]
%11	%000	al, ax, or eax
%00	%001	[ecx]
%01	%001	[ecx+$disp_8$]
%10	%001	[ecx+$disp_{32}$]
%11	%001	cl, cx, or ecx
%00	%010	[edx]
%01	%010	[edx+$disp_8$]
%10	%010	[edx+$disp_{32}$]
%11	%010	dl, dx, or edx
%00	%011	[ebx]
%01	%011	[ebx+$disp_8$]
%10	%011	[ebx+$disp_{32}$]
%11	%011	bl, bx, or ebx
%00	%100	Scaled indexed *(sib)* mode
%01	%100	*sib* + $disp_8$ mode
%10	%100	*sib* + $disp_{32}$ mode
%11	%100	ah, sp, or esp
%00	%101	Displacement-only mode (32-bit displacement)
%01	%101	[ebp+$disp_8$]
%10	%101	[ebp+$disp_{32}$]
%11	%101	ch, bp, or ebp
%00	%110	[esi]
%01	%110	[esi+$disp_8$]
%10	%110	[esi+$disp_{32}$]
%11	%110	dh, si, or esi
%00	%111	[edi]
%01	%111	[edi+$disp_8$]
%10	%111	[edi+$disp_{32}$]
%11	%111	bh, di, or edi

There are a couple of interesting things to note about Tables 10-2 and 10-3. First, there are two different forms of the [*reg*+*disp*] addressing modes: one form with an 8-bit displacement and one form with a 32-bit displacement. Addressing modes whose displacement falls in the range −128..+127 require only a single byte after the opcode to encode the displacement. Instructions with a displacement that falls within this range will be shorter and sometimes faster than instructions whose displacement values are not within this range and thus require the addition of four bytes after the opcode.

The second thing to note is that there is no [ebp] addressing mode. If you look in Table 10-3 where this addressing mode logically belongs (where *r/m* is %101 and *mod* is %00), you'll find that its slot is occupied by the 32-bit displacement-only addressing mode. The basic encoding scheme for addressing modes didn't allow for a displacement-only addressing mode, so Intel "stole" the encoding for [ebp] and used that for the displacement-only mode. Fortunately, anything you can do with the [ebp] addressing mode you can also do with the [ebp+*disp₈*] addressing mode by setting the 8-bit displacement to zero. True, such an instruction is a little bit longer than it would otherwise need to be if the [ebp] addressing mode existed, but the same capabilities are still there. Intel wisely chose to replace this particular register indirect addressing mode because they anticipated that programmers would use it less often than they would use the other register indirect addressing modes.

Another thing you'll notice missing from this table are addressing modes of the form [esp], [esp+*disp₈*], and [esp+*disp₃₂*]. Intel's designers borrowed the encodings for these three addressing modes to support the *scaled indexed addressing* modes they added to their 32-bit processors in the 80x86 family.

If *r/m* = %100 and *mod* = %00, then this specifies an addressing mode of the form [reg1₃₂+reg2₃₂*n]. This scaled index addressing mode computes the final address in memory as the sum of reg2 multiplied by n (n = 1, 2, 4, or 8) and reg1. Programs most often use this addressing mode when reg1 is a pointer holding the base address of an array of bytes (n = 1), words (n = 2), double words (n = 4), or quad words (n = 8) and reg2 holds the index into that array.

If *r/m* = %100 and *mod* = %01, then this specifies an addressing mode of the form [reg1₃₂+reg2₃₂*n + *disp₈*]. This scaled index addressing mode computes the final address in memory as the sum of reg2 multiplied by n (n = 1, 2, 4, or 8), reg1, and the 8-bit signed displacement (sign extended to 32 bits). Programs most often use this addressing mode when reg1 is a pointer holding the base address of an array of records, reg2 holding the index into that array, and *disp₈* providing the offset to a desired field in the record.

If *r/m* = %100 and *mod* = %10, then this specifies an addressing mode of the form [reg1₃₂+reg2₃₂*n + *disp₃₂*]. This scaled index addressing mode computes the final address in memory as the sum of reg2 multiplied by n (n = 1, 2, 4, or 8), reg1, and the 32-bit signed displacement. Programs most often use this addressing mode to index into static arrays of bytes, words, double words, or quad words.

If values corresponding to one of the *sib* modes appear in the *mod* and *r/m* fields, then the addressing mode is a scaled indexed addressing mode with a second byte (the *sib*) following the *mod-reg-r/m* byte, though don't forget that the *mod* field still specifies a displacement size of zero, one, or four bytes. Figure 10-17 shows the layout of this extra *sib*, and Table 10-4, Table 10-5, and Table 10-6 explain the values for each of the *sib* fields.

Figure 10-17: The sib (scaled index byte) layout

Table 10-4: Scale Values

Scale Value	Index*Scale Value
%00	Index*1
%01	Index*2
%10	Index*4
%11	Index*8

Table 10-5: Register Values for *sib* Encoding

Index Value	Register
%000	EAX
%001	ECX
%010	EDX
%011	EBX
%100	Illegal
%101	EBP
%110	ESI
%111	EDI

Table 10-6: Base Register Values for *sib* Encoding

Base Value	Register
%000	EAX
%001	ECX
%010	EDX
%011	EBX
%100	ESP
%101	Displacement only if *mod* = %00, EBP if *mod* = %01 or %10
%110	ESI
%111	EDI

The *mod-reg-r/m* and *sib* bytes are complex and convoluted, no question about that. The reason these addressing mode bytes are so convoluted is that Intel reused its 16-bit addressing circuitry when it switched to the 32-bit format rather than simply abandoning the 16-bit circuitry at that point. There were good hardware reasons for doing this, but the result is a complex scheme for specifying addressing modes.

Note that if the *r/m* field of the *mod-reg-r/m* byte contains %100 and *mod* does not contain %11 the addressing mode is a *sib* mode rather than the expected [esp], [esp+*disp₈*], or [ESP+*disp₃₂*] mode. In this case the compiler or assembler will emit an extra *sib* byte immediately following the *mod-reg-r/m* byte. Table 10-7 lists the various combinations of legal scaled indexed addressing modes on the 80x86.

Table 10-7: The Scaled Indexed Addressing Modes

mod	Index	Legal Scaled Indexed Addressing Modes[1]
%00	%000	$[base_{32}+eax*n]$
Base ≠ %101	%001	$[base_{32}+ecx*n]$
	%010	$[base_{32}+edx*n]$
	%011	$[base_{32}+ebx*n]$
	%100	n/a[2]
	%101	$[base_{32}+ebp*n]$
	%110	$[base_{32}+esi*n]$
	%111	$[base_{32}+edi*n]$
%00	%000	$[disp_{32}+eax*n]$
Base = %101[3]	%001	$[disp_{32}+ecx*n]$
	%010	$[disp_{32}+edx*n]$
	%011	$[disp_{32}+ebx*n]$
	%100	n/a
	%101	$[disp_{32}+ebp*n]$
	%110	$[disp_{32}+esi*n]$
	%111	$[disp_{32}+edi*n]$
%01	%000	$[disp_8+base_{32}+eax*n]$
	%001	$[disp_8+base_{32}+ecx*n]$
	%010	$[disp_8+base_{32}+edx*n]$
	%011	$[disp_8+base_{32}+ebx*n]$
	%100	n/a
	%101	$[disp_8+base_{32}+ebp*n]$
	%110	$[disp_8+base_{32}+esi*n]$
	%111	$[disp_8+base_{32}+edi*n]$

Table 10-7: The Scaled Indexed Addressing Modes (continued)

mod	Index	Legal Scaled Indexed Addressing Modes[1]
%10	%000	$[disp_{32}+base_{32}+eax*n]$
	%001	$[disp_{32}+base_{32}+ecx*n]$
	%010	$[disp_{32}+base_{32}+edx*n]$
	%011	$[disp_{32}+base_{32}+ebx*n]$
	%100	n/a
	%101	$[disp_{32}+base_{32}+ebp*n]$
	%110	$[disp_{32}+base_{32}+esi*n]$
	%111	$[disp_{32}+base_{32}+edi*n]$

[1] The $base_{32}$ register can be any of the 80x86 32-bit general-purpose registers, as specified by the base field.

[2] The 80x86 does not allow a program to use the ESP as an index register.

[3] The 80x86 doesn't support a $[base_{32}+ebp*n]$ addressing mode, but you can achieve the same effective address using $[base_{32}+ebp*n+disp_8]$ with an 8-bit displacement value of zero.

In each of the addressing modes appearing in Table 10-7, the *mod* field of the *mod-reg-r/m* byte specifies the size of the displacement (zero, one, or four bytes). The base and index fields of the *sib* specify the base and index registers, respectively. Note that this addressing mode does not allow the use of the ESP register as an index register. Presumably, Intel left this particular mode undefined to provide the ability to extend the addressing modes to three bytes in a future version of the CPU, although doing so seems a bit extreme.

Just as the *mod-reg-r/m* encoding replaced the [ebp] addressing mode with a displacement only mode, the *sib* addressing format replaces the [EBP+*index**scale] mode with a displacement plus index mode (that is, no base register). If it turns out that you really need to use the [EBP+*index**scale] addressing mode, you will have to use the [*disp8*+EBP+*index**scale] mode instead, specifying a one-byte displacement value of zero.

10.4.2   Encoding the add Instruction — Some Examples

To figure out how to encode an instruction using this complex scheme, some examples may prove useful. Therefore, let's look at how to encode the 80x86 add instruction using various addressing modes. The add opcode is either $00, $01, $02, or $03, depending on the direction and size bits in the opcode (see Figure 10-15). Figures 10-18 through 10-25 on the next three pages show how to encode various forms of the add instruction using different addressing modes.

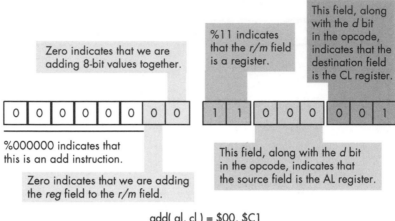

Zero indicates that we are adding 8-bit values together.

%11 indicates that the r/m field is a register.

This field, along with the *d* bit in the opcode, indicates that the destination field is the CL register.

| 0 | 0 | 0 | 0 | 0 | 0 | 0 | 0 | 1 | 1 | 0 | 0 | 0 | 0 | 0 | 1 |

%000000 indicates that this is an add instruction.

Zero indicates that we are adding the *reg* field to the *r/m* field.

This field, along with the *d* bit in the opcode, indicates that the source field is the AL register.

add(al, cl) = $00, $C1

Figure 10-18: Encoding the add(al, cl); instruction

There is an interesting side effect of the *mod-reg-r/m* organization and resulting from how the direction bit works: some instructions have two different legal opcodes. For example, we could also encode the add(al,cl); instruction shown in Figure 10-18 as $02, $C8 by reversing the positions of the AL and CL registers in the *reg* and *r/m* fields and then setting the *d* bit (bit 1) in the opcode to one. This applies to all instructions with two register operands and a direction bit, such as the add(eax,ecx); instruction in Figure 10-19, which can also be encoded as $03, $C8.

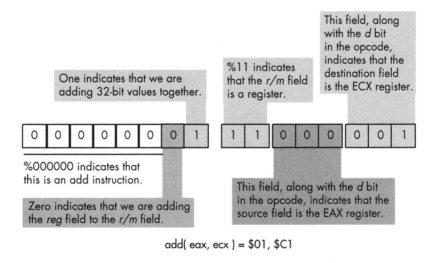

One indicates that we are adding 32-bit values together.

%11 indicates that the r/m field is a register.

This field, along with the *d* bit in the opcode, indicates that the destination field is the ECX register.

| 0 | 0 | 0 | 0 | 0 | 0 | 0 | 1 | 1 | 1 | 0 | 0 | 0 | 0 | 0 | 1 |

%000000 indicates that this is an add instruction.

Zero indicates that we are adding the *reg* field to the *r/m* field.

This field, along with the *d* bit in the opcode, indicates that the source field is the EAX register.

add(eax, ecx) = $01, $C1

Figure 10-19: Encoding the add(eax, ecx); instruction

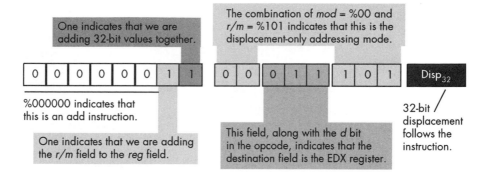

add(disp, edx) = $03, $1D, $ww, $xx, $yy, $zz

Note: $ww, $xx, $yy, $zz represent the four displacement byte values, with $ww being the LO byte and $zz being the HO byte.

Figure 10-20: Encoding the add(disp, edx); instruction

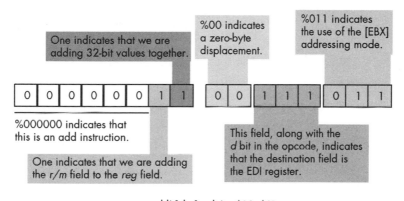

add([ebx], edi) = $03, $3B

Figure 10-21: Encoding the add([ebx], edi); instruction

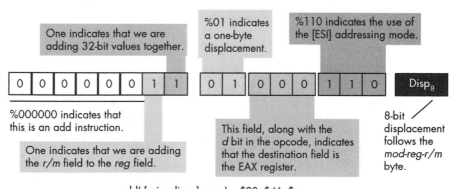

add([esi + disp$_8$], eax) = $03, $46, $xx

Figure 10-22: Encoding the add([esi+disp$_8$], eax); instruction

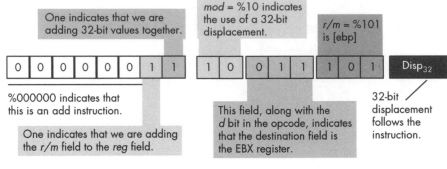

add([ebp + disp$_{32}$], ebx) = $03, $9D, $ww, $xx, $yy, $zz

Note: $ww, $xx, $yy, $zz represent the four displacement byte values, with $ww being the LO byte and $zz being the HO byte.

Figure 10-23: Encoding the add([ebp+disp$_{32}$], ebx); instruction

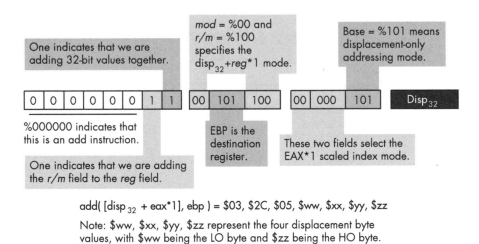

add([disp$_{32}$ + eax*1], ebp) = $03, $2C, $05, $ww, $xx, $yy, $zz

Note: $ww, $xx, $yy, $zz represent the four displacement byte values, with $ww being the LO byte and $zz being the HO byte.

Figure 10-24: Encoding the add([disp32+eax*1], ebp); instruction

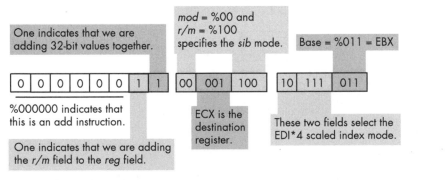

add([ebx + edi*4], ecx) = $03, $0C, $BB

Figure 10-25: Encoding the add([ebx+edi*4], ecx); instruction

10.4.3 Encoding Immediate Operands

You may have noticed that the *mod-reg-r/m* and *sib* bytes don't contain any bit combinations you can use to specify that an instruction contains an immediate operand. The 80x86 uses a completely different opcode to specify an immediate operand. Figure 10-26 shows the basic encoding for an add immediate instruction.

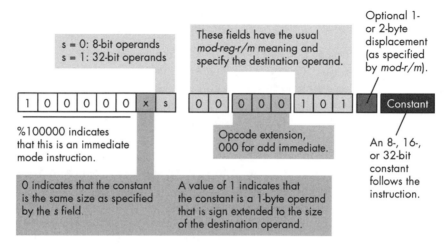

Figure 10-26: Encoding an add immediate instruction

There are three major differences between the encoding of the add immediate instruction and the standard add instruction. First, and most important, the opcode has a one in the HO bit position. This tells the CPU that the instruction has an immediate constant. This one change alone, however, does not tell the CPU that it must execute an add instruction, as you'll see shortly.

The second difference is that there is no direction bit in the opcode. This makes sense because you cannot specify a constant as a destination operand. Therefore, the destination operand is always the location specified by the *mod* and *r/m* bits in the *mod-reg-r/m* field.

In place of the direction bit, the opcode has a sign extension (x) bit. For 8-bit operands, the CPU ignores the sign extension bit. For 16-bit and 32-bit operands, the sign-extension bit specifies the size of the constant following the add instruction. If the sign extension bit contains zero, the constant is already the same size as the operand (either 16 or 32 bits). If the sign-extension bit contains one, the constant is a signed 8-bit value, and the CPU sign extends this value to the appropriate size before adding it to the operand. This little trick often makes programs quite a bit shorter because one commonly adds small constants to 16- or 32-bit destination operands.

The third difference between the add immediate and the standard add instruction is the meaning of the *reg* field in the *mod-reg-r/m* byte. Because the instruction implies that the source operand is a constant and the *mod-r/m* fields specify the destination operand, the instruction does not need to use the *reg* field to specify an operand. Instead, the 80x86 CPU uses these three bits as an opcode extension. For the add immediate instruction, these three bits must contain zero, and another bit pattern would correspond to a different instruction.

Note that when adding a constant to a memory location, any displacement associated with the memory location immediately precedes the constant data in the instruction sequence.

10.4.4   Encoding 8-, 16-, and 32-Bit Operands

When Intel designed the 8086, they used one opcode bit (s) to specify whether the operand sizes were 8 or 16 bits. Later, when they extended the 80x86 architecture to 32 bits with the introduction of the 80386, they had a problem: with this single operand size bit they could only encode two sizes, but they needed to encode three (8, 16, and 32 bits). To solve this problem, they used an *operand-size prefix byte*.

Intel studied its instruction set and came to the conclusion that in a 32-bit environment, programs were likely to use 8-bit and 32-bit operands far more often than 16-bit operands. Therefore, Intel decided to let the size bit (s) in the opcode select between 8- and 32-bit operands, as the previous sections describe. Although modern 32-bit programs don't use 16-bit operands very often, they do need them now and then. To allow for 16-bit operands, Intel lets you prefix a 32-bit instruction with the operand size prefix byte, whose value is $66. This prefix byte tells the CPU that the operands contain 16-bit data rather than 32-bit data.

You do not have to explicitly put an operand-size prefix byte in front of your 16-bit instructions; the assembler or compiler will take care of this automatically for you. However, do keep in mind that whenever you use a 16-bit object in a 32-bit program, the instruction is one byte longer because of the prefix value. Therefore, you should be careful about using 16-bit instructions if size, and, to a lesser extent, speed are important.

10.4.5   Alternate Encodings for Instructions

As noted earlier in this chapter, one of Intel's primary design goals for the 80x86 was to create an instruction set to allow programmers to write very short programs in order to save memory, which was precious at the time. One way they did this was to create alternative encodings of some very commonly used instructions. These alternative instructions were shorter than their standard counterparts, and Intel hoped that programmers would make extensive use of the shorter versions, thus creating shorter programs.

A good example of these alternative instructions are the `add(constant,accumulator);` instructions, where the accumulator is AL, AX, or EAX. The 80x86 provides 1-byte opcodes for `add(constant,al);` and `add(constant,eax );`, which are $04 and $05, respectively. With a 1-byte opcode and no *mod-reg-r/m* byte, these instructions are one byte shorter than their standard add immediate counterparts. The `add(constant,ax);`

instruction requires an operand size prefix, so its opcode is effectively two bytes if you count the prefix byte. This, however, is still one byte shorter than the corresponding standard add immediate.

You do not have to specify anything special to use these instructions. Any decent assembler or compiler will automatically choose the shortest possible instruction it can use when translating your source code into machine code. However, you should note that Intel only provides alternative encodings for the accumulator registers. Therefore, if you have a choice of several instructions to use and the accumulator registers are among these choices, the AL, AX, and EAX registers are often your best bet. However, this option is usually only available to assembly language programmers.

10.5 Implications of Instruction Set Design to the Programmer

Upon initial inspection, it would seem that instruction set design is of little interest to programmers who simply want to write great code, rather than design their own instruction sets. However, only by knowing the computer's architecture and, in particular, how the CPU encodes machine instructions, can a programmer make the most efficient use of the machine's instructions. By studying instruction set design, a programmer can gain a clear understanding of the following:

- Why some instructions are shorter than others
- Why some instructions are faster than others
- Which constant values the CPU can handle efficiently
- Whether constants are more efficient than memory locations
- Why certain arithmetic and logical operations are more efficient than others
- Which types of arithmetic expressions are more easily translated into machine code than other types
- Why code is less efficient if it transfers control over a large distance in the object code

. . . and so on.

By studying instruction set design, a programmer becomes more aware of the implications of the code they write (even in a high-level language) with respect to efficient operation on the CPU. Armed with this knowledge, the programmer can write great code.

10.6 For More Information

Like the previous chapter, this chapter deals with issues of computer architecture. There are many college and professional texts on computer architecture available that will provide additional information about instruction set design and the choices and trade-offs one must make when designing an instruction set. Patterson and Hennessy's *Computer Architecture: A Quantitative Approach* is one of the better regarded texts on this subject (though it is a bit heavily biased towards RISC architectures). The data books for your particular CPU will discuss the instruction encoding for that CPU and detail the operation of each machine instruction the CPU supports. A good text on assembly language programming may also prove helpful when learning more about instruction set design (such as my text for Intel 80x86 users, *The Art of Assembly Language*). For details on the design of the 80x86 instruction set, you'll want to check out Intel's Pentium manuals, available online at http://www.intel.com. Of course, similar information is available at just about every CPU manufacturer's website.

11

MEMORY ARCHITECTURE
AND ORGANIZATION

This chapter discusses the memory hierarchy — the different types and performance levels of memory found in computer systems. Although programmers often treat all forms of memory as though they were equivalent, using memory improperly can have a negative impact on performance. This chapter discusses how to make the best use of the memory hierarchy within your programs.

11.1   The Memory Hierarchy

Most modern programs benefit by having a large amount of very fast memory. Unfortunately, as a memory device gets larger, it tends to be slower. For example, cache memories are very fast, but they are also small and expensive.

Main memory is inexpensive and large, but is slow, requiring wait states. The memory hierarchy provides a way to compare the cost and performance of memory. Figure 11-1 diagrams one variant of the memory hierarchy.

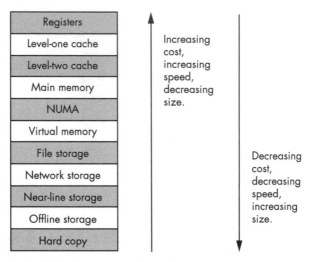

Figure 11-1: The memory hierarchy

At the top level of the memory hierarchy are the CPU's general-purpose *registers*. The registers provide the fastest access to data possible on the CPU. The register file is also the smallest memory object in the hierarchy (for example, the 80x86 has just eight general-purpose registers). Because it is impossible to add more registers to a CPU, registers are also the most expensive memory locations. Even if we count the FPU, MMX/AltaVec, SSE/SIMD, and other CPU registers in this portion of the memory hierarchy, this does not change the fact that CPUs have a very limited number of registers, and the cost per byte of register memory is quite high.

Working our way down, the *level-one cache* system is the next highest performance subsystem in the memory hierarchy. As with registers, the CPU manufacturer usually provides the level-one (L1) cache on the chip, and you cannot expand it. The size is usually small, typically between 4 KB and 32 KB, though this is much larger than the register memory available on the CPU chip. Although the L1 cache size is fixed on the CPU, the cost per cache byte is much lower than the cost per register byte because the cache contains more storage than is available in all the combined registers, and the system designer's cost of both memory types is the price of the CPU.

Level-two cache is present on some CPUs, but not all. For example, most Pentium II, III, and IV CPUs have a level-two (L2) cache as part of the CPU package, but some of Intel's Celeron chips do not. The L2 cache is generally much larger than the L1 cache (for example, 256 KB to 1 MB as compared with 4 KB to 32 KB). On CPUs with a built-in L2 cache, the cache is not expandable. It is still lower in cost than the L1 cache because we amortize the cost of the CPU across all the bytes in the two caches, and the L2 cache is larger.

The *main-memory* subsystem comes below the L2 cache system in the memory hierarchy.[1] Main memory is the general-purpose, relatively low-cost memory found in most computer systems. Typically, this memory is DRAM or some similarly inexpensive memory. However, there are many differences in main memory technology that result in differences in speed. The main memory types include standard DRAM, synchronous DRAM (SDRAM), double data rate DRAM (DDRAM), and Rambus DRAM (RDRAM). Generally, though, you won't find a mixture of these technologies in the same computer system.

Below main memory is the *NUMA* memory subsystem. NUMA, which stands for Non-Uniform Memory Access, is a bit of a misnomer. The term NUMA implies that different types of memory have different access times, and so it is descriptive of the entire memory hierarchy. In Figure 11-1, however, the term NUMA is used to describe blocks of memory that are electronically similar to main memory but, for one reason or another, operate significantly slower than main memory. A good example of NUMA memory is the memory on a video display card. Another example is flash memory, which has significantly slower access and transfer times than standard semiconductor RAM. Other peripheral devices that provide a block of memory to be shared between the CPU and the peripheral usually have slow access times, as well.

Most modern computer systems implement a *virtual memory* scheme that simulates main memory using a mass storage disk drive. A virtual memory subsystem is responsible for transparently copying data between the disk and main memory as needed by programs. While disks are significantly slower than main memory, the cost per bit is also three orders of magnitude lower for disks. Therefore, it is far less expensive to keep data on magnetic storage than in main memory.

File storage also uses disk media to store program data. However, whereas the virtual memory subsystem is responsible for handling data transfer between disk and main memory as programs require, it is the program's responsibility to store and retrieve file-storage data. In many instances, it is a bit slower to use file-storage memory than it is to use virtual memory, hence the lower position of file-storage memory in the memory hierarchy.[2]

Next comes *network storage*. At this level in the memory hierarchy, programs keep data on a different memory system that connects to the computer system via a network. Network storage can be virtual memory, file-storage memory, or a memory system known as *distributed shared memory* (DSM), where processes running on different computer systems share data stored in a common block of memory and communicate changes to that block across the network.

---

[1] Actually, some systems now offer an external level-three cache. External level-three caches are present on some systems where the L1 and L2 caches are part of the CPU package and the system implementor wants to add more cache to the system.

[2] Note, however, that in some degenerate cases virtual memory can be much slower than file access.

Virtual memory, file storage, and network storage are examples of so-called *online memory subsystems.* Memory access within these memory subsystems is slower than accessing the main-memory subsystem. However, when a program requests data from one of these three memory subsystems, the memory device will respond to the request as quickly as its hardware allows. This is not true for the remaining levels in the memory hierarchy.

The *near-line* and *offline storage* subsystems may not be ready to respond to a program's request for data immediately. An offline storage system keeps its data in electronic form (usually magnetic or optical), but on storage media that are not necessarily connected to the computer system that needs the data. Examples of offline storage include magnetic tapes, disk cartridges, optical disks, and floppy diskettes. Tapes and removable media are among the most inexpensive electronic data storage formats available. Hence, these media are great for storing large amounts of data for long periods. When a program needs data from an offline medium, the program must stop and wait for someone or something to mount the appropriate media on the computer system. This delay can be quite long (perhaps the computer operator decided to take a coffee break?).

Near-line storage uses the same types of media as offline storage, but rather than requiring an external source to mount the media before its data is available for access, the near-line storage system holds the media in a special robotic jukebox device that can automatically mount the desired media when a program requests it.

Hard-copy storage is simply a printout, in one form or another, of data. If a program requests some data, and that data is present only in hard-copy form, someone will have to manually enter the data into the computer. Paper, or other hard-copy media, is probably the least expensive form of memory, at least for certain data types.

11.2   How the Memory Hierarchy Operates

The whole point of having the memory hierarchy is to allow reasonably fast access to a large amount of memory. If only a little memory were necessary, we'd use fast static RAM (the circuitry that cache memory uses) for everything. If speed wasn't an issue, we'd use virtual memory for everything. The whole point of having a memory hierarchy is to enable us to take advantage of the principles of *spatial locality of reference* and *temporality of reference* to move often-referenced data into fast memory and leave less-often-used data in slower memory. Unfortunately, during the course of a program's execution, the sets of oft-used and seldom-used data change. We cannot simply distribute our data throughout the various levels of the memory hierarchy when the program starts and then leave the data alone as the program executes. Instead, the different memory subsystems need to be able to adjust for changes in spatial locality or temporality of reference during the program's execution by dynamically moving data between subsystems.

Moving data between the registers and memory is strictly a program function. The program loads data into registers and stores register data into memory using machine instructions like mov. It is strictly the programmer's or compiler's responsibility to keep heavily referenced data in the registers as long as possible, the CPU will not automatically place data in general-purpose registers in order to achieve higher performance.

Programs are largely unaware of the memory hierarchy between the register level and main memory. In fact, programs only explicitly control access to registers, main memory, and those memory-hierarchy subsystems at the file-storage level and below. In particular, cache access and virtual memory operations are generally transparent to the program. That is, access to these levels of the memory hierarchy usually occurs without any intervention on a program's part. Programs simply access main memory, and the hardware and operating system take care of the rest.

Of course, if every memory access that a program makes is to main memory, then the program will run slowly because modern DRAM main-memory subsystems are much slower than the CPU. The job of the cache memory subsystems and of the CPU's cache controller is to move data between main memory and the L1 and L2 caches so that the CPU can quickly access oft-requested data. Likewise, it is the virtual memory subsystem's responsibility to move oft-requested data from hard disk to main memory (if even faster access is needed, the caching subsystem will then move the data from main memory to cache).

With few exceptions, most memory subsystem accesses take place transparently between one level of the memory hierarchy and the level immediately below or above it. For example, the CPU rarely accesses main memory directly. Instead, when the CPU requests data from memory, the L1 cache subsystem takes over. If the requested data is in the cache, then the L1 cache subsystem returns the data to the CPU, and that concludes the memory access. If the requested data is not present in the L1 cache, then the L1 cache subsystem passes the request on down to the L2 cache subsystem. If the L2 cache subsystem has the data, it returns this data to the L1 cache, which then returns the data to the CPU. Note that requests for the same data in the near future will be fulfilled by the L1 cache rather than the L2 cache because the L1 cache now has a copy of the data.

If neither the L1 nor the L2 cache subsystems have a copy of the data, then the request goes to main memory. If the data is found in main memory, then the main-memory subsystem passes this data to the L2 cache, which then passes it to the L1 cache, which then passes it to the CPU. Once again, the data is now in the L1 cache, so any requests for this data in the near future will be fulfilled by the L1 cache.

If the data is not present in main memory, but is present in virtual memory on some storage device, the operating system takes over, reads the data from disk or some other device (such as a network storage server), and passes the data to the main-memory subsystem. Main memory then passes the data through the caches to the CPU in the manner that we've seen.

Because of spatial locality and temporality, the largest percentage of memory accesses take place in the L1 cache subsystem. The next largest percentage of accesses takes place in the L2 cache subsystem. The most infrequent accesses take place in virtual memory.

11.3 Relative Performance of Memory Subsystems

If you take another look at Figure 11-1, you'll notice that the speed of the various memory hierarchy levels increases as you go up. Exactly how much faster is each successive level in the memory hierarchy? To summarize the answer here, the speed gradient is not uniform. The speed difference between any two contiguous levels ranges from "almost no difference" to "four orders of magnitude."

Registers are, unquestionably, the best place to store data you need to access quickly. Accessing a register never requires any extra time, and most machine instructions that access data can access register data. Furthermore, instructions that access memory often require extra bytes (displacement bytes) as part of the instruction encoding. This makes instructions longer and, often, slower.

If you read Intel's instruction timing tables for the 80x86, you'll see that they claim that an instruction like mov(someVar,ecx); is supposed to run as fast as an instruction of the form mov(ebx,ecx);. However, if you read the fine print, you'll find that they make this claim based on several assumptions about the former instruction. First, they assume that someVar's value is present in the L1 cache memory. If it is not, then the cache controller needs to look in the L2 cache, in main memory, or worse, on disk in the virtual memory subsystem. All of a sudden, an instruction that should execute in one nanosecond on a 1-GHz processor (that is, in one clock cycle) requires several milliseconds to execute. That's a difference of over six orders of magnitude. It is true that future accesses of this variable will take place in just one clock cycle because it will subsequently be stored in the L1 cache. But even if you access someVar's value one million times while it is still in the cache, the average time of each access will still be about two cycles because of the large amount of time needed to access someVar the very first time.

Granted, the likelihood that some variable will be located on disk in the virtual memory subsystem is quite low. However, there is still a difference in performance of three orders of magnitude between the L1 cache subsystem and the main memory subsystem. Therefore, if the program has to bring the data from main memory, 999 memory accesses later you're still paying an average cost of two clock cycles to access the data that Intel's documentation claims should happen in one cycle.

The difference in speed between the L1 and L2 cache systems is not so dramatic unless the secondary cache is not packaged together on the CPU. On a 1-GHz processor the L1 cache must respond within one nanosecond if the cache operates with zero wait states (some processors actually introduce wait states in L1 cache accesses, but CPU designers try to avoid this).

Accessing data in the L2 cache is always slower than in the L1 cache, and there is always the equivalent of at least one wait state, and up to eight, when accessing data in the L2 cache.

There are several reasons why L2 cache accesses are slower than L1 accesses. First, it takes the CPU time to determine that the data it is seeking is not in the L1 cache. By the time it determines that the data is not present in the L1 cache, the memory-access cycle is nearly complete, and there is no time to access the data in the L2 cache. Secondly, the circuitry of the L2 cache may be slower than the circuitry of the L1 cache in order to make the L2 cache less expensive. Third, L2 caches are usually 16 to 64 times larger than L1 caches, and larger memory subsystems tend to be slower than smaller ones. All this adds up to additional wait states when accessing data in the L2 cache. As noted earlier, the L2 cache can be as much as one order of magnitude slower than the L1 cache.

The L1 and L2 caches also differ in the amount of data the system fetches when there is a cache miss (see Chapter 6). When the CPU fetches data from or writes data to the L1 cache, it generally fetches or writes only the data requested. If you execute a mov(al,memory); instruction, the CPU writes only a single byte to the cache. Likewise, if you execute the mov(mem32,eax); instruction, the CPU reads exactly 32 bits from the L1 cache. However, access to memory subsystems below the L1 cache does not work in small chunks like this. Usually, memory subsystems move blocks of data, or *cache lines*, whenever accessing lower levels of the memory hierarchy. For example, if you execute the mov(mem32,eax); instruction, and mem32's value is not in the L1 cache, the cache controller doesn't simply read mem32's 32 bits from the L2 cache, assuming that it's present there. Instead, the cache controller will actually read a whole block of bytes (generally 16, 32, or 64 bytes, depending on the particular processor) from the L2 cache. The hope is that the program exhibits spatial locality and therefore that reading a block of bytes will speed up future accesses to adjacent objects in memory. The bad news, however, is that the mov(mem32,eax); instruction doesn't complete until the L1 cache reads the entire cache line from the L2 cache. This excess time is known as *latency*. If the program does not access memory objects adjacent to mem32 in the future, this latency is lost time.

A similar performance gulf separates the L2 cache and main memory. Main memory is typically one order of magnitude slower than the L2 cache. To speed up access to adjacent memory objects, the L2 cache reads data from main memory in blocks (cache lines) to speed up access to adjacent memory elements.

Standard DRAM is three to four orders of magnitude faster than disk storage. To overcome this difference, there is usually a difference of two to three orders of magnitude in size between the L2 cache and the main memory so that the difference in speed between disk and main memory matches the difference in speed between the main memory and the L2 cache. (Having balanced performance characteristics is an attribute to strive for in the memory hierarchy in order to effectively use the different memory levels.)

We will not consider the performance of the other memory-hierarchy subsystems in this chapter, as they are more or less under programmer control. Because their access is not automatic, very little can be said about how frequently a program will access them. However, in Chapter 12 we'll take another look at issues regarding these storage devices.

11.4 Cache Architecture

Up to this point, we have treated the cache as a magical place that automatically stores data when we need it, perhaps fetching new data as the CPU requires it. But how exactly does the cache do this? And what happens when the cache is full and the CPU is requesting additional data not in the cache? In this section, we'll look at the internal cache organization and try to answer these questions, along with a few others.

Because programs only access a small amount of data at a given time, a cache that is the same size as the typical amount of data that programs access can provide very high-speed data access. Unfortunately, the data that programs want rarely sits in contiguous memory locations. Usually the data is spread out all over the address space. Therefore, cache design has to accommodate the fact that the cache must map data objects at widely varying addresses in memory.

As noted in the previous section, cache memory is not organized in a single group of bytes. Instead, cache memory is usually organized in blocks of *cache lines,* with each line containing some number of bytes (typically a small power of two like 16, 32, or 64), as shown in Figure 11-2.

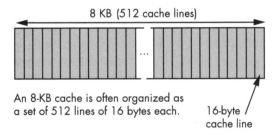

8 KB (512 cache lines)

An 8-KB cache is often organized as a set of 512 lines of 16 bytes each. 16-byte cache line

Figure 11-2: Possible organization of an 8-KB cache

Because of this 512×16-byte cache organization found in Figure 11-2, we can attach a different noncontiguous address to each of the cache lines. Cache line 0 might correspond to addresses \$10000..\$1000F and cache line 1 might correspond to addresses \$21400..\$2140F. Generally, if a cache line is n bytes long, that cache line will hold n bytes from main memory that fall on an n-byte boundary. In the example in Figure 11-2, the cache lines are 16 bytes long, so a cache line holds blocks of 16 bytes whose addresses fall on 16-byte boundaries in main memory (in other words, the LO four bits of the address of the first byte in the cache line are always zero).

When the cache controller reads a cache line from a lower level in the memory hierarchy, where does the data go in the cache? The answer is determined by the caching scheme in use. There are three different cache schemes: *direct-mapped cache*, *fully associative cache*, and *n-way set associative cache*.

11.4.1 Direct-Mapped Cache

In a *direct-mapped cache* (also known as the *one-way set associative cache*), a block of main memory is always loaded into the exact same cache line. Generally, a small number of bits in the data's memory address determines which cache line will hold the data. For example, Figure 11-3 shows how the cache controller could select the appropriate cache line for an 8-KB cache with 512 16-byte cache lines and a 32-bit main-memory address. Because there are 512 cache lines, it requires 9 bits to select one of the cache lines ($2^9 = 512$). This example uses bits 4 through 12 to determine which cache line to use (assuming we number the cache lines from 0 to 511), while bits 0 through 3 of the original memory address determine the particular byte within the 16-byte cache line.

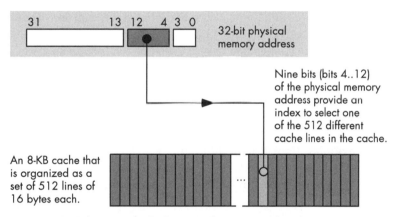

Figure 11-3: Selecting a cache line in a direct-mapped cache

The direct-mapped cache scheme is very easy to implement. Extracting nine (or some other number of) bits from the memory address and using the result as an index into the array of cache lines is trivial and fast. However, direct-mapped caches suffer from a few problems.

Perhaps the biggest problem with a direct-mapped cache is that it may not make effective use of all the cache memory. For example, the cache scheme in Figure 11-3 maps address zero to cache line 0. It also maps addresses $2000 (8 KB), $4000 (16 KB), $6000 (24 KB), and $8000 (32 KB) to cache line 0. In fact, it maps every address that is an even multiple of eight kilobytes to cache line 0. This means that if a program is constantly accessing data at addresses that are even multiples of 8 KB and not accessing any other locations, the system will only use cache line 0, leaving all the other cache lines unused. Each time the CPU requests data at an address that is mapped to cache line 0, but whose corresponding data is not present in cache line 0 (an address that is not an even multiple of 8 KB), the CPU will have to go down to a lower level in the memory hierarchy to access the data. In this extreme case, the cache is effectively limited to the size of one cache line.

11.4.2 Fully Associative Cache

The most flexible cache system is the fully associative cache. In a fully associative cache subsystem, the caching controller can place a block of bytes in any one of the cache lines present in the cache memory. While this is a very flexible system, the flexibility required is not without cost. The extra circuitry to achieve full associativity is expensive and, worse, can slow down the memory subsystem. Most L1 and L2 caches are not fully associative for this reason.

11.4.3 n-Way Set Associative Cache

If a fully associative cache organization is too complex, too slow, and too expensive to implement, but a direct-mapped cache organization isn't as good as we'd like, one might ask if there is a compromise that doesn't have the drawbacks of a direct-mapped approach or the complexity of a fully associative cache. The answer is yes; we can create an *n*-way set associative cache that is a compromise between these two extremes. In an *n*-way set associative cache, the cache is broken up into *sets* of cache lines. The CPU determines the particular set to use based on some subset of the memory address bits, just as in the direct-mapping scheme. Within each cache line set, there are *n* cache lines. The caching controller uses a fully associative mapping algorithm to determine which one of the *n* cache lines within the set to use.

For example, an 8-KB two-way set associative cache subsystem with 16-byte cache lines organizes the cache into 256 cache-line sets with two cache lines each. ("Two-way" means that each set contains two cache lines.) Eight bits from the memory address determine which one of these 256 different sets holds the cache line that will contain the data. Once the cache-line set is determined, the cache controller then maps the block of bytes to one of the two cache lines within the set (see Figure 11-4).

The advantage of a two-way set associative cache over a direct-mapped cache is that two different memory addresses located on 8-KB boundaries (addresses having the same value in bits 4 through 11) can both appear simultaneously in the cache. However, a conflict will occur if you attempt to access a third memory location at an address that is an even multiple of 8 KB.

A two-way set associative cache is much better than a direct-mapped cache and it is considerably less complex than a fully associative cache. However, if you're still getting too many conflicts, you might consider using a four-way set associative cache, which puts four associative cache lines in each cache-line set. In an 8-KB cache like the one in Figure 11-4, a four-way set associative cache scheme would have 128 cache-line sets with four cache lines each. This would allow the cache to maintain up to four different blocks of data without a conflict, each of which would map to the same cache line in a direct-mapped cache.

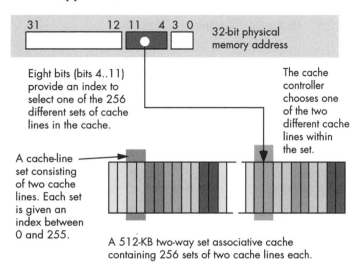

Eight bits (bits 4..11) provide an index to select one of the 256 different sets of cache lines in the cache.

The cache controller chooses one of the two different cache lines within the set.

A cache-line set consisting of two cache lines. Each set is given an index between 0 and 255.

A 512-KB two-way set associative cache containing 256 sets of two cache lines each.

Figure 11-4: A two-way set associative cache

The more cache lines we have in each cache-line set, the closer we come to creating a fully associative cache, with all the attendant problems of complexity and speed. Most cache designs are direct-mapped, two-way set associative, or four-way set associative. The various members of the 80x86 family make use of all three.

11.4.4 Matching the Caching Scheme to the Type of Data Access

Although this chapter has made the direct-mapped cache look bad, it is, in fact, very effective for many types of data. In particular, the direct-mapped cache is very good for data that you access in a sequential rather than random fashion. Because the CPU typically executes instructions in a sequential fashion, instruction bytes can be stored very effectively in a direct-mapped cache. However, because programs tend to access data more randomly than code, a two-way or four-way set associative cache usually makes a better choice for data accesses than a direct-mapped cache.

Because data and machine instruction bytes usually have different access patterns, many CPU designers use separate caches for each. For example, a CPU designer could choose to implement an 8-KB instruction cache and an 8-KB data cache rather than a single 16-KB unified cache. The advantage of dividing the cache size in this way is that the CPU designer could use a caching scheme more appropriate to the particular values that will be stored in each cache. The drawback is that the two caches are now each half the size of a unified cache, which may cause more cache misses than would occur with a unified cache. The choice of an appropriate cache organization is a difficult one and can only be made after analyzing many running programs on the target processor. How to choose an appropriate cache format is beyond the scope of this book, but be aware that it's not a choice you can make just by reading a textbook.

11.4.5 Cache Line Replacement Policies

Thus far, we've answered the question, "Where do we put a block of data in the cache?" An equally important question we've ignored until now is, "What happens if a cache line isn't available when we want to put a block of data in that cache line?"

For a direct-mapped cache architecture, the answer is trivial. The cache controller simply replaces whatever data was formerly in the cache line with the new data. Any subsequent reference to the old data will result in a cache miss, and the cache controller will then have to bring that old data back into the cache by replacing whatever data is in the appropriate cache line at that time.

For a two-way set associative cache, the replacement algorithm is a bit more complex. Whenever the CPU references a memory location, the cache controller uses some subset of the address' bits to determine the cache-line set that should be used to store the data. Using some fancy circuitry, the caching controller determines whether the data is already present in one of the two cache lines in the destination set. If the data is not present, the CPU has to bring the data in from memory. Because the main memory data can go into either cache line, the controller has to pick one of the two lines to use. If either or both of the cache lines are currently unused, the controller simply picks an unused line. However, if both cache lines are currently in use, then the cache controller must pick one of the cache lines and replace its data with the new data.

How does the controller choose which of the two cache lines to replace? Ideally, we'd like to keep the cache line whose data will be referenced first and replace the other cache line. Unfortunately, neither the cache controller nor the CPU is omniscient — they cannot predict which of the lines is the best one to replace.

To understand how the cache controller makes this decision, remember the principle of temporality: if a memory location has been referenced recently, it is likely to be referenced again in the very near future. This implies the following corollary: *if a memory location has not been accessed in a while, it is likely to be a long time before the CPU accesses it again.* Therefore, a good replacement policy that many caching controllers use is the *least recently used* (LRU) algorithm. An LRU policy is easy to implement in a two-way set associative cache system. All you need is to reserve a single bit for each set of two cache lines. Whenever the CPU accesses one of the two cache lines this bit is set to zero, and whenever the CPU accesses the other cache line, this bit is set to one. Then, when a replacement is necessary, this bit will indicate which cache line to replace, as it tracks the last cache line the program has accessed (and, because there are only two cache lines in the set, the inverse of this bit also tracks the cache line that was least recently used).

For four-way (and greater) set associative caches, maintaining the LRU information is a bit more difficult, which is one of the reasons the circuitry for such caches is more complex. Because of the complications that LRU can introduce on these associative caches, other replacement policies are sometimes used. Two of these other policies are *first-in, first-out* (FIFO) and *random*. These are easier to implement than LRU, but they have their own problems, which are beyond the scope of this book, but which a text on computer architecture or operating systems will discuss.

11.4.6 Writing Data to Memory

What happens when the CPU writes data to memory? The simple answer, and the one that results in the quickest operation, is that the CPU writes the data to the cache. However, what happens when the cache line containing this data is subsequently replaced by data that is read from memory? If the modified contents of the cache line are not written to main memory prior to this replacement, then the data that was written to the cache line will be lost. The next time the CPU attempts to access that data it will reload the cache line with the old data that was never updated after the write operation.

Clearly any data written to the cache must ultimately be written to main memory as well. There are two common write policies that caches use: *write-back* and *write-through*. Interestingly enough, it is sometimes possible to set the write policy in software, as the write policy isn't always hardwired into the cache controller. However, don't get your hopes up. Generally the CPU only allows the BIOS or operating system to set the cache write policy, so unless you're the one writing the operating system, you won't be able to control the write policy.

The write-through policy states that any time data is written to the cache, the cache immediately turns around and writes a copy of that cache line to main memory. An important point to notice is that the CPU does not have to halt while the cache controller writes the data from cache to main memory. So unless the CPU needs to access main memory shortly after the write occurs, this writing takes place in parallel with the execution of the program. Furthermore, because the write-through policy updates main memory with the new value as rapidly as possible, it is a better policy to use when two different CPUs are communicating through shared memory.

Still, writing a cache line to memory takes some time, and it is likely that the CPU (or some CPU in a multiprocessor system) will want to access main memory during the write operation, so the write-through policy may not be a high-performance solution to the problem. Worse, suppose the CPU reads from and writes to the memory location several times in succession.

With a write-through policy in place, the CPU will saturate the bus with cache-line writes, and this will have a very negative impact on the program's performance.

The second common cache write policy is the write-back policy. In this mode, writes to the cache are not immediately written to main memory; instead, the cache controller updates main memory at a later time. This scheme tends to be higher performance because several writes to the same cache line within a short time period do not generate multiple writes to main memory.

Of course, at some point the cache controller must write the data in cache to memory. To determine which cache lines must be written back to main memory, the cache controller usually maintains a *dirty bit* within each cache line. The cache system sets this bit whenever it writes data to the cache. At some later time, the cache controller checks this dirty bit to determine if it must write the cache line to memory. For example, whenever the cache controller replaces a cache line with other data from memory, it must first check the dirty bit, and if that bit is set, the controller must write that cache line to memory before going through with the cache-line replacement. Note that this increases the latency time when replacing a cache line. If the cache controller were able to write dirty cache lines to main memory while no other bus access was occurring, the system could reduce this latency during cache line replacement. Some systems actually provide this functionality, and others do not for economic reasons.

11.4.7 Cache Use and Software

A cache subsystem is not a panacea for slow memory access. In order for a cache system to be effective, software must exhibit locality of reference (either spatial or temporal). Fortunately, real-world programs tend to exhibit locality of reference, so most programs will benefit from the presence of a cache in the memory subsystem. But while programs do exhibit locality of reference, this is often accidental; programmers rarely consider the memory-access patterns of their software when designing and coding. Unfortunately, application programmers who work under the assumption that the cache will magically improve the performance of their applications are missing one important point — a cache can actually *hurt* the performance of an application.

Suppose that an application accesses data at several different addresses that the caching controller would map to the exact same cache line. With each access, the caching controller must read in a new cache line (possibly flushing the old cache line back to memory if it is dirty). As a result, each memory access incurs the latency cost of bringing in a cache line from main memory. This degenerate case, known as *thrashing*, can slow down the program by one to two orders of magnitude, depending on the speed of main memory and the size of a cache line. Great code is written with the behavior of the cache in mind. A great programmer attempts to place oft-used variables in adjacent memory cells so those variables tend to fall into the same cache lines. A great programmer carefully chooses data structures (and access patterns to those data structures) to avoid thrashing. We'll take another look at thrashing a little later in this chapter.

Another benefit of the cache subsystem on modern 80x86 CPUs is that it automatically handles many misaligned data references. As you may recall, there is a penalty for accessing words or double-word objects at an address that is not an even multiple of that object's size. As it turns out, by providing some fancy logic, Intel's designers have eliminated this penalty as long as the data object is located completely within a cache line. However, if the object crosses a cache line, there will be a performance penalty for the memory access.

11.5 Virtual Memory, Protection, and Paging

In a modern operating system such as Mac OS, Linux, or Windows, it is very common to have several different programs running concurrently in memory. This presents several problems.

- How do you keep the programs from interfering with each other's memory?

- If one program expects to load a value into memory at address $1000, and a second program also expects to load a value into memory at address $1000, how can you load both values and execute both programs at the same time?

- What happens if the computer has 64 MB of memory, and we decide to load and execute three different applications, two of which require 32 MB and one that requires 16 MB (not to mention the memory that the operating system requires for its own purposes)?

The answers to all these questions lie in the virtual memory subsystem that modern processors support.

Virtual memory on CPUs such as the 80x86 gives each process its own 32-bit address space.[3] This means that address $1000 in one program is physically different from address $1000 in a separate program. The CPU achieves this sleight of hand by mapping the *virtual addresses* used by programs to different *physical addresses* in actual memory. The virtual address and the physical address don't have to be the same, and usually they aren't. For example, program 1's virtual address $1000 might actually correspond to physical address $215000, while program 2's virtual address $1000 might correspond to physical memory address $300000. How can the CPU do this? Easy, by using *paging*.

---

[3] Strictly speaking, you actually get a 36-bit address space on Pentium Pro and later processors, but Windows and Linux limit you to 32 bits, so we'll use that limitation here.

The concept behind paging is quite simple. First, you break up memory into blocks of bytes called *pages*. A page in main memory is comparable to a cache line in a cache subsystem, although pages are usually much larger than cache lines. For example, the 80x86 CPUs use a page size of 4,096 bytes.

After breaking up memory into pages, you use a lookup table to map the HO bits of a virtual address to the HO bits of the physical address in memory, and you use the LO bits of the virtual address as an index into that page. For example, with a 4,096-byte page, you'd use the LO 12 bits of the virtual address as the offset (0..4095) within the page, and the upper 20 bits as an index into a lookup table that returns the actual upper 20 bits of the physical address (see Figure 11-5).

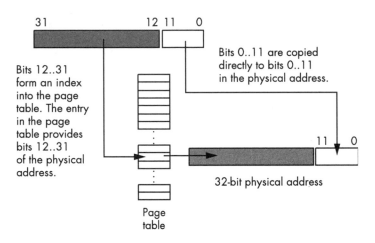

Figure 11-5: Translating a virtual address to a physical address

Of course, a 20-bit index into the page table would require over one million entries in the page table. If each of the over one million entries is a 32-bit value, then the page table would be 4 MB long. This would be larger than most of the programs that would run in memory! However, by using what is known as a multilevel page table, it is very easy to create a page table for most small programs that is only 8 KB long. The details are unimportant here. Just rest assured that you don't need a 4-MB page table unless your program consumes the entire 4 GB address space.

If you study Figure 11-5 for a few moments, you'll probably discover one problem with using a page table — it requires two separate memory accesses in order to retrieve the data stored at a single physical address in memory: one to fetch a value from the page table, and one to read from or write to the desired memory location. To prevent cluttering the data or instruction cache with page-table entries, which increases the number of cache misses for data and instruction requests, the page table uses its own cache, known as the *translation lookaside buffer* (TLB). This cache typically has 32 entries on a

Pentium family processor — enough to handle 128 KB of memory, or 32 pages, without a miss. Because a program typically works with less data than this at any given time, most page-table accesses come from the cache rather than main memory.

As noted, each entry in the page table contains 32 bits, even though the system really only needs 20 bits to remap each virtual address to a physical address. Intel, on the 80x86, uses some of the remaining 12 bits to provide some memory-protection information:

- One bit marks whether a page is read/write or read-only.
- One bit determines whether you can execute code on that page.
- A number of bits determine whether the application can access that page or if only the operating system can do so.
- A number of bits determine if the CPU has written to the page, but hasn't yet written to the physical memory address corresponding to the page entry (that is, whether the page is "dirty" or not, and whether the CPU has accessed the page recently).
- One bit determines whether the page is actually present in physical memory or if it's stored on secondary storage somewhere.

Note that your applications do not have access to the page table (reading and writing the page table is the operating system's responsibility), and therefore they cannot modify these bits. However, operating systems like Windows may provide some functions you can call if you want to change certain bits in the page table (for example, Windows will allow you to set a page to read-only if you want to do so).

Beyond remapping memory so multiple programs can coexist in main memory, paging also provides a mechanism whereby the operating system can move infrequently used pages to secondary storage. Just as locality of reference applies to cache lines, it applies to pages in main memory as well. At any given time, a program will only access a small percentage of the pages in main memory that contain data and instruction bytes and this set of pages is known as the *working set*. Although this working set of pages varies slowly over time, for small periods of time the working set remains constant. Therefore, there is little need for the remainder of the program to consume valuable main memory storage that some other process could be using. If the operating system can save the currently unused pages to disk, the main memory they consume would be available for other programs that need it.

Of course, the problem with moving data out of main memory is that eventually the program might actually need that data. If you attempt to access a page of memory, and the page-table bit tells the memory management unit (MMU) that the page is not present in main memory, the CPU interrupts the program and passes control to the operating system. The operating system then analyzes the memory-access request and reads the corresponding page of data from the disk drive and copies it to some available page in main memory. This process is nearly identical to the process used by a fully associative cache subsystem, except that accessing the disk is much slower than accessing main memory. In fact, you can think of main memory as a fully associative write-back cache with 4,096-byte cache lines, which caches the data that is stored on the disk drive. Placement and replacement policies and other issues are very similar for caches and main memory.

However, that's as far as we'll go in exploring how the virtual memory subsystem works. If you're interested in further information, any decent textbook on operating system design will explain how the virtual memory subsystem swaps pages between main memory and the disk. Our main goal here is to realize that this process takes place in operating systems like Mac OS, Linux, and Windows, and that accessing the disk is very slow.

One important issue resulting from the fact that each program has a separate page table, and the fact that programs themselves don't have access to the page tables, is that programs cannot interfere with the operation of other programs. That is, a program cannot change its page tables in order to access data found in another process's *address space*. If your program crashes by overwriting itself, it cannot crash other programs at the same time. This is a big benefit of a paging memory system.

If two programs want to cooperate and share data, they can do so by placing such data in a memory area that is shared by the two processes. All they have to do is tell the operating system that they want to share some pages of memory. The operating system returns a pointer to each process that points at a segment of memory whose physical address is the same for both processes. Under Windows, you can achieve this by using *memory-mapped files*; see the operating system documentation for more details. Mac OS and Linux also support memory-mapped files as well as some special shared-memory operations; again, see the OS documentation for more details.

Although this discussion applies specifically to the 80x86 CPU, multi-level paging systems are common on other CPUs as well. Page sizes tend to vary from about 1 KB to 64 KB, depending on the CPU. For CPUs that support an address space larger than 4 GB, some CPUs use an *inverted page table* or a *three-level page table*. Although the details are beyond the scope of this chapter, rest assured that the basic principle remains the same — the CPU moves data between main memory and the disk in order to keep oft-accessed data in main memory as much of the time as possible. These other page-table schemes are good at reducing the size of the page table when an application uses only a fraction of the available memory space.

11.6 Thrashing

Thrashing is a degenerate case that can cause the overall performance of the system to drop to the speed of a lower level in the memory hierarchy, like main memory or, worse yet, the disk drive. There are two primary causes of thrashing:

- Insufficient memory at a given level in the memory hierarchy to properly contain the program working sets of cache lines or pages

- A program that does not exhibit locality of reference

If there is insufficient memory to hold a working set of pages or cache lines, the memory system will constantly be replacing one block of data in the cache or main memory with another block of data from main memory or the disk. As a result, the system winds up operating at the speed of the slower memory in the memory hierarchy. A common example of thrashing occurs with virtual memory. A user may have several applications running at the same time, and the sum total of the memory required by these programs' working sets is greater than all of the physical memory available to the programs. As a result, when the operating system switches between the applications it has to copy each application's data, and possibly program instructions, to and from disk. Because switching between programs is often much faster than retrieving data from the disk, this slows the programs down by a tremendous factor.

We have already seen in this chapter that if the program does not exhibit locality of reference and the lower memory subsystems are not fully associative, then thrashing can occur even if there is free memory at the current level in the memory hierarchy. To take our earlier example, suppose an 8-KB L1 caching system uses a direct-mapped cache with 512 16-byte cache lines. If a program references data objects 8 KB apart on *every* access, then the system will have to replace the same line in the cache over and over again with the data from main memory. This occurs even though the other 511 cache lines are currently unused.

When insufficient memory is the problem, you can add memory to reduce thrashing. Or, if you can't add more memory, you can try to run fewer processes concurrently or modify your program so that it references less memory over a given period. To reduce thrashing when locality of reference is causing the problem, you should restructure your program and its data structures to make its memory references physically near one another.

11.7 NUMA and Peripheral Devices

Although most of the RAM in a system is based on high-speed DRAM interfaced directly with the processor's bus, not all memory is connected to the CPU in this manner. Sometimes a large block of RAM is part of a peripheral device, and you communicate with that device by writing data to its RAM. Video display cards are probably the most common example of such a peripheral, but some network interface cards, USB controllers, and other peripherals also work this way. Unfortunately, the access time to the RAM on these peripheral devices is often much slower than the access time to main memory. In this section, we'll use the video card as an example, although NUMA performance applies to other devices and memory technologies as well.

A typical video card interfaces with a CPU via an AGP or PCI bus inside the computer system. The PCI bus typically runs at 33 MHz and is capable of transferring four bytes per bus cycle. Therefore, in burst mode, a video controller card is capable of transferring 132 MB per second, though few would ever come close to achieving this for technical reasons. Now compare this with main-memory access time. Main memory usually connects directly to the CPU's bus, and modern CPUs have an 800-MHz 64-bit-wide bus. If memory were fast enough, the CPU's bus could theoretically transfer 6.4 GB per second between memory and the CPU. This is about 48 times faster than the speed of transferring data across the PCI bus. Game programmers long ago discovered that it's much faster to manipulate a copy of the screen data in main memory and only copy that data to the video display memory whenever a vertical retrace occurs (about 60 times per second). This mechanism is much faster than writing directly to the video card memory every time you want to make a change.

Caches and the virtual memory subsystem operate in a transparent fashion, but NUMA memory does not, so programs that write to NUMA devices must minimize the number of accesses whenever possible (for example, by using an off-screen bitmap to hold temporary results). If you're actually storing and retrieving data on a NUMA device, like a flash memory card, you must explicitly cache the data yourself.

11.8   Writing Software That Is Cognizant of the Memory Hierarchy

Although the memory hierarchy is usually transparent to application programmers, software that is aware of memory performance behavior can run much faster than software that is ignorant of the memory hierarchy. Although a system's caching and paging facilities may perform reasonably well for typical programs, it is easy to write software that would run faster if the caching system were not present. The best software is written to allow it to take maximum advantage of the memory hierarchy.

A classic example of a bad design is the following loop that initializes a two-dimensional array of integer values:

```
int array[256][256];
    . . .
    for( i=0; i<256; ++i )
        for( j=0; j<256; ++j )
            array[j][i] = i*j;
```

Believe it or not, this code runs much slower on a modern CPU than the following sequence:

```
int array[256][256];
    . . .
    for( i=0; i<256; ++i )
        for( j=0; j<256; ++j )
            array[i][j] = i*j;
```

If you look closely, you'll notice that the only difference between the two code sequences is that the i and j indexes are swapped when accessing elements of the array. This small modification can be responsible for an order of magnitude (or two) difference in the run time of these two code sequences! To understand why, first recall that the C programming language uses row-major ordering for two-dimensional arrays in memory. The second code sequence here, therefore, accesses sequential locations in memory, exhibiting spatial locality of reference. The first code sequence does not access sequential memory locations. It accesses array elements in the following order:

```
array[0][0]
array[1][0]
array[2][0]
array[3][0]
    . . .
array[254][0]
array[255][0]
array[0][1]
array[1][1]
array[2][1]
    . . .
```

If integers are four bytes each, then this sequence will access the double-word values at offsets 0; 1,024; 2,048; 3,072; and so on, from the base address of the array. Most likely, this code is going to load only n integers into an n-way set associative cache and then immediately cause thrashing thereafter as each subsequent array element has to be copied from the cache into main memory to prevent that data from being overwritten.

The second code sequence does not exhibit thrashing. Assuming 64-byte cache lines, the second code sequence will store 16 integer values into the same cache line before having to load another cache line from main memory, replacing an existing cache line. As a result, this second code sequence spreads out the cost of bringing the cache line in from memory over 16 memory accesses rather than over a single access, as occurs with the first code sequence. For this, and several other reasons, the second example runs much faster.

There are also several variable declaration tricks you can employ to maximize the performance of the memory hierarchy. First, try to declare together all variables you use within a common code sequence. In most languages, this will allow the language translator to allocate storage for the variables in physically adjacent memory locations, thus supporting spatial locality as well as temporal locality. Second, you should attempt to allocate local variables within a procedure, because most languages allocate local storage on the stack and, as the system references the stack frequently, variables on the stack tend to be in the cache. Third, declare your scalar variables together, and separate from your array and record variables. Access to any one of several adjacent scalar variables generally forces the system to load all of the adjacent objects into the cache. As such, whenever you access one variable, the system usually loads the adjacent variables into the cache as well.

When writing great code, you'll want to study the memory access patterns your program exhibits and adjust your application accordingly. You can toil away for hours trying to achieve a 10 percent performance improvement by rewriting your code in hand-optimized assembly language, but if you modify the way your program accesses memory, it's not unheard of to see an order of magnitude improvement in performance.

11.9   Run-Time Memory Organization

An operating system like Mac OS, Linux, or Windows puts different types of data into different areas (*sections* or *segments*) of main memory. Although it is possible to control the memory organization by running a linker and specifying various parameters, by default Windows loads a typical program into memory using the organization shown in Figure 11-6 (Linux is similar, though it rearranges some of the sections).

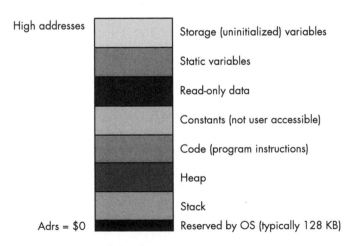

Figure 11-6: Typical Windows run-time memory organization

The operating system reserves the lowest memory addresses. Generally, your application cannot access data (or execute instructions) at the lowest addresses in memory. One reason the OS reserves this space is to help detect NULL pointer references. Programmers often initialize pointers with NULL (zero) to indicate that the pointer is not valid. Should you attempt to access memory location zero under such OSes, the OS will generate a "general protection fault" to indicate that you've accessed a memory location that doesn't contain valid data.

The remaining seven areas in the memory map hold different types of data associated with your program. These sections of memory include:

- The code section, which holds the program's machine instructions.
- The constant section, which holds compiler-generated read-only data.
- The read-only data section, that holds user-defined data that can only be read, never written.
- The static section, which holds user-defined, initialized, static variables.
- The storage section, or BSS section, that holds user-defined uninitialized variables.
- The stack section, where the program keeps local variables and other temporary data.
- The heap section, where the program maintains dynamic variables.

Often, a compiler will combine the code, constant, and read-only data sections because all three sections contain read-only data.

Most of the time, a given application can live with the default layouts chosen for these sections by the compiler and linker/loader. In some cases, however, knowing the memory layout can allow you to develop shorter programs. For example, as the code section is usually read-only, it may be possible to combine the code, constants, and read-only data sections into a single section, thus saving any padding space that the compiler/linker may place between these sections. Although these savings are probably insignificant for large applications, they can have a big impact on the size of a small program.

The following sections discuss each of these memory areas in detail.

11.9.1 Static and Dynamic Objects, Binding, and Lifetime

To understand the memory organization of a typical program, we've first got to define a few terms that will prove useful in our discussion. These terms are *binding, lifetime, static,* and *dynamic.*

Binding is the process of associating an attribute with an object. For example, when you assign a value to a variable, we say that the value is *bound* to that variable at the point of the assignment. The value remains bound to the variable until you bind some other value to it (via another assignment operation). Likewise, if you allocate memory for a variable while the program is running, we say that the variable is *bound* to the address at that point. The variable and address are bound until you associate a different address with the variable. Binding needn't occur at run time. For example, values are bound to constant objects during compilation, and such bindings cannot change while the program is running.

The *lifetime* of an attribute extends from the point when you first bind that attribute to an object to the point when you break that bond, perhaps by binding a different attribute to the object. For example, the lifetime of a variable is from the time you first associate memory with the variable to the moment you deallocate that variable's storage.

Static objects are those that have an attribute bound to them prior to the execution of the application. Constants are good examples of static objects; they have the same value bound to them throughout the execution of the application. Global (program-level) variables in programming languages like Pascal, C/C++, and Ada are also examples of static objects in that they have the same address bound to them throughout the program's lifetime. The lifetime of a static object, therefore, extends from the point at which the program first begins execution to the point when the application terminates. The system binds attributes to a static object before the program begins execution (usually during compilation or during the linking phase, though it is possible to bind values even earlier).

The notion of identifier *scope* is also associated with static binding. The scope of an identifier is that section of the program where the identifier's name is bound to the object. As names exist only during compilation, scope is definitely a static attribute in compiled languages. (In interpretive languages, where the interpreter maintains the identifier names during program execution, scope can be a nonstatic attribute.) The scope of a local variable is generally limited to the procedure or function in which you declare it (or to any nested procedure or function declarations in block structured languages like Pascal or Ada), and the name is not visible outside the subroutine. In fact, it is possible to reuse an identifier's name in a different scope (that is, in a different function or procedure). In such a case as this, the second occurrence of the identifier will be bound to a different object than the first use of the identifier.

Dynamic objects are those that have some attribute assigned to them while the program is running. The program may choose to change that attribute *(dynamically)* while the program is running. The lifetime of that attribute begins when the application associates the attribute with the object and ends when the program breaks that association. If the program associates some attribute with an object and then never breaks that bond, the lifetime of the attribute is from the point of association to the point the program terminates. The system binds dynamic attributes to an object at run time, after the application begins execution.

Note that an object may have a combination of static and dynamic attributes. For example, a static variable will have an address bound to it for the entire execution time of the program. However, that same variable could have different values bound to it throughout the program's lifetime. For any given attribute, however, the attribute is either static or dynamic; it cannot be both.

11.9.2 The Code, Read-Only, and Constant Sections

The code section in memory contains the machine instructions for a program. Your compiler translates each statement you write into a sequence of one or more byte values. The CPU interprets these byte values as machine instructions during program execution.

Most compilers also attach a program's read-only data to the code section because, like the code instructions, the read-only data is already write-protected. However, it is perfectly possible under Windows, Linux, and many other operating systems to create a separate section in the executable file and mark it as read-only. As a result, some compilers do support a separate *read-only* data section. Such sections contain initialized data, tables, and other objects that the program should not change during program execution.

The constant section found in Figure 11-6 typically contains data that the compiler generates (as opposed to a read-only section that contains user-defined read-only data). Most compilers actually emit this data directly to the code section. Therefore, in most executable files, you'll find a single section that combines the code, read-only data, and constant data sections.

11.9.3 The Static Variables Section

Many languages provide the ability to initialize a global variable during the compilation phase. For example, in C/C++ you could use statements like the following to provide initial values for these static objects:

```
static int i = 10;
static char ch[] = ( 'a', 'b', 'c', 'd' };
```

In C/C++ and other languages, the compiler will place these initial values in the executable file. When you execute the application, the operating system will load the portion of the executable file that contains these static variables into memory so that the values appear at the addresses associated with them. Therefore, when the program first begins execution, these static variables will magically have these values bound to them.

11.9.4 The Uninitialized Storage (BSS) Section

Most operating systems will zero out memory prior to program execution. Therefore, if an initial value of zero is suitable and your operating system supports this feature, you don't need to waste any disk space with the static object's initial value. Generally, however, compilers treat uninitialized variables in a static section as though you've initialized them with zero, thus consuming disk space. Some operating systems provide a separate section, the *BSS section*, to avoid this waste of disk space.

The BSS section is where compilers typically put static objects that don't have an explicit value associated with them. BSS stands for *block started by a symbol,* which is an old assembly language term describing a pseudo-opcode one would use to allocate storage for an uninitialized static array. In modern OSes like Windows and Linux, the OS allows the compiler/linker to put all uninitialized variables into a BSS section that simply contains information that tells the OS how many bytes to set aside for the section. When the operating system loads the program into memory, it reserves sufficient memory for all the objects in the BSS section and fills this memory with zeros. It is important to note that the BSS section in the executable file doesn't actually contain any data. Because the BSS section does not require the executable file to consume space for uninitialized zeros, programs that declare large uninitialized static arrays will consume less disk space.

However, not all compilers actually use a BSS section. Many Microsoft languages and linkers, for example, simply place the uninitialized objects in the static data section and explicitly give them an initial value of zero. Although Microsoft claims that this scheme is faster, it certainly makes executable files larger if your code has large, uninitialized arrays (because each byte of the array winds up in the executable file — something that would not happen if the compiler were to place the array in a BSS section).

11.9.5 The Stack Section

The stack is a data structure that expands and contracts in response to procedure invocations and the return to calling routines, among other things. At run time, the system places all automatic variables (nonstatic local variables), subroutine parameters, temporary values, and other objects in the stack section of memory in a special data structure we call the *activation record* (which is aptly named because the system creates an activation record when a subroutine first begins execution, and it deallocates the activation record when the subroutine returns to its caller). Therefore, the stack section in memory is very busy.

Most CPUs implement the stack using a register called the *stack pointer.* Some CPUs, however, don't provide an explicit stack pointer and, instead, use a general-purpose register for this purpose. If a CPU provides an explicit stack-pointer register, we say that the CPU supports a hardware stack; if only a general-purpose register is available, then we say that the CPU uses a software-implemented stack. The 80x86 is a good example of a CPU that provides a hardware stack; the MIPS Rx000 family is a good example of a CPU family that implements the stack in software. Systems that provide hardware stacks can generally manipulate data on the stack using fewer instructions than those systems that implement the stack in software. On the other hand, RISC CPU designers who've chosen to use a software-stack implementation feel that the presence of a hardware stack actually slows down all instructions the CPU executes. In theory, one could make an argument that the RISC designers are right; in practice, though, the 80x86 CPU is one of the fastest CPUs around, providing ample proof that having a hardware stack doesn't necessarily mean you'll wind up with a slow CPU.

11.9.6   The Heap Section and Dynamic Memory Allocation

Although simple programs may only need static and automatic variables, sophisticated programs need the ability to allocate and deallocate storage dynamically (at run time) under program control. In the C and HLA languages, you would use the malloc and free functions for this purpose, C++ provides the new and delete operators, Pascal uses new and dispose, and other languages provide comparable routines. These memory-allocation routines have a few things in common: they let the programmer request how many bytes of storage to allocate, they return a *pointer* to the newly allocated storage (that is, the address of that storage), and they provide a facility for returning the storage space to the system once it is no longer needed, so the system can reuse it in a future allocation call. Dynamic memory allocation takes place in a section of memory known as the *heap*.

Generally, an application refers to data on the heap using pointer variables (either implicitly or explicitly; some languages, like Java, implicitly use pointers behind the programmer's back). As such, we'll usually refer to objects in heap memory as *anonymous variables* because we refer to them by their memory address (via pointers) rather than by a name.

The OS and application create the heap section in memory after the program begins execution; the heap is never a part of the executable file. Generally, the OS and language run-time libraries maintain the heap for an application. Despite the variations in memory management implementations, it's still a good idea for you to have a basic idea of how heap allocation and deallocation operate, because an inappropriate use of the heap management facilities will have a very negative impact on the performance of your applications.

11.9.6.1   Memory Allocation

An extremely simple (and fast) memory allocation scheme would maintain a single variable that forms a pointer into the heap region of memory. Whenever a memory allocation request comes along, the system makes a copy of this heap pointer and returns it to the application; then the heap management routines add the size of the memory request to the address held in the pointer variable and verify that the memory request doesn't try to use more memory than is available in the heap region (some memory managers return an error indication, like a NULL pointer, when the memory request is too great, and others raise an exception). The problem with this simple memory management scheme is that it wastes memory, because there is no mechanism to allow the application to free the memory that anonymous variables no longer require so that the application can reuse that memory later. One of the main purposes of a heap-management system is to perform *garbage collection*, that is, reclaim unused memory when an application finishes using the memory.

The only catch is that supporting garbage collection requires some overhead. The memory management code will need to be more sophisticated, will take longer to execute, and will require some additional memory to maintain the internal data structures the heap-management system uses. Let's consider an easy implementation of a heap manager that supports garbage collection. This simple system maintains a (linked) list of free memory blocks. Each free memory block in the list will require two double-word values: one double-word value specifies the size of the free block, and the other double word contains a link to the next free block in the list (that is, a pointer), see Figure 11-7.

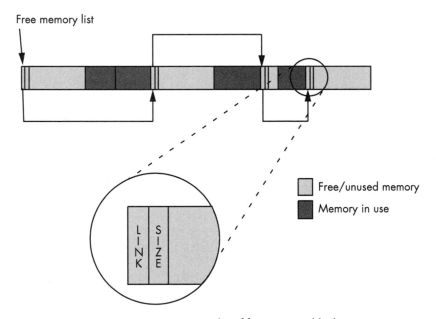

Figure 11-7: Heap management using a list of free memory blocks

The system initializes the heap with a NULL link pointer, and the size field contains the size of the entire free space. When a memory request comes along, the heap manager first determines if there is a sufficiently large block available for the allocation request. To do this, the heap manager has to search through the list to find a free block with enough memory to satisfy the request.

One of the defining characteristics of a heap manager is how it searches through the list of free blocks to satisfy the request. Some common search algorithms are *first-fit* and *best-fit*. The first-fit search, as its name suggests, scans through the list of blocks until it finds the first block of memory large enough to satisfy the allocation request. The best-fit algorithm scans through the entire list and finds the smallest block large enough to satisfy the request. The advantage of the best-fit algorithm is that it tends to preserve larger blocks better than the first-fit algorithm, thereby allowing the system to handle larger subsequent allocation requests when they arrive. The first-fit algorithm, on the other hand, just grabs the first sufficiently large block it finds, even if there is a smaller block that would satisfy the request; as a result, the first-fit algorithm may reduce the number of large free blocks in the system that could satisfy large memory requests.

The first-fit algorithm does have a couple of advantages over the best-fit algorithm, though. The most obvious advantage is that the first-fit algorithm is usually faster. The best-fit algorithm has to scan through every block in the free block list in order to find the smallest block large enough to satisfy the allocation request (unless, of course, it finds a perfectly sized block along the way). The first-fit algorithm, on the other hand, can stop once it finds a block large enough to satisfy the request.

Another advantage to the first-fit algorithm is that it tends to suffer less from a degenerate condition known as *external fragmentation*. Fragmentation occurs after a long sequence of allocation and deallocation requests. Remember, when the heap manager satisfies a memory allocation request, it usually creates two blocks of memory — one in-use block for the request and one free block that contains the remaining bytes in the original block after the request is filled (assuming the heap manager did not find an exact fit). After operating for a while, the best-fit algorithm may wind up producing lots of smaller, leftover blocks of memory that are too small to satisfy an average memory request (because the best-fit algorithm also produces the smallest leftover blocks as a result of its behavior). As a result, the heap manager will probably never allocate these small blocks (fragments), so they are effectively unusable. Although each individual fragment may be small, as multiple fragments accumulate throughout the heap, they can wind up consuming a fair amount of memory. This can lead to a situation where the heap doesn't have a sufficiently large block to satisfy a memory allocation request even though there is enough free memory available (spread throughout the heap). See Figure 11-8 on the next page for an example of this condition.

Desired allocation size

Free/unused memory

Memory in use

Figure 11-8: Memory fragmentation

In addition to the first-fit and best-fit algorithms, there are other memory allocation strategies. Some execute faster, some have less (memory) overhead, some are easy to understand (and some are very complex), some produce less fragmentation, and some have the ability to combine and use noncontiguous blocks of free memory. Memory/heap management is one of the more heavily studied subjects in computer science; there is considerable literature extolling the benefits of one scheme over another. For more information on memory allocation strategies, check out a good book on OS design.

11.9.6.2 Garbage Collection

Memory allocation is only half of the story. In addition to a memory allocation routine, the heap manager has to provide a call that allows an application to return memory it no longer needs for future reuse. In C and HLA, for example, an application accomplishes this by calling the free function.

At first blush, it might seem that free would be a very simple function to write. All it looks like one has to do is append the previously allocated and now unused block onto the end of the free list. The problem with this trivial implementation of free is that it almost guarantees that the heap becomes fragmented to the point of being unusable in very short order. Consider the situation in Figure 11-9.

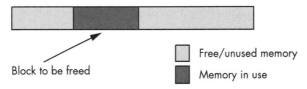

Block to be freed

Free/unused memory

Memory in use

Figure 11-9: Freeing a memory block

If a trivial implementation of free simply takes the block to be freed and appends it to the free list, the memory organization in Figure 11-9 produces three free blocks. However, because these three blocks are all contiguous, the heap manager should really coalesce these three blocks into a single free block; doing so allows the heap manager to satisfy a larger request. Unfortunately, from an overhead perspective, this coalescing operation requires our simple heap manager to scan through the free block list in order to determine whether there are any free blocks adjacent to the block the system is freeing. While it's possible to come up with a data structure that reduces the effort needed to coalesce adjacent free blocks, such schemes generally involve the use of additional overhead bytes (usually eight or more) for each block on the heap. Whether or not this is a reasonable trade-off depends on the average size of a memory allocation. If the applications that use the heap manager tend to allocate small objects, the extra overhead for each memory block could wind up consuming a large percentage of the heap space. However, if the most allocations are large, then the few bytes of overhead will be of little consequence.

11.9.6.3   The OS and Memory Allocation

The performance of the algorithms and data structures the heap manager uses are only a part of the performance problem. Ultimately, the heap manager needs to request blocks of memory from the operating system. In one possible implementation, the operating system handles all memory allocation requests. Another possibility is that the heap manager is a run-time library routine that links with your application; the heap manager requests large blocks of memory from the operating system and then doles out pieces of this block as memory requests arrive from the application.

The problem with making direct memory allocation requests to the OS is that OS API calls are often very slow. If an application calls the operating system for every memory request it makes, the performance of the application will probably suffer if the application makes several memory allocation and deallocation calls. OS API calls are very slow, because they generally involve switching between kernel mode and user mode on the CPU (which is not fast). Therefore, a heap manager that the operating system implements directly will not perform well if your application makes frequent calls to the memory allocation and deallocation routines.

Because of the high overhead of an operating system call, most languages implement their own version of malloc and free (or whatever they call them) within the language's run-time library. On the very first memory allocation, the malloc routine will request a large block of memory from the operating system, and then the application's malloc and free routines will manage this block of memory themselves. If an allocation request comes along that the malloc function cannot fulfill in the block it originally created, then malloc will request another large block (generally much larger than the request) from the operating system, and add that block to the end of its free list. Because the calls to the application's malloc and free routines only call the operating system on an occasional basis, this dramatically reduces the overhead associated with OS calls.

However, you should keep in mind that the procedure illustrated in the previous paragraph is very implementation and language specific; so it's dangerous for you to assume that malloc and free are relatively efficient when writing software that requires high-performance components. The only portable way to ensure a high-performance heap manager is to develop an application-specific set of routines yourself.

Most standard heap management functions perform reasonably for a typical program. For your specific application, however, it may be possible to write a specialized set of functions that are much faster or have less memory overhead. If your application's allocation routines are written by someone who has a good understanding of the program's memory allocation patterns, the allocation and deallocation functions may be able to handle the application's requests in a more efficient manner. Writing such routines is beyond the scope of this book (please see an OS textbook for more details), but you should be aware of this possibility.

11.9.6.4   Heap Memory Overhead

A heap manager often exhibits two types of overhead: performance (speed) and memory (space). Until now, the discussion has mainly dealt with the performance characteristics of a heap manager; now it's time to turn our attention to the memory overhead associated with the heap manager.

Each block the system allocates is going to require some amount of overhead above and beyond the storage the application requests. At the very least, each block the heap manager allocates requires a few bytes to keep track of the block's size. Fancier (higher-performance) schemes may require additional bytes, but a typical number of overhead bytes will be between 4 and 16. The heap manager can keep this information in a separate internal table, or it can attach the block size and any other memory-management information directly to the blocks it allocates.

Saving this information in an internal table has a couple of advantages. First, it is difficult for the application to accidentally overwrite the information stored there; attaching the data to the heap memory blocks themselves doesn't protect as well against the application wiping out this control information with buffer overruns or underruns (thus corrupting the memory manager's data structures). Second, putting memory-management information in an internal data structure allows the memory manager to determine whether a given pointer is valid (whether it points at some block of memory that the heap manager believes it has allocated).

The advantage of attaching the control information to each block the heap manager allocates is that it is very easy to locate this information, because the memory manager typically places this information immediately before the allocated block. When the heap manager maintains this information in an internal table, it may require a search operation of some sort in order to locate the information.

Another issue that affects the overhead associated with the heap manager is the allocation *granularity*. Although most heap managers will allow you to allocate storage in blocks as small as one byte, most memory managers will actually allocate some minimum number of bytes greater than one. This minimum amount is the *allocation granularity* the memory manager supports. Generally, the engineer designing the memory-allocation functions chooses a granularity that will guarantee that any object allocated on the heap will begin at a reasonably aligned memory address for that object.

As such, most heap managers allocate memory blocks on a 4-, 8-, or 16-byte boundary. For performance reasons, many heap managers begin each allocation on a typical cache-line boundary, usually 16, 32, or 64 bytes.

Whatever the granularity, if the application requests some number of bytes that is less than the heap manager's granularity, or that is not a multiple of the granularity value, the heap manager will allocate extra bytes of storage so that the complete allocation is an even multiple of the granularity value. Therefore, there may be a few unrequested bytes tacked on to each allocation request to fill out the minimum-sized block the heap manager allocates. Of course, this amount varies by heap manager (and possibly even by version of a specific heap manager), so an application should never assume that it has more memory available than it requests; doing so would be silly, anyway, because the application could simply have requested more memory in the initial allocation call if it needed more.

The extra memory the heap manager allocates to ensure that the request is a multiple of the granularity size results in another form of fragmentation called *internal fragmentation*. Like external fragmentation, internal fragmentation results in the loss of small amounts of memory throughout the system that cannot satisfy future allocation requests. Assuming random sized memory allocations, the average amount of internal fragmentation that will occur on each allocation is half the granularity size. Fortunately, the granularity size is quite small for most memory managers (typically 16 bytes or fewer), so after thousands and thousands of memory allocations you'll only lose a couple dozen or so kilobytes to internal fragmentation.

Between the costs associated with allocation granularity and the memory control information, a typical memory request may require between 4 and 16 bytes, plus whatever the application requests. If you are making large memory allocation requests (hundreds or thousands of bytes), the overhead bytes won't consume a large percentage of memory on the heap. However, if you allocate lots of small objects, the memory consumed by internal fragmentation and control information may represent a significant portion of your heap area. For example, consider a simple memory manager that always allocates blocks of data on 4-byte boundaries and requires a single 4-byte length value that it attaches to each allocation request for control purposes. This means that the minimum amount of storage the heap manager will require for each allocation is eight bytes. If you make a series of `malloc` calls to allocate a single byte, the application will not be able to use almost 88 percent of the memory it allocates. Even if you allocate 4-byte values on each allocation request, the heap manager consumes 67 percent of the memory for overhead purposes. However, if your average allocation is a block of 256 bytes, the overhead only requires about 2 percent of the total memory allocation. Moral of the story: The larger your allocation request, the less impact the control information and internal fragmentation will have on your heap.

Computer science journals contain lots of examples of software engineering studies where the authors determined that memory allocation and deallocation requests caused a significant loss of performance in their systems. In such studies, the authors often obtained performance improvements of 100 percent or better by simply implementing their own simplified, application-specific, memory-management algorithms rather than calling the standard run-time library or OS kernel memory allocation code. Let's hope this section has made you aware of this potential problem in your own code.

11.10 For More Information

Like the previous couple of chapters, this chapter deals with computer architecture issues. Almost any decent college textbook on computer architecture will go into considerable depth discussing caches and the memory hierarchy. Patterson and Hennessy's *Computer Architecture: A Quantitative Approach* is one of the better-regarded texts on this subject. For information about virtual memory management, a good operating systems textbook will be useful as well. For information about the specific paging mechanism and support for virtual memory that your particular CPU provides, see the CPU manufacturer's data books for the CPU.

12

INPUT AND OUTPUT (I/O)

A typical program has three basic tasks: input, computation, and output. This book has so far concentrated on the computational aspects of the computer system, but now it is time to discuss input and output.

This chapter will focus on the primitive input and output activities of the CPU, rather than on the abstract file or character input/output (I/O) that high-level applications usually employ. It will discuss how the CPU transfers bytes of data to and from the outside world, paying special attention to the performance issues behind I/O operations. As all high-level I/O activities are eventually routed through the low-level I/O systems, you must understand how low-level input and output works on a computer system if you want to write programs that communicate efficiently with the outside world.

12.1 Connecting a CPU to the Outside World

The first thing to learn about the I/O subsystem is that I/O in a typical computer system is radically different from I/O in a typical high-level programming language. At the primitive I/O levels of a computer system, you will rarely find machine instructions that behave like Pascal's writeln, C++'s cout, C's printf, or even like the HLA stdin and stdout statements. In fact, most I/O machine instructions behave exactly like the 80x86's mov instruction. To send data to an output device, the CPU simply moves that data to a special memory location, and to read data from an input device, the CPU moves data from the device's address into the CPU. I/O operations behave much like memory read and write operations, except that there are usually more wait states associated with I/O operations.

We can classify I/O ports into five categories based on the CPU's ability to read and write data at a given port address. These five categories of ports are read-only, write-only, read/write, dual I/O, and bidirectional.

A *read-only port* is obviously an *input port*. If the CPU can only read the data from the port, then the data must come from some source external to the computer system. The hardware typically ignores any attempt to write data to a read-only port, but it's never a good idea to write to a read-only port because some devices may fail if you do so. A good example of a read-only port is the status port on a PC's parallel printer interface. Data from this port specifies the current status of the printer, while the hardware ignores any data written to this port.

A *write-only port* is always an *output port*. Writing data to such a port presents the data for use by an external device. Attempting to read data from a write-only port generally returns whatever garbage value happens to be on the data bus. You generally cannot depend on the meaning of any value read from a write-only port. An output port typically uses a latch device to hold data to be sent to the outside world. When a CPU writes to a port address associated with an output latch, the latch stores the data and makes it available on an external set of signal lines (see Figure 12-1).

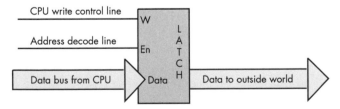

Figure 12-1: A typical output port

A perfect example of an output port is a parallel printer port. The CPU typically writes an ASCII character to a byte-wide output port that connects to the DB-25F connector on the back of the computer's case. A cable transmits this data to the printer, where it arrives on the printer's input port (from the printer's perspective, it is reading the data from the computer system).

A processor inside the printer typically converts this ASCII character to a sequence of dots that it prints on the paper.

Note that output ports can be write-only or read/write. The port in Figure 12-1, for example, is a write-only port. Because the outputs on the latch do not loop back to the CPU's data bus, the CPU cannot read the data the latch contains. Both the address decode line (En) and the write control line (W) must be active for the latch to operate. If the CPU tries to read the data located at the latch's address the address decode line is active but the write control line is not, so the latch does not respond to the read request.

A *read/write port* is an output port as far as the outside world is concerned. However, the CPU can read as well as write data to such a port. Whenever the CPU reads data from a read/write port, it reads the data that was last written to the port allowing a programmer to retrieve that value. The act of reading data from the port does not affect the data presented to the external peripheral device.[1]

Figure 12-2 shows how to create a port that you can both read from and write to. The data written to the output port loops back to a second latch. Placing the address of these two latches on the address bus asserts the *address decode lines* on both latches. Therefore, to select between the two latches, the CPU must also assert either the read line or the write line. Asserting the read line (as will happen during a read operation) will enable the lower latch. This places the data previously written to the output port on the CPU's data bus, allowing the CPU to read that data.

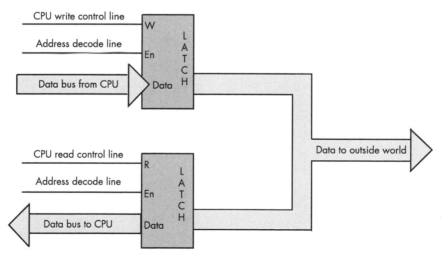

Figure 12-2: An output port that supports read/write access

Note that the port in Figure 12-2 is not an input port — true input ports read data from external pins. Although the CPU can read data from this latch, the organization of this circuit simply allows the CPU to read the data

---

[1] Historically, "peripheral" meant any device external to the computer system itself. This book will use the modern form of this term to simply imply any device that is not part of the CPU or memory.

it previously wrote to the port, thus saving the program from maintaining this value in a separate variable if the application needs to know what was written to the port. The data appearing on the external connector is output only, and one cannot connect real-world input devices to these signal pins.

A *dual I/O port* is also a read/write port, but when you read a dual I/O port, you read data from an external input device rather than the last data written to the output side of the port's address. Writing data to a dual I/O port transmits data to some external output device, just as writing to a write-only port does. Figure 12-3 shows how you could interface a dual I/O port with the system.

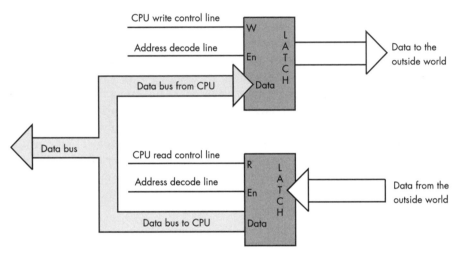

Figure 12-3: An input port and output device that share the same address (a dual I/O port)

Note that a dual I/O port is actually created using two ports — a read-only port and a write-only port — that share the same port address. Reading from the address accesses the read-only port, and writing to the address accesses the write-only port. Essentially, this port arrangement uses the read and write (R/W) control lines to provide an extra address bit that specifies which of the two ports to use.

A *bidirectional port* allows the CPU to both read and write data to an external device. To function properly, a bidirectional port must pass various control lines, such as read and write enable, to the peripheral device so that the device can change the direction of data transfer based on the CPU's read/write request. In effect, a bidirectional port is an extension of the CPU's bus through a bidirectional latch or buffer.

Generally, a given peripheral device will utilize multiple I/O ports. The original PC parallel printer interface, for example, uses three port addresses: a read/write I/O port, a read-only input port, and a write-only output port. The read/write port is the data port on which the CPU can read the last ASCII character written through that port. The input port returns control signals from the printer, which indicate whether the printer is ready to accept another character, is offline, is out of paper, and so on. The output port transmits control information to the printer. Later model PCs substituted a bidirectional port for the data port, allowing data transfer from and to a device through the parallel port. The bidirectional data port improved performance for various devices such as disk and tape drives connected to the PC's parallel port.

12.2 Other Ways to Connect Ports to the System

The examples given thus far may leave you with the impression that the CPU always reads and writes peripheral data using the data bus. However, while the CPU generally transfers the data it has read from input ports across the data bus, it does not always use the data bus when writing data to output ports. In fact, a very common output method is to simply access a port's address directly without writing any data to it. Figure 12-4 illustrates a very simple example of this technique using a set/reset (S/R) flip-flop. In this circuit, an address decoder decodes two separate addresses. Any read or write access to the first address sets the output line high; any read or write access to the second address clears the output line. This circuit ignores the data on the CPU's data lines, and it also ignores the status of the read and write lines. The only thing that matters is that the CPU accesses one of these two addresses.

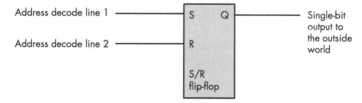

Figure 12-4: Outputting data to a port by simply accessing that port

Another possible way to connect an output port to a system is to connect the read/write status lines to the data input of a D flip-flop. Figure 12-5 shows how you could design such a device. In this diagram, any read of the port sets the output bit to zero, while any write to this port sets the output bit to one.

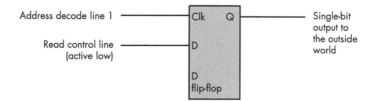

Figure 12-5: Outputting data using the read/write control as the data to output

These examples of connecting peripheral devices directly to the CPU are only two of an amazing number of different designs that engineers have devised to avoid using the data bus. However, unless otherwise noted, the remaining examples in this chapter presume that the CPU reads and writes data to an external device using the data bus.

12.3   I/O Mechanisms

There are three basic I/O mechanisms that computer systems can use to communicate with peripheral devices: memory-mapped input/output, I/O-mapped input/output, and direct memory access (DMA). Memory-mapped I/O uses ordinary locations within the CPU's memory address space to communicate with peripheral devices. I/O-mapped input/output uses an address space separate from memory, and it uses special machine instructions to transfer data between that special I/O address space and the outside world. DMA is a special form of memory-mapped I/O where the peripheral device reads and writes data located in memory without CPU intervention. Each I/O mechanism has its own set of advantages and disadvantages, which we will discuss in the following sections.

How a device connects to a computer system is usually determined by the hardware system engineer at design time, and programmers have little control over this choice. While some devices may present two different interfaces to the system, software engineers generally have to live with whatever interface the hardware designers provide. Nevertheless, by paying attention to the costs and benefits of the I/O mechanism used for communication between the CPU and the peripheral device, you can choose different code sequences that will maximize the performance of I/O within your applications.

12.3.1   Memory-Mapped I/O

A memory-mapped peripheral device is connected to the CPU's address and data lines exactly like regular memory, so whenever the CPU writes to or reads from the address associated with the peripheral device, the CPU transfers data to or from the device. This mechanism has several benefits and only a few disadvantages.

The principle advantage of a memory-mapped I/O subsystem is that the CPU can use any instruction that accesses memory, such as mov, to transfer data between the CPU and a peripheral. For example, if you are trying to access a read/write or bidirectional port, you can use an 80x86 *read/modify/write* instruction, like add, to read the port, manipulate the value, and then write data back to the port, all with a single instruction. Of course, if the port is read-only or write-only, an instruction that reads from the port address, modifies the value, and then writes the modified value back to the port will be of little use.

The big disadvantage of memory-mapped I/O devices is that they consume addresses in the CPU's memory map. Every byte of address space that a peripheral device consumes is one less byte available for installing actual memory. Generally, the minimum amount of space you can allocate to a peripheral (or block of related peripherals) is a page of memory (4,096 bytes on an 80x86). Fortunately, a typical PC has only a couple dozen such devices, so this usually isn't much of a problem. However, it can become a problem with some peripheral devices, like video cards, that consume a large chunk of the address space. Some video cards have 32 MB of on-board memory that they map into the memory address space and this means that the 32 MB address range consumed by the card is not available to the system for use as regular RAM memory.

12.3.2   I/O and the Cache

It goes without saying that the CPU cannot cache values intended for memory-mapped I/O ports. Caching data from an input port would mean that subsequent reads of the input port would access the value in the cache rather than the data at the input port, which could be different. Similarly, with a write-back cache mechanism, some writes might never reach an output port because the CPU might save up several writes in the cache before sending the last write to the actual I/O port. In order to avoid these potential problems, there must be some mechanism to tell the CPU not to cache accesses to certain memory locations.

The solution is found in the virtual memory subsystem of the CPU. The 80x86's page table entries, for example, contain information that the CPU can use to determine whether it is okay to map data from a page in memory to cache. If this flag is set one way, the cache operates normally; if the flag is set the other way, the CPU does not cache up accesses to that page.

12.3.3   I/O-Mapped Input/Output

I/O-mapped input/output differs from memory-mapped I/O, insofar as it uses a special I/O address space separate from the normal memory space, and it uses special machine instructions to access device addresses. For example, the 80x86 CPUs provide the in and out instructions specifically for this purpose. These 80x86 instructions behave somewhat like the mov instruction except that they transmit their data to and from the special I/O address space rather than the normal memory address space. Although the 80x86 processors (and other processors that provide I/O-mapped input/output capabilities, most notably various embedded microcontrollers) use the same physical address bus to transfer both memory addresses and I/O device addresses, additional control lines differentiate between addresses that belong to the normal memory space and those that belong to the special I/O address space. This means that the presence of an I/O-mapped input/output system on a CPU does not preclude the use of memory-mapped I/O in the system. Therefore, if there is an insufficient number of I/O-mapped locations in the CPU's address space, a hardware designer can always use memory-mapped I/O instead (as a video card does on a typical PC).

In modern 80x86 PC systems that utilize the PCI bus (or later variants), special peripheral chips on the system's motherboard remap the I/O address space into the main memory space, allowing programs to access I/O-mapped devices using either memory-mapped or I/O-mapped input/output. By placing the peripheral port addresses in the standard memory space, high-level languages can control those I/O devices even though those languages might not provide special statements to reference the I/O address space. As almost all high-level languages provide the ability to access memory, but most do not allow access to the I/O space, having the PCI bus remap the I/O address space into the memory address space provides I/O access to those high-level languages.

12.3.4 Direct Memory Access (DMA)

Memory-mapped I/O subsystems and I/O-mapped subsystems both require the CPU to move data between the peripheral device and memory. For this reason, we often call these two forms of I/O *programmed I/O*. For example, to store into memory a sequence of ten bytes taken from an input port, the CPU must read each value from the input port and store it into memory.

For very high-speed I/O devices the CPU may be too slow to process this data one byte (or one word or double word) at a time. Such devices generally have an interface to the CPU's bus so they can directly read and write memory, which is known as *direct memory access* because the peripheral device accesses memory directly, without using the CPU as an intermediary. This often allows the I/O operation to proceed in parallel with other CPU operations, thereby increasing the overall speed of the system. Note, however, that the CPU and the DMA device cannot both use the address and data buses at the same time. Therefore, concurrent processing only occurs if the bus is free for use by the I/O device, which happens when the CPU has a cache and is accessing code and data in the cache. Nevertheless, even if the CPU must halt and wait for the DMA operation to complete before beginning a different operation, the DMA approach is still much faster because many of the bus operations that occur during I/O-mapped input/output or memory-mapped I/O consist of instruction fetches or I/O port accesses that are not present during DMA operations.

A typical DMA controller consists of a pair of counters and other circuitry that interfaces with memory and the peripheral device. One of the counters serves as an address register, and this counter supplies an address on the address bus for each transfer. The second counter specifies the number of data transfers. Each time the peripheral device wants to transfer data to or from memory, it sends a signal to the DMA controller, which places the value of the address counter on the address bus. In coordination with the DMA controller, the peripheral device places data on the data bus to write to memory during an input operation, or it reads data from the data bus, taken from memory, during an output operation.[2] After a successful data transfer, the DMA controller increments its address register and decrements the transfer counter. This process repeats until the transfer counter decrements to zero.

12.4 I/O Speed Hierarchy

Different peripheral devices have different data transfer rates. Some devices, like keyboards, are extremely slow when compared to CPU speeds. Other devices, like disk drives, can actually transfer data faster than the CPU can process it. The appropriate programming technique for data transfer depends strongly on the transfer speed of the peripheral device involved in the I/O operation. Therefore, in order to understand how to write the most appropriate code, it first makes sense to invent some terminology to describe the different transfer rates of peripheral devices.

Low-speed devices Devices that produce or consume data at a rate much slower than the CPU is capable of processing. For the purposes of discussion, we'll assume that low-speed devices operate at speeds that are two or more orders of magnitude slower than the CPU.

Medium-speed devices Devices that transfer data at approximately the same rate as, or up to two orders of magnitude slower than, the CPU.

High-speed devices Devices that transfer data faster than the CPU is capable of handling using programmed I/O.

The speed of the peripheral device will determine the type of I/O mechanism used for the I/O operation. Clearly, high-speed devices must use DMA because programmed I/O is too slow. Medium- and low-speed devices may use any of the three I/O mechanisms for data transfer (though low-speed devices rarely use DMA because of the cost of the extra hardware involved).

With typical bus architectures, personal computer systems are capable of one transfer per microsecond or better. Therefore, high-speed devices are those that transfer data more rapidly than once per microsecond. Medium-speed transfers are those that involve a data transfer every 1 to 100 microseconds. Low-speed devices usually transfer data less often than once every 100 microseconds. Of course, these definitions for the speed of low-, medium-, and high-speed devices are system dependent. Faster CPUs with faster buses allow faster medium-speed operations.

Note that one transfer per microsecond is not the same thing as a 1-MB-per-second transfer rate. A peripheral device can actually transfer more than one byte per data transfer operation. For example, when using the 80x86

---

[2] Don't forget that "input" and "output" are from the perspective of the computer system, not the device. Hence, the device writes data during an input operation and reads data during an output operation.

`in( dx, eax );` instruction, the peripheral device can transfer four bytes in one transfer. Therefore, if the device is reaching one transfer per microsecond, the device can transfer 4 MB per second using this instruction.

12.5   System Buses and Data Transfer Rates

Earlier in this book, you saw that the CPU communicates with memory and I/O devices using the system bus. If you've ever opened up a computer and looked inside or read the specifications for a system, you've probably seen terms like *PCI, ISA, EISA*, or even *NuBus* mentioned when discussing the computer's system bus. In this section, we'll discuss the relationship between the CPU's bus and these different system buses, and describe how these different computer system buses affect the performance of a system.

Although the choice of the hardware bus is made by hardware engineers, not software engineers, many computer systems will actually employ multiple buses in the same system. Therefore, software engineers can choose which peripheral devices they use based upon the bus connections of those peripherals. Furthermore, maximizing performance for a particular bus may require different programming techniques than for other buses. Finally, although a software engineer may not be able to choose the buses available in a particular computer system, that engineer can choose which system to write their software for, based on the buses available in the system they ultimately choose.

Computer system buses like PCI (Peripheral Component Interconnect) and ISA (Industry Standard Architecture) are definitions for physical connectors inside a computer system. These definitions describe the set of signals, physical dimensions (i.e., connector layouts and distances from one another), and a data transfer protocol for connecting different electronic devices. These buses are related to the CPU's *local bus*, which consists of the address, data, and control lines, because many of the signals on the peripheral buses are identical to signals that appear on the CPU's bus.

However, peripheral buses do not necessarily mirror the CPU's bus — they often contain several lines that are not present on the CPU's bus. These additional lines let peripheral devices communicate with one another without having to go through the CPU or memory. For example, most peripheral buses provide a common set of interrupt control signals that let I/O devices communicate directly with the system's interrupt controller, which is also a peripheral device. Nor do the peripheral buses include all the signals found on the CPU's bus. For example, the ISA bus only supports 24 address lines compared with the Pentium IV's 36 address lines.

Different peripheral devices are designed to use different peripheral buses. Figure 12-6 shows the organization of the PCI and ISA buses in a typical computer system.

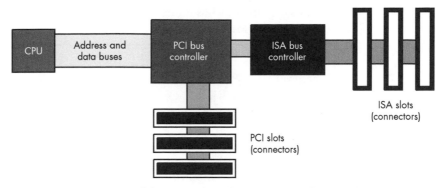

Figure 12-6: Connection of the PCI and ISA buses in a typical PC

Notice how the CPU's address and data buses connect to a PCI bus controller peripheral device, but not to the PCI bus itself. The PCI bus controller contains two sets of pins, providing a *bridge* between the CPU's local bus and the PCI bus. The signal lines on the local bus are not connected directly to the corresponding lines on the PCI bus; instead, the PCI bus controller acts as an intermediary, rerouting all data transfer requests between the CPU and the PCI bus.

Another interesting thing to note is that the ISA bus controller is not directly connected to the CPU. Instead, it is usually connected to the PCI bus controller. There is no logical reason why the ISA controller couldn't be connected directly to the CPU's local bus. However, in most modern PCs, the ISA and PCI controllers appear on the same chip, and the manufacturer of this chip has chosen to interface the ISA bus through the PCI controller for cost or performance reasons.

The CPU's local bus usually runs at some submultiple of the CPU's frequency. Typical local bus frequencies are currently 66 MHz, 100 MHz, 133 MHz, 400 MHz, 533 MHz, and 800 MHz, but they may become even faster. Usually, only memory and a few selected peripherals like the PCI bus controller sit on the CPU's bus and operate at this high frequency.

Because a typical CPU's bus is 64 bits wide and because it is theoretically possible to achieve one data transfer per clock cycle, the CPU's bus has a maximum possible data transfer rate of eight bytes times the clock frequency, or 800 MB per second for a 100-MHz bus. In practice, CPUs rarely achieve the maximum data transfer rate, but they do achieve some percentage of it, so the faster the bus, the more data can move in and out of the CPU (and caches) in a given amount of time.

12.5.1   Performance of the PCI Bus

The PCI bus comes in several configurations. The base configuration has a 32-bit-wide data bus operating at 33 MHz. Like the CPU's local bus, the PCI bus is theoretically capable of transferring data on each clock cycle.

This means that the bus has a theoretical maximum data transfer rate of 4 bytes times 33 MHz, or 132 MB per second. In practice, though, the PCI bus doesn't come anywhere near this level of performance except in short bursts.

Whenever the CPU wishes to access a peripheral on the PCI bus, it must negotiate with other peripheral devices for the right to use the bus. This negotiation can take several clock cycles before the PCI controller grants the CPU access to the bus. If a CPU writes a sequence of values to a peripheral device at a rate of a double word per bus transfer, you can see that the negotiation time actually causes the transfer rate to drop dramatically. The only way to achieve anywhere near the maximum theoretical bandwidth on the bus is to use a DMA controller and move blocks of data in *burst mode*. In this burst mode, the DMA controller negotiates just once for the bus and then makes a large number of transfers without giving up the bus between each one.

There are a couple of enhancements to the PCI bus that improve performance. Some PCI buses support a 64-bit wide data path. This, obviously, doubles the maximum theoretical data transfer rate from four bytes per transfer to eight bytes per transfer. Another enhancement is running the bus at 66 MHz, which also doubles the throughput. With a 64-bit-wide 66-MHz bus you would quadruple the data transfer rate over the performance of the baseline configuration. These optional enhancements to the PCI bus allow it to grow with the CPU as CPUs increase their performance. As this is being written, a high-performance version of the PCI bus, PCI-X, is starting to appear with expected bus speeds beginning at 133 MHz and other enhancements to improve performance.

12.5.2 Performance of the ISA Bus

The ISA bus is a carry-over from the original PC/AT computer system. This bus is 16 bits wide and operates at 8 MHz. It requires four clock cycles for each bus cycle. For this and other reasons, the ISA bus is capable of about only one data transmission per microsecond. With a 16-bit-wide bus, data transfer is limited to about 2 MB per second. This is much slower than the speed at which both the CPU's local bus and the PCI bus operate. Generally, you would only attach low-speed devices, like an RS-232 communications device, a modem, or a parallel printer interface, to the ISA bus. Most other devices, like disks, scanners, and network cards, are too fast for the ISA bus. The ISA bus is really only capable of supporting low-speed and medium-speed devices.

Note that accessing the ISA bus on most systems involves first negotiating for the PCI bus. The PCI bus is so much faster than the ISA bus that the negotiation time has very little impact on the performance of peripherals on the ISA bus. Therefore, there is very little difference to be gained by connecting the ISA controller directly to the CPU's local bus.

12.5.3　The AGP Bus

Video display cards are very special peripherals that need maximum bus performance to ensure quick screen updates and fast graphic operations. Unfortunately, if the CPU has to constantly negotiate with other peripherals for the use of the PCI bus, graphics performance can suffer. To overcome this problem, video card designers created the AGP *(Accelerated Graphics Port)* interface between the CPU's local bus and the video display card, which provides various control lines and bus protocols specifically designed for video display cards.

The AGP connection lets the CPU quickly move data to and from the video display RAM (see Figure 12-7). Because there is only one AGP port per system, only one card can use the AGP slot at a time. The upside of this is that the system never has to negotiate for access to the AGP bus.

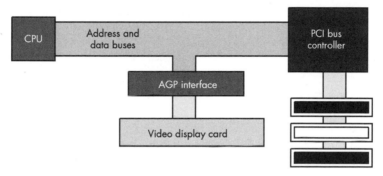

Figure 12-7: The AGP bus interface

12.6　Buffering

If a particular I/O device produces or consumes data faster than the system is capable of transferring data to or from that device, the system designer has two choices: provide a faster connection between the CPU and the device, or slow down the rate of transfer between the two.

If the peripheral device is connected to a slow bus like ISA, a faster connection can be created by using a different, faster bus. Another way to increase the connection speed is by switching to a wider bus like the 64-bit PCI bus, a bus with a higher frequency, or a higher performance bus like PCI-X. System designers can also sometimes create a faster interface to the bus as they have done with the AGP connection. However, once you exhaust these possibilities for improving performance, it can be very expensive to create a faster connection between peripherals and the system.

The other alternative available when a peripheral device is capable of transferring data faster than the system is capable of processing it, is to slow down the transfer rate between the peripheral and the computer system. This isn't always as bad an option as it might seem. Most high-speed devices don't transfer data at a constant rate to the system. Instead, devices typically transfer a block of data rapidly and then sit idle for some length of time. Although the burst rate is high and is faster than what the CPU or memory can handle, the average data transfer rate is usually lower than this. If you could average out the high-bandwidth peaks and transfer some of the data when the peripheral was inactive, you could easily move data between the peripheral and the computer system without resorting to an expensive, high-bandwidth bus or connection.

The trick is to use memory on the peripheral side to buffer the data. The peripheral can rapidly fill this buffer with data during an input operation, and it can rapidly extract data from the buffer during an output operation. Once the peripheral device is inactive, the system can proceed at a sustainable rate either to empty or refill the buffer, depending on whether the buffer is full or empty at the time. As long as the average data transfer rate of the peripheral device is below the maximum bandwidth the system supports, and the buffer is large enough to hold bursts of data going to and from the peripheral, this scheme lets the peripheral communicate with the system at a lower average data transfer rate.

Often, to save costs, the buffering takes place in the CPU's address space rather than in memory local to the peripheral device. In this case, it is often the software engineer's responsibility to initialize the buffer for a peripheral device. Therefore, this buffering isn't always transparent to the software engineer. In some cases, neither the peripheral device nor the OS provide a buffer for the peripheral's data and it becomes the application's responsibility to buffer up this data in order to maintain maximum performance and avoid loss of data. In other cases, the device or OS may provide a small buffer, but the application itself might not process the data often enough to avoid data overruns — in such situations, an application can create a larger buffer that is local to the application to avoid the data overruns.

12.7 Handshaking

Many I/O devices cannot accept data at just any rate. For example, a Pentium-based PC is capable of sending several hundred million characters per second to a printer, but printers are incapable of printing that many characters each second. Likewise, an input device such as a keyboard will never transmit several million keystrokes per second to the system (because it operates at human speeds, not computer speeds). Because of the difference in capabilities between the CPU and many of the system peripherals, the CPU needs some mechanism to coordinate data transfer between the computer system and its peripheral devices.

One common way to coordinate data transfers is to send and receive status bits on a port separate from the data port. For example, a single bit sent by a printer could tell the system whether it is ready to accept more data. Likewise, a single status bit in a different port could specify whether a keystroke is available at the keyboard data port. The CPU can test these bits prior to writing a character to the printer, or reading a key from the keyboard.

Using status bits to indicate that a device is ready to accept or transmit data is known as *handshaking*. It gets this name because the protocol is similar to two people agreeing on some method of transfer by a handshake.

To demonstrate how handshaking works, consider the following short 80x86 assembly language program segment. This code fragment will continuously loop while the HO bit of the printer status register (at input port $379) contains zero and will exit once the HO bit is set (indicating that the printer is ready to accept data):

```
mov( $379, dx );        // Initialize DX with the address of the status port.
repeat

    in( dx, al );       // Get the parallel port status into the AL register.
    and( $80, al );     // Clear Z flag if the HO bit is set.

until( @nz );           // Repeat until the HO bit contains a one.

// Okay to write another byte to the printer data port here.
```

12.8 Time-outs on an I/O Port

One problem with the repeat..until loop in the previous section is that it could spin indefinitely as it waits for the printer to become ready to accept additional input. If someone turns the printer off, or if the printer cable becomes disconnected, the program could freeze up, forever waiting for the printer to become available. Usually, it's a better idea to inform the user when something goes wrong rather than allowing the system to hang. Typically, great programmers handle this problem by including a *time-out* period in the loop, which once exceeded causes the program to alert the user that something is wrong with the peripheral device.

You can expect some sort of response from most peripheral devices within a reasonable amount of time. For example, even in the worst case, most printers will be ready to accept additional character data within a few seconds of the last transmission. Therefore, something is probably wrong if 30 seconds or more have passed without the printer accepting a new character. If the program is written to detect this kind of problem, it can pause, asking the user to check the printer and tell the program to resume printing once the problem is resolved.

Choosing a good time-out period is not an easy task. In doing so, you must carefully balance the irritation of possibly having the program incorrectly claim that something is wrong, with the pain of having the program lock up for long periods when there actually is something wrong. Both situations are equally annoying to the end user.

An easy way to create a time-out period is to count the number of times the program loops while waiting for a handshake signal from a peripheral. Consider the following modification to the repeat..until loop of the previous section:

```
mov( $379, dx );            // Initialize DX with the address of the status port.
mov( 30_000_000, ecx );     // Time-out period of approximately 30 seconds,
                            //   assuming port access time is about 1 microsecond.

HandshakeLoop:

    in( dx, al );           // Get the parallel port status into the AL register.
    and( $80, al );         // Clear Z flag if the HO bit is set.

loopz HandshakeLoop;        // Decrement ECX and loop while ECX <> 0 and
                            //   the HO bit of AL contains a zero.

if( ecx <> 0 ) then

    // Okay to write another byte to the printer data port here.

else

    // We had a time-out condition if we get here.

endif;
```

This code will exit once the printer is ready to accept data or when approximately 30 seconds have expired. You might question the 30-second figure, after all, a software-based loop (counting down ECX to zero) should run at different speeds on different processors. However, don't miss the fact that there is an in instruction inside this loop. The in instruction reads a port on the ISA bus and that means this instruction will take approximately one microsecond to execute (about the fastest operation on the ISA bus). Hence, one million times through the loop will take about a second (plus or minus 50 percent, but close enough for our purposes). This is true almost regardless of the CPU frequency.

12.9 Interrupts and Polled I/O

Polling is the process of constantly testing a port to see if data is available. The handshaking loops of the previous sections provide good examples of polling — the CPU waits in a short loop, testing the printer port's status value until the printer is ready to accept more data, and then the CPU can transfer more data to the printer. Polled I/O is inherently inefficient. If the printer in this example takes ten seconds to accept another byte of data, the CPU spins doing nothing productive for those ten seconds.

In early personal computer systems, this is exactly how a program would behave. When a program wanted to read a key from the keyboard, it would poll the keyboard status port until a key was available. These early computers could not do other processing while waiting for the keyboard.

The solution to this problem is to use what is called an *interrupt mechanism*. An interrupt is triggered by an external hardware event, such as the printer becoming ready to accept another character, that causes the CPU to interrupt its current instruction sequence and call a special *interrupt service routine* (ISR). Typically, an interrupt service routine runs through the following sequence of events:

1. It preserves the current values of all machine registers and flags so that the computation that is interrupted can be continued later.
2. It does whatever operation is necessary to *service* the interrupt.
3. It restores the registers and flags to the values they had before the interrupt.
4. It resumes execution of the code that was interrupted.

In most computer systems, typical I/O devices generate an interrupt whenever they make data available to the CPU, or when they become able to accept data from the CPU. The ISR quickly processes the interrupt request in the background, allowing some other computation to proceed normally in the foreground.

Though interrupt service routines are usually written by OS designers or peripheral device manufacturers, most OSes provide the ability to pass an interrupt to an application via *signals* or some similar mechanism. This allows you to include interrupt service routines directly within an application. You could use this facility, for example, to have a peripheral device notify your application when its internal buffer is full and the application needs to copy data from the peripheral's buffer to an application buffer to prevent data loss.

12.10 Protected Mode Operation and Device Drivers

If you're working on Windows 95 or 98, you can write assembly code to access I/O ports directly. The assembly code shown earlier as an example of handshaking is a good example of this. However, recent versions of Windows and all versions of Linux employ a protected mode of operation. In this mode, direct access to devices is restricted to the OS and certain privileged programs. Standard applications, even those written in assembly language, are not so privileged. If you write a simple program that attempts to send data to an I/O port, the system will generate an illegal access exception and halt your program.

Linux does not allow just any program to access I/O ports as it pleases. Only programs with "super-user" (root) privileges may do so. For limited I/O access, it is possible to use the Linux ioperm system call to make certain I/O ports accessible from user applications. For more details, Linux users should read the "man" page on "ioperm."

12.10.1   Device Drivers

If Linux and Windows don't allow direct access to peripheral devices, how does a program communicate with these devices? Clearly, this *can* be done, because applications interact with real-world devices all the time. It turns out that specially written modules, known as *device drivers*, are able to access I/O ports by special permission from the OS. A complete discussion of writing device drivers is well beyond the scope of this book, but an understanding of how device drivers work may help you understand the possibilities and limitations of I/O under a *protected-mode* OS.

A device driver is a special type of program that links with the OS. A device driver must follow some special protocols, and it must make some special calls to the OS that are not available to standard applications. Furthermore, in order to install a device driver in your system, you must have administrator privileges, because device drivers create all kinds of security and resource allocation problems, and you can't have every hacker in the world taking advantage of rogue device drivers running on your system. Therefore, "whipping out a device driver" is not a trivial process and application programs cannot load and unload drivers at will.

Fortunately, there are only a limited number of devices found on a typical PC, so you only need a limited number of device drivers. You would typically install a device driver in the OS at the same time you install the device, or, if the device is built into the PC, at the same time you install the OS. About the only time you'd really need to write your own device driver is when building your own device, or in special cases when you need to take advantage of some device's capabilities that standard device drivers don't handle.

The device driver model works well with low-speed devices, where the OS and device driver can respond to the device much more quickly than the device requires. The model is also great for use with medium- and high-speed devices where the system transmits large blocks of data to and from the device. However, the device driver model does have a few drawbacks, and one is that it does not support medium- and high-speed data transfers that require a high degree of interaction between the device and the application.

The problem is that calling the OS is an expensive process. Whenever an application makes a call to the OS to transmit data to the device, it can potentially take hundreds of microseconds, if not milliseconds, before the device driver actually sees the application's data. If the interaction between the device and the application requires a constant flurry of bytes moving back and forth, there will be a big delay if each transfer has to go through the OS. The important point to note is that for applications of this sort, you will need to write a special device driver that can handle the transactions itself rather than continually returning to the application.

12.10.2 Communicating with Device Drivers and "Files"

For the most part, communicating with a peripheral device under a modern OS is exactly like writing data to a file or reading data from a file. In most OSes, you open a "file" using a special file name like COM1 (the serial port) or LPT1 (the parallel port) and the OS automatically creates a connection to the specified device. When you are finished using the device, you "close" the associated file, which tells the OS that the application is done with the device so other applications can use it.

Of course, most devices do not support the same semantics that do disk files do. Some devices, like printers or modems, can accept a long stream of unformatted data, but other devices may require that you preformat the data into blocks and write the blocks to the device with a single write operation. The exact semantics depend upon the particular device. Nevertheless, the typical way to send data to a peripheral is to use an OS "write" function to which you pass a buffer containing some data, and the way to read data from a device is to call an OS "read" function to which you pass the address of some buffer into which the OS will place the data it reads.

Of course, not all devices conform to the *stream-I/O* data semantics of file I/O. Therefore, most OSes provide a *device-control API* that lets you pass information directly to the peripheral's device driver to handle the cases where a stream-I/O model fails.

Because it varies by OS, the exact details concerning the OS API interface are a bit beyond the scope of this book. Though most OSes use a similar scheme, they are different enough to make it impossible to describe them in a generic fashion. For more details, consult the programmer's reference for your particular OS.

12.11 Exploring Specific PC Peripheral Devices

This chapter has so far introduced I/O in a very general sense, without spending too much time discussing the particular peripheral devices present in a typical PC. It some respects, it's dangerous to discuss real devices on modern PCs because the traditional ("legacy") devices that are easy to understand are slowly disappearing from PC designs. As manufacturers introduce new PCs, they are removing many of the legacy peripherals like parallel and serial ports that are easy to program, and they are replacing these devices with complex peripherals like USB and FireWire. Although a detailed discussion on programming these newer peripheral devices is beyond the scope of this book, you need to understand their behavior in order to write great code that accesses these devices.

Because of the nature of the peripheral devices appearing in the rest of this chapter, the information presented applies only to IBM-compatible PCs. There simply isn't enough space in this book to cover how particular I/O devices behave on different systems. Other systems support similar I/O devices, but their hardware interfaces may be different from what's presented here. Nevertheless, the general principles still apply.

12.12 The Keyboard

The PC's keyboard is a computer system in its own right. Buried inside the keyboard's case is an 8042 microcontroller chip that constantly scans the switches on the keyboard to see if any keys are held down. This processing occurs in parallel with the normal activities of the PC, and even though the PC's 80x86 is busy with other things, the keyboard never misses a keystroke.

A typical keystroke starts with the user pressing a key on the keyboard. This closes an electrical contact in a switch, which the keyboard's microcontroller can sense. Unfortunately, mechanical switches do not always close perfectly clean. Often, the contacts bounce off one another several times before coming to rest with a solid connection. To a microcontroller chip that is reading the switch constantly, these bouncing contacts will look like a very quick series of keypresses and releases. If the microcontroller registers these as multiple keystrokes, a phenomenon known as *keybounce* may result, a problem common to many cheap and old keyboards. Even on the most expensive and newest keyboards, keybounce can be a problem if you look at the switch a million times a second, because mechanical switches simply cannot settle down that quickly. A typical inexpensive key will settle down within five milliseconds, so if the keyboard scanning software polls the key less often than this, the controller will effectively miss the keybounce. The practice of limiting how often one scans the keyboard in order to eliminate keybounce is known as *debouncing*.

The keyboard controller must not generate a new key code sequence every time it scans the keyboard and finds a key held down. The user may hold a key down for many tens or hundreds of milliseconds before releasing it, and we don't want this to register as multiple keystrokes. Instead, the keyboard controller should generate a single key code value when the key goes from the up position to the down position (a *down key* operation). In addition to this, modern keyboards provide an *autorepeat* capability that engages once the user has held down a key for a given time period (usually about half a second), and it treats the held key as a sequence of keystrokes as long as the user continues to hold the key down. However, even these autorepeat keystrokes are regulated to allow only about ten keystrokes per second rather than the number of times per second the keyboard controller scans all the switches on the keyboard.

Upon detecting a down keystroke, the microcontroller sends a keyboard *scan code* to the PC. The scan code is *not* related to the ASCII code for that key; it is an arbitrary value IBM chose when the PC's keyboard was first developed. The PC keyboard actually generates *two* scan codes for every key you press. It generates a *down code* when you press a key down and an *up code* when you release the key. Should you hold the key down long enough for the autorepeat operation to begin, the keyboard controller will send a sequence of down codes until you release the key, at which time the keyboard controller will send a single up code.

The 8042 microcontroller chip transmits these scan codes to the PC, where they are processed by an interrupt service routine for the keyboard. Having separate up and down codes is important because certain keys (like SHIFT, CTRL, and ALT) are only meaningful when held down. By generating up codes for all the keys, the keyboard ensures that the keyboard ISR knows which keys are pressed while the user is holding down one of these *modifier* keys. Exactly what the system does with these scan codes depends on the OS, but usually the OS's keyboard device driver will translate the scan code sequence into an appropriate ASCII code or some other notation that applications can work with.

12.13 The Standard PC Parallel Port

The original IBM PC design provided support for three parallel printer ports that IBM designated LPT1:, LPT2:, and LPT3:. With laser and ink jet printers still a few years in the future, IBM probably envisioned machines that could support a standard dot matrix printer, a daisy wheel printer, and maybe some other auxiliary type of printer for different purposes. Surely, IBM did not anticipate the general use that parallel ports have received or they would probably have designed them differently. Today, the PC's parallel port controls keyboards, disk drives, tape drives, SCSI adapters, Ethernet (and other network) adapters, joystick adapters, auxiliary keypad devices, other miscellaneous devices, and, oh yes, printers.

The current trend is to eliminate the parallel port from systems because of connector size and performance problems. Nevertheless, the parallel port remains an interesting device. It's one of the few interfaces that hobbyists can use to connect the PC to simple devices they've built themselves. Therefore, learning to program the parallel port is a task many hardware enthusiasts take upon themselves.

In a unidirectional parallel communication system, there are two distinguished sites: the transmitting site and the receiving site. The transmitting site places its data on the data lines and informs the receiving site that data is available; the receiving site then reads the data lines and informs the transmitting site that it has taken the data. Note how the two sites synchronize their access to the data lines — the receiving site does not read the data lines until the transmitting site tells it to, and the transmitting site does not place a new value on the data lines until the receiving site removes the data and tells the transmitting site that it has the data. In other words, this form of parallel communications between the printer and computer system relies on handshaking to coordinate the data transfer.

The PC's parallel port implements handshaking using three control signals in addition to the eight data lines. The transmitting site uses the *strobe* (or data strobe) line to tell the receiving site that data is available. The receiving site uses the *acknowledge* line to tell the transmitting site that it has taken the data. A third handshaking line, *busy*, tells the transmitting site that the receiving site is busy and that the transmitting site should not attempt to send data. The busy signal differs from the acknowledge signal, insofar as acknowledge tells the system that the receiving site has accepted the data just sent and processed it. The busy line tells the system that the receiving site cannot accept any new data just yet; the busy line does not imply that the last character sent has been processed (or even that a character was sent).

From the perspective of the transmitting site, a typical data transmission session looks something like the following:

1. The transmitting site checks the busy line to see if the receiving site is busy. If the busy line is active, the transmitter waits in a loop until the busy line becomes inactive.
2. The transmitting site places its data on the data lines.
3. The transmitting site activates the strobe line.
4. The transmitting site waits in a loop for the acknowledge line to become active.
5. The transmitting site sets the strobe inactive.
6. The transmitting site waits in a loop for the receiving site to set the acknowledge line inactive, indicating that it recognizes that the strobe line is now inactive.
7. The transmitting site repeats steps 1–6 for each byte it must transmit.

From the perspective of the receiving site, a typical data transmission session looks something like the following:

1. The receiving site sets the busy line inactive when it is ready to accept data.
2. The receiving site waits in a loop until the strobe line becomes active.
3. The receiving site reads the data from the data lines.
4. The receiving site activates the acknowledge line.
5. The receiving site waits in a loop until the strobe line goes inactive.
6. The receiving site (optionally) sets the busy line active.
7. The receiving site sets the acknowledge line inactive.
8. The receiving site processes the data.
9. The receiving site sets the busy line inactive (optional).
10. The receiving site repeats steps 2–9 for each additional byte it receives.

By carefully following these steps, the receiving and transmitting sites coordinate their actions so that the transmitting site doesn't attempt to put several bytes on the data lines before the receiving site consumes them, and so the receiving site doesn't attempt to read data that the transmitting site has not sent.

12.14 Serial Ports

The RS-232 serial communication standard is probably the most popular serial communication scheme in the world. Although it suffers from many drawbacks, speed being the primary one, its use is widespread, and there are thousands of devices you can connect to a PC using an RS-232 serial interface. Though the use of the serial port is rapidly being eclipsed by USB use, many devices still use the RS-232 standard.

The original PC system design supports concurrent use of up to four RS-232 compatible devices connected through the COM1:, COM2:, COM3:, and COM4: ports. For those who need to connect additional serial devices, you can buy interface cards that let you add 16 or more serial ports to the PC.

In the early days of the PC, DOS programmers had to directly access the 8250 Serial Communications Chip (SCC) to implement RS-232 communications in their applications. A typical serial communications program would have a serial port ISR that read incoming data from the SCC and wrote outgoing data to the chip, as well as code to initialize the chip and to buffer incoming and outgoing data. Though the serial chip is very simple compared to modern peripheral interfaces, the 8250 is sufficiently complex that many programmers would have difficulty getting their serial communications software working properly. Furthermore, because serial communications was rarely the main purpose of the application being written, few programmers added anything beyond the basic serial communications features needed for their applications.

Fortunately, today's application programmers rarely program the SCC directly. Instead, OSes such as Windows or Linux provide sophisticated serial communications device drivers that application programmers can call. These drivers provide a consistent feature set that all applications can use, and this reduces the learning curve needed to provide serial communication functionality. Another advantage to the OS device driver approach is that it removes the dependency on the 8250 SCC. Applications that use an OS device driver will automatically work with different serial communication chips. In contrast, an application that programs the 8250 directly will not work on a system that uses a USB to RS-232 converter cable. However, if the manufacturer of that USB to RS-232 converter cable provides an appropriate device driver for an OS, applications that do serial communications via that OS will automatically work with the USB/serial device.

An in-depth examination of RS-232 serial communications is beyond the scope of this book. For more information on this topic, consult your OS programmer's guide or pick up one of the many excellent texts devoted specifically to this subject.

12.15   Disk Drives

Almost all modern computer systems include some sort of disk drive unit to provide online mass storage. At one time, certain workstation vendors produced *diskless workstations*, but the relentless drop in price and increasing storage space of fixed (aka "hard") disk units has all but obliterated the diskless computer system. Disk drives are so ubiquitous in modern systems that most people take them for granted. However, for a programmer to take a disk drive for granted is a dangerous thing. Software constantly interacts with the disk drive as a medium for application file storage, so a good understanding of how disk drives operate is very important if you want to write efficient code.

12.15.1   Floppy Drives

Floppy disks are rapidly disappearing from today's PCs. Their limited storage capacity (typically 1.44 MB) is far too small for modern applications and the data those applications produce. It is hard to believe that barely 25 years ago a 143 KB (that's *kilo*bytes, not megabytes or gigabytes) floppy drive was considered a high-ticket item. However, except for floptical drives (discussed in Section 12.15.4, "Zip and Other Floptical Drives"), floppy disk drives have failed to keep up with technological advances in the computer industry. Therefore, we'll not consider these devices in this chapter.

12.15.2   Hard Drives

The fixed disk drive, more commonly known as the hard disk, is without question the most common mass storage device in use today. The modern hard drive is truly an engineering marvel. Between 1982 and 2004, the capacity of a single drive unit has increased over 50,000-fold, from 5 MB to over 250 GB. At the same time, the minimum price for a new unit has dropped from $2,500 (U.S.) to below $50. No other component in the computer system has enjoyed such a radical increase in capacity and performance along with a comparable drop in price. (Semiconductor RAM probably comes in second, and paying the 1982 price today would get you about 4,000 times the capacity.)

While hard drives were decreasing in price and increasing in capacity, they were also becoming faster. In the early 1980s, a hard drive subsystem was doing well to transfer 1 MB per second between the drive and the CPU's memory; modern hard drives transfer more than 50 MB per second. While this increase in performance isn't as great as the increase in performance of memory or CPUs, keep in mind that disk drives are mechanical units on which the laws of physics place greater limitations. In some cases, the dropping costs of hard drives has allowed system designers to improve their performance by using disk arrays (see Section 12.15.3, "RAID Systems," for details). By using certain hard disk subsystems like disk arrays, it is possible to achieve 320-MB-per-second transfer rates, though it's not especially cheap to do so.

"Hard" drives are so named because their data is stored on a small, rigid disk that is usually made out of aluminum or glass and is coated with a magnetic material. The name "hard" differentiates these disks from floppy disks, which store their information on a thin piece of flexible Mylar plastic.

In disk drive terminology, the small aluminum or glass disk is known as a *platter*. Each platter has two surfaces, front and back (or top and bottom), and both sides contain the magnetic coating. During operation, the hard drive unit spins this platter at a particular speed, which these days is usually 3,600; 5,400; 7,200; 10,000; or 15,000 revolutions per minute (RPM). Generally, though not always, the faster you spin the platter, the faster you can read data from the disk and the higher the data transfer rate between the disk and the system. The smaller disk drives that find their way into laptop computers typically spin at much slower speeds, like 2,000 or 4,000 RPM, to conserve battery life and generate less heat.

A hard disk subsystem contains two main active components: the disk platter(s) and the read/write head. The read/write head, when held stationary, floats above concentric circles, or *tracks*, on the disk surface (see Figure 12-8). Each track is broken up into a sequence of sections known as *sectors* or *blocks*. The actual number of sectors varies by drive design, but a typical hard drive might have between 32 and 128 sectors per track (again, see Figure 12-8). Each sector typically holds between 256 and 4,096 bytes of data, and many disk drive units let the OS choose between several different sector sizes, the most common choices being 512 bytes and 4,096 bytes.

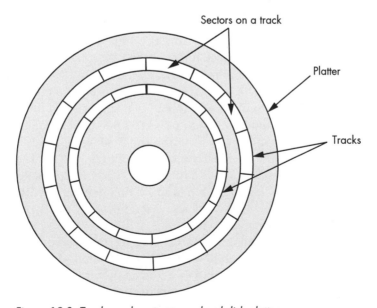

Figure 12-8: Tracks and sectors on a hard disk platter

The disk drive records data when the read/write head sends a series of electrical pulses to the platter, which translates those electrical pulses into magnetic pulses that the platter's magnetic surface retains. The frequency at which the disk controller can record these pulses is limited by the quality of the electronics, the read/write head design, and the quality of the magnetic surface.

The magnetic medium is capable of recording two adjacent bits on its disk surface and then differentiating between those two bits during a later read operation. However, as you record bits closer and closer together, it becomes harder and harder to differentiate between them in the magnetic domain. *Bit density* is a measure of how closely a particular hard disk can pack data into its tracks — the higher the bit density, the more data you can squeeze onto a single track. However, to recover densely packed data requires faster and more expensive electronics.

The bit density has a big impact on the performance of the drive. If the drive's platters are rotating at a fixed number of revolutions per minute, then the higher bit density, the more bits will rotate underneath the read/write head during a fixed amount of time. Larger disk drives tend to be faster than smaller disk drives because they often employ a higher bit density.

By moving the disk's read/write head in a roughly linear path from the center of the disk platter to the outside edge, the system can position a single read/write head over any one of several thousand tracks. Yet the use of only one read/write head means that it will take a fair amount of time to move the head among the disk's many tracks. Indeed, two of the most often quoted hard disk performance parameters are the read/write head's *average seek time* and *track-to-track seek time*.

A typical high-performance disk drive will have an average seek time between five and ten milliseconds, which is half the amount of time it takes to move the read/write head from the edge of the disk to the center, or vice versa. Its track-to-track seek time, on the other hand, is on the order of one or two milliseconds. From these numbers, you can see that the acceleration and deceleration of the read/write head consumes a much greater percentage of the track-to-track seek time than it consumes of the average seek time. It only takes 20 times longer to traverse 1,000 tracks than it does to move to the next track. And because moving the read/write heads from one track to the next is usually the most common operation, the track-to-track seek time is probably a better indication of the disk's performance. Regardless of which metric you use, however, keep in mind that moving the disk's read/write head is one of the most expensive operations you can do on a disk drive so it's something you want to minimize.

Because most hard drive subsystems record data on both sides of a disk platter, there are two read/write heads associated with each platter — one for the top of the platter and one for the bottom. And because most hard drives incorporate multiple platters in their disk assembly in order to increase storage capacity (see Figure 12-9), a typical drive will have multiple read/write heads (two heads for each platter).

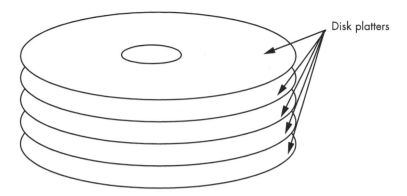

Disk platters

Figure 12-9: Multiple platter hard disk assembly

The various read/write heads are physically connected to the same actuator. Therefore, each head sits above the same track on its respective platter, and all the heads move across the disk surfaces as a unit. The set of all tracks over which the read/write heads are currently sitting is known as a *cylinder* (see Figure 12-10).

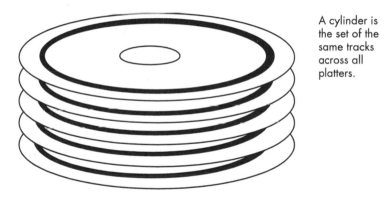

A cylinder is the set of the same tracks across all platters.

Figure 12-10: A hard disk cylinder

Although using multiple heads and platters increases the cost of a hard disk drive, it also increases the performance. The performance boost occurs when data that the system needs is not located on the current track. In a hard disk subsystem with only one platter, the read/write head would need to move to another track to locate the data. But in a disk subsystem with multiple platters, the next block of data to read is usually located within the same cylinder. And because the hard disk controller can quickly switch between read/write heads electronically, doubling the number of platters in a disk subsystem nearly doubles the track seek performance of the disk unit because it winds up doing half the number of seek operations. Of course, increasing the number of platters also increases the capacity of the unit, which is another reason why high-capacity drives are often higher-performance drives as well.

With older disk drives, when the system wants to read a particular sector from a particular track on one of the platters, it commands the disk to position the read/write heads over the appropriate track, and the disk drive then waits for the desired sector to rotate underneath. But by the time the head settles down, there's a chance that the desired sector has just passed under the head, meaning the disk will have to wait for almost one complete rotation before it can read the data. On the average, the desired sector appears halfway across the disk. If the disk is rotating at 7,200 RPM (120 revolutions per second), it requires 8.333 milliseconds for one complete rotation of the platter, and, if on average the desired sector is halfway across the disk, 4.2 milliseconds will pass before the sector rotates underneath the head. This delay is known as the *average rotational latency* of the drive, and it is usually equivalent to the time needed for one rotation, divided by two.

To see how this can be a problem, consider that an OS usually manipulates disk data in sector-sized chunks. For example, when reading data from a disk file, the OS will typically request that the disk subsystem read a sector of data and return that data. Once the OS receives the data, it processes the data and then very likely makes a request for additional data from the disk. But what happens when this second request is for data that is located on the next sector of the current track? Unfortunately, while the OS is processing the first sector's data, the disk platters are still moving underneath the read/write heads. If the OS wants to read the next sector on the disk's surface and it doesn't notify the drive immediately after reading the first sector, the second sector will rotate underneath the read/write head. When this happens, the OS will have to wait for almost a complete disk rotation before it can read the desired sector. This is known as *blowing revs* (revolutions). If the OS (or application) is constantly blowing revs when reading data from a file, file system performance suffers dramatically. In early "single-tasking" OSes running on slower machines, blowing revs was an unpleasant fact. If a track had 64 sectors, it would often take 64 revolutions of the disk in order to read all the data on a single track.

To combat this problem, the disk-formatting routines for older drives allow the user to *interleave sectors*. Interleaving sectors is the process of spreading out sectors within a track so that logically adjacent sectors are not physically adjacent on the disk surface (see Figure 12-11).

The advantage of interleaving sectors is that once the OS reads a sector, it will take a full sector's rotation time before the logically adjacent sector moves under the read/write head. This gives the OS time to do some processing and to issue a new disk I/O request before the desired sector moves underneath the head. However, in modern multitasking OSes, it's difficult to guarantee that an application will gain control of the CPU so that it can respond before the next logical sector moves under the head. Therefore, interleaving isn't very effective in such multitasking OSes.

To solve this problem, as well as improve disk performance in general, most modern disk drives include memory on the disk controller that allows the controller to read data from an entire track. By avoiding interleaving the controller can read an entire track into memory in one disk revolution, and once the track data is cached in the controller's memory, the controller can communicate disk read/write operations at RAM speed rather than at disk rotation speeds, which can dramatically improve performance. Reading the first sector from a track still exhibits rotational latency problems, but once the disk controller reads the entire track, the latency is all but eliminated for that track.

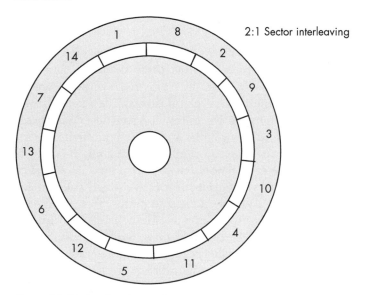

Figure 12-11: Interleaving sectors

A typical track may have 64 sectors of 512 bytes each, for a total of 32 KB per track. Because newer disks usually have between 512 KB and 8 MB of on-controller memory, the controller can buffer as many as 100 or so tracks in its memory. Therefore, the disk-controller cache not only improves the performance of disk read/write operations on a single track, it also improves overall disk performance. And the disk-controller cache not only speeds up read operations, but write operations as well. For example, the CPU can often write data to the disk controller's cache memory within a few micro-seconds and then return to normal data processing while the disk controller moves the disk read/write heads into position. When the disk heads are finally in position at the appropriate track, the controller can write the data from the cache to the disk surface.

From an application designer's perspective, advances in disk subsystem design have attempted to reduce the need to understand how disk drive geometries (track and sector layouts) and disk-controller hardware affect the application's performance. Despite these attempts to make the hardware transparent to the application, though, software engineers wanting to write great code must always remain cognizant of the underlying operation of the disk drive. For example, sequential file operations are usually much faster than random-access operations because sequential operations require fewer head seeks. Also, if you know that a disk controller has an on-board cache, you can write file data in smaller blocks, doing other processing between the block operations, to give the hardware time to write the data to the disk surface. Though the techniques early programmers used to maximize disk performance don't apply to modern hardware, by understanding how disks operate and how they store their data, you can avoid various pitfalls that produce slow code.

12.15.3   RAID Systems

Because a modern disk drive typically has between 8 and 16 heads, you might wonder if it is possible to improve performance by simultaneously reading or writing data on multiple heads. While this is certainly possible, few disk drives utilize this technique. The reason is cost. The read/write electronics are among the most expensive, bulky, and sensitive circuitry on the disk drive controller. Requiring up to 16 sets of the read/write electronics would be prohibitively expensive and would require a much larger disk-controller circuit board. Also, you would need to run up to 16 sets of cables between the read/write heads and the electronics. Because cables are bulky and add mass to the disk head assembly, adding so many cables would affect track seek time. However, the basic concept of improving performance by operating in parallel is sound. Fortunately, there is another way to improve disk drive performance using parallel read and write operations: the *redundant array of inexpensive disks* (RAID) configuration.

The RAID concept is quite simple: you connect multiple hard disk drives to a special host controller card, and that adapter card simultaneously reads and writes the various disk drives. By hooking up two disk drives to a RAID controller card, you can read and write data about twice as fast as you could with a single disk drive. By hooking up four disk drives, you can almost improve average performance by a factor of four.

RAID controllers support different configurations depending on the purpose of the disk subsystem. So-called *Level 0 RAID* subsystems use multiple disk drives simply to increase the data transfer rate. If you connect two 150-GB disk drives to a RAID controller, you'll produce the equivalent of a 300-GB disk subsystem with double the data transfer rate. This is a typical configuration for personal RAID systems — those systems that are not installed on a file server.

Many high-end file server systems use *Level 1 RAID* subsystems (and other higher-numbered RAID configurations) to store multiple copies of the data across the multiple disk drives, rather than to increase the data transfer rate between the system and the disk drive. In such a system, should one disk fail, a copy of the data is still available on another disk drive. Some even higher-level RAID subsystems combine four or more disk drives to increase the data transfer rate and provide redundant data storage. This type of configuration usually appears on high-end, high-availability file server systems.

RAID systems provide a way to dramatically increase disk subsystem performance without having to purchase exotic and expensive mass storage solutions. Though a software engineer cannot assume that every computer system in the world has a fast RAID subsystem available, certain applications that could not otherwise be written can be created using RAID. When writing great code, you shouldn't specify a fast disk subsystem like RAID from the beginning, but it's nice to know you can always fall back to its specification if you've optimized your code as much as possible and you still cannot get the data transfer rates your application requires.

12.15.4   Zip and Other Floptical Drives

One special form of floppy disk is the *floptical disk.* By using a laser to etch marks on the floppy disk's magnetic surface, floptical manufacturers are able to produce disks with 100 to 1,000 times the storage of normal floppy disk drives. Storage capacities of 100 MB, 250 MB, 750 MB, and more, are possible with the floptical devices. The Zip drive from Iomega is a good example of this type of media. These floptical devices interface with the PC using the same connections as regular hard drives (IDE, SCSI, and USB), so they look just like a hard drive to software. Other than their reduced speed and storage capacity, software can interact with these devices as it does with hard drives.

12.15.5   Optical Drives

An *optical* drive is one that uses a laser beam and a special photosensitive medium to record and play back digital data. Optical drives have a couple of advantages over hard disk subsystems that use magnetic media:

- They are more shock resistant, so banging the disk drive around during operation won't destroy the drive unit as easily as a hard disk.

- The media is usually removable, allowing you to maintain an almost unlimited amount of offline or near-line storage.

- The capacity of an individual optical disk is fairly high compared to other removable storage solutions, such as floptical drives or cartridge hard disks.

At one time, optical storage systems appeared to be the wave of the future because they offered very high storage capacity in a small space. Unfortunately, they have fallen out of favor in all but a few niche markets because they also have several drawbacks:

- While their read performance is okay, their write speed is very slow: an order of magnitude slower than a hard drive and only a few times faster than a floptical drive.

- Although the optical medium is far more robust than the magnetic medium, the magnetic medium in a hard drive is usually sealed away from dirt, humidity, and abrasion. In contrast, optical media is easily accessible to someone who really wants to do damage to the disk's surface.

- Seek times for optical disk subsystems are much slower than for magnetic disks.

- Optical disks have limited storage capacity, currently less than a couple gigabytes.

One area where optical disk subsystems still find use is in *near-line storage subsystems*. An optical near-line storage subsystem typically uses a *robotic jukebox* to manage hundreds or thousands of optical disks. Although one could argue that a rack of high-capacity hard disk drives would provide a more space efficient storage solution, such a hard disk solution would consume far more power, generate far more heat, and require a more sophisticated interface. An optical jukebox, on the other hand, usually has only a single optical drive unit and a robotic disk selection mechanism. For archival storage, where the server system rarely needs access to any particular piece of data in the storage subsystem, a jukebox system is a very cost-effective solution.

If you wind up writing software that manipulates files on an optical drive subsystem, the most important thing to remember is that read access is much faster than write access. You should try to use the optical system as a "read-mostly" device and avoid writing data as much as possible to the device. You should also avoid random access on an optical disk's surface, as the seek times are very slow.

12.15.6   CD-ROM, CD-R, CR-R/W, DVD, DVD-R, DVD-RAM, and DVD-R/W Drives

CD and DVD drives are also optical drives. However, their widespread use and their sufficiently different organization and performance when compared with standard optical drives means that they warrant a separate discussion.

CD-ROM was the first optical drive subsystem to achieve wide acceptance in the personal computer market. CD-ROM disks were based on the audio CD digital recording standard, and they provided a large amount of storage (650 MB) when compared to hard disk drive storage capacities at the time (typically 100 MB). As time passed, of course, this relationship reversed. Still, CD-ROMs became the preferred distribution vehicle for most commercial applications, completely replacing the floppy disk medium for this purpose. Although a few of the newer applications contain so much data that it is inconvenient to ship them on one or two CD-ROM disks, the vast majority of applications can be delivered just fine on CD-ROM, so this will probably remain the preferred software distribution medium for most applications.

Although the CD-ROM format is a very inexpensive distribution medium in large quantities, often only costing a few cents per disk, it is not an appropriate distribution medium for small production runs. The problem is that it typically costs several hundreds or thousands of dollars to produce a disk master (from which the run of CD-ROMs are made), meaning that CD-ROM is usually only a cost-effective distribution medium when the quantity of disks being produced is at least in the thousands.

The solution was to invent a new CD medium, CD-Recordable (CD-R), which allowed the production of *one-off* CD-ROMs. CD-R uses a write-once optical disk technology, known euphemistically as WORM (write-once, read-many). When first introduced, CD-R disks cost about $10–$15. However, once the drives reached critical mass and media manufacturers began producing blank CD-R disks in huge quantities, the bulk retail price of CD-Rs fell to about $0.25. As a result, CD-R made it possible to distribute a fair amount of data in small quantities.

One obvious drawback to CD-R is the "write-once" limitation. To overcome this limitation, the CD-Rewriteable (CD-RW) drive and medium were created. CD-RW, as its name suggests, supports both reading and writing. Unlike optical disks, however, you cannot simply rewrite a single sector on CD-RW. Instead, to rewrite the data on a CD-RW disk you must first erase the whole disk.

Although the 650 MB of storage on a CD seemed like a gargantuan amount when CDs were first introduced, the old maxim that data and programs expand to fill up all available space certainly held true. Though CDs were ultimately expanded from 650 MB to 700 MB, various games (with embedded video), large databases, developer documentation, programmer development systems, clip art, stock photographs, and even regular applications reached the point where a single CD was woefully inadequate. The DVD-ROM (and later, DVD-R, DVD-RW, DVD+RW, and DVD-RAM) disk reduced this problem by offering between 3 GB and 17 GB of storage on a single disk. Except for the DVD-RAM format, one can view the DVD formats as faster, higher-capacity versions of the CD formats. There are some clear technical differences between the two formats, but most of them are transparent to the software.

The CD and DVD formats were created for reading data in a continuous stream from the storage medium, called *streaming data*. The track-to-track head movement time required when reading data stored on a hard disk, creates a big gap in the streaming sequence that is unacceptable for audio and video applications. Therefore, CDs and DVDs record information on a single, very long track that forms a spiral across the surface of the whole disk. This allows the CD or DVD player to continuously read a stream of data by simply moving the laser beam along the disk's single spiral track at a continuous rate.

Although having a single track is great for streaming data, it does make it a bit more difficult to locate a specific sector on the disk. The CD or DVD drive can only approximate a sector's position by mechanically repositioning the laser beam to some point on the disk. Once the drive approximates the position, it must actually read data from the disk surface to determine where the laser is positioned, and then do some fine-tuning adjustments of the laser position in order to find the desired sector. As a result, searching for a specific sector on a CD or DVD disk can take an order of magnitude longer than searching for a specific sector on a hard disk.

From the programmer's perspective, the most important thing to remember when writing code that interacts with CD or DVD media is that random-access is verboten. These media were designed for sequential streaming access, and seeking for data on such media will have a negative impact on application performance. If you are using these disks to deliver your application and its data to the end user, you should have the user copy the data to a hard disk before use if high-performance random access is necessary.

12.16 Tape Drives

Tape drives are also popular mass storage devices. Traditionally, personal computer owners have used tape drives to back up data stored on hard disk drives. For many years, tape storage was far more cost-effective than hard disk storage on a cost-per-megabyte basis. Indeed, at one time there was an order of magnitude difference in cost per megabyte between tape storage and magnetic disk storage. And because tape drives held more data than most hard disk drives, they were more space-efficient too.

However, because of competition and technological advances in the hard disk drive marketplace, tapes have lost these advantages. Hard disk drives are now exceeding 250 GB in storage, and the optimum price point for hard disks is about $0.50 per gigabyte. Tape storage today costs far more per megabyte than hard disk storage. Plus, only a few tape technologies allow one to store 250 GB on a single tape, and those that do (such as Digital Linear Tape, or DLT) are extremely expensive. It's not surprising that tape drives are seeing less and less use these days in home PCs and are typically found only in larger file server machines.

Back in the days of mainframes, application programs interacted with tape drives in much the same way that today's applications interact with hard disk drives. A tape drive, however, is not an efficient random access device. That is, although software can read a random set of blocks from a tape, it cannot do so with acceptable performance. Of course, in the days when most applications ran on mainframes, applications generally were not interactive, and the CPUs were much slower. As such, the standard for "acceptable performance" was different.

In a tape drive, the read/write head is fixed, and the tape transport mechanism moves the tape past the read/write head linearly, from the beginning of the tape to the end of the tape, or vice versa. If the beginning of the tape is currently positioned over the read/write head and you want to read data at the end of the tape, you have to move the entire tape past the read/write head to get to the desired data. This can be very slow, requiring tens or even hundreds of seconds, depending on the length and format of the tape. Compare this with the tens of milliseconds it takes to reposition a hard disk's read/write head. Therefore, to perform well on a tape drive, software has to be written with special awareness of the limitations of a sequential access device. In particular, data should be read or written sequentially on a tape to produce the highest performance.

Originally, data was written to tapes in blocks (much like sectors on a hard disk), and the drives were designed to allow quasi-random access to the tape's blocks. If you've ever seen an old science fiction movie with the old-style reel-to-reel drives, with the reels constantly stopping, starting, stopping, reversing, stopping, and continuing, you were seeing "random access" in action. Such tape drives were very expensive because they required powerful motors, finely tooled tape-path mechanisms, and so on. As hard drives became larger and less expensive, applications stopped using tape as a data manipulation medium and used tape only for offline storage. Using a tape drive was simply too slow for normal application work. As a result, most systems started using tape drives only in sequential mode for backing up data from hard disks.

Because sequential data access on tape does not require the heavy-duty mechanics of the original tape drives, the tape drive manufactures sought to make a lower-cost product suitable for sequential access only. Their solution was the *streaming* tape drive, which was designed to keep the data constantly moving from the CPU to the tape, or vice versa. For example, while backing up the data from a hard disk to tape, a streaming tape drive treats the data like a video or audio recording and just lets the tape run, constantly writing the data from the hard disk to the tape. Because of the way streaming tape drives work, very few applications deal directly with the tape unit. Today, it's very rare for anything other than a tape backup utility program, run by the system administrator, to access the tape hardware.

12.17 Flash Storage

An interesting storage medium that has recently become popular because of its compact form factor[3] is flash storage media. The flash medium is actually a semiconductor device, based on the electrically erasable programmable read-only memory (EEPROM) technology, which, despite its name, is both readable and writable. Unlike regular semiconductor memory, flash storage is *non-volatile*, meaning that it maintains its data even in the absence of power. Like other semiconductor technologies, flash storage is purely electronic and doesn't require any motors or other electro-mechanical devices for proper operation. Therefore, flash storage devices are more reliable and shock resistant, and they use far less power than mechanical

---

[3] In this context, "form factor" means *shape and size.*

storage solutions such as disk drives. This makes flash storage solutions especially valuable in portable battery-powered devices like PDAs, electronic cameras, MP3 playback devices, and portable recorders.

Flash storage modules now provide between 2 MB and several gigabytes of storage, and their optimal price point is at about $0.25 per megabyte. This makes them far more expensive per bit than hard disk storage, which means that their use as a storage medium is diminished.

Flash devices are sold in many different form factors. OEMs (original equipment manufacturers) can buy flash storage devices that look like other semiconductor chips and then mount these devices directly on their circuit boards. However, most flash memory devices sold today are built into one of several standard forms including PC Cards, CompactFlash cards, smart memory modules, memory sticks, or USB/flash modules. For example, a digital camera user might remove a CompactFlash card from their camera, insert it into a special CompactFlash card reader on their PC, and access their photographs just as they would files on a disk drive.

Memory in a flash storage module is organized in blocks of bytes, not unlike sectors on a hard disk. Unlike regular semiconductor memory, or RAM, you cannot write individual bytes in a flash storage module. Although you can generally read an individual byte from a flash storage device, to write to a particular byte you must first erase the entire block on which it resides. The block size varies by device, but most OSes will treat these flash blocks like a disk sector for the purposes of reading and writing. Although the basic flash storage device itself could connect directly to the CPU's memory bus, most common flash storage packages (such as Compact Flash cards and Memory Sticks) contain electronics that simulate a hard disk interface, and you access the flash device just as you would a hard disk drive.

One interesting aspect to flash memory devices, and EEPROM devices in general, is that they have a limited write lifetime. That is, you may only write to a particular memory cell in a flash memory module a certain number of times before that cell begins to have problems retaining the information. In early EEPROM/flash devices, this was a big concern because the average number of write cycles before failures would begin occurring was around 10,000. That is, if some software wrote to the same memory block 10,000 times in a row, the EEPROM/flash device would probably develop a bad memory cell in that block, effectively rendering the entire chip useless. On the other hand, if the software wrote just once to 10,000 separate blocks, the device could still take 9,999 additional writes to each memory cell. Therefore, the OSes of these early devices would try to spread out write operations across the entire device to minimize damage. Although modern flash devices still exhibit this problem, technological advances have reduced it almost to the point where we can ignore it. A modern flash memory cell supports an average of about a million write cycles before it will go bad. Furthermore, today's OSes simply mark bad flash blocks, the same way they mark bad sectors on a disk, and will skip a block once they determine that it has gone bad.

Being electronic, flash devices do not exhibit rotational latency times at all, and they don't exhibit much in the way of seek times. There is a tiny amount of time needed to write an address to a flash memory module, but it is nothing compared to the head seek times on a hard disk. Despite this, flash memory is generally nowhere near as fast as typical RAM. Reading data from a flash device itself usually takes microseconds (rather than nanoseconds), and the interface between the flash memory device and the system may require additional time to set up a data transfer. Worse still, it is common to interface a flash storage module to a PC using a USB flash reader device, and this often reduces the average read time per byte to hundreds of microseconds.

Write performance is even worse. To write a block of data to flash, you must write the data, read it back, compare it to the original data, and rewrite it if they don't match. Writing a block of data to flash can take several tens or even hundreds of milliseconds.

As a result, flash memory modules are generally quite a bit slower than high-performance hard disk subsystems. Technological advances are improving their performance, a process that is mainly being driven by high-end digital camera users who want to be able to snap as many pictures as possible in a short time. Though flash memory performance will probably not catch up with hard disk performance any time soon, it should steadily improve as time passes.

12.18   RAM Disks and Semiconductor Disks

Another pair of interesting mass storage devices you'll find are the RAM and semiconductor disks. A RAM disk is just an application that treats a large block of the computer system's memory as though it were a disk drive, simulating blocks and sectors using memory arrays. A *semiconductor disk* is a device consisting of RAM memory and a controller that interfaces with the system using a traditional disk interface. Semiconductor disks usually have their own power supply (including a battery backup system) so that they maintain memory integrity when you turn off the PC. The use of a standard disk interface and a separate, uninterruptible, power supply are what differentiate true semiconductor disks from software-based RAM disks.

The advantage of memory-based disks is that they are very high performance. RAM disks and semiconductor disks do not exhibit the time delays associated with head seek time and rotational latency that you find on hard, optical, and floppy drives. Their interface to the CPU is also much faster, so data transfer times are very high, often running at the maximum bus speed. It is hard to imagine a faster storage technology than a RAM or semiconductor disk.

RAM and semiconductor disks, however, have two disadvantages: cost and volatility. The cost per byte of storage in a semiconductor disk system is very high. Indeed, byte-for-byte, semiconductor storage is as much as 1,000 times more expensive than magnetic hard disk storage. Because of the high cost of semiconductor storage, semiconductor disks usually have low storage capacities, typically no more than a couple of gigabytes. And, semiconductor disks are volatile — they lose their memory unless they are powered at all times. A battery-backed, uninterruptible power supply can help prevent memory loss during power failures, but you cannot disconnect a semiconductor disk from the power line for an extended period of time and expect the data to persist. This generally means that semiconductor disks are great for storing temporary files and files you'll copy back to some permanent storage device before shutting down the system. Because of their low-latency, high data transfer rates, and relatively low storage capacity, semiconductor disks are excellent for use as *swap storage* for a virtual memory subsystem. They are not particularly well suited for maintaining important information over long periods of time.

The popularity of semiconductor disks tends to rise and fall with motherboard and CPU designs. Semiconductor disks tend to be more popular when it is physically impossible to extend the amount of memory in a given computer system. Semiconductor disks tend to be less popular when a computer system allows memory expansion. The reason for this is simple: It is far less expensive to increase the RAM in a typical computer system and use a software-based RAM disk than it is to add a semiconductor disk to the system. A software-based RAM disk is usually faster than a semiconductor disk because the system can access the RAM disk at memory bus speeds rather than at disk controller speeds. In fact, there are only two disadvantages to RAM disks: their memory is volatile, and every byte you allocate to a RAM disk is one less byte available for your applications. In a few systems, these two disadvantages prevent the use of RAM disks. For most uses, however, if there is a little extra unused RAM in the system, and the user is careful to copy important data from the RAM disk to nonvolatile storage before shutting off the system, a software-based RAM disk can be a very cost-effective solution.

The problems with software-based RAM disk solutions begin when you have added all the RAM your system can support, and your applications require most of the memory in the system. Back when CPUs had a 16-bit address space, users quickly reached the point where they had installed as much as 64 KB of memory on their machines (2^{16} bytes is 64 KB). When the 8088/8086 rolled around with a 20-bit address bus, it wasn't long before users had installed the maximum amount of memory in those machines too. Ditto for CPUs with a 24-bit address bus, allowing a maximum of 16 MB of memory. Once CPUs started supporting 32-bit address buses, it seemed like the amount of memory one could install in the system had hit infinity, but today we're once again bumping up against that limit. It's not uncommon now to find machines with the maximum amount of memory already installed, particularly since motherboards often limit the amount of RAM that can be installed on a system even though the system CPU can address a much larger amount of RAM.

Semiconductor disks become practical when you've installed the maximum amount of RAM in your system and the applications or OS are making use of that memory, so that there isn't a large block of memory lying around that you can use for a RAM disk. Because the semiconductor disk's memory exists outside the CPU's address space, it does not impact the memory limits that apply to motherboard designs.

12.19   SCSI Devices and Controllers

The *Small Computer System Interface* (SCSI, pronounced "scuzzy") is a peripheral interconnection bus used to connect high-speed peripheral devices to personal computer systems. Designed in the early 1980s, the SCSI bus was popularized by its introduction on the Apple Macintosh computer system in the middle 1980s. The original SCSI interface supported an 8-bit bidirectional data bus and was capable of transferring 5 MB of data per second, which was considered "high-performance" for hard disk subsystems of that era. Although the performance of that early SCSI interface is quite slow by modern standards, SCSI has gone through several revisions over the years and remains a high-performance peripheral interconnection system. Today's SCSI devices are capable of transferring 320 MB per second.

Although the SCSI interconnection system is most commonly used for disk drive subsystems, SCSI was designed to support a whole host of PC peripherals using a cable connection. Indeed, as SCSI became popular during the late 1980s and into the 1990s, you could find printers, scanners, imaging machines, phototypesetters, network, and display adapters, and many other devices interfacing with the SCSI bus. However, the popularity of the SCSI bus as a general-purpose peripheral bus has diminished since the appearance of the USB and FireWire peripheral connection systems. Except for very high performance disk drive subsystems and some very specialized peripheral devices, few new peripherals use the SCSI interface.

To understand why SCSI's popularity is waning, one must consider the problems SCSI users have faced over the years. When SCSI was first introduced, the SCSI bus supported concurrent connection of the SCSI adapter card and up to seven actual peripheral devices. To connect multiple devices, one first ran a cable from the host controller card to the first peripheral device. To connect a second device, one ran a cable from a second connector on the first device to the second device. To connect a third device, one ran a cable from a separate connector on the second device to the third device, and so on. At the end of this "daisy chain" of devices, one attached a special terminating device to the last connector of the last peripheral device. Without the special "terminator" at the end of the SCSI chain, many SCSI systems would work unreliably, if at all.

As a "convenience" to their customers, many peripheral manufacturers built the terminating circuitry into their devices. Unfortunately, connecting multiple terminators in the middle of the SCSI chain was just as bad as not having a terminator in the SCSI system. Though most manufacturers who designed the terminating circuitry into their peripherals often provided an option to disable the terminator, some did not. Ensuring that those devices with the active terminator circuitry were at the end of the SCSI chain was often cumbersome, and even if a device provided an option to enable or disable the terminator, knowing the appropriate "dip-switch" settings was a problem if the documentation wasn't handy. As a result, many computer owners had problems with a chain of SCSI devices not working properly in their system.

On the original SCSI bus, the computer system owner had to assign each device one of eight numeric "addresses" from zero to seven, with address seven generally reserved for the host controller card. If two devices in the SCSI chain had the same address, they wouldn't operate properly. This made moving SCSI peripherals from one computer system to another somewhat difficult, because the address of the device being moved was usually already taken by another device on the new system.

The original SCSI bus had other limitations as well. First, it only supported seven peripheral devices. When SCSI was first designed, this wasn't usually a problem because common SCSI peripherals like hard drives and scanners were very expensive, costing thousands of dollars each. Connecting more than seven devices wasn't something your average computer owner would have done back then. But, as the price of hard drives and other SCSI peripherals came down, the seven-peripheral limit became burdensome. Second, SCSI was not, and still is not, *hot swappable*. That is, you cannot unplug a peripheral device while power is applied to the system, nor may you connect a new peripheral to the SCSI bus while the power is on. Doing so could cause electrical damage to the SCSI controller, the peripheral, or even some other peripheral on the SCSI bus. As SCSI peripherals came down in price and people began connecting multiple devices to their computer systems, the desire to unplug a device from one system and plug it into another grew, but SCSI did not support this mode of operation.

Despite all these bad features, SCSI's popularity grew. To maintain that popularity, SCSI was modified over time to improve its functionality. SCSI-2, the first modification, doubled the speed from 5 MHz to 10 MHz, thus doubling the data transfer rate on the bus. This was necessary because the speed of high-performance devices like disk drives increased so much that the original SCSI interface was actually slowing them down. The next improvement was to increase the size of the bidirectional SCSI data bus from 8 bits to 16 bits. This not only doubled the data transfer rate from 10 MB per second to 20 MB per second, it also increased the number of peripherals one could place on the bus from 7 to 15. Variations of SCSI-2 were known as *Fast SCSI* (10 MHz), *Wide SCSI* (16 bits), and *Fast and Wide SCSI* (16 bits at 10 MHz).

It should come as no surprise that SCSI-3 followed SCSI-2. SCSI-3 offers a veritable smorgasbord of different connection options while maintaining compatibility with the older standards. Although SCSI-3 (using names like Ultra, Ultra Wide, Ultra2, Wide Ultra2, Ultra3, and Ultra320) still operates as a 16-bit bus in the parallel cable mode, and it still supports a maximum of 15 peripherals, it is vastly improved. SCSI-3 increased the operating speed of the bus and the maximum permissible physical distance across which SCSI peripherals could be chained. To make a long story short, SCSI-3 operates at speeds of up to 160 MHz, allowing the SCSI bus to transfer data in bursts up to 320 MB per second (that is, faster than many PCI bus interconnects!).

SCSI was originally a parallel interface. Today, SCSI supports three different interconnection standards: SCSI Parallel Interface (SPI), Serial SCSI across FireWire, and Fibre Channel Arbitrated Loop. The SPI is the original definition that most people associate with the SCSI interface. SCSI parallel cables contain either 8 or 16 data lines, depending on the type of SCSI interface in use. This makes SCSI cables bulky, heavy, and expensive. The parallel SCSI interface also limits the maximum length of the SCSI chain in the system to just a few meters. These concerns, especially the economic ones, are why modern computer systems only use SCSI peripherals when extremely high performance is necessary.

An important fact to note about SCSI is that it is not a master/slave interconnection system. That is, the computer system does not own the bus and doesn't necessarily direct the traffic between various peripherals on the bus. SCSI is a truc *peer-to-peer bus,* and any two peripherals on the bus may communicate with one another. Indeed, it's possible (though unusual) for two computer systems to share the same SCSI bus. This peer-to-peer operation can improve the performance of the overall system tremendously. To illustrate this point, consider a tape backup system. In practice, most tape backup programs read a block of data from a disk drive into the computer's memory and then write that block of data from the computer's memory to the tape drive. On the SCSI bus (in theory, at least), it is possible to have the tape and disk drives communicate directly with one another. The tape backup software would send two commands, one to the disk drive and one to the tape drive, telling the disk drive to transfer the block of data directly to the tape drive rather than going through the computer system. Not only does this reduce the number of transfers across the SCSI bus by half, speeding up the transfer, but it also frees up the computer's CPU to do other things. In reality, few tape backup systems work this way, but there are many examples where two peripherals communicate with one another across the SCSI bus without using the computer as an intermediary. Software that programs SCSI peripherals to operate this way (rather than running the data through the computer's memory) is a good example of *great programming.*

SCSI is interesting insofar as it is not only an electrical interconnection, but a *protocol* as well. One does not communicate with a SCSI peripheral device by writing some data to a couple of registers on the SCSI interface card, causing that data to travel down the SCSI cable to the peripheral device. Although SCSI is a parallel interface like the parallel printer port, it doesn't communicate with SCSI peripheral devices like the parallel port communicates with printer devices. To use SCSI, you build up a data structure in memory containing a SCSI command, command parameters, any data you may want to send to the SCSI peripheral, and possibly a pointer with the memory address where the SCSI controller should store any data the peripheral device returns. Once you construct this data structure, you normally provide the SCSI controller with the data structure's address, and the SCSI controller then fetches the command from system memory and sends it to the appropriate peripheral device on the SCSI bus.

As SCSI hardware has evolved over the years, so has the SCSI protocol, the SCSI *command set*. SCSI was never intended to serve as just a hard disk interface, and the breadth of peripherals that SCSI supports has steadily increased over the years along with the advent of new types of computer peripherals. To accommodate these new and unanticipated uses for the SCSI bus, SCSI's designers created a device-independent command protocol that could be easily extended as new devices were invented. Contrast this with certain device interfaces such as the original Integrated Disk Electronics (IDE) interface, which was suitable only for disk drives.

The SCSI protocol transmits a packet containing the peripheral's address, the command, and the command's data. The SCSI-3 standard has roughly grouped these commands into the following classes:

- Controller commands for RAID arrays (SCC)
- Enclosure services commands (SES)
- Graphics commands for printers (SGC)
- Hard disk interface commands (the SCSI block commands, or SBC)
- Management server commands (MSC)
- Multimedia commands for devices such as DVD drives (MMC)
- Object-based storage commands (OSD)
- Primary commands (SPC)
- Reduced block commands for simplified hard drive subsystems (RBC)
- Stream commands for tape drives (SSC)

What do these commands look like? Unlike traditional interfaces such as serial and parallel, one does not necessarily write SCSI "commands" to registers on the SCSI controller chip. Indeed, SCSI commands are generally intended for devices on the SCSI bus, not for the SCSI host controller (which is often called the *SCSI host adapter*). The job of the host controller, from the programmer's perspective, is to place SCSI commands onto the SCSI bus for use by other peripherals and to fetch commands and data from the SCSI bus intended for the host system. Although the SCSI commands themselves are standardized, the actual interface to the SCSI host controller is not. Different host controller manufacturers use different hardware to connect their SCSI controller chips to the host computer system, so how you talk to a SCSI controller chip is different, depending on the particular host controller device. Because SCSI controllers are *very* complex and difficult to program, and because there is no "standard" SCSI interface chip, programmers are faced with having to write several different variants of their software to control SCSI devices.

To correct this situation, SCSI host controller manufacturers like Adaptec have created specialized device driver modules that provide a uniform interface to their devices. Rather than writing data directly to a SCSI chip, a programmer creates an in-memory data structure with SCSI commands to be placed on the SCSI bus, calls the device driver software, and lets the device driver transfer the SCSI commands to the SCSI bus. There are several nice things about this approach:

- It frees the programmer from having to learn the complexities of each particular host controller.

- It allows different manufacturers to provide a compatible interface to their SCSI controller devices.

- It allows manufacturers to create a single optimized driver that properly supports the capabilities of their device, rather than allowing individual programmers to write possibly mediocre code for the device.

- It allows manufacturers to change the hardware of future versions of their device without destroying compatibility with existing software.

This concept was carried forward into modern OSes. Today, SCSI host controller manufacturers write *SCSI miniport drivers* for OSes like Windows. These miniport drivers provide a hardware-independent interface to the host controller so that the OS can simply say, "Here is a SCSI command. Put it on the SCSI bus."

One big advantage of the SCSI interface is that it provides parallel processing of SCSI commands. That is, a host system can place several different SCSI commands on the bus, and different peripheral devices can process those commands simultaneously. Some devices, like disk drives, can even accept multiple commands at once and process those commands in the order that is most efficient. As an example, suppose that a disk drive is currently near block 1,000. If the system sends block read requests for blocks 5,000; 4,560; 3,000; and 8,000; the disk controller can rearrange these requests and satisfy them in the most efficient order (probably 3,000; 4,560; 5,000; and then 8,000) as it moves the read/write head across the surface of the disk. This results in a big performance improvement on multitasking OSes that process requests for disk I/O from several different applications simultaneously.

SCSI is also a great interface for RAID systems because SCSI is one of the few disk controller interfaces that supports a large number of drives on the same interface. Indeed, because no modern hard drive is capable of equaling SCSI data transfer rates, the only way to achieve SCSI's 320-MB-per-second transfer rate is with a RAID subsystem. Very high performance drives are capable of sustaining only about 80-MB-per-second data transfer rates, and that's only in burst mode. In an ideal world where the SCSI protocol did not consume any overhead, you would have to connect four such drives to a RAID/SCSI controller to achieve the theoretical maximum data transfer rate on the SCSI bus.[4] A very high performance RAID controller would sit between the SCSI bus and the actual hard drives. Lower-cost RAID systems can be created by connecting the disks directly to the SCSI bus and using special software to send disk I/O operations to different disks on the SCSI bus. Such systems don't require special hardware, but they don't achieve the maximum throughput that is possible on SCSI either; not that they run particularly slowly, mind you.

The SCSI command set is very powerful, and it is designed for high-performance applications. It is sufficiently large and complex that space limitations prevent its inclusion here. Readers interested in a deeper look at SCSI programming should refer to *The Book of SCSI* (by Gary Field, Peter M. Ridge, et al., published by No Starch Press). The complete SCSI specifications appear at various sites on the Web. A quick search for "SCSI specifications" on AltaVista, Google, or any other decent Web search engine should turn up several copies of the specifications.

12.20 The IDE/ATA Interface

Although the SCSI interface is very high performance, it is also expensive. A SCSI device requires a sophisticated and fast processor in order to handle all the operations that are possible on the SCSI bus. Furthermore, because SCSI devices can operate on a peer-to-peer basis (that is, one peripheral may talk to another without intervention from a host computer system), each SCSI device must carry around a considerable amount of sophisticated software in ROM on the device's controller board. Adding all the extra functionality needed to support full SCSI when all you want to do is to attach a single hard disk to a personal computer system is a bit of overkill. During the middle to late 1980's, several computer and disk manufacturers got together to discuss a less expensive, though standardized, interface that would let them connect inexpensive disk drives to personal computers. The result of this initiative was the IDE (Integrated Drive Electronics) interface.

The point behind SCSI was to off load as much work as was reasonably possible to the device controller, freeing up the host computer to do other activities. But all this extra complexity and cost to improve system performance was going to waste because in typical personal computer systems the host computer was usually waiting for the data transfer to complete. So the computer was sitting idle while the SCSI disk drive was busy processing the SCSI command. The idea behind the IDE interface was to lower the cost of the disk drive by using the host computer's CPU to do the processing. Because the CPU was usually idle (during SCSI transfers) anyway, this

---

[4] In reality, of course, there is some overhead consumed by the SCSI protocol itself. Hence, the SCSI bus would actually be saturated with fewer than 20 high-performance drives.

seemed like a good use of resources. IDE drives, because they were often hundreds of dollars less than SCSI drives, became incredibly popular on personal computer systems.

The original IDE drive specification was very limited compared to the SCSI interface. First, it supported only two drives chained together (modern systems provide two IDE interfaces, a primary channel and a secondary channel, that support up to four devices). Second, the IDE specification was created only for disk drives; it was not a general-purpose peripheral interface bus like SCSI. And third, cable lengths for the IDE interface effectively limited IDE devices to residing in the same case as the CPU. Nevertheless, the much lower cost of the IDE interface and of IDE drives ensured its popularity.

Soon after the introduction of the IDE interface, peripheral manufacturers discovered that there were other devices that they'd like to connect to the IDE interface. Though the IDE interface was designed specifically for mass storage devices, and wouldn't work well with non-storage devices like scanners and printers, there were many types of storage devices other than hard disks (such as CD-ROMs, tape drives, and Zip drives) for which the IDE interface represented a cheap alternative to SCSI. Furthermore, because most PCs were being shipped with IDE interfaces, manufacturers of non-hard-disk mass storage devices were drooling over the possibility of connecting to an interface found on all new personal computer systems. Because the original IDE specification was geared specifically to hard disk drives and was not particularly well suited for other types of storage devices, the committee that designed the IDE interface went back to work and developed the *AT Attachment with Packet Interface* (IDE/ATAPI), which is usually shortened to ATA *(Advanced Technology Attachment)*. Like SCSI, the ATA standard has gone through several revisions and improvements over the years.

Originally, IDE was designed to work on a 33-MHz PCI bus and was theoretically capable of transferring 33 MB per second. Later revisions of the ATA standard (ATA-66, ATA-100, and ATA-133) were capable of transferring data at 66 MB, 100 MB, and 133 MB per second. One might think that with these speeds (which far outstrip the speed of the physical disk drives) the ATA interface would be comparable to SCSI in performance. However, there are two reasons why the ATA interface is still slower than SCSI. First, the host processor is still involved in many of the operations, and it may take several host computer operations across the IDE/ATA interface to accomplish what a SCSI device could do on its own. Second, SCSI supports RAID much better than the ATA interface does. For the average home user, though, the modern IDE/ATA interface provides very good performance. One easy way to compare ATA and SCSI is to note that the most recent ATA specification tends to have performance equal to the previous SCSI generation.

The ATAPI specification (in its sixth version as of December 2001) extends the IDE specification to support a wide range of mass storage devices, including tape drives, Zip drives, CD-ROMs, DVDs, removable cartridge drives, and more. In order to extend the IDE interface to support all these different storage devices, the designers of the ATAPI specification adopted a packet command format that is very similar to, and in some cases is identical to, the SCSI packet command format. One big difference between SCSI and ATA is the fact that the hardware interface for ATA is far more standardized. This allows, for example, a single BIOS routine to boot from an IDE device regardless of who manufactured the interface chip. Indeed, the major differences between various IDE/ATAPI interface chips are simply the particular ATAPI specification to which the chip adheres: ATAPI-2, ATAPI-3, ATAPI-4, ATAPI-5, or ATAPI-6. So, in theory at least, it's possible for application programmers to communicate directly with the IDE/ATAPI interface and control the mass storage device directly.

In modern protected-mode OSes like Windows or Linux, however, an application programmer is never allowed to talk directly to the hardware. In theory, it would be possible to write a *miniport driver* for IDE to simulate the way the SCSI interface works. In practice, however, the OS vendor generally supplies a software library that provides an API (application programming interface) to the IDE/ATAPI devices. The application programmer can then make function calls to the API, passing appropriate parameters, and the underlying library routines take care of the remaining tasks associated with actually talking to the hardware.

Programming ATAPI devices in a modern system is quite similar to programming SCSI devices. You load up a memory-based data structure with a command code and a set of parameters, and then pass the memory structure to a driver library function that passes the data across the ATAPI interface to the target storage device. If such a low-level library is not available, and your OS allows it, you can program the ATAPI interface device to grab this data (generally using DMA on modern systems). The full ATAPI-6 specification is almost 500 pages long; obviously, we do not have sufficient space to cover the specification in any kind of detail. If you are interested in a more detailed look at the IDE/ATAPI specifications, search for "ATAPI specifications" with your favorite Internet search engine.

Modern machines use a serial ATA (SATA) controller. This is a high-performance serial version of the venerable IDE/ATAPI parallel interface. However, to the programmer, SATA looks exactly like ATAPI.

12.21 File Systems on Mass Storage Devices

Very few applications access mass storage devices directly. That is, applications do not generally read and write tracks, sectors, or blocks on a mass storage device. Instead, most applications open, read, write, and otherwise manipulate files on the mass storage device. The OS's *file manager* is responsible for abstracting away the physical configuration of the underlying storage device and providing a convenient storage facility for multiple independent files on a single device.

On the earliest computer systems, application software was responsible for tracking the physical position of data on a mass storage device because there was no file manager available to handle this function for them. Such applications were able to maximize their performance by carefully considering the layout of data on the disk. For example, software could manually interleave data across various sectors on a track to give the CPU time to process data between reading and writing those sectors on the track. Such software was often many times faster than comparable software using a generic file manager. Later, when file managers were commonly available, some application authors still managed their files on a storage device for performance reasons. This was especially true back in the days of floppy disks, when low-level software written to manipulate data at the track and sector level often ran ten times faster than the same application using a file manager system.

In theory, today's software could benefit from this as well, but you rarely see such low-level disk access in modern software for several reasons. First, writing software that manipulates a mass storage device at such a low level locks you into using that one particular device. That is, if your software manipulates a disk with 48 sectors per track, 12 tracks per cylinder, and 768 cylinders per drive, that same software will not work optimally (if at all) on a drive with a different sector, track, and cylinder layout. Second, accessing the drive at a low level makes it difficult to share the device among different applications, something that can be especially costly on a multitasking system that may have multiple applications sharing the device at once. For example, if you've laid out your data on various sectors on a track to coordinate computation time with sector access, your work is lost when the OS interrupts your program and gives some other application its timeslice, thus consuming the time you were counting on to do any computations prior to the next data sector rotating under the read/write head. Third, some of the features of modern mass storage devices, such as on-board caching controllers and SCSI interfaces that present a storage device as a sequence of blocks rather than as something with a given track and sector geometry, eliminate any advantage such low-level software might have had at one time. Fourth, modern OSes typically contain file buffering and block caching algorithms that provide good file system performance, obviating the need to operate at such a low level. Finally, low-level disk access is very complex and writing such software is difficult.

The earliest file manager systems stored files sequentially on the disk's surface. That is, if each sector/block on the disk held 512 bytes and a file was 32 KB long, that file would consume 64 consecutive sectors/blocks on the disk's surface. In order to access that file at some future time, the file manager only needed to know the file's starting block number and the number of blocks it occupied. Because the file system had to maintain these two pieces of information somewhere in nonvolatile storage, the obvious place was on the storage media itself, in a data structure known as the *directory*. A disk directory is an array of values starting at a specific location on the disk that the OS can reference when an application requests a specific file. The file manager can search through the directory for the file's name and extract its starting block and length. With this information, the file system can provide the application with access to the file's data.

One advantage of the sequential file system is that it is very fast. The OS can read or write a single file's data very rapidly if the file is stored in sequential blocks on the disk's surface. But a sequential file organization has some big problems, too. The biggest and most obvious drawback is that you cannot extend the size of a file once the file manager places another file at the next block on the disk. Disk fragmentation is another big problem. As applications create and delete many small and medium-sized files, the disk fills up with small sequences of unused sectors that, individually, are too small for most files. It was common on sequential file systems to find disks that had sufficient free space to hold some data, but that couldn't use that free space because it was spread all over the disk's surface in small pieces. To solve this problem, users had to run disk compaction programs to coalesce all the free sectors and move them to the end of the disk by physically rearranging files on the disk's surface. Another solution was to copy files from one full disk to another empty disk, thereby collecting the many small, unused sectors together. Obviously, this was extra work that the user had to do, work that the OS should be doing.

The sequential-file storage scheme really falls apart when used with multitasking OSes. If two applications attempt to write file data to the disk concurrently, the file system must place the starting block of the second application's file beyond the last block required by the first application's file. As the OS has no way of determining how large the files can grow, each application has to tell the OS the maximum length of the file when the application first opens the file. Unfortunately, many applications cannot determine, beforehand, how much space they will need for their files. So the applications have to guess the file size when opening a file. If the estimated file size is too small, either the program will have to abort with a "file full" error, or the application will have to create a larger file, copy the old data from the "full" file to the new file, and then delete the old file. As you can imagine this is horribly inefficient, and definitely not great code.

To avoid such performance problems, many applications grossly overestimate the amount of space they need for their files. As a result, they wind up wasting disk space when the files don't actually use all the data allocated to them, a form of *internal fragmentation*. Furthermore, if applications truncate their files when closing them, the resulting free sections returned to the OS tend to fragment the disk into small, unusable blocks of free space, a problem known as *external fragmentation*. For these reasons, sequential storage on the disk was replaced by more sophisticated storage-management schemes in modern OSes.

Most modern file-allocation strategies allow files to be stored across arbitrary blocks on the disk. Because the file system can now place bytes of the file in any free block on the disk, the problems of external fragmentation and the limitation on file size are all but eliminated. As long as there is at least one free block on the disk, you can expand the size of any file. However, along with this flexibility comes some extra complexity. In a sequential file system, it was easy to locate free space on the disk — by noting the starting block numbers and sizes of the files in a directory, it was possible to easily locate a free block large enough to satisfy the current disk allocation request, if such a block was available. But with a file system that stores files across arbitrary blocks, scanning the directory and noting which blocks a file uses is far too expensive to compute, so the file system has to keep track of the free and used blocks. Most modern OSes use one of three data structures — a set, a table (array), or a list — to keep track of which sectors are free and which are not. Each of these schemes has its advantages and disadvantages, and you'll find all three schemes in use in modern OSes.

12.21.1 Maintaining Files Using a Free-Space Bitmap

The free-space bitmap scheme uses a set data structure to maintain a set of free blocks on the disk drive. If a block is a member of the free-block set, the file manager can remove that block from the set whenever it needs another block for a file. Because set membership is a Boolean relationship (you're either in the set or you're not), it takes exactly one bit to specify the set membership of each block.

Typically, a file manager will reserve a certain section of the disk to hold a bitmap that specifies which blocks on the disk are free. The bitmap will consume some integral number of blocks on the disk, with each block consumed being able to represent a specific number of other blocks on the disk, which can be calculated by multiplying the block size (in bytes) by 8 (bits per byte). For example, if the OS uses 4,096-byte blocks on the disk, a bit map consisting of a single block can track up to 32,768 other blocks on the disk. To handle larger disks, you need a larger bitmap. The disadvantage of the bitmap scheme is that as disks get large, so does the bitmap. For example, on a 120-gigabyte drive with 4,096-byte blocks, the bitmap will be almost four megabytes long. While this is a small percentage of the total disk capacity, accessing a single bit in a bitmap this large can be clumsy. To find a free block, the OS has to do a linear search through this four-megabyte bitmap. Even if you keep the bitmap in system memory (which is a bit expensive, considering that you have to do it for each drive), searching through the bitmap every time you need a free sector is an expensive proposition. As a result, you don't see this scheme used much on larger disk drives.

One advantage (and also a disadvantage) of the bitmap scheme is that the file manager only uses it to keep track of the free space on the disk, but it does not use this data to track which sectors belong to a given file. As a result, if the free sector bitmap is damaged somehow, nothing is permanently lost. It's easy to reconstruct the free-space bitmap by searching through all the directories on the disk and computing which sectors are in use by the files in those directories (with the remaining sectors, obviously, being the free ones). Although such a computation is somewhat time consuming, it's nice to have this ability when disaster strikes.

12.21.2   File Allocation Tables

Another way to track disk sector usage is with a table of sector pointers. In fact, this scheme is the most common one in use today because it is the scheme employed by MS-DOS and various versions of Microsoft Windows. An interesting facet of the *file allocation table* (FAT) scheme is that it combines both free-space management and file-sector allocation management into the same data structure, ultimately saving space when compared to the bitmap scheme, which uses separate data structures for free-space management and file-sector allocation. Furthermore, unlike the bitmap scheme, FAT doesn't require an inefficient linear search to find the next available free sector.

The FAT is really nothing more than an array of self-relative pointers (or indexes, if you prefer) into itself, setting aside one pointer for each sector/block on the storage device. When a disk is first initialized, the first several blocks on the disk's surface are reserved for objects like the root directory and the FAT itself, and then the remaining blocks on the disk are the free space. Somewhere in the root directory is a free-space pointer that specifies the next available free block on the disk. Assuming the free-space pointer initially contains the value 64, implying that the next free block is block 64, the FAT entries at indexes 64, 65, 65, and so on, would contain the following values, assuming there are n blocks on the disk, numbered from zero to $n - 1$:

FAT Index	FAT Entry Value
. . .	. . .
64	65
65	66
66	67
67	68
. . .	. . .
$n - 2$	$n - 1$
$n - 1$	0

The entry at block 64 tells you the next available free block on the disk, 65. Moving on to entry 65, you'll find the value of the next available free block on the disk, 66. The last entry in the FAT contains a zero (block zero contains meta-information for the entire disk partition and is never available).

Whenever an application needs one or more blocks to hold some new data on the disk's surface, the file manager grabs the free-space pointer value and then continues going through the FAT entries for however many blocks are required to store the new data. For example, if each block is 4,096 bytes long and the current application is attempting to write 8,000 bytes to a file, the file manager will need to remove two blocks from the free-block list. To do so, the file manager needs to go through the following steps:

1. Get the value of the free-space pointer.

2. Save the value of the free-space pointer so that the file manager will know the first free sector it can use.

3. Continue going through the FAT entries for the number of blocks required to store the application's data.

4. Extract the FAT entry value of the last block where the application needs to store its data, and set the free-space pointer to this value.

5. Store a zero over the FAT entry value of the last block that the application uses, thus marking the end to the list of blocks that the application needs.

6. Return the original value of the free-space pointer (as it was prior to these steps) into the FAT as the pointer to the list of blocks in the FAT that are now allocated for the application.

After the block allocation scheme in our earlier example, the application has blocks 64 and 65 at its disposal, the free-space pointer contains 66, and the FAT looks like this:

FAT Index	FAT Entry Value
. . .	. . .
64	65
65	0
66	67
67	68
. . .	. . .
$n - 2$	$n - 1$
$n - 1$	0

Don't get the impression that entries in the FAT *always* contain the index of the next entry in the table. As the file manager allocates and deallocates storage for files on the disk, these numbers tend to become scrambled. For example, if an application winds up returning block 64 to the free list but holds on to block 65, the free-space pointer would contain the value 64, and the FAT would wind up having the following values:

FAT Index	FAT Entry Value
. . .	. . .
64	66
65	0
66	67
67	68
. . .	. . .
$n - 2$	$n - 1$
$n - 1$	0

As noted earlier, one advantage of the FAT data structure is that it combines both the free-space management and the file block lists into a single data structure. This means that each file doesn't have to carry around a list of the blocks its data occupies. Instead, a file's directory entry needs to have only a single pointer value that specifies an index into the FAT where the first block of the file's data can be found. The remaining blocks that the file's data consumes can be found by simply stepping through the FAT. One important advantage that the FAT scheme has over the set (bitmap) scheme is that once the disk using a FAT file system is full, no blocks on the disk are used to maintain information about which blocks are free. Even when there are no free blocks available, the bitmap scheme still consumes space on the disk to track the free space. But the FAT scheme replaces the entries originally used to track free blocks with the file-block pointers. When the disk is full, none of the values that originally maintained the free-block list are consuming space on the disk because all of those values are now tracking blocks in files. In that case, the free-space pointer would contain zero (to denote an empty free space list) and all the entries in the FAT would contain chains of block indexes for file data.

However, the FAT scheme does have a couple of disadvantages. First, unlike the bitmap in a set scheme file system, the table in a FAT file system represents a single point of failure. If the FAT is somehow destroyed, it can be very difficult to repair the disk and recover files; losing some free space on a disk is a problem, but losing track of where one's files are on the disk is a *major* problem. Furthermore, because the disk head tends to spend more time in the FAT area of a storage device than in any other single area on the disk, the FAT is the most likely part of a hard disk to be damaged by a head crash, or the most likely part of a floppy or optical drive to exhibit excessive wear. This has been a sufficiently big concern that some FAT file systems provide an option to maintain an extra copy of the file allocation table on the disk.

Another problem with the FAT is that it's usually located at a fixed place on the disk, usually at some low block number. In order to determine which block or blocks to read for a particular file, the disk heads must move to the FAT, and if the FAT is at the beginning of the disk, the disk heads will constantly be seeking to and from the FAT across large distances. This massive head movement is slow, and, in fact, tends to wear out the mechanical parts of the disk drive sooner. In newer versions of Microsoft OSes, the FAT-32 scheme eliminates part of this problem by allowing the FAT to be located somewhere other than the beginning of the disk, though still at a fixed location. Application file I/O performance can be quite low with a FAT file system unless the OS caches the FAT in main memory, which can be dangerous if the system crashes, because you could lose track of all file data whose FAT entries have not been written to disk.

The FAT scheme is also inefficient when doing random access on a file. To read from offset m to offset n in a file, the file manager must divide n by the block size to obtain the block offset into the file containing the byte at offset n, divide m by the block size to obtain its block offset, and then sequentially search through the FAT chain between these two blocks to find the sector(s) containing the desired data. This linear search can be expensive if the file is a large database with many thousands of blocks between the current block position and the desired block position.

Yet another problem with the FAT file system, though this one is rather esoteric, is that it doesn't support sparse files. That is, you cannot write to byte 0 and byte 1,000,000 of a file without also allocating every byte of data in between the two points on the disk surface. Some non-FAT file managers will only allocate the blocks where an application has written data. For example, if an application only writes data to bytes 0 and 1,000,000 of a file, the file manager would only allocate two blocks for the file. If the application attempts to read a block that has not been previously allocated (for example, if the application in the current example attempts to read the byte at byte offset 500,000 without first writing to that location), the file manager will simply return zeros for the read operation without actually using any space on the disk. The way a FAT is organized, it is not possible to create sparse files on the disk.

12.21.3 List-of-Blocks File Organization

To overcome the limitations of the FAT file system, advanced OSes such as Windows NT/2000/XP and various flavors of Unix use a list-of-blocks scheme rather than a FAT. Indeed, the list scheme enjoys all the advantages of a FAT system (such as efficient, nonlinear free-block location, and efficient storage of the free-block list), and it solves many of FAT's problems.

The list scheme begins by setting aside several blocks on the disk for the purpose of keeping (generally) 32-bit pointers to each of the free blocks on the disk. If each block on the disk holds 4,096 bytes, a block can hold 1,024 pointers. Dividing the number of blocks on the disk by 1,024 determines the number of blocks the free-block list will initially consume. As you'll soon see, the system can actually use these blocks to store data once the disk fills up, so there is no storage overhead associated with the blocks consumed by the free-block list.

If a block in the free-block list contains 1,024 pointers, then the first 1,023 pointers contain the block numbers of free blocks on the disk. The file manager maintains two pointers on the disk: one that holds the block number of the current block containing free-block pointers, and one that holds an index into that current block. Whenever the file system needs a free block, it obtains the index for one from the free list block by using these two pointers. Then the file manager increments the index into the free-block list to the next available entry in the list. When the index increments to 1,023 (the 1,024th item in the free-block list), the OS does not use the pointer entry value at index 1,023 to locate a free block. Instead, the file manager uses this pointer as the address of the next block containing a list of free-block pointers on the disk, and it uses the current block, containing a now-empty list of block pointers, as the free block. This is how the file manager reuses the blocks originally designated to hold the free-block list. Unlike the FAT, the file manager does not reuse the pointers in the free-block list to keep track of the blocks belonging to a given file. Once the file manager uses up all the free-block pointers in a given block, the file manager uses that block for actual file data.

Unlike the FAT, the list scheme does not merge the free-block list and the file list into the same data structure. Instead, a separate data structure for each file holds the list of blocks associated with that file. Under typical Unix and Linux file systems, the directory entry for the file actually holds the first 8 to 16 entries in the list (see Figure 12-12). This allows the OS to track short files (up to 32 KB or 64 KB) without having to allocate any extra space on the disk.

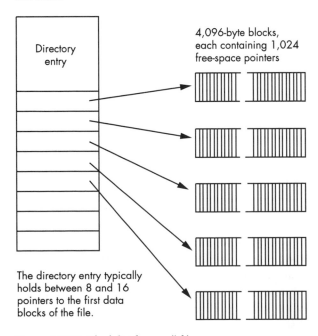

Figure 12-12: Block list for small files

OS research on various flavors of Unix suggests that the vast majority of files are small, and embedding several pointers into the directory entry provides an efficient way to access small files. Of course, as time passes, the average file size seems to increase. But as it turns out, block sizes tend to increase as well. When this average file size research was first done, the typical block size was 512 bytes, but today a typical block size is 4,096 bytes. During that time, then, average file sizes could have increased by a factor of eight without, on average, requiring any extra space in the directory entries.

For medium sized files up to about 4 MB, the OS will allocate a single block with 1,024 pointers to the blocks that store the file's data. The OS continues to use the pointers found in the directory entry for the first few blocks of the file, and then it uses a block on the disk to hold the next group of block pointers. Generally, the last pointer in the directory entry holds the location of this block (see Figure 12-13).

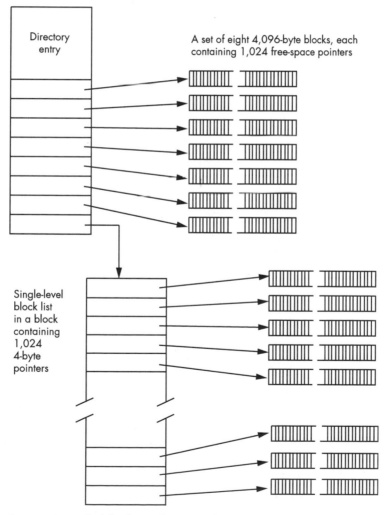

Figure 12-13: Block list for medium-sized files

For files larger than about 4 MB, the file system switches to a three-tiered block scheme, which works for file sizes up to 4 GB. In this scheme, the last pointer in the directory entry stores the location of a block of 1,024 pointers, and each of the pointers in this block holds the location of an additional block of 1,024 pointers, with each pointer in this block storing the location of a block that contains actual file data. See Figure 12-14 for the details.

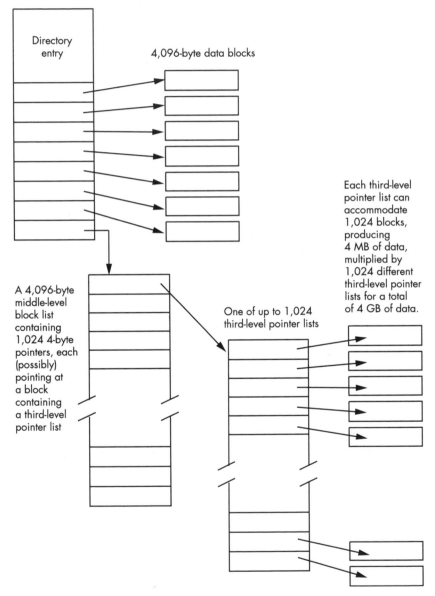

Figure 12-14: Three-level block list for large files (up to 4 GB)

One advantage to this tree structure is that it readily supports sparse files. That is, an application can write to block 0 and block 100 of a file without having to allocate data blocks for every block in between those two points. By placing a special block pointer value (typically zero) in the intervening entries in the block list, the OS can determine whether a block is not present in the file. Should an application attempt to read such a missing block in the file, the OS can simply return all zeros for the empty block. Of course, once the application writes data to a block that hadn't been previously allocated, the OS must copy the data to the disk and fill in the appropriate block pointer in the block list.

As disks became larger, the 4 GB file limit imposed by this scheme began to create some problems for certain applications, such as video editors, large database applications, and Web servers. One could easily extend this scheme 1,000 times — to 4 terabytes (TB) — by adding another level to the block-list tree. The only problem with this approach is that the more levels of indirection you have, the slower random file access becomes, because the OS may have to read several blocks from the disk in order to get a single block of data. (When it has one level, it is practical to cache the block-pointer list in memory, but with two and three levels, it is impractical to do this for every file). Another way to extend the maximum value size 4 GB at a time is to use multiple pointers to second-tier file blocks (for example, take the original 8 to 16 pointers in the directory and have all or most of them point at second-tier block list entries rather than directly at file data blocks). Although there is no current standard way to extend beyond three levels, rest assured that as the need arises, OS designers will develop schemes they can use to acccss large files in an efficient manner.

12.22 Writing Software That Manipulates Data on a Mass Storage Device

Understanding how different mass storage devices behave is important if you want to write high-performance software that manipulates files on these devices. Although modern OSes attempt to isolate applications from the physical realities of mass storage, an OS can only do so much for you. Furthermore, an OS cannot predict how your particular application will access files on a mass storage device, so the OS cannot optimize access for your specific application; instead, the OS optimizes file access for applications that exhibit typical file-access patterns. The less typical your application's file I/O is, the less likely you'll get the best performance out of the system. In this section, we'll look at how you can coordinate your file access activities with the OS to achieve the best performance.

12.22.1 File Access Performance

Although disk drives and most other mass storage devices are often thought of as "random access" devices, the fact is that mass storage access is usually more efficient when done in a sequential fashion. Sequential access on a disk drive is relatively efficient because the OS can move the read/write head one track at a time (assuming the file appears in sequential blocks on the disk). This is much faster than accessing one block on the disk, moving the read/write head to some other track, accessing another block, moving the head again, and so on. Therefore, you should avoid random file access in an application if it is possible to do so.

You should also attempt to read or write large blocks of data on each file access rather than reading or writing small amounts more frequently. There are two reasons for this. First, OS calls are not fast, so if you make half as many calls by reading or writing twice as much data on each access, the application will often run twice as fast. Second, the OS must read or write whole disk blocks. If your block size is 4,096 bytes, but you just write 2,000 bytes to some block and then seek to some other position in the file outside that block, the OS will actually have to read the entire 4,096-byte block from the disk, merge in the 2000 bytes, and then finally write the entire 4,096 bytes back to the disk. This happens because the OS must read and write entire blocks; it cannot transfer partial blocks between the disk and memory. Contrast this with a write operation that writes a full 4,096 bytes — in this case, the OS wouldn't have to read the data from the disk first; it would only have to write the block. Writing full blocks improves disk access performance by a factor of two because writing partial blocks requires the OS to first read the block, merge the data, and then write the block; by writing whole blocks the read operation is unnecessary. Even if your application doesn't write data in increments that are even multiples of the disk's block size, writing large blocks improves performance. If you write 16,000 bytes to a file in one write operation, the OS will still have to write the last block of those 16,000 bytes using a read-merge-write operation, but it will write the first three blocks using only write operations.

If you start with a relatively empty disk, the OS will generally attempt to write the data for new files in sequential blocks. This organization is probably most efficient for future file access. However, as the system's users create and delete files on the disk, the blocks of data for individual files may start to be spread out in a nonsequential fashion. In a very bad case, the OS may wind up allocating a few blocks here and a few blocks there all across the disk's surface. As a result, even sequential file access can behave like slow random file access. This situation, known as *file fragmentation*, can dramatically decrease file system performance. Unfortunately, there is no way for an application to determine if its file data is fragmented across the disk surface and, even if it could, there would be little that it could do about the situation.

Although utilities exist to *defragment* the blocks on the disk's surface, an application generally cannot request the execution of these utilities. Furthermore, "defragger" utilities are generally quite slow.

Although applications rarely get the opportunity to defragment their data files during normal program execution, there are some rules you can follow to reduce the probability that your data files will become fragmented. The best advice you can follow is to always write file data in large chunks. Indeed, if you can write the whole file in a single write operation, do so. In addition to speeding up access to the OS, writing large amounts of data tends to cause sequential blocks to be allocated for the data. When you write small blocks of data to the disk, other applications in a multitasking environment could also be writing to the disk concurrently. In such a case, the OS may interleave the block allocation requests for the files being written by several different applications making it unlikely that a particular file's data will be written in sequential blocks on the disk's surface. It is important to try to write a file's data in sequential blocks, even if you plan to access portions of that data randomly, since searching for random records in a file that is written to contiguous blocks generally requires far less head movement than searching for random records in a file whose blocks are scattered all over the place.

If you're going to create a file and then access its blocks of data repeatedly, whether randomly or sequentially, it's probably a good idea to preallocate the blocks on the disk if you have an idea about how large the file will grow. If you know, for example, that your file's data will not exceed one megabyte, you could write a block of one million zeros to the disk before your application starts manipulating the file. By doing so, you help ensure that the OS will write your file to sequential blocks on the disk. Though you pay a price to write all those zeros to begin with (an operation you wouldn't normally do, presumably), the savings in read/write head-seek times could easily make up for the time spent preallocating the file. This scheme is especially useful if an application is reading or writing two or more files concurrently (which would almost guarantee the interleaving of the blocks for the various files).

12.22.2   Synchronous and Asynchronous I/O

Because most mass storage devices are mechanical, and, therefore, subject to mechanical delays, applications that make extensive use of such devices are going to have to wait for them to complete read/write operations. Most disk I/O operations are *synchronous*, meaning that an application that makes a call to the OS will wait until that I/O request is complete before continuing subsequent operations.

However, most modern OSes also provide an *asynchronous I/O* capability, in which the OS begins the application's request and then returns control to the application without waiting for the I/O operation to complete. While the

I/O operation proceeds, the application promises not to do anything with the data buffer specified for the I/O request. Then, when the I/O operation completes, the OS somehow notifies the application. This allows the application to do additional computation while waiting for the I/O operation to complete, and it also allows the application to schedule additional I/O operations while waiting for the first operation to complete. This is especially useful when accessing files on multiple disk drives in the system, which is usually only possible with SCSI and other high-end drives.

12.22.3   The Implications of I/O Type

Another important consideration when writing software that manipulates mass storage devices is the type of I/O you're performing. *Binary I/O* is usually faster than *formatted text I/O*. The difference between the two has to do with the format of the data written to disk. For example, suppose you have an array of 16 integer values that you want to write to a file. To achieve this, you could use either of the following two C/C++ code sequences:

```
FILE *f;
int array[16];
    . . .
// Sequence #1:

fwrite( f, array, 16 * sizeof( int ));
    . . .
// Sequence #2:

for( i=0; i < 16; ++i )
    fprintf( f, "%d ", array[i] );
```

The second sequence looks like it would run slower than the first because it uses a loop to step through each element of the array, rather than a single call. But although the extra execution overhead of the loop does have a small negative impact on the execution time of the write operation, this efficiency loss is minor compared to the real problem with the second sequence. Whereas the first code sequence writes out a 64-byte memory image consisting of 16 32-bit integers to the disk, the second code sequence converts each of the 16 integers to a string of characters and then writes each of those strings to the disk. This integer-to-string conversion is relatively slow and will greatly impact the performance of the code. Furthermore, the fprintf function has to interpret the format string ("%d") at run time, thus incurring an additional delay.

The advantage of formatted I/O is that the resulting file is both human readable and easily read by other applications. However, if you're using a file to hold data that is only of interest to your application, you can improve the efficiency of your software by writing data as a memory image, rather than first converting it to human-readable text.

12.22.4 Memory-Mapped Files

Some OSes allow you to use what are known as *memory-mapped files*. Memory-mapped files use the OS's virtual memory capabilities to map memory addresses in the application space directly to blocks on the disk. Because modern OSes have highly optimized virtual memory subsystems, piggy-backing file I/O on top of the virtual memory subsystem can produce very efficient file access. Furthermore, memory-mapped file access is very easy. When you open a memory-mapped file, the OS returns a memory pointer to some block of memory. By simply accessing the memory locations referenced by this pointer, just as you would any other in-memory data structure, you can access the file's data. This makes file access almost trivial, while often improving file-manipulation performance, especially when file access is random.

One of the reasons that memory-mapped files are so much more efficient than regular files is that the OS only reads the list of blocks belonging to memory-mapped files once. It then sets up the system's memory-management tables to point at each of the blocks belonging to the file. After opening the file, the OS rarely has to read any file metadata from the disk. This greatly reduces superfluous disk access during random file access. It also improves sequential file access, though to a lesser degree. Memory-mapped file access is very efficient because the OS doesn't constantly have to copy data between the disk, internal OS buffers, and application data buffers.

Memory-mapped file access does have some disadvantages. First, you cannot map gigantic files entirely into memory, at least on contemporary PCs that have a 32-bit address bus and set aside a maximum of 4 GB per application. Generally, it is not practical to use a memory-mapped access scheme for files larger than 256 MB, though this will change as more CPUs with 64-bit addressing capabilities become available. It is also not a good idea to use memory-mapped files when an application already uses an amount of memory that approaches the amount of RAM physically present in the system. Fortunately, these two situations are not typical, so they don't limit the use of memory-mapped files much.

However, there is another problem with memory-mapped files that is rather significant. When you first create a memory-mapped file, you have to tell the OS the maximum size of that file. If it is impossible to determine the file's final size, you'll have to overestimate it and then truncate the file when you close it. Unfortunately, this wastes system memory while the file is open. Memory-mapped files work well when you're manipulating files in read-only fashion or you're simply reading and writing data within an existing file without extending the file's size. Fortunately, you can always create a file using traditional file-access mechanisms and then use memory-mapped file I/O to access the file later.

Finally, almost every OS does memory-mapped file access differently, and there is little chance that memory-mapped file I/O code will be portable between OSes. Nevertheless, the code to open and close memory-mapped files is quite short, and it's easy enough to provide multiple copies of the code for the various OSes you need to support. Of course, actually accessing the file's data consists of simple memory accesses, and that's independent of the OS. For more information on memory-mapped files, consult your OS's API reference. Given the convenience and performance of memory-mapped files, you should seriously consider using them whenever possible in your applications.

12.23 The Universal Serial Bus (USB)

The *Universal Serial Bus* (USB) is not a peripheral port in the traditional sense (like an RS-2323 serial communications controller). Rather than using it to connect your computer to some peripheral device, USB is a mechanism that allows you to use a single interface to connect a wide variety of different peripheral devices to a PC, similar to SCSI. The USB supports *hot-pluggable devices*, meaning that you can plug and unplug devices without shutting down the power or rebooting your machine, and it supports *plug-and-play devices*, meaning that the OS will automatically load a device driver, if available, once you plug in a device. This flexibility comes at a cost, however. Programming devices on the USB is considerably more complex than programming a serial or parallel port. You cannot communicate with USB peripherals by reading or writing a few device registers.

12.23.1 USB Design

To understand the motivation behind USB, consider the situation PC users faced when Windows 95 first arrived, nearly 14 years after the introduction of the IBM PC. The IBM PC's designers provided the PC with a variety of peripheral interconnects that were common on personal computers and minicomputers in the late 1970s. However, they did not anticipate, nor did they particularly allow for, the wide variety of peripheral devices that people would invent to attach to PCs in the following decades. They also did not count on any individual PC owners connecting more than a few different peripheral devices to their machines. Certainly three parallel ports, four serial ports, and a single hard disk drive should have been sufficient!

By the time Windows 95 was introduced, people were connecting their PCs to all kinds of crazy devices, including sound cards, video digitizers, digital cameras, advanced gaming devices, scanners, telephones, mice, digitizing tablets, SCSI devices, and literally hundreds of other devices the original PC's designers hadn't dreamed of. The creators of these devices interfaced their hardware to the PC using peripheral I/O port addresses, interrupts, and DMA channels that were originally intended for other devices. The problem with this approach was that there were a limited number of port addresses, interrupts, and DMA channels, and there were a large number of devices that competed for these resources. In an attempt to alleviate conflicts between devices, the device manufacturers added "jumpers" to their cards that would allow the purchaser to select from a small set of different port addresses, interrupts, and DMA channels, so as not to conflict with other devices. Creating a conflict-free system was a complex process, and it was impossible to achieve with some combinations of peripherals. In fact, one of the big selling points of the Apple Macintosh during this period was that you could easily connect multiple peripheral devices without worrying about device conflicts. What was needed was a new peripheral connection system that supported a large number of devices without conflicts. USB was the answer.

USB allows the connection of up to 127 devices simultaneously by using a 7-bit address. USB reserves the 128th slot, address zero, for auto-configuration purposes. In real life, it's doubtful that one would ever successfully connect so many devices to a single PC, but it's good to know that USB has a fair amount of potential for growth, unlike the original PC's design.

Despite the name, USB isn't a true "bus" in the sense of allowing several devices to communicate with one another. The USB is a *master-slave* connection, with the PC always acting as master and the peripherals acting as slaves. This means, for example, that a camera cannot talk directly to a printer across the USB. To transmit information from a digital camera to a printer, both of which are connected to a PC, the camera must first send its data to the PC before the PC can pass the data along to the printer. The PCI, ISA, and FireWire (IEEE 1394) buses allow two devices to communicate with one another in a *peer-to-peer* fashion, independent of the host's CPU, but USB wasn't designed to allow this method of communication (to keep down the cost of peripherals and the USB interface chips in those peripheral devices).[5]

USB also keeps peripheral costs down by moving as much complexity as possible to the host (PC) side of the connection. The thinking here is that the PC's CPU will offer much higher performance than the low-cost micro-controllers found in most USB peripheral devices. This means that writing software to be embedded in a USB peripheral isn't much more work than using another interface. On the other hand, writing USB software on the host (PC) side is very complex. So complex, in fact, that it isn't realistic to expect programmers to write software that directly communicates over the USB. Instead, the OS supplier must provide a USB host controller *stack* that enables communication with USB devices and most application programmers talk to those devices using the OS's device driver interface. Even those programmers who need to write custom USB device drivers for their particular device don't talk directly to the USB hardware. Instead, they make OS calls to the USB host controller stack with requests for their particular device. Because a typical USB host controller stack is generally around 20,000 to 50,000 lines of C code and requires several years of development, there is

---

[5] Recently, the USB Interface Group (or USB-IF) has defined an extension to the USB known as *USB On-The-Go* that allows a limited amount of pseudo-peer-to-peer operation. However, this scheme doesn't truly support peer-to-peer operation; what it really does is allow different peripherals to take turns being the master on the USB.

little chance of programming USB devices on a system that does not provide a native USB stack (such as MS-DOS).

12.23.2 USB Performance

The initial USB design supported two different types of peripherals — slow and fast. Slow devices could transfer up to 1.5 Mbps (megabits per sec) across the USB, while fast devices were capable of transferring up to 12 Mbps. The reason for supporting two speeds was cost. Cost-sensitive devices could be built inexpensively as low-speed devices. Non–cost-sensitive devices could use the 12 Mbps data rate. The USB 2.0 specifications added a high-speed mode supporting up to 480 Mbps data transfer rates, at considerable extra complexity and cost.

USB will not dedicate the entire 1.5 Mbps, 12 Mbps, or 480 Mbps available bandwidth to one peripheral. Instead, the host controller stack *multiplexes* the data on the USB, effectively giving each peripheral a "time slice" of the bus. The USB operates with a one-millisecond clock. At the start of each millisecond period, the USB host controller begins a new USB *frame*, and during a frame, each peripheral may transmit or receive a packet of data. Packets vary in size, depending on the speed of the device and the transmission time, but a typical packet size contains between 4 and 64 bytes of data. If you're transferring data between four peripherals at an equal rate, you'd typically expect the USB stack to transmit one packet of data between the host and each peripheral in a *round-robin* fashion, taking care of the first peripheral first, the second peripheral second, and so on. Like time slicing in a multitasking OS, this data transfer mechanism gives the appearance of transferring data concurrently between the host and every USB peripheral, even though there can be only one transmission on the USB at a time.

Although USB provides a very flexible and expandable system, keep in mind that as you add more peripherals to the bus, you reduce the maximum amount of bandwidth available to each device. For example, if you connect two disk drives to the USB and access both drives simultaneously, the two drives must share the available bandwidth on the USB. For USB 1.*x* devices, this produces a noticeable speed degradation. For USB 2.*x* devices, the available bandwidth is sufficiently high (typically higher than what two disk drivers can sustain) that you will not notice the performance degradation. Theoretically, you could use multiple host controllers to provide multiple USB buses in a system (with full bandwidth available on each bus). But this addresses only part of the performance problem.

Another performance consideration is the overhead of the USB host controller stack. Although the USB 1.*x* hardware may be capable of 12 Mbps bandwidth, there is some "dead" time during which no transmission takes place on the USB because the host controller stack consumes a fair amount of time setting up data transfers. In some USB systems, achieving half the theoretical USB bandwidth is the best you can hope for, because the host controller stack uses so much of the available CPU time setting up the transfer and moving data around. On some embedded systems using slower processors (such as 486, StrongArm, or MIPS) running an embedded USB 1.x host controller device, this can be a real problem. Fortunately, on modern PCs with USB 2.x controllers, the host controller only consumes a small percentage of the USB bandwidth.

If a particular host controller stack is incapable of maintaining the full USB bandwidth, it usually means that the CPU can't process USB information as fast as the USB produces it. This generally implies that the CPU's processing capabilities are saturated, and no time is available for other computations, either. Remember, USB leaves all the complex computations for the host controller on the USB, and executing code in the USB stack on the host requires CPU cycles. It is quite possible for the host controller to get so involved processing USB traffic that overall system performance for non-USB traffic suffers.

12.23.3 Types of USB Transmissions

The USB supports four different types of data transmissions: control, bulk, interrupt, and isochronous. Note that it is the peripheral manufacturer, not the application programmer, that determines the data transfer mechanism between the host and a given peripheral device. That is, if a device uses the isochronous data transfer mode to communicate with the host PC, a programmer cannot decide to use bulk transfers instead. Indeed, the application program may not even be aware of the underlying transmission scheme, as long as the software can handle the rate at which the device produces or consumes the data.

USB generally uses control transmissions to initialize a peripheral device. In theory, you could use control transmissions to pass data between the peripheral and the host, but very few devices use control transmissions for that purpose. USB guarantees correct delivery of control transmissions and also guarantees that at least 10 percent of the USB bandwidth is available for control transmissions to prevent *starvation*, a situation where a particular transmission never occurs because some higher-priority transmission is always taking place. USB control transmissions are generally used to read and write data from and to a peripheral's registers. For example, if you have a USB-to-serial converter device, you would typically use control transfers to set the baud rate, number of data bits, parity, number of stop bits, and so on, just as you would store data into the 8250 SCC's register set.

As the name implies, USB *bulk* transmissions are used to transmit large blocks of data between the host and a peripheral device. Bulk transmissions are available only on full-speed (12 Mbps) and high-speed (480 Mbps) devices, not on low-speed ones. On full-speed devices, a bulk transmission generally carries between 4 and 64 bytes of data per packet; on high-speed devices you can transmit up to 1,023 bytes per packet. USB guarantees correct delivery of a bulk packet between the host and the peripheral device, but it does not guarantee timely delivery. If the USB is handling a large number of other transmissions, it may take a while for a bulk transmission to complete. In fact, theoretically, a bulk transmission might never occur if the USB is sufficiently busy with the right combination of isochronous, interrupt, and control transmissions. In practice, however, most USB stacks do set aside a small amount of guaranteed bandwidth for bulk transmissions (generally about 2 to 2.5 percent) so that starvation doesn't occur.

USB intends bulk transmissions to be used by devices that transmit a fair amount of data that must transfer correctly yet doesn't necessarily need to be transferred quickly. For example, when transferring data to a printer or between a computer and a disk drive, correct transfer is far more important than is a timely transfer. Sure, it may be annoying to wait what seems like forever to save a file to a USB disk drive, but operating slowly is much better than operating quickly and writing incorrect data to the disk file.

Some devices require both correct data transmission and a timely delivery of the data. The *interrupt* transfer type provides this capability. Despite the name, interrupt transfers do not involve interrupts on the computer system. In fact, with only two exceptions (initial connection and power-up notification), peripheral devices never communicate with the host across USB unless the host explicitly requests information from the device. The host *polls* all devices on the USB — the devices do not interrupt the host when they have data available. A peripheral device may request how often the host polls it, choosing an interval from 1 to 255 milliseconds, but the host may legally poll the device more often than the device requests.

In order to guarantee correct and timely delivery of interrupt transmissions between a host and a peripheral device, the USB host controller stack must *reserve* a portion of the USB bandwidth whenever an application opens a device for interrupt transmission. For example, if a particular device wants to be serviced every millisecond and needs to transmit 16 bytes per packet, the USB host controller stack must reserve a little bit more than 128 Kbps (kilobits per second) of bandwidth (16 bytes × 8 bits per byte × 1,000 packets per second) from the total bandwidth available. You need to reserve a little bit more than this because there is some protocol overhead on the bus as well. We'll not worry about the actual figure here other than to suggest that the overhead is probably at least 10 to 20 percent and could be more depending upon how the USB stack is written.

Because there is a limited amount of bandwidth available on the USB, and because interrupt transmissions consume a fixed amount of that bandwidth whenever you open a device for use, it is clearly not possible to have an arbitrary number of interrupt transmissions active at any one time. Once the USB bandwidth (minus the 10 percent that USB reserves for control transmissions) is consumed, the stack refuses to allow the activation of any new interrupt transmissions.

Interrupt transmission packets are between 4 and 64 bytes long, though most of the time they fall into the low end of this range. Many devices use interrupt transmissions to notify the host CPU that some data is available, and then the host can read the actual data from the device using a bulk transmission. Of course, if the amount of data to be transmitted between the host and the peripheral is small, then the peripheral may transmit the data as part of the interrupt's data payload to avoid a second transmission. Keyboards, mice, joysticks, and similar devices are examples of peripherals that typically transmit their data as part of the interrupt packet payload. Disk drives, scanners, and other such devices are good examples of peripherals that use interrupt transmissions to notify the host that data is available and then use bulk transfers to actually move the data around.

Isochronous transfers are the fourth transfer type that USB supports. Like interrupt transfers, isochronous transfers (or just *iso* transfers) require a timely delivery. Like bulk transfers, iso transfers generally involve larger data packets. However, unlike the other three transfer types, iso transfers do not guarantee correct delivery between the host and the peripheral device. Timely delivery is so important for iso transfers that if a packet arrives late, it may as well not arrive at all. Peripheral devices such as audio input (microphones) and output (speakers) and video cameras use isochronous transmissions. If you lose a packet, or if a packet is transmitted incorrectly between the peripheral and host, you'll get a momentary glitch on the video display or in the audio signal, but the results are not disastrous as long as such problems don't occur too frequently.

Like interrupt transfers, isochronous transfers consume USB bandwidth. Whenever you open a connection to an isochronous USB peripheral device, that device requests a certain amount of bandwidth. If the bandwidth is available, the USB host controller stack reserves that amount of bandwidth for the device until the application is finished with the device. If sufficient bandwidth is not available, the USB stack notifies the application that it cannot use the desired device until more bandwidth is available, and the user will have to stop using other iso and interrupt devices to free up some bandwidth.

12.23.4   USB Device Drivers

Most OSes that provide a USB stack support dynamic loading and unloading of USB device drivers, also known as *client drivers* in USB terminology. Whenever you attach a USB device to the USB, the host system gets a signal that tells it that the *bus topology* has changed (that is, there is a new device on the USB). The host controller scans for the new device, a process known as *enumeration*, and then reads some configuration information from the peripheral. Among other things, this configuration information tells the USB stack the type of the device, the manufacturer, and model information. The USB host stack uses this information to determine which device driver to load into memory. If the USB stack cannot find a suitable driver, it will generally open up a dialog box requesting help from the user; if the user cannot provide the path to an appropriate driver, the system will simply ignore the new device. Similarly, when the user unplugs a device, the USB stack will unload the appropriate device driver from memory if it's not also being used for some other device.

To simplify device-driver implementation for many common devices, such as keyboards, disk drives, mice, and joysticks, the USB standard defines certain device classes. Peripheral manufacturers who create devices that adhere to one of these standardized device classes don't have to supply a device driver with their equipment. Instead, the class drivers that come with the USB host controller stack provide the only interface necessary. Examples of class drivers include HID (Human Interface Devices, such as keyboards, mice, and joysticks), STORAGE (disk, CD, and tape drives), COMMUNICATIONS (modems and serial converters), AUDIO (speakers, microphones, and telephony equipment), and PRINTERS. A peripheral manufacturer always has the option of supplying their own specialized features that add several bells and whistles to their product, but a customer can often get basic functionality with some existing class driver by simply plugging in the device without installing a device driver specifically for the new peripheral.

12.24 Mice, Trackpads, and Other Pointing Devices

Along with disk drives, keyboards, and display devices, pointing devices are probably the most common peripherals you'll find on modern personal computers. Pointing devices are actually among the more simple peripheral devices, providing a very simple data stream to the computer. Pointing devices generally come in two categories: those that return the relative position of the pointer and those that return the absolute position of the pointing device. A relative position is simply the change in position since the last time the system read the device; an absolute position is some set of coordinate values within a fixed coordinate system. Mice, trackpads, and trackballs are examples of devices that return relative coordinates; touch screens, light pens, pressure-sensitive tablets, and joysticks are examples of devices that return absolute coordinates. Generally, it's easy to translate an absolute coordinate system to a relative one, but a bit more problematic to convert a relative coordinate system to an absolute one. This latter conversion requires a constant reference point that may become meaningless if, for example, someone lifts a mouse off the surface and sets it down elsewhere. Fortunately, most windowing systems work with relative coordinate values from pointing devices, so the limitations of pointing devices that return relative coordinates are not a problem.

Early mice were typically opto-mechanical devices that rotated two encoding wheels that were oriented along the X- and Y-axes of the mouse body. Usually, both of these wheels were encoded to send 2-bit pulses whenever they would move a certain distance. One bit told the system that the wheel had moved a certain distance, and the other bit told the system which direction the wheel had moved.[6] By constantly tracking the four bits (two bits for each axis) from the mouse, the computer system

---

[6] Actually, this is a bit of a simplification, but we will ignore that fact here.

could determine the mouse's distance and direction traveled, and keep a very accurate calculation of the mouse's position in between application requests for that position.

One problem with having the CPU track each mouse movement is that when moved quickly, mice can generate a constant and high-speed stream of data. If the system is busy with other computations, it might miss some of the incoming mouse data and would therefore lose track of the mouse's position. Furthermore, using the host CPU to keep track of the mouse position consumes CPU time that could be put to better use doing application computations.

As a result, mouse manufacturers decided early on to incorporate a simple microcontroller in the mouse package. This simple microcontroller keeps track of the physical mouse movements and responds to system requests for mouse coordinate updates, or at the very least generates interrupts on a periodic basis when the mouse position changes. Most modern mice connect to the system via the USB and respond with positional updates to system requests that occur about every eight milliseconds.

Because of the wide acceptance of the mouse as a GUI pointing device, computer manufacturers have created many other devices that serve the same purpose. The motivation behind developing most of these devices has been to increase portability — mice aren't the most convenient pointing devices to attach to a laptop computer system on the road. Trackballs, strain gauges (the little "stick" you'll find between the G and H keys on many laptops), trackpads, trackpoints, and touch screens are all examples of devices that manufacturers have attached to portable computers and PDAs to create more portable pointing devices. Though these devices vary with respect to their convenience to the end user, to the OS they can all look like a mouse. So, from a software perspective, there is little difference between these devices.

In modern OSes, the application rarely interfaces with a pointing device directly. Instead, the OS is responsible for tracking the mouse position and updating cursors and other mouse effects in the system. The OS typically notifies an application when some sort of pointing device event occurs that the application should consider. Though applications may query the pointing device's status, as a normal state of affairs they don't manage the pointing device's position. In response to a query from an application, the OS will return the position of the system cursor and the state of the buttons on the pointing device. The OS may also notify the application whenever a pointer device event, such as a button press, occurs.

12.25 Joysticks and Game Controllers

The analog game adapter created for the IBM PC allowed users to connect up to four resistive potentiometers and four digital switch connections to the PC. The design of the PC's game adapter was obviously influenced by the analog input capabilities of the Apple II computer, the most popular computer available at the time the PC was developed. IBM's analog input design, like Apple's, was designed to be dirt-cheap. Accuracy and performance were not a concern at all. In fact, you can purchase the electronic parts to build your own version of the game adapter, at retail, for less than three dollars. Unfortunately, IBM's low-cost design in 1981 produces some major performance problems for high-speed machines and high-performance game software in the 2000s.

Few modern systems incorporate the original electronics of the IBM PC game controller because of the inherent inefficiencies of reading them. Rather, most modern game controllers contain the analog electronics that convert physical position into a digital value directly inside the controller, and then interface to the system via USB. Microsoft Windows and other modern OSes provide a special game-controller device-driver interface that allows applications to determine what facilities the game controller has and also sends the data to those applications in a standardized form. This allows game-controller manufacturers to provide many special features that were not possible when using the original PC game-controller interface. Modern applications read game-controller data just as though they were reading data from a file or some other character-oriented device like a keyboard. This vastly simplifies the programming of such devices while improving overall system performance.

Microsoft Windows also provides a special game controller API that provides a high-performance interface to various types of game controllers on the system. Similar library modules exist for other OSes as well. Some "old-time" game programmers feel that calling such code is inherently inefficient and that great code always controls the hardware directly. This concept is a bit outdated. First, most modern OSes don't allow applications direct access to hardware even if the programmer wants such access. Second, software that talks directly to the hardware won't work with as wide a variety of devices as software that lets the OS handle the hardware for it. Back in the days when there were a small number of standardized peripherals for the PC, it was possible for a single application to directly program all the different devices the program would access. In modern systems, however, there are far too many devices for an individual program to deal with. This is just as true for game-controller devices as it is for other types of devices. Finally, keep in mind that most OS device drivers are probably going to be written more efficiently by the manufacturer's programmers or the OS developer's programmers than you could write them yourself.

Because newer game controllers are no longer constrained by the design of the original IBM PC game-controller card, they provide a wide range of capabilities. Refer to the relevant game controller and OS documentation for information on how to program the API for the device.

12.26 Sound Cards

The original IBM PC included a built-in speaker that the CPU could program using an on board timer chip that could produce a single frequency tone. To produce a wide range of sound effects required programming a single bit connected directly to the speaker, something which consumed nearly all available CPU time. Within a couple of years of the PC's arrival, various manufacturers like Creative Labs created a special interface board that provided higher quality PC audio output that didn't consume anywhere near the CPU resources.

The first sound cards to appear for the PC didn't follow any standards because no such standards existed at the time. Creative Labs' *Sound Blaster* card became the defacto standard because it had reasonable capabilities and sold in very high volumes. At the time, there was no such thing as a device driver for sound cards, so most applications were programming the registers directly on the sound card. Initially, the fact that so many applications were written for the Sound Blaster card meant that anyone wanting to use most audio applications also had to purchase Creative Labs' sound card. However, before too long this advantage was negated, as other sound card manufacturers quickly copied the Sound Blaster design. All of these manufacturers became stuck with their designs, for they knew that any new features added to their designs would not be supported by any of the available audio software.

Sound card technology stagnated until Microsoft introduced multimedia support into Windows. Once Windows fully supported audio cards in a device-independent fashion, sound card technology improved dramatically. The original audio cards were capable of mediocre music synthesis, suitable only for cheesy video game sound effects. Some boards supported 8-bit telephone-quality audio sampling, but the audio was definitely not high fidelity. Once Windows provided a standardized interface for audio, the sound card manufacturers began producing high-quality sound cards for the PC. Immediately, "CD-quality" cards appeared that were capable of recording and playing back audio at 44.1 KHz and 16 bits. Higher-quality sound cards began adding "wave table" synthesis hardware that produced realistic synthesis of musical instruments. Synthesizer manufacturers like Roland and Yamaha produced sound cards with the same electronics found in their high-end synthesizers. Today, professional recording studios use PC-based digital audio recording systems to record original music with 24-bit resolution at 96 KHz, arguably producing better results than all but the finest analog recording systems. Of course, such systems are not cheap, costing many thousands of dollars. They're definitely not your typical sound card that retails for under $100.

12.26.1 How Audio Interface Peripherals Produce Sound

Modern audio interface peripherals[7] generally produce sound in one of three different fashions: analog (FM synthesis), digital-wave-table synthesis, or digital playback. The first two schemes produce musical tones and are the basis for most computer-based synthesizers, while the third scheme is used to play back audio that was digitally recorded.

The FM-synthesis scheme is an older, lower-cost, music-synthesis mechanism that creates musical tones by controlling various oscillators and other sound-producing circuits on the sound card. The sound produced by such devices is usually very low quality, reminiscent of the types of sounds associated with early video games; there is no mistaking such sound synthesis for an actual musical instrument. While some very low-end sound cards still use FM synthesis as their main sound-producing mechanism, few modern audio peripherals continue to provide this form of synthesis for anything other than producing "synthetic" sounds.

Modern sound cards that provide musical synthesis capabilities tend to use what has become known as *wave table synthesis*. With wave-table synthesis, the audio manufacturer will typically record and digitize several notes from an actual musical instrument. They program these digital recordings into read-only memory (ROM) that they assemble into the audio interface circuit. When an application requests that the audio interface play some note on a given musical instrument, the audio hardware will play back the recording from ROM producing a very realistic sound. To someone who is not intimately familiar with what the actual instrument sounds like, wave-table synthesis can produce some extremely realistic sounds.

However, wave table synthesis is not simply a digital playback scheme. To record over 100 different instruments, each with a several octave range, would require a tremendous amount of ROM storage. Although ROM isn't outrageously expensive, providing hundreds of megabytes of ROM with an audio synthesizer device for a PC would be prohibitively expensive. Therefore, most manufacturers of such devices will actually resort to using software embedded on the audio interface card to take a small number of digitized waveforms stored in ROM and raise or lower them by some integral number of octaves. This allows manufacturers to record and store only a single octave (12 notes) for each instrument. In fact, it is theoretically possible to use software to convert only a single recorded note into any other note, and some synthesizers do exactly that to reduce costs. However, in practice, the more notes the manufacturer records, the better the quality of the resulting sound. Some of the higher-end audio boards will record several octaves on complex musical instruments (like a piano) but record only a few notes on some lesser-used, less-complex sound-producing objects. This is especially true for sound effects like gunshots, explosions, crowd noise, and other less-critical sounds.

---

[7] The term "sound card" hardly applies anymore because many personal computers include the audio controller directly on the motherboard, and many high-end audio interface systems interface via USB or FireWire, or require multiples boxes and interface cards.

Pure digital playback is used for two purposes: playing back arbitrary audio recordings and performing very high-end musical synthesis, known as *sampling*. A sampling synthesizer is, effectively, a RAM-based version of a wave-table synthesizer. Rather than storing digitized instruments in ROM, a sampling synthesizer stores them in system RAM. Whenever an application wants to play a given note from a musical instrument, the system fetches the recording for that note from system RAM and sends it to the audio circuitry for playback. Like wave-table synthesis methods, a sampling synthesizer can convert digitized notes up and down octaves, but because the system doesn't have the cost-per-byte constraints associated with ROM, the audio manufacturer can usually record a wider range of samples from real-world musical instruments. Generally, sampling synthesizers provide a microphone input to create your own samples. This allows you, for example, to play a song by recording a barking dog and generating a couple octaves of "dog bark" notes on the synthesizer. Third parties often sell "sound fonts" containing high-quality samples of popular musical instruments.

The other use for pure digital playback is as a digital audio recorder. Almost every modern sound card has an audio input that will theoretically record "CD-quality" sound in stereo.[8] This allows the user to record an analog signal and play it back verbatim, like a tape recorder. With sufficient outboard gear, it's even possible to make your own musical recordings and burn your own music CDs, though to do so you'd want something a little bit fancier than a typical Sound Blaster card — something at least as advanced as the DigiDesign Digi-001 or M-Audio system.

12.26.2   The Audio and MIDI File Formats

There are two standard mechanisms for playing back sound in a modern PC: audio file playback and MIDI file playback. Audio files contain digitized samples of the sound to play back. While there are many different audio file formats (for example, WAV and AIF), the basic idea is the same — the file contains some header information that specifies the recording format (such as 16-bit 44.1 KHz, or 8-bit 22 KHz) and the number of samples, followed by the actual sound samples. Some of the simpler file formats allow you to dump the data directly to a typical sound card after proper initialization of the card; other formats may require a minor data translation prior to having the sound card process the data. In either case, the audio file format is essentially a hardware-independent version of the data one would normally feed to a generic sound card.

One problem with sound files is that they can grow rather large. One minute of stereo CD-quality audio requires just less than 10 MB of storage. A typical three- to four-minute song requires between 25 MB and 40 MB. Not only would such a file take up an inordinate amount of RAM, but it

---

[8] "CD quality" simply means that the board's digitizing electronics are capable of capturing 44,100 16-bit samples every second. Usually the analog circuitry on the board does not have sufficiently high quality to pass this audio quality through to the digitizing circuitry. Hence, very few PC sound cards today are truly capable of "CD-quality" recording.

consumes a fair amount of storage on the software's distribution CD as well. If you're playing back a unique audio sequence that you've had to record, you have no choice but to use this space to hold the sequence. However, if you're playing back an audio sequence that consists of a series of repeated sounds, you can use the same technique that sampling synthesizers use and store only one instance of each sound, then use some sort of index value to indicate which sound you want to play. This can dramatically reduce the size of a music file.

This is exactly the idea behind the MIDI *(Musical Instrument Digital Interface)* file format. MIDI is a standard protocol for controlling music synthesis and other equipment. Rather than holding audio samples, a MIDI file simply specifies the musical notes to play, when to play them, how long to play them, which instrument to play them on, and so on. Because it only takes a few bytes to specify all this information, a MIDI file can represent an entire song very compactly. High-quality MIDI files generally range from about 20 KB to 100 KB for a typical three- to four-minute song. Contrast this with the 20 MB to 45 MB an audio file of the same length would require. Most sound cards today are capable of playing back *General MIDI* (GM) files using an on-board wave-table synthesizer or FM synthesis. General MIDI is a standard that most synthesizer manufacturers use to control their equipment, so its use is very widespread and GM files are easy to obtain. If you want to play back music that doesn't contain vocals or other nonmusical elements, MIDI can be very efficient.

One problem with MIDI is that the quality of the playback is dependent upon the quality of the sound card the end user provides. Some of the more expensive audio boards do a very good job of playing back MIDI files. Some of the lower-cost boards, including, unfortunately, a large number of systems that have the audio interface built on to the motherboard, produce cartoonish sounding recordings. Therefore, you need to carefully consider using MIDI in your applications. On the one hand, MIDI offers the advantages of smaller files and faster processing. On the other hand, on some systems the audio quality will be quite low, making your application sound bad. You have to balance the pros and cons of these approaches for your particular application.

Because most modern audio cards are capable of playing back "CD-quality" recordings, you might wonder why the sound card manufacturers don't collect a bunch of samples and simulate one of these sampling synthesizers. Well, they do. Roland, for example, provides a program it calls the *Virtual Sound Canvas* that does a good simulation of its hardware Sound Canvas module in software. These virtual synthesizers produce very high quality output. However, that quality comes at a price — CPU cycles. Virtual synthesizer programs consume a large percentage of the CPU's capability, thus leaving less power for your applications. If your applications don't need the full power of the CPU, these virtual synthesizers provide a very high-quality, low-cost solution to this problem.

Another solution is to connect an outboard synthesizer module to your PC via a MIDI interface port and send the MIDI data to a synthesizer to play. This solution is acceptable if you know your target audience will have such a device, but few people outside of musicians would own one, so requiring the hardware severely limits your customer base.

12.26.3   Programming Audio Devices

One of the best things about audio in modern applications is that there has been a tremendous amount of standardization. File formats and audio hardware interfaces are very easy to use in modern applications. Like most other peripheral interface issues, few modern programs will control audio hardware directly, because OSes like Windows and Linux provide device drivers that handle this chore for you. To produce sound in a typical Windows application requires little more than reading data from a file that contains the sound information, and writing that data to another file that transmits the data to the device driver that interfaces with the actual audio hardware.

One other issue to consider when writing audio-based software is the availability of multimedia extensions in the CPU you're using. The Pentium and later 80x86 CPUs provide the MMX instruction set. Other CPU families provide comparable instruction set extensions (such as the AltaVec instructions on the PowerPC). Although the OS probably uses these extended instructions in the device driver, it's quite possible to employ these multimedia instructions in your own applications as well. Unfortunately, using these extended instructions usually involves assembly language programming, because few high-level languages provide efficient access to them. Therefore, if you're going to be doing high-performance multimedia programming, assembly language is probably something you want to learn. See my book *The Art of Assembly Language* for additional details on the Pentium's MMX instruction set.

12.27   For More Information

To program a particular peripheral device, you will need to obtain the data sheets for that device directly from its manufacturer. Most manufacturers maintain their data sheets on the Web these days, so getting the information is usually a simple matter of finding their Web page. Some manufacturers do consider the interface to their devices to be proprietary and refuse to share this information (this is particularly true of video card manufacturers), but by and large it's relatively easy to get the information you need.

Semiconductor manufacturers are especially generous with the information they supply on their websites. Furthermore, common peripheral devices like the 8250 serial communications chip have dozens of websites dedicated to programming them. A quick search on the Net will turn up considerable information for the more common interface devices.

For USB, FireWire, and TCP/IP (network) protocol stacks, there is considerable information available on the Net. For example, http://www.usb.org contains all the technical specifications for the USB protocol as well as programming information for various common USB host controller chip sets. Similar information exists for FireWire.

You'll be able to find considerable example code that controls most peripheral devices on the Net as well. This even includes some complex protocols such as USB, FireWire, and TCP/IP. For example, the open source Linux OS provides complete TCP/IP and USB host controller stacks in source form. This code is not easy reading and is tens of thousands of lines long, but if you're dead-set on creating this kind of code, the Linux (and other open source) offerings make a good starting point.

THINKING LOW-LEVEL, WRITING HIGH-LEVEL

The goal of this volume, *Understanding the Machine,* was to get you thinking at the level of the machine. Of course, one way to force yourself to write code at the machine level is to write your applications in assembly language. When you've got to write code statement by statement in assembly language, you're going to have a pretty good idea of the cost associated with every statement.

Unfortunately, using assembly language isn't a realistic solution for most applications. The disadvantages of assembly language have been well publicized (and blown out of proportion) over the past several decades, so most people are quite familiar with the drawbacks, real or imagined. Assembly just isn't an option for most people.

Though writing code in assembly language forces you to think down at the machine level, writing code in a high-level language does not force you to think at a high level of abstraction. There is nothing preventing you from thinking in low-level terms while writing high-level code. The goal of this book was to provide you with the background knowledge you need to do exactly that — think in low-level terms while writing high-level code. By learning how the computer represents data, you've learned how high-level language data types translate to the machine level. By learning how the CPU executes machine instructions, you've learned the costs of various operations in your high-level language applications. By learning about memory performance, you've learned how to organize your high-level language variables and other data to maximize cache and memory access. There's only one piece missing from this puzzle: "Exactly *how* does a particular compiler map high-level language statements to the machine level?" Unfortunately, that topic is sufficiently large that it deserves an entire book on its own. And that's the purpose of the next volume in the Write Great Code series: *Thinking Low-Level, Writing High-Level.*

Write Great Code: Thinking Low-Level, Writing High-Level will pick up right where this volume leaves off. *Thinking Low-Level, Writing High-Level* will teach you how each statement in a typical high-level language maps to machine code, how you can choose between two or more high-level sequences to produce the best possible machine code, and how to analyze that machine code to determine its quality and the quality of the high-level code that produced it. And while doing all of this, it will give you a greater appreciation of how compilers do their job and how you can assist them in doing their job better.

Congratulations on your progress thus far towards knowing how to write great code. See you in volume 2.

ASCII CHARACTER SET

Binary	Hex	Decimal	Character
0000_0000	00	0	NULL
0000_0001	01	1	CTRL A
0000_0010	02	2	CTRL B
0000_0011	03	3	CTRL C
0000_0100	04	4	CTRL D
0000_0101	05	5	CTRL E
0000_0110	06	6	CTRL F
0000_0111	07	7	bell
0000_1000	08	8	backspace
0000_1001	09	9	TAB
0000_1010	0A	10	line feed
0000_1011	0B	11	CTRL K
0000_1100	0C	12	form feed
0000_1101	0D	13	RETURN
0000_1110	0E	14	CTRL N
0000_1111	0F	15	CTRL O
0001_0000	10	16	CTRL P
0001_0001	11	17	CTRL Q
0001_0010	12	18	CTRL R
0001_0011	13	19	CTRL S

Binary	Hex	Decimal	Character
0001_0100	14	20	CTRL T
0001_0101	15	21	CTRL U
0001_0110	16	22	CTRL V
0001_0111	17	23	CTRL W
0001_1000	18	24	CTRL X
0001_1001	19	25	CTRL Y
0001_1010	1A	26	CTRL Z
0001_1011	1B	27	CTRL [
0001_1100	1C	28	CTRL \
0001_1101	1D	29	ESC
0001_1110	1E	30	CTRL ^
0001_1111	1F	31	CTRL _
0010_0000	20	32	space
0010_0001	21	33	!
0010_0010	22	34	"
0010_0011	23	35	#
0010_0100	24	36	$
0010_0101	25	37	%
0010_0110	26	38	&
0010_0111	27	39	'
0010_1000	28	40	(
0010_1001	29	41	)
0010_1010	2A	42	*
0010_1011	2B	43	+
0010_1100	2C	44	,
0010_1101	2D	45	-
0010_1110	2E	46	.
0010_1111	2F	47	/
0011_0000	30	48	0
0011_0001	31	49	1
0011_0010	32	50	2
0011_0011	33	51	3
0011_0100	34	52	4
0011_0101	35	53	5
0011_0110	36	54	6
0011_0111	37	55	7

Binary	Hex	Decimal	Character
0011_1000	38	56	8
0011_1001	39	57	9
0011_1010	3A	58	:
0011_1011	3B	59	;
0011_1100	3C	60	<
0011_1101	3D	61	=
0011_1110	3E	62	>
0011_1111	3F	63	?
0100_0000	40	64	@
0100_0001	41	65	A
0100_0010	42	66	B
0100_0011	43	67	C
0100_0100	44	68	D
0100_0101	45	69	E
0100_0110	46	70	F
0100_0111	47	71	G
0100_1000	48	72	H
0100_1001	49	73	I
0100_1010	4A	74	J
0100_1011	4B	75	K
0100_1100	4C	76	L
0100_1101	4D	77	M
0100_1110	4E	78	N
0100_1111	4F	79	O
0101_0000	50	80	P
0101_0001	51	81	Q
0101_0010	52	82	R
0101_0011	53	83	S
0101_0100	54	84	T
0101_0101	55	85	U
0101_0110	56	86	V
0101_0111	57	87	W
0101_1000	58	88	X
0101_1001	59	89	Y
0101_1010	5A	90	Z
0101_1011	5B	91	[

Binary	Hex	Decimal	Character
0101_1100	5C	92	\
0101_1101	5D	93	]
0101_1110	5E	94	^
0101_1111	5F	95	_
0110_0000	60	96	`
0110_0001	61	97	a
0110_0010	62	98	b
0110_0011	63	99	c
0110_0100	64	100	d
0110_0101	65	101	e
0110_0110	66	102	f
0110_0111	67	103	g
0110_1000	68	104	h
0110_1001	69	105	i
0110_1010	6A	106	j
0110_1011	6B	107	k
0110_1100	6C	108	l
0110_1101	6D	109	m
0110_1110	6E	110	n
0110_1111	6F	111	o
0111_0000	70	112	p
0111_0001	71	113	q
0111_0010	72	114	r
0111_0011	73	115	s
0111_0100	74	116	t
0111_0101	75	117	u
0111_0110	76	118	v
0111_0111	77	119	w
0111_1000	78	120	x
0111_1001	79	121	y
0111_1010	7A	122	z
0111_1011	7B	123	{
0111_1100	7C	124		
0111_1101	7D	125	}
0111_1110	7E	126	~
0111_1111	7F	127	

INDEX

Extended Binary Coded Decimal
Interchange Code
(EBCDIC), 107
extended precision floating-point
format, 71, 74
extending instruction set with prefix
byte, 279
extension
sign, 27–29
zero, 27–29
external fragmentation
on a hard disk drive, 376
in a memory manager, 323
extracting bit fields, 62

F

falling edge of a clock, 150
false, 192
Fast and Wide SCSI, 368
faster processing, 235
FAT (file allocation table), 378
free-space management, 380
implementation, 378
fault, 317
fetched bytes, 240
Fibre Channel Arbitrated Loop
(FCAL) and SCSI, 369
field
aligning in record, 184
C bit, 58
encoding, 61, 282
extracting bit, 62
inserting data into bit, 62
in a record/structure, 181
file
access performance, 386
AIF, 401
block, 375, 382, 383, 387
formats, 401
formatted I/O to disk, 388
fragmentation, 376, 386
GM (general MIDI), 402
I/O performance, 386
managers, 374
memory-mapped, 312, 389
MIDI, 401
organization, 381
size, 383
sparse, 381, 385

storage in memory, 297
WAV, 401
file allocation table. *See* FAT
file system
free-space bitmaps in, 377
on mass storage devices, 374
operating system, 374
sequential, 376
financial transactions and fixed-point
arithmetic, 35
fine-grained parallelism, 257
FireWire, 367, 369
first-fit memory allocation, 323
first-in, first-out (FIFO) cache
replacement policy, 307
fixed drives, 352. *See also* disk drives
fixed-point
arithmetic, 35
binary formats, 34
representation, 33–34
flag
register, 232
zero, 230
flash memory device, 364
flash storage modules, 363
flip-flop, D (data), 221
flip-flop, S/R (set/reset), 220
latch, 221
as output port (S/R), 333
unstable, 221
float data type (C/C++), 72
floating-point
accuracy, 68
addition, 81–82
arithmetic, 33, 65, 66
exceptions in, 79
IEEE rounding, 84
limitations of, 65
calculation, 67
error accumulation, 68
order of evaluation, 68
comparisons, 69
denormalized values, 76
division, 92, 97
fpdiv function, 93, 97
by zero, 79
double-precision format
(IEEE), 74
dynamic range, 66
error accumulation, 68

N

NaN (not-a-number), 78–79
NAND
    logical, 196
    universal Boolean function, 213
NAND gate, 213
    constructing an AND gate, 214
    constructing an OR gate, 214
    implementation of any Boolean
        function, 213
    implementing a D flip-flop
        with, 222
    inverter built from a, 213
    set/reset flip-flop constructed
        from, 220
NAND operation, 196
    AND logic functions, 213
    constructing logic functions
        using, 213
nanoseconds, 150
n-bit adder, 215
nearest floating-point operation, 77
near-line storage subsystems, 298, 360
negation, logical, 192
negation algorithm, 25
network storage, 297
Neumann, John von, 134
new memory allocation
    function, 164
    operator (C++ or Pascal), 321
nibble, 22
non-80x86 processors, 143
Non-Uniform Memory Access, 297.
        See also NUMA
non-volatile storage, 363
NOR
    logical, 196
    operation, 196
normalized values, 75
NOT
    instruction (Y86), 269, 276
    logical, 196
    operation, 46, 47, 192, 196
    precedence in a Boolean
        expression, logical, 194
    truth table, 47
not-a-number (NaN)
    quiet, 78
    signaling, 78
notation, scientific, 66

notation system, 11
notification of interrupts, 345
NuBus, 338
NUL character, 112
null pointer references, 317
NUMA (Non-Uniform Memory
        Access), 297
    peripheral devices and, 313
number, 10
    abstract concept of, 10
    of Boolean functions, 195
    packed fields encoding, 61
    representation of, 10
    of values representable with bit
        strings, 24
number system
    Arabic, 11
    base-2, 13
    base-8, 13
    base-10, 11
    binary, 13
    decimal positional, 11–13
    hexadecimal, 15
    nonpositional, 11
    octal, 18
    positional, 11–12
    radix (base), 12
    two's complement, 24
numbers
    comparing, 69
    defined, 10
    dynamic range in floating-
        point, 66
    eager approach to comparing, 71
    function, 197
    generating minterms from
        binary, 199
    logical operations on binary, 47
    miserly approach to
        comparing, 71
    odd, 26
    properties of binary, 25
    signed and unsigned, 24
    truncation, 77
numerals
    Arabic, 11
    Roman, 10
numeric abstraction, 10
numeric digits
    in ASCII character set, 105
    ASCII codes for, 106

read-only
> ports, 330
> sections in a program, 319

real data type (FORTRAN), 72

real estate and CPU design, 260

receiving data via a parallel port, 350

record, 181
> activation, 320
> aligning fields, 184
> application binary interface, 184
> base address, 183
> C/C++, 182
> case variant, 147
> difference between unions and
>> records/structs, 187
> dot operator, 183
> fields, 181
> HLA, 182
> length, 184
> memory storage, 183
> packed, 184
> padding bytes, 184
> Pascal
>> case variant record, 186
>> declarations, 181
> Pascal/Delphi, 181
> variant section, 186

recorders, digital audio, 401

recording on a hard disk drive, 354

records and structs
> dot operator, 183
> memory storage of, 183

rectangle, 208
> in Boolean truth map, 206
> formed by ones, 207

redundant array of inexpensive disks
> (RAID), 358

reel-to-reel tape drives, 363

reference
> locality of, 153, 300
> NULL pointer, 317
> spatial locality of, 153, 298, 300
> temporal locality of, 153
> temporality of, 298

reference counting for strings, 117

reg field
> in 80x86 instruction
>> encoding, 282
> encodings, 282

reg values for 80x86 scaled indexed
> addressing modes, 285

register
> condition codes, 232
> electronic implementation, 222
> flags, 232
> instruction pointer, 228
> in memory hierarchy, 296
> program performance and, 300
> shift, 222
> stack pointer, 320

register built from D flip-flops, 4-bit
> shift, 223

register implemented with eight
> D flip-flops, 8-bit, 222

register renaming, 254

register values
> for *sib* encoding, 285
> for *sib* encoding, base, 285

relative coordinate pointing
> devices, 396

relative performance of memory
> subsystems, 300

replacement policy
> LRU (least recently used)
>> cache, 306
> random cache, 307

representation
> arrays in memory, 172
> base-8, 18
> binary, 11
> binary-coded decimal (BCD), 31
> in a byte, BCD data, 31–32
> of character sets, list, 120
> of character sets, powerset, 120
> converting
>> between decimal and
>>> binary, 14
>> between hexadecimal and
>>> binary, 17
>> between octal and binary, 18
> dates, 55
> English, of numeric quantities, 10
> fixed-point, 33–34
> floating-point, 80
> of fractional values, rational, 38
> hexadecimal, 10, 15
> hexadecimal digit, 22
> HLA character set, 120
> HLA hexadecimal, 16
> internal and external numeric, 10
> internal numeric, 21
> MASM hexadecimal, 16

U

Ultra SCSI, 368
unconditional jumps, 277
undefined opcodes, 278
underflow, numeric, 80
Unicode, 109–10
unidirectional parallel
        communications, 349
uninitialized storage (BSS)
        section, 319
union, 147, 185
    aliases, 188
    on big endian machine, 148
    C/C++ declarations, 186
    data type, discriminant, 147
    discriminant, 185
    field offsets in a union, 185
    HLA declarations, 187
    on little endian machine, 148
    memory storage, 187
    object disassembly, 189
    other uses, 188
    in Pascal/Delphi/Kylix, 186
    versus a record (struct), 148
unique Boolean functions, 195
universal Boolean function
        (NAND), 213
Universal Serial Bus. *See* USB
unnormalized values, 76
unpacking data, 60
unsigned numbers, 24
unstable flip-flop operation, 221
unused bus cycles, 240
up codes on the keyboard, 348
uppercase characters, 105
usage frequency, 267
USB (Universal Serial Bus), 146,
        351, 390
    audio, 395
    bandwidth, 394
    client drivers, 395
    communications devices, 396
    control transmissions, 393
    design, 390
    device classes, 396
    device drivers, 395
    enumeration, 395
    flash modules, 364
    host controller stack, 391
    interrupt transfers, 394
    isochronous transfers, 395
    performance, 392
    polling operation on, 394
    printer devices, 396
    protocol, frames in, 392
    round-robin polling on, 392
    starvation on, 393
    storage devices, 396
    transmission types, 393
U.S. Social Security numbers, 60

V

values
    adding binary, 40
    adding integer to a pointer, 166
    comparing pointer, 164
    converting binary to decimal, 14
    denormalized, 75
    dividing binary, 43
    fractional, 33
    multiplying binary, 42
    normalized, 75
    numeric, 11
    rational representation of
        fractional, 38
    representable with bit strings, 24
    scale, 285
    signed integer, 24
    special floating-point, 78
    subtracting binary, 41
    unnormalized, 76
    unsigned integer, 24
variable
    accessing pointer, 159
    anonymous, 164, 321
    automatic, 170
    OR truth table for two, 204
    truth table format for function
        of three, 195
variable section, static, 319
variable-length instructions, 264
variant records, 147
very long instruction word (VLIW)
        architecture, 255
virtual address, 309
virtual memory, 297, 309
    protection and paging, 309
    subsystem, swap storage for a, 366
Virtual Sound Canvas, 402
virtual synthesizers, 402

THE ART OF ASSEMBLY LANGUAGE

by RANDALL HYDE

SEPTEMBER 2003, 928 PP. W/CD
$59.95 ($89.95 CAN)
ISBN 1-886411-97-2

Presents assembly language from the high-level programmer's point of view, so you can start writing meaningful programs within days. The High Level Assembler (HLA) that accompanies the book is the first assembler that allows you to write portable assembly language programs that run under either Linux or Windows with nothing more than a recompile. The CD-ROM includes the HLA and the HLA Standard Library, all the source code from the book, and over 50,000 lines of additional sample code, all well-documented and tested. The code compiles and runs as-is under Windows and Linux.

HACKING
The Art of Exploitation

by JON ERICKSON

NOVEMBER 2003, 264 PP.
$39.95 ($59.95 CAN)
ISBN 1-59327-007-0

A comprehensive introduction to the exploitation techniques and creative problem-solving methods known as "hacking." Explains technical aspects of hacking such as stack based overflows, heap based overflows, string exploits, return-into-libc, shellcode, and cryptographic attacks on 802.11b.

"The seminal hacker's handbook." — SecurityForums.com

HOW NOT TO PROGRAM IN C++
111 Broken Programs and 3 Working Ones, or Why Does 2+2=5986?

by STEVE OUALLINE

APRIL 2003, 280 PP.
$24.95 ($37.95 CAN)
ISBN 1-886411-95-6

Over 100 fun and challenging C++ puzzles that will make you a better programmer. Find the bugs in these broken programs and become a better programmer. Based on real-world errors, the puzzles range from easy (one wrong character) to mind twisting (errors with multiple threads). Match your wits against the author's and polish your language skills as you try to fix broken programs. Clues help along the way, and answers are provided at the back of the book.

THE WEB PROGRAMMER'S DESK REFERENCE
A Complete Cross-Reference to HTML, CSS, and JavaScript

by LÁZARO ISSI COHEN *&* JOSEPH ISSI COHEN

AUGUST 2004, 1123 PP.
$59.95 ($83.95 CAN)
ISBN 1-59327-011-9

The only book to serve as a single point of reference to all three primary web programming languages: HTML, CSS (Cascading Style Sheets), and JavaScript. Begins with a web programming primer that gives beginning and intermediate programmers an understanding of the core elements of HTML, CSS, and JavaScript, then moves on to a reference section that lists every element of HTML, CSS, and JavaScript. Each listing includes the latest syntax and functionality, compatibility with other elements, and cross-browser compatibility issues.

THE SPAM LETTERS

by JONATHAN LAND

JUNE 2004, 232 PP.
$14.95 ($19.95 CAN)
ISBN 1-59327-032-1

You may have read about Jonathan Land's running dialogs with spam writers in *Entertainment Weekly*, the *New York Times*, or on Slashdot. He combines his favorite exchanges here to create this collection of brilliant and entertaining correspondence, and it's a laugh riot. Land masquerades as a multitude of characters as he carries on exchanges with spammers, and some of them even fall for his ruses. If you hate spam, you'll love *The Spam Letters*.

PHONE:
800.420.7240 OR
415.863.9900
MONDAY THROUGH FRIDAY,
9 A.M. TO 5 P.M. (PST)

FAX:
415.863.9950
24 HOURS A DAY,
7 DAYS A WEEK

EMAIL:
SALES@NOSTARCH.COM

WEB:
HTTP://WWW.NOSTARCH.COM

MAIL:
NO STARCH PRESS
555 DE HARO ST, SUITE 250
SAN FRANCISCO, CA 94107
USA

UPDATES

Visit **http://www.nostarch.com/greatcode.htm** for updates, errata, and other information.